Infertility and Non-Traditional Family Building

Rebecca Feasey

Infertility and Non-Traditional Family Building

From Assisted Reproduction to Adoption in the Media

Rebecca Feasey
The School of Creative Industries
Bath Spa University
Bath, UK

ISBN 978-3-030-17789-8   ISBN 978-3-030-17787-4   (eBook)
https://doi.org/10.1007/978-3-030-17787-4

© The Editor(s) (if applicable) and The Author(s) 2019
This work is subject to copyright. All rights are solely and exclusively licensed by the Publisher, whether the whole or part of the material is concerned, specifically the rights of translation, reprinting, reuse of illustrations, recitation, broadcasting, reproduction on microfilms or in any other physical way, and transmission or information storage and retrieval, electronic adaptation, computer software, or by similar or dissimilar methodology now known or hereafter developed.
The use of general descriptive names, registered names, trademarks, service marks, etc. in this publication does not imply, even in the absence of a specific statement, that such names are exempt from the relevant protective laws and regulations and therefore free for general use.
The publisher, the authors, and the editors are safe to assume that the advice and information in this book are believed to be true and accurate at the date of publication. Neither the publisher nor the authors or the editors give a warranty, express or implied, with respect to the material contained herein or for any errors or omissions that may have been made. The publisher remains neutral with regard to jurisdictional claims in published maps and institutional affiliations.

Cover image: Matt Anderson Photography / Getty images
Cover design: eStudioCalamar

This Palgrave Macmillan imprint is published by the registered company Springer Nature Switzerland AG
The registered company address is: Gewerbestrasse 11, 6330 Cham, Switzerland

For You

PREFACE

As I came to write the final pages of an earlier book on motherhood and popular television (Feasey 2016), it seemed clear that I would follow up with an accompanying volume dedicated to an examination of fatherhood on the small screen. However, although the book proposal sits poised, ready for sending in a folder entitled 'future research', it has not as yet been sent to publishers. Somewhere between finishing a volume on motherhood and writing a proposal on fatherhood and the media I found myself distracted, distracted by a short blog post that I had written about the codes, conventions and clichés of the 40-something celebrity infertility story (Feasey 2014). There was a book that I wanted to read about the representation of infertility, pregnancy loss and non-traditional mothering in the media, but that book did not exist, so I set myself the task of writing what I felt to be a much-needed volume on an important media representation. Important in part because infertility and pregnancy loss continue to have an impact on women, couples and families on both sides of the Atlantic, in part because many of these individuals and families speak of a sense of alienation and isolation as they live through these experiences, and in part because there is currently little formal education on fertility in schools, six forms or colleges (Fertility Fest 2018; Hepburn 2018; Harper et al. 2019). A recent survey conducted by the British Fertility Society among 16- to 24-year-olds 'found that young people today have a largely inaccurate understanding of how the fertility life cycle works. This is likely to be one of the key reasons why infertility and sub-fertility are now considered to be a major public health issue by the World Health Organization' (British Fertility Society 2018a, b). The media could play a valuable part

viii   PREFACE

in informing its audience about fertility, infertility, pregnancy loss and non-traditional family building, and, as such, it is crucial that we understand how these texts and voices communicate, or otherwise, messages about health and hearth.

A cursory glance at potential book covers demonstrates how society struggles to make sense of the notion of infertility and non-traditional family building. Searching for images under titles such as fertility and infertility provided me with sad women and heterosexual couples holding negative pregnancy tests, elated women and heterosexual couples holding positive pregnancy tests, a myriad of ways of depicting an empty womb, barren landscapes, injection needles and empty pushchairs. Each one in turn plays its part in foregrounding the importance of motherhood to female identity, adult maturity and the wider pronatal society. It is to this debate that I now turn … I hope you can accept the abstract snowflakes.

Bath Spa University, Bath, UK   Rebecca Feasey

References

British Fertility Society. 2018a. Modern Families Education Project. *British Fertility Society*. Accessed April 12, 2019. https://britishfertilitysociety.org.uk/fei/#link5.

British Fertility Society. 2018b. Fertility Fest—The Modern Families Project. *British Fertility Society*. Accessed April 12, 2019. https://www.fertilityfest.com/the-modern-families-project.

Feasey, Rebecca. 2014. From Heartache to Happiness: The Codes, Conventions and Clichés of the 40-something Celebrity Infertility Story. *MaMSIE*. Accessed April 12, 2019. http://mamsie.org/2014/11/10/from-heartache-to-happiness-the-codes-conventions-and-cliches-of-the-40-something-celebrity-infertility-story/.

Feasey, Rebecca. 2016. *Mothers on Mothers: Maternal Readings of Popular Television*. Oxford: Peter Lang.

Fertility Fest. 2018. Fertility Fest. *Fertility Fest*. Accessed April 12, 2019. https://www.fertilityfest.com.

Harper, Joyce, Jessica Hepburn, Gabby Vautier, Emma Callander, Tian Glasgow, Adam Balen, and Jacky Boivin. 2019. Feasibility and Acceptability of Theatrical and Visual Art to Deliver Fertility Education to Young Adults. *Human Fertility* 1: 1–7.

Hepburn, Jessica. 2018. Jessica Hepburn. *Jessica Hepburn*. Accessed April 12, 2019. https://www.jessicahepburn.com.

Contents

1 Introduction: Infertility and Non-Traditional Family Building   1

2 Infertility: Private Confessions in a Public Arena   37

3 Assisted Reproduction: Family, Fortunes and Fertility Clinics   87

4 Pregnancy Loss: Shame and Silence over a Shared Experience   143

5 Adoption: Eligibility, Assessment and Selection   189

6 Conclusion: Future Research Directions   249

Useful Websites UK   259

Index   261

CHAPTER 1

Introduction: Infertility and Non-Traditional Family Building

Motherhood: From Representations to Societal Expectations

Film, television and media studies have long been interested in depictions of women in a range of screen, print and online platforms. More recently, the emergence of media-motherhood studies has paid particular attention to the representation of women as maternal figures in the entertainment arena (Douglas and Michaels 2005; Feasey 2012, 2018). However, what is missing from such research is an exploration of unsuccessful or unconventional pregnancy stories, non-traditional family building and narratives of non-traditional motherhood. I am using the term non-traditional here to refer to a myriad of family building options that involve medical support and/or third-party intervention, ranging from intrauterine insemination (IUI) and in vitro fertilisation (IVF), through womb transplants and adoption. In this way, non-traditional families can be straight or gay, experiencing primary, secondary or social infertility; genetically related or otherwise.

While notions of fertility, fecundity, the politics of reproduction and the impact of modern technology have been acknowledged in the field of motherhood studies (Berridge and Portwood-Stacer 2014; Feasey 2014), they remain a small part of a growing field of study. Indeed, there has been little sustained research on infertility and non-traditional mothering. Research on non-traditional family building and new reproductive

© The Author(s) 2019
R. Feasey, *Infertility and Non-Traditional Family Building*,
https://doi.org/10.1007/978-3-030-17787-4_1

technologies are rarely acknowledged beyond lesbian motherhood in Andrea O'Reilly's 800-page edited volume *Maternal Theory: Essential Readings* (2007). O'Reilly's seminal collection captures decades of maternal theorising, yet routinely overlooks the themes that I am introducing here, namely, the representation of infertility and non-traditional mothering within and beyond popular media culture. Over the last three decades the topic of motherhood has emerged as a significant area of academic debate, with themes ranging from sexuality, peace, religion, public policy, literature, health, work, care work, young mothers, feminist mothering, mothers and sons, mothers and daughters, the motherhood movement, race and ethnicity for example. Although work on the role of lesbian mothering, co-mothering and adoption does exist, such research tends to be short chapters or isolated journal articles in larger volumes dedicated to more traditional maternal experiences and/or debates concerning feminist mothering (Lewin 1994; DiLapi 1999; Ryan 2008). Although this work offers a fascinating and much needed consideration of non-traditional motherhood, wider debates concerning infertility continue to be overlooked within the field of gender, film, television and media motherhood studies.

Motherhood is often assumed to be a 'normal' element of adulthood and indeed a 'natural' part of a woman's life. Vivian Kraaij, Nadi Garnefski and Maya Schroevers make this point when they tell us that having children is an essential stage of life for *most* people (Kraaij et al. 2009, p. 19, emphasis added). This pronatal stance is echoed on screen as television titles routinely close with maternal outcomes. We are told that in recent years 'two generically different HBO programs, namely Girls (2012–2017) and True Detective (2015) 'each concluded their series or recent season with a "strong" female character whose life is apparently rounded out through maternity or the promise of maternity' (Hosey 2019). At the same time, characters who are diagnosed with infertility on the big screen 'are portrayed as incomplete … until they become positioned as normative by becoming natural mothers and situated within a heterosexual couple dyad' (Le Vay 2019, p. 190). Irrespective of screen size and 'regardless of a woman's goals or accomplishments' the media makes it clear that women must become mothers 'in order to be truly fulfilled' (Hosey 2019).

Kristina Engwall and Helen Peterson have gone so far as to suggest that women without children are viewed with 'doubt, suspicion and even disgust' (Engwall and Peterson cited in Le Vay 2019, p. 161). Contemporary society judges 'women on their ability or desire to procreate' (Striff 2005,

p. 190), and irrespective of whether women become mothers, motherhood is 'central to the ways in which they are defined by others and to their perceptions of themselves' (Phoenix and Woollett 1991, p. 13).

Feminists have spent decades fighting for political, economic and social equality; and much of the second wave movement looked to remove women from what was understood to be the shackles of the domestic sphere. Demands for universal free childcare made it clear that motherhood in general, and stay-at-home motherhood in particular was part of a patriarchal society that held women back, or rather, maintained the seemingly 'natural' status quo that divided genders along the lines of public and private spheres. These discussions are useful, and in many regards, crucial, to a contemporary feminist debate at a time when more young women than ever before are entering higher education, looking to narrow the gender pay gap, getting married later and having children later still. However, there is a growing group for whom the feminist debate about motherhood, and by extension, maternal domesticity, is at best null and void and, at worst, alienating. For those affected by an infertility diagnosis and a desire to experience pregnancy and motherhood, feminist debates concerning access to contraception and abortion might appear misguided and misplaced. Popular news articles at the height of the second-wave feminist movement have been accused of ignoring the needs of those affected by an infertility diagnosis. It has been argued that 'in an era of birth control, the Pill and the Population Explosion [women affected by infertility are] too often forgotten or simply dismissed as unimportant' (cited in Marsh and Ronner 1999, p. 216). Only a few feature articles of the period 'suggested that in such a culture the infertile might feel as disenfranchised as had the voluntarily childless in the previous generation' (Ibid., pp. 215–216). More recently, feminist positions relating to infertility in general and assisted reproduction in particular have been divided between those that view treatments and technologies 'as coercive and abusive, pressuring women to conform to … norms of womanhood through having children', those who 'embrace technologies as a source of empowerment' and those again who 'view it as a method by which to fix/repair infertility by literally constructing biology' (Le Vay 2019, p. 40).

While those women who choose not to mother may struggle against reductive definitions of womanhood as motherhood as they circulate in contemporary society, women affected by infertility are left to navigate the 'shame and stigma' that is said to follow a diagnosis (Edge 2015, p. 100). One woman speaks for many when she 'recounts finding out that she cannot have a child … as a loss of her womanhood' (Bronstein and Knoll 2015). These feelings are common because infertility is seldom discussed in polite conversation; it is routinely overlooked by those without first-hand experience and it is rarely commented on by those affected.

The History of Infertility

In previous centuries, there was little knowledge or understanding of the process of human reproduction, and as such 'various ideas about the origin of infertility have existed throughout Western history' (Van Balen 2002, p. 79). These ideas seem to fluctuate, as does the terminology to account for our changing understanding of them.

In his enlightening book-length volume on the rhetoric of infertility, Robin Jensen looks at the ways in which infertility 'has been defined in and across technical, mainstream, and lay communities' during specific historical moments (Jensen 2016, p. 3). We are reminded that in Europe and the American colonies of the seventeenth and eighteenth centuries, agrarian societies relied on large families to plant seeds, harvest crops and tend to cattle. At this time, the 'barren' woman, unable to produce children and thus serve the greater community, was seen to be at fault for her 'inability to metaphorically flower or bear fruit' (Ibid., p. 21). These women were blamed for their reproductive problems and were encouraged to 'engage in diet and exercise related self-treatments' before taking herbal remedies and practicing religious prayer in order to aid conception (Ibid., p. 21). In the nineteenth century, the barren woman was recast as a sterile body suffering from mechanical failure and in need of repair by the medical community. During this period, women's bodies were understood as 'a compilation of objective parts' and as such, women lacked the necessary agency to 'prevent, cause or cure their own reproductive problems' (Ibid., p. 33). Unlike the barren women before them, those suffering from sterility were not instructed to follow specific diets, encouraged to take particular remedies or asked to pray, but rather, 'the "cure" for sterility … had to do with the expert techniques of the surgeon, observing, cutting, removing, opening, expanding, and excising patients' bodies to achieve normalcy and function' (Ibid., p. 34). The shift in reproductive metaphors from the organic to the mechanical demonstrates a change in accountability and personal responsibility for the woman in question. While the barren woman was accused of 'everything from … consuming the wrong types of food to cavorting with the devil' (Ibid., p. 34) a woman diagnosed as sterile was not similarly accountable because she 'had no control over the mechanical success of human reproduction' (Ibid., p. 34). To coincide with increasing industrialisation, the language of sterility came to present human reproduction as a machine-operated manufacturing process.

However, the mid-twentieth-century language of psychogenic infertility put the blame for involuntary childlessness back at the feet of those women who were experiencing reproductive difficulties. Psychogenic infertility is a condition whereby psychological factors interfere with the body's ability to conceive (Sandelowski 1990; Boivin et al. 2011). During the 1940s and 1950s, medical practitioners and broader channels of discourse were looking to women's mental health as the cause of their reproductive difficulties, irrespective of whether they were physiological or biochemical in nature. Drawing on the work of Lana Thompson, Jensen reminds us of the long history of presenting women's psychology and intelligence through the 'lens of their reproductive body parts' (Thompson cited in Jensen 2016, p. 128). Presenting a woman's reproductive failing or success as a presentation of their minds gave the medical community scope to diagnose infertility based on 'a woman's underlying hostility, immaturity, or general unwillingness to accept her femininity' (Jensen 2016, p. 128). Medical and psychological writers of the period observed that 'assisting the infertile to become parents could be thwarting nature's wishes, given the high incidence of obstetrical and psychological problems in this group of patients' (Sandelowski 1990, p. 494). William Kroger, a specialist in the fields of gynaecology and psychiatry, made the point that 'aiding the emotionally immature infertile woman to become fertile could "open up the proverbial hornet's nest" and lead to neurotic children, broken homes, and divorce' (Kroger cited in Sandelowski 1990, p. 494). Brooke Edge makes the point that

> stereotypes of infertile women as selfish, neurotic, and unfit to raise children—align with cultural conceptions of what makes a woman a bad mother. This is particularly true when considering the 'bad mother's' opposite: the ideal of the 'intensive mother' … [a]dditionally, the key element of intensive mothers as naturally comfortable with and suited for motherhood draws a strict boundary between good mothers and infertile women who wish to become mothers. (Edge 2015, p. 141)

In a speech to the American Society for the Study of Sterility, Kroger concluded that infertility might best be understood as 'nature's first line of defense against the union of potentially defective germ plasm', later referring to the successful treatment of infertility as a 'hollow triumph' due to the fact that, in line with the psychogenic model, these pregnancies would lead to further increases in emotional pathology (Kroger cited in Sandelowski 1990, p. 494).

It was not until the early 1980s with the emergence and development of IVF treatments that the discourse changed again, with infertility being recast as a 'medical abnormality' (Wohlmann 2014). With increasing insights being gained into the 'workings of the human body and the processes of fertilization and implantation' the numbers of unexplained infertility cases were seen to steadily decrease (Van Balen 2002, p. 85). Thus, with growing numbers of somatic explanations of infertility emerging from the biomedical community, earlier psychogenic models were seen to be challenged and dismissed. This is not to say that women affected by reproductive problems do not experience feelings of guilt as it relates to their diagnosis, but rather, that current biomedical research is not assigning blame (Madsen of The Road to Baby Madsen: Our IVF Journey 2014; Brian 2015).

INFERTILITY: CONTEMPORARY DEFINITIONS AND DEMOGRAPHICS

Today, biomedical definitions of infertility are routinely founded on a specified time period of regular unprotected intercourse without pregnancy success (HFEA 2004, p. 9). According to the World Health Organization (WHO), infertility is 'a disease of the reproductive system defined by the failure to achieve a clinical pregnancy after 12 months or more of regular unprotected sexual intercourse' (WHO 2018). The UK's National Institute for Health and Care Excellence (NICE) guidelines previously referred to infertility as a 'failure to conceive after regular unprotected sexual intercourse for 2 years in the absence of known reproductive pathology' (NICE cited in Arya 2011, p. 541). However, they have more recently replaced this definition with a recommendation that a 'woman of reproductive age who has not conceived after 1 year of unprotected vaginal sexual intercourse, in the absence of any known cause of infertility, should be offered further clinical assessment and investigation along with her partner' with earlier referral to a specialist if 'the woman is aged 36 years or over' (NICE 2018a).

In the US, infertility is generally defined as 'not being able to ... conceive ... after one year ... of unprotected sex' (CDC 2018a). Women who have never experienced a pregnancy are understood to be affected by primary infertility, whereas those who have conceived in the past but are presently unable to conceive are diagnosed with secondary infertility (NHS 2018a). However, while WHO, NICE and the Centers for Disease Control and Prevention (CDC) define infertility as a problem with conception, elsewhere the term has been used to refer to women who are either unable to conceive after a year or more of unprotected intercourse *or* those who are unable to 'carry a pregnancy to term' (Garner cited in Needleman 1987, p. 136). While biomedical discourses use the term infertility to describe a heterosexual couple who are unable to conceive after a specified period of time, the term sub-fertility has more recently been employed because it draws attention to the fact that few couples are wholly infertile, rather, many are sub-fertile, meaning that 'they have problems that make conception difficult, if not highly unlikely, without medical help' (HFEA cited in Throsby 2004, p. 175). However, it is difficult to locate exact data.

Although the Office for National Statistics (ONS) compiles robust data concerning live births, stillbirths, infant, neonatal and perinatal deaths, infertility is not accounted for in this same way. Moreover, it is difficult to compile objective data on global infertility due to inconsistent definitions, diagnosis and reporting. For example, reporting on the UK alone, we are told that 'one in six *or* one in seven couples' are affected by fertility problems (HFEA 2011, p. 7, emphasis added; NHS 2018a). And although we are informed that one in eight American couples has trouble getting pregnant or sustaining a pregnancy (Resolve 2018), an 'estimated 25 percent of all American women and their partners will experience an episode of infertility during their lifetime' (CDC cited in Sterling 2013, p. 6). Irrespective of which figure is taken here, it is clear that the majority of couples are able to conceive naturally, and yet, there are a myriad of reasons why conception can be unsuccessful.

Although it only needs one healthy sperm to fertilise the ovum there are potential issues relating to the fallopian tubes, the quality of the egg, the thickness of the uterine lining, the position of the uterus, ovulation and the production of hormones (Scully 2014, p. 39). The UK's National Health Service (NHS) provides information on some of the most common causes of infertility, namely scarring from surgery, cervical mucus problems, fibroids, endometriosis and chemotherapy for women and poor-quality semen, low or abnormal sperm, testicular surgery, hypogonadism and anti-inflammatory medicines for men (NHS 2018b). The term infertility therefore covers a wide and diverse range of physiological problems; that said, there is also a diagnosis that relates to the couple rather than the individual, namely, idiopathic infertility, in which the cause of infertility is unknown and unexplained (Tomlins 2003, p. 17). The UK's health service informs us that approximately one quarter of all cases of infertility are unexplained, where no cause can be found in either partner (NHS 2018b).

Infertility is currently understood 'as a medical condition and managed within the medical model of diagnosis and treatment' (Sterling 2013, p. 28). However, although the standard medical model offers few grey areas concerning health and illness, in that the body is either 'disease-free, normally functioning and we are healthy or there is a presence of some disease or malfunction and we are ill' (Burr 2015, p. 42), infertility sits somewhat uncomfortably between the two. Infertility 'remains ambiguous medically as it is variously conceptualized as itself a disease, a symptom of disease, a cause of disease, a consequence of disease, and as not a disease at all' (Sandelowski and de Lacey 2002, p. 35). We are asked to consider if a woman who struggles to conceive but has no underlying organic pathology to explain her infertility is indeed suffering from an illness or disease.

This is not to say that infertility cannot be caused by an illness such as cancer or thyroid disorders or by biological defects in the reproductive system, but rather that infertility is not limited to these disorders or defects, and these disorders or defects are not necessarily incompatible with conception and pregnancy. Infertility is less a rigid medical ailment and more a 'flexible social process' (Sterling 2013, p. 242), a 'fluid social experience' (Ibid., p. 43) and 'a dynamic, socially conditioned process that is continuously in flux' (Ibid., p. 29). Those individuals who 'experience difficulty getting pregnant must determine on their own whether or not they are "infertile" and exactly what this means for them' (Ibid., p. 43). After all, there isn't 'a clear demarcation between infertility and fertility' or between infertility and maternity, because women can move from one condition to the other through reproductive choices and changing circumstances (Sandelowski 1990, p. 477; Sandelowski 1993). Women can seek specialist fertility treatment, foster, adopt or take on step- and co-mothering roles. In short, 'it is possible to be "infertile" and yet to be mothering children—either socially or within a biological relationship' (Letherby 1999, p. 371). Perhaps this is where we have to make distinctions between the biological diagnosis of infertility and the experience of social infertility.

Social infertility is a term that 'originally described the experiences of single women and lesbian couples who may not fit the "traditional" definition of infertility but need procreative assistance to have a child' (Sterling 2013, pp. 6–7). However, the broader definition of social infertility has extended so as to include long-distance couples and couples who work away from the family home for extended periods of time (Throsby 2004, p. 14). The notion of social infertility then can 'extend the concept of infertility as a process of self-identification to include those for whom "trying for a baby", in the sense of regular, unprotected heterosexual intercourse, is not an option' (Ibid., p. 14). Yet although some individuals affected by infertility have found social infertility to be 'a helpful term', others suggest that it is 'degrading' and 'offensive to those who are *truly* infertile' (The She Is Project 2015, emphasis added). More recently, the ontological category of anticipated infertility has been introduced, whereby cancer sufferers or healthy young women without an infertility diagnosis choose to freeze their eggs in anticipation of future fertility problems (Martin 2010; Mundy 2019). Either way, research looks to prevent, detect and manage infertility for those affected by a diagnosis (Macaluso et al. 2010).

Outside of biomedical literature, memoirs and diaries that deal with the topic of infertility, in what is commonly termed 'repro-lit' (Miller 2008, p. 79), tend to offer a different definition of infertility, namely the 'active but frustrated desire for a biologically related child' (Throsby 2004, p. 14). This definition separates 'physiological impediments to reproduction from the experience of infertility', making it an accessible definition for those affected by both medical and social models (Ibid., p. 14). Moreover, this description has what are said to be advantages over medical definitions because it 'opens up a range of possibilities for resolution', be it becoming a biological parent, fostering, adopting, or living without children (Ibid., p. 14). In short, one can 'stop identifying as infertile without having a baby' (Ibid., p. 14).

Assisted Reproduction: Treatments, Techniques and Technologies

For those affected by an infertility diagnosis, irrespective of the definition or experience, they might look to assisted reproduction as a way of creating or extending their family. While assisted reproduction is the name given to treatments that can help a woman get pregnant without having sexual intercourse (NICE 2018b), there exists an exhaustive glossary of clinical and laboratory terminology (Zegers-Hochschild et al. 2009). Artificial insemination is the 'broad term that refers to a number of different ways of artificially getting sperm to the right place for it to fertilise an egg, be it partner, husband or donor' (Tomlins 2003, p. 99). More specifically, IUI is the placing of sperm inside the womb and IVF is when an egg is fertilised by sperm in a test tube or elsewhere outside the body. IVF with intracytoplasmic sperm injection (ICSI) is commonly used in severe cases of male-factor infertility, involving the injection of a single sperm directly into the oocyte cytoplasm/mature egg. Furthermore, preimplantation genetic diagnosis (PGD) is the process of removing a cell from an in vitro fertilisation embryo for genetic testing to help identify genetically abnormal embryos before transferring a healthy embryo to the uterus. Donor insemination and/or egg donation are also available, all of which are regulated and controlled by the Human Fertilisation and Embryology Authority (HFEA) (HFEA 2018a) in the UK (NICE 2018a, b; HFEA 2018b, c; VARTA 2018).

While assisted reproduction refers to the myriad of treatment options available, ranging from 'the relatively easy and straightforward *artificial insemination* ... to the far more complex and invasive *in vitro fertilisation*' (Tomlins 2003, p. 95, emphasis in original), assisted reproductive technology speaks of 'medically assisted reproduction and comprises all treatments or procedures that include the *in vitro* handling of both human oocytes and sperm or of embryos for the purpose of establishing a pregnancy' (De Neubourg and Devroe 2016, p. 149, emphasis in original). Therefore, medically assisted reproductive technologies do not include assisted or artificial insemination 'using sperm from either a woman's partner or a sperm donor' (Ibid., p. 149) or 'procedures in which a woman takes medicine only to stimulate egg production without the intention of having eggs retrieved' (Mutcherson 2017, p. 175). The CDC makes the point when it tells us that assisted reproductive technologies include 'all fertility treatments in which both eggs and embryos are handled' (CDC

2018b), going on to state that the 'procedures involve surgically removing eggs from a woman's ovaries, combining them with sperm in the laboratory, and returning them to the woman's body or donating them to another woman' (Ibid.).

Due to the treatment options and technologies on offer we have been told that 'few conditions result in absolute sterility' (Tomlins 2003, p. 60). After all,

> even in the worst instances—where there are no eggs or no sperm—it may be possible to conceive using eggs or sperm of a donor. It is far more likely, though, you will have a problem with ovulation, with hormone levels, blocked tubes, or a problem with the quality or quantity of sperm—all of which may be treatable. (Ibid., p. 60)

And it was blocked fallopian tubes that led to Lesley Brown seeking out fertility specialists before giving birth to the first ever baby born using IVF in the UK back in 1978. Although the preceding decade had been fuelled by intense debate concerning 'both the ethics of the endeavour and its practicability' (Throsby 2004, p. 1), the

> safe arrival of Louise Brown confirmed that it was indeed possible to successfully remove an egg from a woman's body, fertilise it in a petri dish and transfer it to the uterus via the cervix, resulting in a pregnancy that was capable of continuing to term. (Ibid., p. 1)

After struggling for nine years with an infertility diagnosis linked to blocked fallopian tubes, a natural IVF cycle found parents Lesley and John Brown delivering a healthy baby girl. However, it is important to note that they were not the first couple to undergo the procedure (Crowe 1990, p. 35). We are told that the first 'transfer of a human embryo fertilised by IVF took place in December 1971, and the first IVF pregnancy was confirmed in 1975, although this turned out to be ectopic and was therefore terminated. A second embryo transfer shortly afterwards failed to implant' (Throsby 2004, p. 7). Moreover, when, in 1978, Lesley and John Brown were selected for treatment, they were not the only couple chosen; there were three women who underwent the procedure, and yet it is the birth of Louise Brown that made the national and international headlines (Ibid., pp. 7–8)—perhaps unsurprising when we discover that the other two women failed to conceive. Indeed, the early IVF pioneers were so concerned about poor or negative public reaction to their new procedure that those couples who underwent experimental cycles 'had to agree to an abortion if the developing foetus was discovered to be malformed' in any way (Throsby 2004, p. 4, Challoner 1999, p. 41).

Louise Brown was presented as the first successful 'test tube baby' in the UK, while in 1981 Elizabeth Carr became the first IVF baby born in the US, and the fifteenth in the world. Like Lesley Brown before her, Judith Carr had been unable to conceive due to complications with her fallopian tubes caused by earlier unsuccessful pregnancies (Cohn 1981). Since that time, more than 250,000 babies have been born as a result of IVF in the UK alone, with one commentator going as far as suggesting that we will soon witness 'one in ten' of all births in Britain being the result of fertility treatments (Morgan 2015). Moreover, over one million babies have been born in the US using IVF and alternative assisted reproductive techniques. Louise and Elizabeth make up two of the five million babies born worldwide through assisted reproductive technologies (Press Association 2016).

Assisted reproductive technologies are routinely drawn on when less invasive procedures or cheaper pharmaceutical options have failed (Boggs 2017), and yet, although these varied treatments are routinely used to help those affected by an infertility diagnosis to conceive, they can also be used for social infertility and where communicable diseases put partners at risk of infection through intercourse. Since the birth of Louise Brown back in the late 1970s, people accessing assisted reproductive treatments and technologies do not necessarily have an infertility diagnosis. After all, an infertility diagnosis may apply to a heterosexual couple as a single unit even if only one individual in that couple is infertile. Moreover, unpartnered individuals or lesbian or gay couples may technically be fertile but require assistance to achieve pregnancy (Martin 2010, p. 529; Tri Health 2018). Nor is an infertility diagnosis necessarily relevant for those who use IVF paired with PGD to select for or against particular genetic traits (Ibid., p. 529). Those assisted reproductive treatments and techniques that have been 'created to aid the infertile achieving pregnancy have expanded to allow other categories of people have *biologically related* children' (Martin 2010, p. 529, emphasis added).

Although there are differences between treatment options and medical procedures as they relate to IUI and IVF, for example, for the remainder of this volume, I am going to draw on NICE guidelines and use assisted reproduction to refer to any and all treatments, be they invasive or otherwise, that 'can help a woman get pregnant without having sexual intercourse' (NICE 2018a), while making it clear when I am paying particular attention to assisted reproductive technologies such as IVF.

Infertility Diagnosis and Treatment

For those women who postponed motherhood and still have a healthy egg supply or those who are trying for children decades earlier, many of those diagnosed with infertility are affected by ovulation problems. And for each of these women, the first stage of treatment might be to prescribe a fertility medication such as clomifene, tamoxifen, metformin or gonadotrophin (NHS 2019). Although it can be difficult to garner the success rates of such fertility medicines, specialists suggest that clomifene, a medication which encourages ovulation, offers an '80 percent chance of ovulating, usually within the first three months' and because of 'this ovulation boost, most women have a 50 percent chance of getting pregnant within the first six months' after beginning the prescribed medication (Attain Fertility 2018). However, the drug is only helpful if 'you still have an ample egg supply' (Ibid.). We are reminded of the risk of age-related infertility because if 'you are over 35 and your egg supply is low or dwindling' such medication may not help you get pregnant (Ibid.). Although these drugs may cause 'side effects, such as nausea, vomiting, headaches and hot flushes' (NHS 2019), taking them is relatively simple and can be scheduled relatively effortlessly into a working day. That is not necessarily the case, however, for those women for whom clomifene has not been successful, for whom assisted reproduction, and specifically reproductive technologies are the only realistic options left for a chance of conception and/ or pregnancy.

As already stated, there are myriads of assisted reproductive treatment and technology options available to those affected by an infertility diagnosis, be it IUI, IVF or IVF with intracytoplasmic sperm injection, the use of either donor insemination or egg donation, traditional/straight or gestational/host surrogacy. And although each option comes with its own strengths, limitations and stages of treatment 'the majority of people going down the IVF or [ICSI] path will pass through' various stages known as downregulation, stimulation, egg collection, fertilisation and transfer (Scully 2014, pp. 99–102). These stages might appear daunting at first glance, and there is evidence from women experiencing treatment that it is difficult to navigate alongside other working or caring responsibilities (Ibid., p. 96).

We are informed that the 'daily practices of IVF, and particularly the administration of the hormonal drug treatments that precede the more high-profile clinical moments of egg collection, fertilisation and embryo transfer, take place in the wider social context within which people live, work and socialise' (Throsby 2004, p. 109; Tomlins 2003, pp. 102–134). We find that 'many women undergoing fertility treatment stay in unchallenging and unsatisfying careers for many years', in part to help enable the logistics and in part because they expect to be 'leaving to have a baby … and returning part-time' (Throsby 2004, p. 155). Moreover, we are reminded not just of the logistical difficulties, but also the physical toll of treatment. After all,

> IVF is a physical, corporeal experience which literally … as well as discursively marks the body. In a culture which values physical appearance as an essential expression of femininity, this creates an additional burden for women whose feminine identity is already under threat as a result of not having conceived. (Ibid., p. 154)

The long-standing and ubiquitous 'beauty myth' encourages women to judge themselves and one another against unrealisable ideals of appearance and attractiveness (Wolf 1991). While pregnant women are encouraged to align their post-pregnancy bodies with their pre-pregnant physiques (Dworkin and Wachs 2004, pp. 610–624), for those women who are going through a cycle, or multiple cycles, of IVF treatment, their physical appearance and thus their very feminine identity is in question. After all, at the same time as a woman might be experiencing hot flashes, headaches, mood swings, depression, anxiety, joint, abdominal and breast pain, dizziness, nausea, injection site soreness and menstrual spotting (Gurevich 2019), she might also be suffering from acne, weight gain and hair loss (Casella 2018). Although the former can, with discomfort, be hidden from view, the latter are much more difficult to mask. For those women who are open about their IVF treatments, there is an explanation and thus justification for their physical changes, but not so for those women who seek to keep their infertility and accompanying treatments private.

Women today have access to a vast array of interventions including IUI, IVF, ICSI, surgical sperm removal, embryo freezing, blastocyst transfer, assisted hatching, egg donation and surrogacy. Indeed, family-building options are 'very much tailored to the individual and the issues that have been diagnosed' (Scully 2014, p. 99). However, while such options are available, they cannot guarantee a successful conception. By way of an example, IVF procedures fail more than they succeed. Evidence shows that 'the chance of getting pregnant from an individual IVF cycle in Britain still only stands at about 21 per cent' for women under the age of 35 (Winston 2018) and yet 'the cyclical nature of IVF presents a persistent and seductive maybe-next-time promise' (Throsby 2004, p. 8). Women undergoing IVF treatment routinely liken the experience to 'being on a treadmill from which there is no easily apparent exit point' (Ibid., p. 8). Because treatments and medicines available are increasing all the time, be it womb transplants (The New Scientist 2018), restorative reproductive medicines (Moran 2018) or the future possibility of extending egg health (Science Daily 2018), women are encouraged to believe that conception and pregnancy success will follow.

HIERARCHIES OF FAMILY BUILDING

Just as women affected by an infertility diagnosis speak of societal judgement, so too, women who utilise medical support and/or third-party intervention in order to create or increase their family are also found wanting. In her seminal work on the experience of motherhood, infertility and involuntary childlessness, Gayle Letherby foregrounds a social hierarchy of appropriate family-building practices when she states, quite bluntly, that 'real' families are 'genetically related' (Letherby 1999, p. 367). That said, even though contemporary Western society presents biological children as the preferred norm, genetic lineage is not always the key component in the construction of a family. David Schneider's (1980) anthropological research on kinship in Western society in general and American society in particular makes it clear that the biological framework that is routinely viewed as 'the natural foundation for the analysis of family and marriage relationships around the world—is, actually, an ethnocentric construct' (Ottenheimer 2001, p. 202)—a construct that is based on Eurocentric notions of reproduction, but not one that is necessarily shared worldwide. Although literature on kinship has been confounded by changes to assisted reproductive treatments and technologies (Akesson 2002), there is the suggestion that, in Western society at least, 'the means of achieving relatedness may have changed' but 'the rigorous emphasis on the family and on the biogenetic basis of American kinship remains essentially unchanged' (Ragoné 2004, p. 342).

Amy Klein, who writes a fertility column for *The New York Times*, experienced this hierarchy of appropriate family building first hand, when, after four miscarriages and nine rounds of IVF, she became pregnant. We are told that others affected by an infertility diagnosis were desperate to know what this 44-year-old woman had done to conceive so that they might follow her example, be it counselling, medication or meditation. However, when she mentioned that she became pregnant with donor eggs, she was met with disappointment rather than congratulations. Klein comments that although she was carrying what she felt to be her child, made from her husband's sperm and donor eggs, she was seen as having 'failed to achieve the holy grail of fertility treatment: having a child with my own and my husband's DNA' (Klein 2015). Klein goes on to outline what she sees and experiences as the hierarchy of conception:

> Obviously, the easiest and least costly is just plain sex. Then there's IVF—These 'test-tube babies' use the mother's oocytes and father's sperm, so they're genetically related to both parents, not to mention carried by the mother: equal in almost every way to natural conception. Lower on the totem pole is what's called 'third-party reproduction'. … Everyone knows about sperm donation, with thousands of banks where you can choose a guy like from an online dating profile; single mothers are not ashamed to admit creating a child using their own genes combined with those of a (tall, hot, smart) stranger. … Surrogacy, in which a woman outside the relationship carries the couple's embryo until birth, has also made it to the mainstream. … The only thing that still seems to be a secret in these uber-confessional days is women who use donor eggs. (Ibid.)

Erica Haimes argues that since 'motherhood is at the centre of "family-ness," to subvert motherhood is to subvert the family' (Haimes cited in Letherby 1999, p. 368), and I would suggest that, on the back of Klein's experiences, it continues to be genetic motherhood rather than the broader maternal role that is central here. It is the use of donor eggs that is said to be disrupting the maternal order, even though between 10 and 15 per cent of all babies born through IVF used donated gametes or embryos in the UK and US respectively (Klein 2015). Post-constructionists have coined the term 'reproductive misfit' (Lam 2016, p. 303) as a way of describing those women who rely on assisted or artificial reproductive treatments and technologies in order to 'transcend the limitations of their bodies' (Le Vay 2019, p. 155).

Infertility Visibility: The Roles and Responsibilities of the Media

Although infertility has existed since time immemorial, it is only with the advent of assisted treatments and technologies that it has become more visible. Likewise, although adoption has been understood as a way of building and extending families for generations, it is only relatively recently, with the decline of newborns in need of adoption and the growing numbers of older children awaiting permanence, that adoption too has become more visible. Likewise, although miscarriage and pregnancy loss have always been very common experiences for women, they are experiences that can be, and routinely have been, kept from public view, at least until an online trend that sought to break the 'conspiracy of silence' (Kohn and Moffitt 2000, p. 133). The fact that stars, celebrities and recognisable faces from the entertainment arena have spoken about infertility, pregnancy loss and non-traditional mothering in recent years provides some evidence of the ways in which these topics are starting to enter the public consciousness. However, it might also explain why, until relatively recently, there has been little in the way of media representations. As such, this work offers less of a compare–contrast through different decades or generations, but tends to focus its attention around the turn of the millennium, when the media started to acknowledge not just the topics in hand, but their interest to an invested audience.

Infertility and non-traditional family building are visible in the mainstream media environment. Indeed, Jennifer Maher has noted that irrespective of whether you are watching *Children of Men* (2006), *Juno* (2007), *Knocked Up* (2007) or *What to Expect When You're Expecting* (2012), 'reproduction—accidental, thwarted, eliminated by environmental disaster, or made possible by … medicine—is a near-obsessive theme' (Maher 2014, p. 854). Add to this list, *The Odd Life of Timothy Green* (2012), *The New Normal* (2012–13), *The Girl on the Train* (2016), *The Light Between Oceans* (2016), *The Handmaid's Tale* (2017–) and *Private Life* (2018), and it is clear that the topic of infertility and non-traditional family building continues to find a home in the entertainment arena. Likewise, those celebrity infertility or international adoption narratives that saturate the tabloid and gossip sector, touring art and photographic exhibitions such as Home Time (2008), theatrical plays such as *The Quiet House* (2016), podcasts such as BBC Radio 4's *The Adoption* (2017), blogs such as Bubbles and Bumps (2018) and fertility art festivals such as Fertility Fest (2018) go further to remind audiences that the themes in question span screens, auditoriums, sound waves, social and print media. And although infertility and non-traditional family building have 'been studied from historical, sociological, and medical perspectives', it remains evident that 'little has been written about representations of infertility in popular media' (Edge 2015, p. 11). This is surprising given that 'popular representations are a powerful force in the social world and [in the] cultural construction of reproduction' (Franklin cited in Le Vay 2019, p. 217). Individuals are routinely introduced to alternative family-building options through popular media culture, and for those who fail to 'actively seek alternative information about reproductive issues' there is little other frame of reference here (Shalev and Lemish 2013, p. 322).

Alongside a consideration of the legal and medical aspects of reproduction, an examination of the ways in which representations of infertility and non-traditional family building via assisted reproductive technologies and adoption are depicted in the media is crucial as these texts can be seen to inform, educate and inspire audiences, or, alternatively, mislead and miscommunicate. These popular stories and accompanying statistics have the power and scope to quash the silence surrounding infertility and pregnancy loss while breaking the taboo that continues to envelop much non-traditional family building. In her infertility memoir Anne-Marie Scully tells us that it is easy to get 'angry' at how little fertility issues are discussed in contemporary society (Scully 2014, p. 66), and yet popular media texts have the ability to engender a dialogue around reproductive disruption and non-traditional family building.

In their work on televisual depictions of surrogacy Shirley Shalev and Dafna Lemish argue that 'the media have become a key factor in an individual's decision-making process regarding reproductive issues' while remaining 'crucial to the success of public family planning programs' (Shalev and Lemish 2013, p. 322). After all, audiences 'construct their understandings of the world, including their beliefs about medicine, health [and] disease … from their interactions with culture', with popular media culture being of significance here (Sterling 2013, p. 21; Ashton and Feasey 2014). Evelina Sterling makes this point when she states that the depiction of infertility both 'shapes and reflects the overall infertility experience itself' (Sterling 2013, p. 27).

In one IVF message board, members comment that 'society as a whole gets most of its "information" (big quotes there) from our fabulous media, and so most people whose lives haven't been touched by infertility feel uncomfortable with it' (wondercat 2010). There is scepticism about the ways in which popular media culture, with the rare exception of Disney's animated children's feature *UP* (2009), presents the lived reality of infertility and non-traditional family building. Myriad media texts, from blogs and vlogs to factual television, can be seen to form a consensus in their depiction of women affected by an infertility diagnosis, because while they routinely depict these women as mothers on the back of successful assisted reproductive treatments, in so doing, they routinely fail to address the full physical, emotional, logistical and financial reality of that particular path to parenthood. So too, they overlook the lived reality of alternative futures without children (it81 2010).

Although one might argue that the various stages of adoption are presented on screen and in social media in a more candid fashion, televisual closure is routinely the matching process rather than the experiences of adoptive parenting or the stark reality of the many children awaiting permanence. The point here then is that while the entertainment arena appears keen to engage with the themes of infertility and non-traditional family building, their partial nature and self-selecting depictions are ignoring the lived reality of these experiences and are thus doing little to negotiate the shame and secrecy that too often accompany an infertility diagnosis and alternative paths to parenthood. With this in mind, this volume examines the representation of infertility, the use of assisted reproductive treatments and technologies, pregnancy loss and adoption in a variety of media texts ranging from social media to television documentaries, paying particular attention to those frames and formats that can be grouped together as first-person, documentary and factual. After all, it is these texts first and foremost that have a responsibility to their audiences as compared to their more escapist and dramatic media counterparts.

However, rather than look at these texts in isolation, this book shifts between mainstream film, television, radio and journalism, official websites, forums, think pieces, editorial-opinion writing, online blogs, vlogs, anonymous postings and academic writing from the fields of media, motherhood and gender studies. In order to make sense of the ways in which a topic such as infertility or adoption is understood, it is important to acknowledge those popular and professional discourses that are in circulation, considering the ways in which social, medical, journalistic and personal paratexts help inform our understanding of the themes and discourses in question (Gray 2003; Barker 2004; Darweesh 2014). This is not about offering a hierarchy of personal, popular or professional credibility, but rather, to draw attention to the discourses in broader circulation here. In this way, I am not looking to offer an 'exceptionally knowledgeable' reading (Hermes 1995); rather, I am more interested in acknowledging the ways in which ancillary materials can be understood as part of a broader discussion about infertility and non-traditional family building.

Facts and figures, detailed data and case studies exist for women who are interested in finding out about infertility, IVF, stillbirth, ectopic and molar pregnancies, miscarriage and adoption. Moreover, a myriad of factual and fictional texts exist across a diverse range of media formats and platforms that address the broader debates that stem from an infertility diagnosis. And yet, with an abundance of research and representations to hand, women continue to speak of a lack of awareness about infertility in general and their own fertility in particular (Shapiro 2012, Nargund cited in Adams 2015; Levy and Farrar 2018; British Fertility Society 2018a, b). It is important that we look at the ways in which infertility and its surrounding channels of discourse are being represented in popular media culture, be it medical advice, self-help narratives, film and television texts, blogs, vlogs, social media and the documentary tradition.

A wealth of contemporary research exists for those working within reproductive endocrinology or gynaecology, although medical volumes have little crossover access or appeal to media students or popular readers. Alternatively, infertility memoirs and self-help support books are routinely written with the interested and invested reader in mind. These books all document the pain and occasional shame of life as a woman affected by an infertility diagnosis in the current pronatal period, celebrity or otherwise, offering personal stories from those who have navigated the path to motherhood through assisted reproductive treatments. They are written for those women who, after having been diagnosed with infertility, choose to take decisive action in their quest for a maternal role. Although fictional novels exist that deal with similar themes and narratives, readers remain interested in these confessional volumes as they offer hope, support and a level of authenticity in their words, stories and outcomes. While the medical books are penned specifically for physicians working in reproductive medicine, these first-person volumes are written with the involuntarily childless woman in mind. And although both the medical and confessional volumes serve a meaningful role for their readers, neither has accounted for the role of infertility in the media, and the ways in which such images and stories are in dialogue with both the medical and confessional discourses relating to non-traditional family building.

In *The Empty Cradle: Infertility in America from Colonial Times to the Present* (1999), historian Margaret Marsh and obstetrician-gynaecologist Wanda Ronner look to unmask the complex relationship between science and society. They draw on medical, confessional and popular media discourses ranging from intimate diaries and letters, patient records, medical literature and mass circulation magazines such as *Hygieia* (a health magazine published by the American Medical Association), *Reader's Digest*, *Parents* and *Good Housekeeping* in order to make sense of the social and scientific dimensions of infertility over the past three centuries (Marsh and Ronner 1999). The book has been applauded for giving voice to those affected by both the physiological and cultural conditions of infertility, and yet, there is scope here to update the work in question and to consider it in light of more recent debates, family-building options and media texts now available.

Scope and Structure of the Book

This is the first book-length volume to examine the broad-ranging depiction of infertility and non-traditional family building in the media. Although fascinating work does exist to account for celebrity infertility narratives (Feasey 2014; Osborne-Thompson 2014) and the representation of infertile bodies in the blogosphere (Hepworth 2015) and reality programming (Edge 2014) respectively, such work has so far been limited to individual film, television and media research articles, medical accounts, personal blog posts or chapters in broader edited collections relating to maternal experiences. At the time of writing, Lulu Le Vay's enlightening volume on the reproduction of normative family on television has just been published (Le Vay 2019), and although the work offers a fascinating insight into the representation and audience reception of surrogacy storylines in soap opera and reality programming, for example, it's focus leaves little scope for broader debates relating to non-traditional family building as they exist within or beyond the television schedules.

Moreover, there are numerous volumes written for and by embryologists, physicians and those involved with researching or handling assisted reproductive technologies, but it is difficult for anyone outside of these fields to access or navigate due to the terminology used and the data being presented. The themes are timely, pertinent and of importance, but they are neither approachable nor situated in their wider social, cultural or entertainment context. This volume will acknowledge the themes, debates, case studies and clinical practices as they relate to reproductive medicine and make them accessible for a broader readership before interrogating the ways in which such practices, technologies and case studies are depicted on screen, in print and on social media platforms.

The book will introduce the clinical and medical terms that are relevant to a discussion of infertility and non-traditional mothering, alongside statistics relating to infertility, pregnancy loss, assisted reproductive treatments and technologies, surrogacy, fostering and adoption in both the UK and the US, before considering the ways in which contemporary media texts make reference to these conditions and practices. I have drawn on reports, case studies and media texts from both sides of the Atlantic, and while statistics relating to infertility, treatments available, the feelings of women affected by a diagnosis and media representations are shared, much of the wider medical, legal and ethical contexts differ.

Maternal possibilities have changed in recent years and, as such, it is important that the volume acknowledges such changes, developments, emerging treatments and techniques in relation to the wider social landscape. The book examines the representation of those women who have experienced or are shown to be experiencing infertility or miscarriage, have used artificial reproductive technologies or who have or are trying to build a family through surrogacy or adoption. It is crucial to discover where these images are seen, where the personal and professional stories, opinion editorials and thought pieces are heard, and where the relevant demographic data can be encountered in the contemporary media environment, using these findings to appeal for more attention to be paid to the topic of infertility and non-traditional family building within both the public service and commercial media sector alike.

In terms of structure, Chap. 2 introduces the reader to UK, US and worldwide infertility statistics before paying particular attention to the rise in infertility blogs and confessional first-person accounts of otherwise private infertility stories. Infertility blogs, or what I will term family building blogs, are routinely dedicated to the experiences not of infertility *per se*, but of the public performance of fertility treatments, a public performance of pain and endurance, which routinely ends with a much-anticipated final maternal post. Indeed, long-running family building blogs that do not offer a happy ending in the form of a healthy newborn are few and far between; those that do not seek treatment are even rarer in the blogosphere. Therefore, an examination of confessional storytelling allows us to consider the ways in which family building blogging might be considered both beneficial and problematic for authors and audiences alike.

Chapter 3 looks at both the medical reality and media depictions of assisted reproductive treatments and technologies, paying particular attention to IVF, egg and sperm donations and surrogacy arrangements. The medical community is continuing to expand the possibility of family building for postmenopausal women and women born without wombs, cancer patients, single parents and gay and lesbian families. With such possibilities in mind, it is crucial that we consider the medical, legal and ethical frameworks that underpin such new and emerging family-building opportunities alongside the media depictions of those families. Myriad televisual documentaries have explored the topic of infertility in general and age-related infertility in particular, and it is important to make sense of the narratives that are being depicted in such factual entertainment as it is routinely presented to the women in the audience. The documentary tradition has a long and ubiquitous history of non-partisan reporting and objectivity. As such, it is crucial that such infotainment introduces not only the facts and treatment options on offer for those diagnosed with infertility, but also the success rates for those participants within and beyond the programme.

Chapter 4 looks at the representation of miscarriage, stillbirth, ectopic and molar pregnancies as they exist in social media, paying particular attention to those women who have begun to speak out about pregnancy loss on the back of generations of silence and isolation. Miscarriage is a routine and very common experience and yet it remains an experience rarely shared. Women are said to be ill informed about both the frequency and medical reality of miscarriage, as such; it is important to consider the ways in which women who make early pregnancy announcements on social media are helping, and otherwise, to negotiate miscarriage myths and offer a support network at a time when young people more than ever before are looking to the digital world for health advice and information.

Moving from miscarriage to adoption, Chap. 5 draws attention to the number of children in care, those in need of permanence and the ways in which both Britain and America are seen to market their 'harder to place' children for the attention of prospective adopters. Media texts that span message boards and multi-part documentaries make it clear that adoption is the last acceptable option for those women affected by an infertility diagnosis who have exhausted the possibility of biological children via assisted reproductive treatment options. A wealth of government reports, charity groups, personal profiles and shared forums look to inform, educate and indeed recruit potential adoptive families, and although they do well to offer clear advice on who can be approved for adoption, there remains a question here about how open these sites are being about the lived experience of adopting children with a history of trauma, abuse and neglect.

Although the volume seeks to explore a variety of media texts and contexts, I am aware that there are as many omissions as there are inclusions, and, as such, the concluding chapter presents a synthesis of the broader themes, debates and representations offered throughout the book, restating the case for considering the depiction of infertility, loss and non-traditional family building while foregrounding future case studies and research directions.

Everything included in the book, be it public health messages, government reports or popular media materials, is readily available in both the UK and US, so my argument is not that information relating to infertility and non-traditional family building is unavailable, but rather that this information is only accessed when needed. Women only tend to search for medical advice or support networks when they or someone close to them has been affected by an infertility diagnosis, and my point here is simply that we need to expand that audience, extend the conversation and bring the debate into a broader educational and entertainment arena. With this in mind, I am keen to map the public health messages alongside the media representations; and, as such, the ensuing chapters rely on the NHS Choices website, CDC data, adoption networks, pregnancy loss associations and blog threads, for example. It is important to present such material in order to fully understand and thus engage with the details, data and descriptions being presented here.

Although the book will look to find an audience with undergraduate students, postgraduate students and scholars from the fields of film, television, media, gender and motherhood studies, there exists a broader aim for the work. After all, the findings may help prepare specialists—be they family physicians, obstetricians, gynaecologists, IVF consultants, counsellors or alternative health-care professionals who work with women affected by an infertility diagnosis—to understand the ways in which media representations help to shape discourses and individual narratives of infertility and non-traditional family building. In addition, the work could inform professional health campaigners interested in public education initiatives about effective infertility dialogue and communication. Although the reality of infertility by way of the aforementioned family-building options is not hidden, it continues to be shrouded in secrecy, and I would hope that the work presented here goes some way towards encouraging public service broadcasters, creatives and researchers to speak to women about both the commonality and reality of these experiences, and in so doing, educate future generations so that we might break the long-standing and stifling silence surrounding infertility (Hepburn 2018; MFM 2018).

For those already familiar with the medical facts, figures and statistics as they relate to primary or secondary infertility, the symptoms, causes and diagnosis of miscarriage, or the different steps and stages experienced on the path to adoption, for example, you may wish to skip through the opening contextualising sections and jump to the media representations. If, however, you are not as yet familiar with the medical and social framework, I would recommend starting at the beginning.

LANGUAGE AND TERMINOLOGY

Before turning to the statistics, themes and media texts that inform the volume, it is important to explain some of the terms that are used and others that are sidestepped, namely *childlessness*, pregnancy *loss*, *family building* and the notion of *suffering*.

In the first instance, involuntary *childlessness* is used to refer to those women who desire a child but who have not been able to conceive or carry a pregnancy to term. However, the term seems to suggest that you are 'missing' something from life if you are living without children, and although this is a linguistic concern, the current alternative, *childfree*, appears celebratory, when for those women who desire children, the experience is anything but (Letherby 1994, pp. 525–532, 2003, pp. 50–65). Likewise, the phrase pregnancy *loss* as a way of speaking about miscarriage, stillbirth, ectopic and molar pregnancies seems too light a word for what can be a traumatic and devastating experience. For many women, *losing* something seems trivial, ephemeral and avoidable, and, as such, the term *loss* is deemed inappropriate. But again, we are struggling for sensitive alternatives. The notion of pregnancy or reproductive disruption exists, but that is a term that accounts for a wealth of ways in which 'the standard linear narrative of conception, birth, and the progress of the next generation is interrupted' from births of children with congenital health problems to abortion (Van Balen and Inhorn 2002, p. 4). Therefore, although I tend to write about the specifics of miscarriage, stillbirth, ectopic and molar pregnancies, on occasion when I am making reference to a shared experience of unsuccessful pregnancy, I will, for lack of a more appropriate term, employ the word *loss*.

Miscarriage is a very common experience and stillbirth itself is a common experience in the UK and US, while the former is understood as a natural loss of pregnancy materials, the latter is acknowledged as the loss of an unborn baby, but we tend not to refer to the women who have experienced such losses as mothers (Edelman 2017) unless they go on to have later successful pregnancies. I do not address these women as mothers even though they carried their, in many cases, longed-for children, not because I am insensitive to their experiences, but because I am trying to offer clarity in my argument about those who struggle to conceive, those who struggle to stay pregnant and those who end treatment. We refer to women as mothers who have successfully used a gestational surrogate, because even though they have not themselves carried their babies to term, they are mothers, performing predictable motherwork, unlike those women who have experienced pregnancy but not to term.

A key theme throughout this book is non-traditional *family building*. Although the term is useful in its ability to foreground a desire to conceive or adopt, I am mindful of the fact that I am positioning the family in question as a couple who have, or are planning to have, children. After all, we live in a pronatal society whereby the term family is rarely used to talk about couples, be they short- or long-term, in civil partnerships or married. In short, a couple is not read as a family unit until they have children, preferably biological children, soon after marriage (Scully 2014: 67). Although the term *family building* is not unproblematic in this regard, the alternative, family extension, is rarely used within the blogosphere, vlogopshere, the documentary tradition or wider channels of discourse. Moreover, the term family extension itself assumes a couple rather than a single mother or father by choice. My point here then is that although we need to be mindful of the limitations of the term *family building*, its alternative, family extension, is differently problematic.

Furthermore, I am sensitive to the ways in which women are routinely presented as *suffering* with or from infertility, a phrase routinely employed in existing literature (Bronstein and Knoll 2015), and although I am in no way looking to diminish the pain and trauma that many women go through at the point of diagnosis, as they look to assisted reproductive options, adoption or a life without children, it is not a phrase that accurately reflects the experience of infertility. For those women who are content to live a *childless* existence on the back of an infertility diagnosis, the term *suffering* is not in keeping with their life choices. Even for those women who are in their own words devastated by an infertility diagnosis and desperate for children, their infertile body is not a body in pain or discomfort. Rather, it is the fact that the body is incapable of conceiving or carrying a pregnancy to term that can lead to emotional distress, while assisted reproductive treatments and technologies can bring with them both mental and physical pain. In this same way, I want to avoid referring to women as infertile, as if their fertility somehow stands for or defines them. From this estimation then, I routinely talk about women being diagnosed with infertility or of women being affected by an infertility diagnosis.

I refer, throughout this work, to females who are diagnosed with infertility irrespective of the fact that infertility, be it medical and/or social, affects men and women, gay and straight, single by choice, those who are involuntarily single, long-term partners and married couples. This is not in an effort to dismiss the experience of male-factor infertility or to ignore individual female bodies, but rather to acknowledge that infertility 'the world over, remains largely a *woman's* problem' (Van Balen and Inhorn 2002, p. 19; Earle and Letherby 2003, p. 2). Men and women are equally likely to be affected by an infertility diagnosis (Kumar and Singh 2015) and yet 'people think of complications with conceiving as gendered female' (Edge 2015, p. 4).

Evelina Sterling makes the point when she tells us that '[e]ven though there are as many infertile men as women, women have traditionally borne the brunt of the medical, social, and cultural burdens when a couple fails to become pregnant' because '[t]hroughout history, reproductive health has been "women's business"' (Sterling 2013, p. 15). Indeed, '[e]ven when the root of the infertility is male, treatment to address that condition most often entails invasive work on the woman's body' (Edge 2015, p. 4). As Karen Throsby notes, 'the distribution of practical tasks in obtaining, organising and undergoing treatment ... is fundamentally "woman's work"' (Throsby 2004, p. 137). Assisted reproductive treatments are performed on and to the female body, irrespective of which partner has been diagnosed, as one family building blogger states, with tongue only gently in cheek,

> [u]s girls get the shitty end of the stick when it comes to fertility treatment, we have to go to all of the doctor's appointments, drop our pants for strang-

ers in white coats, repeatedly do blood tests, have cameras wiggled around us, take horrid hormone injections and then deal with the emotional consequences ... and that's before you even get pregnant! (Simone of Bubbles and Bumps 2017)

Irrespective of the diagnosis 'women are usually the ones who initiate treatment, receive treatment and cope with the difficulties associated with infertility regardless of the diagnosis' (Sterling 2013, p. 130; Greil cited in Wohlmann 2014). Moreover, as the book will demonstrate, it is women who routinely tweet, post, write as bloggers and appear in those televisual texts dedicated to the diagnosis in question. Likewise, women are more proactive than their male counterparts in seeking assisted reproductive treatments and researching the adoption process (Becker 2000; Greil 2002).

Lastly, when referring to those women who experience the 'shitty end of the stick' by way of assisted reproductive technologies and treatments, I routinely speak of them as women first and foremost. The term patient can be misleading as the majority of women who are affected by an infertility diagnosis are not sick and are therefore not looking to be restored to the status quo as is common in a 'restitution narrative' (Throsby 2004, p. 15). Likewise, the terms customer, client, consumer or user are accurate in as much as they refer to the experience of employing a medical service on offer, but they are routinely steeped in the language of marketing and public relations (McLaughlin 2009). I am not overlooking the roles and responsibilities of those companies, teams, couples or individuals who offer, sell or consume; I am simply trying to note that these phrases do not fully address the 'complexities of the service-recipient relationship' (Ibid., p. 1101) in assisted reproductive transactions, surrogacy or adoption arrangements to which I will now turn.

REFERENCES

Adams, Stephen. 2015. NHS Chief Warns Women Not to Wait until 30 to Have Baby as Country Faces a Fertility Timebomb. *The Mail on Sunday*. Accessed April 12, 2019. http://www.dailymail.co.uk/news/article-3104023/NHS-chief-warns-women-not-wait-30-baby-country-faces-fertility-timebomb.html.

Akesson, Lynn. 2002. Bound by Blood? New Meanings of Kinship and Individuality in Discourses of Genetic Counseling. In *New Directions in Anthropological Kinship*, ed. Linda Stone, 125–138. Oxford: Rowman and Littlefield.

Arya, Jitendra. 2011. *Health Naturally: Nature Cure for Common Diseases*. Arya Publications.

Ashton, Dan, and Rebecca Feasey. 2014. This is Not How Cancer Looks: Celebrity Diagnosis and Death in the Tabloid Media. *Journalism: Theory, Practice and Criticism—Celebrity News* 15 (2): 237–251.

Attain Fertility. 2018. Clomid Success Rates. *Attain Fertility.* Accessed April 12, 2019. https://attainfertility.com/article/clomid-success-rates.

Barker, Martin. 2004. News, Reviews, Clues, Interviews and Other Ancillary Materials—A Critique and Research Proposal. *Scope.* Accessed April 12, 2019. https://www.nottingham.ac.uk/scope/documents/2004/february-2004/barker.pdf.

Becker, Gay. 2000. *The Elusive Embryo: How Women and Men Approach New Reproductive Technologies.* Los Angeles: University of California Press.

Berridge, Susan, and Laura Portwood-Stacer. 2014. Introduction: *Gender, Media and Assisted Reproductive Technologies. Feminist Media Studies* 14 (5): 868.

Boggs, Belle. 2017. The Price of Infertility. *The Cut.* Accessed April 12, 2019. https://www.thecut.com/2016/09/price-of-infertility-ivf-cost-c-v-r.html.

Boivin, Jacky, E. Griffiths, and C. Venetis. 2011. Emotional Distress in Infertile Women and Failure of Assisted Reproductive Technologies: Meta-analysis of Prospective Psychosocial Studies. *BMJ* 342. Accessed April 12, 2019. http://www.bmj.com/content/342/bmj.d223.

Brian, Kate. 2015. Kate's Story—Unexplained Infertility. *Fertility Matters.* Accessed April 12, 2019. http://fertilitymatters.org.uk/real-life-stories/kates-story/.

British Fertility Society. 2018a. Modern Families Education Project. *British Fertility Society.* Accessed April 12, 2019. https://britishfertilitysociety.org.uk/fei/#link5.

———. 2018b. Fertility Fest—The Modern Families Project. *British Fertility Society.* Accessed April 12, 2019. https://www.fertilityfest.com/the-modern-families-project.

Bronstein, Jenny, and Maria Knoll. 2015. Blogging Motivations of Women Suffering from Infertility. *Information Research* 20: 2. Accessed April 12, 2019. http://www.informationr.net/ir/20-2/paper669.html#.WpAK1mZFnVo.

Burr, Vivien. 2015. *Social Constructionism—Third Edition.* New York: Routledge.

Casella, Rachael. 2018. The Side Effects of IVF. *My Love of Life Blog.* Accessed April 12, 2019. https://www.mylifeoflove.com/blogme/2018/4/13/the-side-effects-of-ivf.

CDC. 2018a. Infertility FAQs: What is Infertility? *Centers for Disease Control and Prevention.* Accessed April 12, 2019. https://www.cdc.gov/reproductivehealth/infertility/index.htm.

———. 2018b. What is Assisted Reproductive Technology? *Centers for Disease Control and Prevention.* Accessed April 12, 2019. https://www.cdc.gov/art/whatis.html.

Challoner, Jack. 1999. *Baby Makers: The History of Artificial Conception.* London: Channel 4 Books.

Cohn, Victor. 1981. First U.S. Test-Tube Baby Is Born. *Washington Post*. Accessed April 12, 2019. https://www.washingtonpost.com/archive/politics/1981/12/29/first-us-test-tube-baby-is-born/a6f3de2f-422f-43bd-9b45-0d798ed18e8e/?utm_term=.faa6a8b824b5.

Crowe, Christine. 1990. Whose Mind Over Whose Matter? Women, *in vitro* Fertilisation and the Development of Scientific Knowledge. In *The New Reproductive Technologies*, ed. Maureen McNeil, Ian Varcoe, and Steven Yearley, 27–57. London: Palgrave Macmillan.

Darweesh, S. 2014. Codes of Conduct: Understanding Paratextuality and How the Critical Reception of Girls Uncovered Ideological Codes in American Culture. PhD diss., Utrecht University. Accessed April 12, 2019. https://dspace.library.uu.nl/handle/1874/298045.

De Neubourg, Diane, and Sarah Devroe. 2016. Fertility Treatment in the Modern Age: Possibilities and Anaesthesia. In *Oxford Textbook of Obstetric Anaesthesia*, ed. Vicki Clark, Marc Van de Velde, and Roshan Fernando, 149–156. Oxford: Oxford University Press.

DiLapi, Elena. 1999. Lesbian Mothers and the Motherhood Hierarchy. In *Homosexuality and the Family*, ed. Patricia Dean, 101–122. London: Routledge.

Douglas, Susan, and Meredith Michaels. 2005. *The Mommy Myth: The Idealization of Motherhood and How it Has Undermined All Women*. London: Free Press.

Dworkin, Shari, and Faye Wachs. 2004. Getting Your Body Back: Postindustrial Fit Motherhood in Shape Fit Pregnancy Magazine. *Gender & Society* 18 (5): 610–624.

Earle, Sarah, and Gayle Letherby. 2003. Introducing Gender, Identity and Reproduction. In *Gender, Identity and Reproduction: Social Perspectives*, ed. Sarah Earle and Gayle Letherby, 1–12. London: Palgrave Macmillan.

Edelman, Joni. 2017. What If You Never Hold Your Baby? Are You Still A Mother? *Ravishly*. Accessed April 12, 2019. https://ravishly.com/what-if-you-never-hold-your-baby-are-you-still-mother.

Edge, Brooke. 2014. Infertility On E!: Assisted Reproductive Technologies and Reality Television. *Feminist Media Studies* 14 (5): 873–876.

———. 2015. Barren or Bountiful? Analysis of Cultural Values in Popular Media Representations of Infertility. PhD diss., University of Colorado. Accessed April 12, 2019. https://scholar.colorado.edu/jour_gradetds/25/.

Feasey, Rebecca. 2012. *From Happy Homemaker to Desperate Housewives: Motherhood and Popular Television*. London: Anthem.

———. 2014. From Heartache to Happiness: The Codes, Conventions and Clichés of the 40-something Celebrity Infertility Story. *MaMSIE*. Accessed April 12, 2019. http://mamsie.org/2014/11/10/from-heartache-to-happiness-the-codes-conventions-and-cliches-of-the-40-something-celebrity-infertility-story/.

—. 2018. Good, Bad or Just Good Enough: Representations of Motherhood and the Maternal Role on the Small Screen. *MaMSIE*. Accessed April 12, 2019. https://www.mamsie.bbk.ac.uk/articles/10.16995/sim.234/.

Fertility Fest. 2018. Fertility Fest. *Fertility Fest*. Accessed April 12, 2019. https://www.fertilityfest.com.

Gray, Jonathan. 2003. New Audiences, New Textualities: Anti-Fans and Non-Fans. *International Journal of Cultural Studies* 6 (1): 64–81.

Greil, Arthur. 2002. Infertile Bodies: Medicalization, Metaphor, and Agency. In *Infertility Around the Globe: New Thinking on Childlessness, Gender and Reproductive Technologies*, ed. Marcia Inhorn and Frank Van Balen, 101–118. Berkeley and Los Angeles: University of California Press.

Gurevich, Rachel. 2019. Side Effects and Risks of Fertility Drugs: From Headaches to Twins, Hot Flashes to Mood Swings. *verywellfamily*. Accessed April 12, 2019. https://www.verywellfamily.com/what-are-the-potential-risks-of-fertility-drugs-1960190.

Hepburn, Jessica. 2018. Jessica Hepburn. *Jessica Hepburn*. Accessed April 12, 2019. https://www.jessicahepburn.com.

Hepworth, Rosemary. 2015. Infertility Blogging, Body, and the Avatar. In *Feminist Erasures: Challenging Backlash Culture*, ed. Kumarini Silva and Kaitlynn Mendes, 198–218. London: Palgrave Macmillan.

Hermes, Joke. 1995. *Reading Women's Magazines*. London: Polity Press.

HFEA. 2004. Your Guide to Infertility: HFEA Directory of Clinics 2003/2004. *Human Fertilisation and Embryology Authority*. 1–107. Accessed April 12, 2019. https://www.yumpu.com/en/document/view/33524642/your-guide-to-infertility-hfea-directory-of-clinics-2003-04-human-.

—. 2011. Fertility Treatment in 2011: Trends and Figures. *Human Fertilisation and Embryology Authority*. Accessed April 12, 2019. https://www.hfea.gov.uk/media/2079/hfea-fertility-trends-2011.pdf.

—. 2018a. Welcome to the HFEA. *Human Fertilisation and Embryology Authority*. Accessed April 12, 2019. https://www.hfea.gov.uk.

—. 2018b. Pre-implantation Genetic Diagnosis. *Human Fertilisation and Embryology Authority*. Accessed April 12, 2019. https://www.hfea.gov.uk/treatments/embryo-testing-and-treatments-for-disease/pre-implantation-genetic-diagnosis-pgd/.

—. 2018c. Explore Fertility Treatments. *Human Fertilisation and Embryology Authority*. Accessed April 12, 2019. https://www.hfea.gov.uk/treatments/.

Hosey, Sara. 2019. *Home is Where the Hurt is: Media Depictions of Wives and Mothers*. London: McFarland.

It81. 2010. Infertility in More Movies. *ivf-infertility.com*. Accessed April 12, 2019. http://www.ivf-infertility.com/phpBB3/viewtopic.php?p=307028.

Jensen, Robin. 2016. *Infertility: Tracing the History of a Transformative Term*. University Park, PA: Pennsylvania State University Press.

Klein, Amy. 2015. Is That My Baby? Sperm Donation is Socially Acceptable but Donor Eggs Still Provoke a Wave of Unease about Blood Relations and Motherhood. *Aeon*. Accessed April 12, 2019. https://aeon.co/essays/why-are-donor-eggs-almost-taboo-among-fertility-options.

Kohn, Ingrid, and Perry-Lynn Moffitt. 2000. *A Silent Sorrow: Pregnancy Loss: Guidance and Support for You and Your Family*. London: Routledge.

Kraaij, Vivian, Nadia Garnefski, and Maya Schroevers. 2009. Coping, Goal Adjustment, and Positive and Negative Affect in Definitive Infertility. *Journal of Health Psychology* 14 (1): 18–26.

Kumar, Naina, and Amit Singh. 2015. Trends of Male Factor Infertility, an Important Cause of Infertility: A Review of Literature. *Journal of Human Reproductive Sciences* 8 (4): 191–196.

Lam, Carla. 2016. Thinking Through Constructionism: Reflections on (Reproductive) Disembodiment and Misfits. *Studies in Social Justice* 10 (2): 289–307.

Le Vay, Lulu. 2019. *Surrogacy and the Reproduction of Normative Family on TV*. London: Palgrave Macmillan.

Letherby, Gayle. 1994. Mother or Not, Mother or What: Problems of Definition and Identity. *Women's Studies International Forum* 17 (5): 525–532.

———. 1999. Other than Mother and Mothers as Others: The Experience of Motherhood and Non-Motherhood in Relation to Infertility and Involuntary Childlessness. *Women's Studies International Forum* 22 (3): 359–372.

———. 2003. Battle of the Gametes: Cultural Representations of 'Medically' Assisted Conception. In *Gender, Identity and Reproduction: Social Perspectives*, ed. Sarah Earle and Gayle Letherby, 50–65. London: Palgrave Macmillan.

Levy, Claire and Farrar, Ruth. 2018. *Infertility, The Media & Me*. Film.

Lewin, Ellen. 1994. Negotiating Lesbian Motherhood: The Dialectics of Resistance and Accommodation. In *Mothering: Ideology, Experience, and Agency*, ed. Evelyn Nakano Glenn, Grace Chang, and Linda Rennie Forcey, 333–354. London: Routledge.

Macaluso, Maurizio, Tracie Wright-Schnapp, Anjani Chandra, Robert Johnson, Catherine Satterwhite, and Amy Pulver. 2010. A Public Health Focus on Infertility Prevention, Detection, and Management. *Fertility and Sterility* 93 (1): 16e1–16e10.

Madsen, Charlotte. 2014. Infertility on Film and Television—Part 3: *Parenthood* and *Sex and the City*. *The Road To Baby Madsen: Our IVF Journey*. Accessed April 12, 2019. http://roadtobabymadsen.blogspot.com/2014/07/infertility-on-film-and-television-part.html.

Maher, Jennifer. 2014. Something Else Besides a Father. *Feminist Media Studies* 14 (5): 853–867.

Marsh, Margaret, and Wanda Ronner. 1999. *The Empty Cradle: Infertility in America from Colonial Times to the Present*. London: Johns Hopkins University Press.

Martin, Lauren. 2010. Anticipating Infertility: Egg Freezing, Genetic Preservation, and Risk. *Gender & Society* 24 (4): 526–545.

McLaughlin, Hugh. 2009. What's in a Name? *The British Journal of Social Work* 39 (6): 1101–1117.

MFM. 2018. Innovation in Sex Education. *My Fertility Matters Project*. Accessed April 12, 2019. http://www.mfmprojectuk.org.

Miller, Cheryl. 2008. Blogging Infertility. *The New Atlantis: A Journal of Technology & Society* 19 (Winter): 79–90.

Moran, Hannah. 2018. New Fertility Treatment Offers Fresh Hope to Women after Failed IVF. *Evoke*. Accessed April 12, 2019. https://evoke.ie/2018/09/04/health/new-fertility-treatment-fresh-hope.

Morgan, Polly. 2015. One in Ten British Babies Will Soon be Born via IVF. So Why is It Taboo? *The Spectator*. Accessed April 12, 2019. https://www.spectator.co.uk/2015/10/women-are-still-scared-to-talk-about-ivf-lets-change-that/.

Mundy, Liza. 2019. Eggs on Ice. *Scientific American* 320 (5): 52–57.

Mutcherson, Kimberley. 2017. Procreative Rights in a Postcoital World. In *The Oxford Handbook of Reproductive Ethics*, ed. Leslie Francis, 159–181. Oxford: Oxford University Press.

Needleman, Sima. 1987. Infertility and In Vitro Fertilisation: The Social Workers Role. *Health and Social Work* 12 (2): 135–143.

New Scientist. 2018. First Baby Born Thanks to Womb Transplant from Deceased Donor. *New Scientist*. Accessed April 12, 2019. https://www.newscientist.com/article/2187397-first-baby-born-thanks-to-womb-transplant-from-deceased-donor/

NHS. 2018a. Overview: Infertility. *NHS*. Accessed April 12, 2019. https://www.nhs.uk/conditions/infertility/.

———. 2018b. Causes: Infertility. *NHS*. Accessed April 12, 2019. https://www.nhs.uk/conditions/infertility/causes/.

———. 2019. Treatment: Infertility. *NHS*. Accessed April 12, 2019. https://www.nhs.uk/conditions/infertility/treatment/.

NICE. 2018a. Fertility Problems: Assessment and Treatment—Recommendations. *National Institute for Health and Care Excellence*. Accessed April 12, 2019. https://www.nice.org.uk/guidance/cg156/chapter/recommendations.

———. 2018b. Fertility Problems: Assessment and Treatment: Assisted Reproduction. *National Institute for Health and Care Excellence*. Accessed April 12, 2019. https://www.nice.org.uk/guidance/cg156/ifp/chapter/assisted-reproduction.

O'Reilly, Andrea. 2007. *Maternal Theory: Essential Readings*. Toronto: Demeter Press.

Osborne-Thompson, Heather. 2014. Seriality and Assisted Reproductive Technologies in Celebrity Reality Television. *Feminist Media Studies* 14 (5): 877–880.

Ottenheimer, Martin. 2001. The Current Controversy in Kinship. *Czech Sociological Review* 9 (2): 201–210.

Phoenix, Ann, and Anne Woollett. 1991. Motherhood: Social Construction, Politics and Psychology. In *Motherhood, Meanings, Practices and Ideologies*, ed. Ann Phoenix and Anne Woollett, 13–27. London: Sage.

Press Association. 2016. More Than 250,000 UK Babies Born Through IVF. *The Guardian*. Accessed April 12, 2019. https://www.theguardian.com/society/2016/nov/04/more-than-250000-uk-babies-born-ivf.

Ragoné, Helena. 2004. Surrogate Motherhood and American Kinship. In *Kinship and Family: An Anthropological Reader*, ed. Robert Parkin and Linda Stone, 342–361. Oxford: Blackwell.

Resolve. 2018. Fast Facts: Who Has Infertility. *Resolve*: The National Infertility Association. Accessed April 12, 2019. https://resolve.org/infertility-101/what-is-infertility/fast-facts/.

Ryan, Maura. 2008. An Open Letter to the Lesbians Who Have Mothered Before Me. In *Mothering in the Third Wave*, ed. Amber Kinser, 31–37. Toronto: Demeter Press.

Sandelowski, Margarete. 1990. Failures of Volition: Female Agency and Infertility in Historical Perspective. *Signs* 15 (3): 475–499.

———. 1993. *With Child in Mind. Studies of the Personal Encounter with Infertility*. Philadelphia: University of Pennsylvania Press.

Sandelowski, Margarete, and Sheryn de Lacey. 2002. The Uses of a Disease: Infertility as Rhetorical Vehicle. In *Infertility around the Globe: New Thinking on Childlessness, Gender, and Reproductive Technologies*, ed. Marcia Inhorn and Frank Van Balen, 33–51. Berkeley: University of California Press.

Schneider, David. 1980. *American Kinship: A Cultural Account*. London: University of Chicago Press.

Science Daily. 2018. Fertility Breakthrough: New Research Could Extend Egg Health with Age. *Science Daily*. Accessed April 12, 2019. https://www.sciencedaily.com/releases/2018/02/180222125659.htm.

Scully, Anne-Marie. 2014. *Motherhoodwinked: An Infertility Memoir*. CreateSpace Independent Publishing Platform.

Shalev, Shirley, and Dafna Lemish. 2013. Infertile Motherhood. *Feminist Media Studies* 13 (2): 321–336.

Shapiro, Connie. 2012. Eventual Mons-To-Be: Heads Up! *Hopefully Yours, Connie*. Accessed April 12, 2019. http://connieshapiro13.blogspot.com.

Simone of Bubbles and Bumps. 2017. Time to Chat Sperm: 3 Simple Ways to Improve Sperm Quality. *Bubbles and Bumps*. Accessed April 12, 2019. http://www.bubblesandbumps.com/vlog-time-to-chat-sperm-3-simple-ways-to-improve-sperm-quality/.

Sterling, Evelina. 2013. From No Hope to Fertile Dreams: Procreative Technologies, Popular Media, and the Culture of Infertility. PhD diss., Georgia State University. Accessed April 12, 2019. https://scholarworks.gsu.edu/cgi/viewcontent.cgi?article=1069&context=sociology_diss.

Striff, Erin. 2005. Infertile Me: The Public Performance of Fertility Treatments in Internet Weblogs. *Women & Performance: A Journal of Feminist Theory* 15 (2): 189–205.

The She Is Project. 2015. Social Infertility—Tania's Story. *The She Is Project*. Accessed April 12, 2019. http://thesheisproject.org/2015/08/social-infertility/.

Tri Health. 2018. Gay Health: Having Children. *Tri Health: Doncaster's Sexual Health Service for People Aged 19 and Over*. Accessed April 12, 2019. http://www.doncastertrihealth.co.uk/gay-health-having-children/.

Throsby, Karen. 2004. *When IVF Fails: Feminism, Infertility and the Negotiation of Normality*. Basingstoke: Palgrave Macmillan.

Tomlins, Jacqueline. 2003. *The Infertility Handbook: A Guide to Making Babies*. Sydney: Allen & Unwin.

Van Balen, Frank. 2002. The Psychologization of Infertility. In *Infertility Around the Globe: New Thinking on Childlessness, Gender and Reproductive Technologies*, ed. Marcia Inhorn and Frank Van Balen, 79–98. London: University of California Press.

Van Balen, Frank, and Marcia Inhorn. 2002. Introduction: Interpreting Infertility: A View from the Social Sciences. In *Infertility Around the Globe: New Thinking on Childlessness, Gender and Reproductive Technologies*, ed. Marcia Inhorn and Frank Van Balen, 3–32. London: University of California Press.

VARTA. 2018. Types of Assisted Reproductive Treatment. *Victorian Assisted Reproductive Treatment Authority*. Accessed April 12, 2019. https://www.varta.org.au/information-support/assisted-reproductive-treatment/types-assisted-reproductive-treatment.

WHO. 2018. Sexual and Reproductive Health: Infertility Definitions and Terminology. *World Health Organisation*. Accessed April 12, 2019. http://www.who.int/reproductivehealth/topics/infertility/definitions/en/.

Winston, Robert. 2018. Professor Robert Winston: Couple Being Misled Over Chances of IVF Success. *The Yorkshire Post*. Accessed April 12, 2019. https://www.yorkshirepost.co.uk/news/professor-robert-winston-couple-being-misled-over-chances-of-ivf-success-1-9246529.

Wohlmann, Anita. 2014. Illness Narrative and Self-Help Culture—Self-Help Writing on Age-Related Infertility. *European Journal of Life Writing* 3: 19–41. Accessed April 12, 2019. http://ejlw.eu/article/view/90/246.

Wolf, Naomi. 1991. *The Beauty Myth: How Images of Beauty are Used Against Women*. London: Vintage.

Wondercat. 2010. Infertility in More Movies. *ivf-infertility.com*. Accessed April 12, 2019. http://www.ivf-infertility.com/phpBB3/viewtopic.php?p=307028.

Zegers-Hochschild, F., G.D. Adamson, J. de Mouzon, O. Ishihara, R. Mansour, K. Nygren, E. Sullivan, and S. Vanderpoel. 2009. International Committee for Monitoring Assisted Reproductive Technology (ICMART) and the World Health Organization (WHO) revised glossary of ART Terminology. *Fertility and Sterility* 92 (5): 1520–1524.

CHAPTER 2

Infertility: Private Confessions in a Public Arena

INTRODUCTION

Around one in seven couples may have difficulty conceiving in the UK (NHS 2018) and one in eight in the US (Resolve 2018a), with between 50 and 80 million couples worldwide affected by fertility problems (WHO 2018; United Nations 2015). With these figures in mind, this chapter will focus on the depiction of infertility, paying particular attention to the rise in infertility blogs and confessional first-person accounts of otherwise private infertility stories. By looking at niche forms of confessional storytelling in sites such as The Life of a[n] Infertile Myrtle, Not Just a Beauty Blogger, Bubbles and Bumps, and Don't Count Your Eggs, this chapter will outline the ways in which women affected by an infertility diagnosis offer a candid yet entertaining account of infertility that is seldom spoken about in the wider media environment, considering the ways in which such commentary could be considered meaningful both within and beyond the blogosphere.

Although this volume seeks to cover a number of blog titles and individual posts, I am aware that readers will question the inclusion of some texts and the exclusion of others. I have chosen a number of family building blogs throughout this chapter because they are accessible and available to interested and invested parties scouring the Internet for personal accounts, private confessions, emotional support and medical guidance. I reference a number of the blogs included in the 'Creating a Family'

© The Author(s) 2019
R. Feasey, *Infertility and Non-Traditional Family Building*,
https://doi.org/10.1007/978-3-030-17787-4_2

37

blogroll as they are presented as the 'best of the best' by the American infertility, adoption and foster care education and support non-profit organisation (Creating a Family 2018a, b). As for those blogs that are not sign-posted on the 'Creating a Family' blogroll, they are chosen for their ease of access and representativeness rather than for any particular originality or uniqueness in tone, appearance or content. This is not to say that I have presented an exhaustive overview of the titles available; indeed, at the time of writing we are invited to look at the 'Top 75 Infertility Blogs and Websites On IVF, IUI & ICSI in 2019 … from [the] thousands of top Infertility blogs' available (Feedspot 2019). Therefore, I would ask readers to take the blogs presented here as a starting point for future debates as titles emerge, develop and flourish, rather than as an attempt to present a rigid or static overview of the media form in question.

GRIEF AND ANGER IN REPRO-LIT

With motherhood understood as a marker of adult female maturity and appropriate femininity, infertility is experienced both as a medical challenge and a social concern for women affected by a diagnosis. Women living with infertility are routinely told that involuntary childlessness is a tragedy which is 'unequalled in any sphere of life' (Winston cited in Throsby 2004, p. 40) and therefore that if they are unable to get pregnant they 'should be immobilized by deep grief' (Reimer and Sahagian 2016, p. 243). We are reminded that these women can 'experience levels of psychological distress similar to patients with grave medical conditions, such as cancer or those going through cardiac rehabilitation' (Hinton et al. 2010, p. 436). In a pronatal culture, women who are unable to get pregnant or stay pregnant are devalued, stigmatised and presented as failing to adhere to 'acceptable boundaries of "proper" womanhood' (Edge 2015, p. 138). Few women 'expect to face infertility' and, as such, a diagnosis can lead some to question their family roles, relationships, life choices and identities (Sterling 2013, p. 88). In her research on procreative technologies, popular media and the culture of infertility, Evelina Sterling tells us that

> most people go through a series of intense feelings after being diagnosed with infertility, including anger, sadness, grief, guilt and self-blame. Individuals are hit at their very core as infertility challenges basic beliefs,

faith and hope in the 'normal' workings of our bodies, and may leave people feeling broken and defective. (Ibid., p. 3)

Infertility is understood as a pathology, and yet rather than pathologise the fallopian tubes or uterus, for example, it is the woman herself, the whole woman, who is defined by the term as she is positioned in opposition to 'hegemonic social constructions of gender norms' (Edge 2015, p. 101). And although this notion of infertility as a pathology is meaningful to a discussion of both medical infertility and social infertility, it is the woman diagnosed with Polycystic Ovarian Syndrome, Premature Ovarian Failure, Endometriosis, Pelvic Inflammatory Disease, Intrauterine Fibroids or Asherman's Syndrome to name but a few female-factor infertility problems who is most at risk of feeling like a 'second class citizen' (Scully 2014, p. 58).

Although there is clearly no single, monolithic way to experience infertility, feelings of stress and desperation pepper myriad narrative accounts for those women who have written publicly about their experiences in the new and growing genre of 'repro-lit' (Miller 2008, p. 79). Women talk of trying to balance feelings of hope and acceptance, seeing themselves as 'parents-in waiting' (Mamo 2013, p. 227) rather than as an involuntarily infertile woman without children; and although there might appear a fine line between the two, the former speaks of possibility, the latter, resignation. Although many repro-lit authors speak of their pledge to 'not let infertility break' them, family pressure and societal expectation often lead to isolation and subsequent depression (Scully 2014, p. 60). Naomi from the Embrace Fertility blog makes this point when she confesses that after '20 months of trying to conceive and following a failed stimulated IUI cycle I hit rock bottom and was signed off work with extreme anxiety and depression stemming from infertility' (Naomi of Embrace Fertility 2014). Time is routinely presented as the enemy of women affected by a diagnosis. In her book-length infertility memoir, Anne-Marie Scully tells us that as the days, weeks and 'months rolled on, I had simply become more and more worn down' and that '[e]very month when I got my period I would feel another little piece fall away, until eventually there was no joy or happiness left in me' (Scully 2014, p. 60). One woman experiencing involuntary childlessness makes it clear that 'for those who have never experienced infertility or the intense desire for a child, it is easy to pigeonhole as obsessive or desperate those who have' (Menard cited in Sterling 2013, p. 87). And although there are examples where women have challenged such stereotypes, we find that 'personal accounts overwhelming[ly] portrayed women experiencing infertility as desperate and unfulfilled, willing to do anything to have a baby' (Sterling 2013, p. 87; Hepburn 2017).

Authors are candid about the devastation that infertility causes on their domestic and working lives; relationships become tense, friendships strained and concentration in the workplace slips (Scully 2014, p. 60). Women who were once capable, caring, compassionate and optimistic speak of their shame as these feelings were replaced by fear, anger, injustice, loneliness and jealousy. Injustice that seemingly everyone around them can get pregnant, easily and effortlessly; fear that they will never find happiness without a maternal role and feelings of jealousy as they interact with pregnant women, new mothers, existing and experienced mothers—in short, the majority of the female population (Malik and Coulson 2008, p. 106; Scully 2014, p. 68). The 'obligatory introduction' to the Forever Infertile blog tells us that the outwardly serene writer has 'turned into a bitter hag who resents anyone who is able to get pregnant, stay pregnant, and sail through pregnancy and childbirth without a care in the world' (Kitten 2012). Likewise, Scully tells us that

> [j]ealousy wasn't an emotion that I had ever been familiar with. Of course, I had often felt envious of other people in the past for being more intelligent, better looking, more talented or having more money—all the usual trivial things. However, feeling jealous of my friends and every other pregnant woman I saw was a more sinister emotion than simple envy, and it didn't sit well with me at all. I hate the fact that I was jealous. I had always associated jealousy with bitter, angry people who were unhappy in their own lives. It took a while for me to realize that I had become one of them too. (Scully 2014, p. 64)

These feelings of jealousy meant that women not only extracted themselves from baby showers, christenings and first birthday parties, but also from wider social events, for fear of women congregating to discuss the minutiae of looking after babies, children or teenagers. One woman spoke ironically of her exclusion and dislocation during large family gatherings, because although she was surrounded by her extended family unit, she was never quite sure where she 'stood' literally and figuratively 'within the strongly gender-divided space' when the men left the kitchen after dinner to talk about sport and the women stayed and discussed maternal roles and mothering responsibilities (Throsby 2004, p. 131). Even with

National Infertility Associations providing 'compassionate support and information about infertility' (Resolve 2018b) many women still find infertility to be a lonely place because it can be 'hard to find others in your "real life" who are living this experience' (Creating a Family 2018b).

It is not unusual to find that women diagnosed with infertility start to withdraw from friends and family, but what this means is that 'in addition to feeling the loss of the babies I had dreamed of, I also felt the loss of my friends who I had previously shared everything with, increasing my isolation' (Scully 2014, p. 64). Women refer to themselves as the odd one out, lepers and pariahs (Hinton et al. 2010, p. 438). The popular and long-running infertility blogger of A Little Pregnant says of herself: 'Once a freak, always a freak, and don't you fucking forget it' (cited in Striff 2005, p. 201).

With these feelings in mind, it is perhaps unsurprising to find that a Google search for 'infertility stigma' offers 84 times more returns than the same search for 'infertility support' (Sable 2014). Infertility is 'a disruption in the social fabric of women's lives' because it 'is inconsistent with the normative conversation as well as the anticipated trajectories of family life' (McCarthy 2008, p. 324). In short, we are encouraged to view infertility as a 'major negative life event which has deleterious effects on women's … subjective well-being' (Abbey et al. 1992, p. 408). This is not to suggest that every woman experiences an infertility diagnosis in this way, or that it is a permanent position, but its potential impact must be understood and acknowledged within and beyond the media environment. It is often noted that when 'a life changing event occurs, one of the most recognized means of coping is to talk to people with shared experiences' and infertility is no different (Scully 2014, p. 79). In terms of finding happiness and fulfilment without a traditional maternal role, women speak of a desire to look to role models in their social, work or family groups, but it seems that even when one looks for these women, 'there are very few of them out there' (Ibid., p. 76). By way of example, Scully tells us that she

> once attended a panel session at a Women in Business event in the hope that there would be a few women who didn't have children speaking about what a success they had made of their lives. I couldn't have been more wrong. As it turned out, most of the panelists were successful career women who were also mothers. Inevitably, the conversation turned to the topic of juggling children and a career, as if being able to do that was the definition of success for a woman … there didn't seem to be any room in these people's minds

for a woman who had children but not a career, or a woman like me with a career but no children. It seemed essential to have both in order to consider yourself a successful woman. (Ibid., p. 76)

Struggling to find role models and fearful of reprisals in close-knit social circles, 'the partner becomes the sole confidante ... for many infertile couples' (Malik and Coulson 2008, p. 106) as they speak of going 'down the road alone, with only each other for support' (Scully 2014, p. 80). While many repro-lit authors speak eloquently, openly and at length about the various ways in which their experiences of infertility put a strain on their relationship, Julia Selby sums it up for many when she states that the infertility diagnosis was a 'third party' in her marriage. We are told that this 'third party was sad, angry, and very frustrated. He came with us to dinner, the bathroom, and the bedroom. He filled the silences and was often the instigator behind most of our arguments. And he was getting bigger all the time' (Selby 2015, p. 54). Women affected by an infertility diagnosis speak of their struggles to find confidants or role models at home or work, and yet, disclosure can be difficult, especially when the subject is as personal and potentially painful as involuntary childlessness.

Scully acknowledges that it is easy to get angry at how little fertility issues are discussed in society (Scully 2014, p. 66), and, as such, it is worth looking at the ways in which popular media culture addresses the topic, so as to either offer support, comfort or camaraderie for those living with the diagnosis. Sterling looks at the changing ways in which infertility is presented in mainstream print media. We are told that when popular and scientific journalists for *Time, Newsweek, Health* and *Psychology Today* touched on the theme of infertility in the 1990s, it was routinely in relation to the notion of prevention. The concern here is that these titles presented a link between sexually transmitted diseases and unexplained infertility, even when clinical research of the period showed no change in infertility among young women due to sexually transmitted infections, birth control or the environment (Sterling 2013, p. 50). During the 2000s, the majority of journalists changed their focus by linking an infertility diagnosis to exercise, diet and stress, even though researchers had little in the way of evidence to support the connections being presented here (Ibid., p. 51). In nearly 80 per cent of over 500 popular print articles assessed in Sterling's study, infertility was presented as a preventable diagnosis, with women in particular being 'portrayed as deserving of their infertility ... through lifestyle choices and past decision-making' (Ibid.,

p. 57). To conclude her analysis, Sterling informs us that 'clinical researchers provided very little data to popular media as to which factors directly affect fertility' allowing the popular press to revert to earlier models of psychogenic infertility, whereby women were once again at fault for their diagnosis (Ibid., p. 57).

In the same way that exercise, diet and stress were said to be factors in an infertility diagnosis, so too was age-related infertility. In this way, Sterling's work can be seen as another voice in a growing body of research that suggests that the popular media environment encourages women to self-blame for their involuntary childlessness (Sterling 2013; Marsh and Ronner 1999). *Newsweek* told its readers that advanced maternal age was 'the most formidable enemy of fertility' (cited in Sterling 2013, p. 60), with countless articles echoing this sentiment. Infertility doctors announced that 'women's lack of knowledge about how age affects fertility—is the single biggest cause [of] infertility' (Carter cited in Sterling 2013, p. 104). Such medical professionals were said to 'be alarmed by what they viewed as a widespread lack of understanding about age as a risk factor for infertility—and a false sense of security about what science can do' (Sterling 2013, p. 64). The American Society for Reproductive Medicine initiated a media campaign informing women about age-related infertility (Ibid., p. 64). However, America is not alone in its efforts because while Australian ministers were warning women that 'putting off childbirth' results in 'an increase in infertility, miscarriage and foetal abnormalities' (Chapman cited in Gatrell 2008, p. 48), NHS fertility specialists in the UK have been heard lobbying for better education on age-related infertility in schools (Adams 2015; British Fertility Society 2018a, b; MFM 2018).

What is interesting here is the ways in which age-related infertility is discussed only in relation to women's reproductive health. Indeed, very few campaigns associate infertility or miscarriage with older fatherhood; rather, the media tend to 'allay fears about older fatherhood by telling readers since a man continually produces new sperm every day, his age does not influence his fertility' (Sterling 2013, p. 68). Examples of sexagenarian, septuagenarian and octogenarian fatherhood from the celebrity sphere are routinely provided as evidence, be it Rod Stewart (60), Clint Eastwood (66), Ronnie Wood (68), Tony Randall (78), Julio Iglesias (87), Anthony Quinn (81) or Saul Bellow (84).

Female fertility is reduced at 35 and reduced dramatically after 40, and as fertility decreases, the chances of miscarriage increase. For those women over 35 who carry their baby to term there 'is a higher incidence of haemorrhage [...] hypertension, pre-eclamptic toxaemia and diabetes' (Khanapure and Bewley 2007, p. 21) and 'more problems with abnormal labour patterns and a ... higher risk of caesarean section' (Ibid., p. 21). We find that 'older women have an increased incidence of preterm delivery and are more likely to deliver under 32 weeks' gestation with a consequent increased risk of prenatal mortality' (Ibid., p. 21). Moreover, we are informed that 'maternal mortality also increases several fold for older women compared with the younger pregnant patient' (Ibid., p. 21). Older mothers, particularly aged 35 and upwards, have an increased risk of a Down's Syndrome baby, ectopic pregnancy, placental problems, high blood pressure, aneuploidy, stillbirth and low-birth-weight babies (Bonifazi cited in Feasey 2012, p. 131; Wood cited in Feasey 2012, p. 131).

Continuing education within and beyond the media is key, not as stark warnings on billboards, nor scaremongering statistics in patient surgeries, but as part of existing sex and relationship education in schools. Professor Allan Pacey, outgoing chair of the British Fertility Society, makes this point when he suggests that 'pupils should receive "age appropriate" information on infertility from primary school to university' (Pacey cited in Adams 2015). Without education, audiences are left relying on the entertainment medium for their information and understanding.

From this perspective it is worth noting that infertility has been addressed on radio (Bullock 2015) and in a range of mainstream film genres, ranging from family films (*The Odd Life of Timothy Green* 2012) and comedy (*The BabyMakers* 2012) to comedy romance (*Baby Mama* 2008) and drama (*Secrets and Lies* 1996, *The Good Girl* 2002), thrillers (*The Girl on a Train* 2016), science fiction (*Children of Men* 2006) and horror (*Grace* 2009). On the small screen, the subject has long been depicted in the sitcom genre (*Friends* 1994–2004, *How I Met Your Mother* 2005–14, *The Mindy Project* 2012–17), reality programming (*Giuliana & Bill* 2009–, *Keeping Up with the Kardashians* 2007–, *Tia & Tamera* 2011–13), dystopian fiction (*The Handmaids Tale* 2017–) and drama, be it hospital drama (*Inconceivable* 2005–), romantic drama (*Private Practice* 2007–13), comedy drama (*Sex and the City* 1998–2004) or crime drama (*Top of the Lake: China Girl* 2017). Lulu Le Vay has gone as far as to suggest that third-party-assisted conception in particular 'is pure maternal melodramatic gold' (Le Vay 2019, p. 234).

Science, Sympathy and Repro-Lit

The theme of involuntary childlessness has sparked debate and discussion from news media to screen representations. Similarly, the topic has been seen to dominate self-help volumes, memoirs and auto-pathographies. And while news magazines in general, and media campaigns in particular, might be charged with inciting infertility fear in a generation of women, the 'long-form personal narrative fused with life coaching' that has come to inform 'repro-lit' appears keen to negotiate such narratives by way of detailed personal accounts of age-related infertility (Tuhus-Dubrow 2013). We are told that the 'selling point is not that their challenges are exceptional, but that they are common … [t]hey do, however, claim to bring something special to readers—some wisdom gleaned through happenstance or research—that equips them (and by extension, us) to meet life's [infertility] challenges' (Ibid.). After all, such writing is 'motivated by an impulse to overcome a crisis and, simultaneously, to help others who suffer from similar conditions' (Wohlmann 2014).

Existing work on the emergence and rise of self-help culture in the 1970s tells us that an 'increased interest in and public attention to advice literature is fostered by a culture of anxiety and insecurity' (Wohlmann 2014), foregrounding changing family and working patterns as key to a growing sense of uncertainty. While 'lifelong marriage is replaced by increasing divorce rates' (Ibid.), the expectation of a job for life has been usurped by 'short-term employment' (Ibid.). The result we are told is that individuals 'feel required to engage in constant makeover and self-transformation to stay marriageable and employable' (Ibid.; Riley et al. 2019). Concerns over Western health-care organisations are said to have been sparked by a 'widespread loss of confidence in experts [and] the declining belief in centralist solutions to social problems', both of which have been said to play a part in the growing self-help market (Wohlmann 2014). Moreover, it has been noted that the burgeoning market of self-help volumes 'coincid[ed] with the rising popularity of illness narratives written from an autobiographical perspective' (Ibid. 2014).

A growing number of female, first-person, confessional volumes on the topic of infertility have emerged since the millennium. Writing in 2019, an Amazon search for 'infertility' produces over 5000 books, but while less than 1000 of these volumes are filed under 'Gynaecology and Obstetrics', over 3000 are filed under the 'Health, Family & Lifestyle' banner. In short, a wealth of 'repro-lit' has emerged in recent decades on the topic of infertility in general and age-related infertility in particular.

Julia Indichova, author of *Inconceivable: A Woman's Triumph Over Despair and Statistics* (2001) and founder of FertileHeart.com, recounts her own infertility story, interwoven with similar stories shared by other women. We are told that 'these additional narratives' render her work 'an account of collective experience' (Wohlmann 2014). Indeed, extant literature on illness narratives speak of authors navigating self-exploration and service to the community (Couser 1997, p. 15), with infertility authors negotiating similar territory here. Anita Wohlmann reminds us that at the same time that self-help authors are looking to their books as 'learning projects of self-discovery' they are also looking to 'share what [they] learned with others' (Wohlmann 2014). We are told that the dual motives of self-help and counsel are about control. We find that in order to 'overcome the uncertainty of their individual situations, the authors emancipate from their roles as passive patients and become experts themselves' (Ibid.). Women affected by an infertility diagnosis make the point that 'one of the hardest parts of infertility is the lack of control you feel as … there is no set course of action you can follow to get the end result. By actively seeking information and support you feel like you are doing something to achieve your goal' (Female, 33 cited in Malik and Coulson 2008, p. 109).

Indichova speaks about her experiences of infertility after being diagnosed with a very high level of follicle-stimulating hormone. She speaks of taking advice from the medical community and a myriad of non-traditional healers who encouraged her to try 'acupuncture, unidentifiable black-and-white pellets, herb soup, foul-smelling fruit [and] even making love on red sheets' (Indichova 2001, inside cover). The author tells us that she only met with reproductive success when she became proactive in her research on reproductive medicine. She read sociological studies, interviewed other women struggling with infertility, doctors, psychological experts and even business leaders in the field of fertility science before formulating her own 'mind body program' (Indichova 2001). We are told that after 'eight caffeine-free, nutrient-rich, yoga-laden months, complemented by visualization exercises' Indichova was pregnant (Ibid., inside cover), irrespective of the fact that 'five reproductive endocrinologists told her that there was no documented case of anyone in her hormonal condition' ever conceiving without intervention (Ibid.).

While medical texts and traditional pathographies routinely make the themes of diagnosis, illness and treatment accessible to the public, Indichova's self-help volume seeks to present the patient as expert. Her book is said to be the first to be 'written about infertility from the patient's point of view' (Indichova 2018a) and since that time, a number of repro-lit authors have emulated this style of writing. Such authors choose to present themselves as ethnographers, memoirists, biographers and investigators who combine their own voice with those of other women, in what are referred to as 'letters from the front' (Wohlmann 2014). Such writing tends to seek and share knowledge while quantifying personal experiences. The accounts of women's shared stories are routinely counterbalanced with facts, statistics, knowledge of biomedical technologies and a foreword by an eminent medical figure.

In *A Few Good Eggs: Two Chicks Dish on Overcoming the Insanity of Infertility* (2006), Julia Vargo and Maureen Regan inform us that their book was intended 'as a wakeup call to their peers' (cited in Sterling 2013, p. 67) because when they each found themselves in their late thirties trying to have a baby, they felt like walking science experiments (Vargo and Regan 2006, p. 2). What is interesting here is the way in which the authors and readers unite in their understanding of the codes and conventions of the genre in question, weaving together science and sympathy for an interested and invested audience. One reader tells us that 'for anyone attempting to navigate the pitfalls and vast amount of information on the infertility journey, this book is one of the key items you need to have … it explains every fertility issue you might come across, in a humorous, easy to understand way. With lots of real life stories to make it more interesting, and to give you hope!' (Natja 2011). Likewise, the authors are thanked because readers 'found it very helpful not only for medical terms but emotional support too' (Jamie 2015). The book is awarded a full 5 star rating on Amazon because 'it gives you a lot of information about different procedures, but also offers emotional consolation' (Bui 2009). And again, in the now predictable trope of a genre text, *A Few Good Eggs* contains not one, but two forewords by eminent clinical professors, while also offering a disclaimer related to the proactive procreative methods suggested in the book. Vargo and Regan tell 30 and 40-something readers that

> just because we've stopped the clock on our surface doesn't mean we've beaten Mother Nature at the game she invented or that Father Time has stopped the clock inside our bodies. You may look great on the outside, but you are still old on the inside, which means everything when it comes to reproduction. (Vargo and Regan 2006, p. 32)

The authors encourage other women who are currently experiencing age-related infertility to seek immediate medical assistance so that they, like the authors before them, get to experience a happy ending. Promotional materials for the book highlight the maternal status rather than the writing credentials of the women in question as we are introduced to 'a 45-year-old mother of two miracle children ages 3 and 6 who started trying to conceive when [she] was 35' and a '44 year old [who] suffered from secondary infertility, with a 12 year old and 23 month old' (INCIID 2005).

Whether these are seen as inspiring books for those affected by an infertility diagnosis or frustrating volumes about yet another successful pregnancy against the age-related infertility odds, repro-lit rarely produces stories about living with infertility, without children. Rather, infertility stories are routinely narratives about overcoming reproductive problems in the quest for biological children. As such, writing on infertility should more routinely be reframed as writing on family building. Indichova uses her own miraculous pregnancy to inspire others, through her fertileheart workshops, webinars and forums, where she tells interested audiences that they are 'more fertile than [they] ever imagined' (Indichova 2018b). Self-help writing on infertility in general and the happy ending epilogue in particular have become something of a cliché in the genre, so much so that Julie Selby tells the reader at the beginning of her book that 'if you are going through infertility and do not want to hear yet another story with a happy ending, you should stop here. I totally get it. I was one of the lucky ones' (Selby 2015, p. IX).

Many repro-lit authors speak of a shift from passive patient to active fertility subject, as they discover reputable research from the field, alongside other, perhaps less traditional, tried or tested avenues of fertility assistance. Many of these self-help writers speak of a need to maintain hope, irrespective of whether that came in the shape of a medical appointment, old wives' tale, new supplement or fortune teller (Ibid., pp. 27–30). Women didn't just change their diet, work or bedroom patterns, but also their health and beauty regimes in an attempt to improve egg quality. Selby tells us that being proactive is crucial after a diagnosis of infertility, because you 'need to feel that [you] are doing something, anything, in fact, to improve [your] chances. All you need is one story of how it worked out for someone else and you are ready to give it a go' (Ibid., p. 63). In terms of a new vitamin supplement recommended by one online forum, Selby tells us that 'I had no idea if these would help. Some studies said yes, some said no, but I didn't care. I needed to rebuild a sense of hope and right now these were the items that were going to do that' (Ibid., p. 55). She tells us that 'like most other infertiles, I felt like I knew more, had researched more, and was as up to speed on my "medical" condition as anyone could be' (Ibid., p. 93). Scully echoes this when she tells us that she had stepped up her research by learning 'all about endometriosis, polycystic ovaries, luteal phase defects, immune disorders and blocked fallopian tubes as potential causes of infertility' (Scully 2014, p. 31).

Repro-lit has its roots in Indichova's self-help memoir, and like Indichova herself, many existing and forthcoming infertility authors have set up web portals and message boards (Indichova 2018a). However, it is 'blogging that has provided the most popular and heterogeneous outlet for the infertile' (Miller 2008, p. 79). And perhaps one should add altruistic. After all, while extant literature on the practice tells us that one of the most common motivations for blogging about pregnancy and childcare is gaining attention, with the goal of becoming a career blogger (Sohr-Preston et al. 2016), those blogging from the standpoint of infertility are said to be motivated by the desire for self-expression and a will to educate others (Ibid.). Writing on pathographies, Thomas Couser draws on the term 'duplicity of self-help' to draw attention to both the 'individualist "urge for self-exploration" and a focus on the communal which is expressed in "a desire to serve those with the same condition"' (Couser cited in Wohlmann 2014). Likewise, Arthur Frank argues that, for 'wounded storytellers … storytelling is for an other as much as it is for oneself' (Frank cited in Wohlmann 2014). In 'illness writing and self-help culture, the seeming opposites of individual self-reliance and mutual aid correlate and overlap' (Wohlmann 2014). And this duplicity remains relevant in helping to understand why infertility bloggers take their stories online.

Infertility and Family Building Blogs

The blogosphere offers those affected by involuntary childlessness 'a place to chronicle their personal stories, create communities, seek support, and raise awareness about their condition' (Miller 2008, p. 79). Unlike the aforementioned authors who found traditional publication opportunities for their book-length volumes, blogging is a more immediate and available form of writing. Bea, the author of Infertile Fantasies: Dreams about the Nightmare of Infertility, says 'one of the great things about technology today is it's democratization … you don't have to be a professional writer or film school graduate to tell your story online—anyone can do it, and even if it's of interest to only a small percentage of people in the world, they can find you' (Bea cited in Miller 2008, p. 79). We find that 'inexpensive technology' allows 'immediacy and accessibility' for bloggers (Wells 2011, p. 204). Sarah Preston, Alyssa Lacour, Tyler Brent, Timothy Dugas and Lauren Jordan echo this point when they say that 'initially, keeping a blog required knowledge of programming, but with [the] introduction of user-friendly free services ... anyone with internet access can start and maintain a blog' (Sohr-Preston et al. 2016, p. 8). In their work on the gendered blogosphere, Jenna Abetz and Julia Moore make the point that

> [t]he internet affords constant, connected communication and personalization in ways that were not possible in the past. ... Digitally networked communities, with [their] participatory potential, promised freedom from hierarchical and unidirectional mass media in favour of horizontal and deterritorial many-to-many patterns of information flows. ... Early theorizations of the internet espoused a democratizing vision for the medium, where a person could easily create content and be exposed to a plurality of ideas in the public sphere. (Abetz and Moore 2018, p. 266)

It has been noted that bloggers with an intimate knowledge of the frustrations and alienation that often accompany the experience of infertility 'may be particularly drawn to blogging as a means of passing on the knowledge collected over the course of their struggles and to articulate feelings and insights brought on by those struggles' (Sohr-Preston et al. 2016, p. 18). This is not to say that infertility bloggers are a monolithic group; after all, they do not necessarily share a common diagnosis relating to infertility. We are told that there are

> blogs devoted to almost every aspect of and response to infertility: donor insemination, donor eggs, surrogacy, in vitro fertilization, intrauterine insemination, and adoption. There are blogs written by gay and lesbian parents, single mothers by choice, and by couples who have successfully conceived after infertility. (Miller 2008, p. 79)

The Internet has provided a wide range of opportunities to discover and disseminate a wealth of information, focusing on health in general and infertility narratives in particular. Although a wealth of formal centres, trusts, clinics, networks and associations exist to offer online support for those diagnosed with infertility, it is the blogs—those websites that take the form of an online diary or journal (presenting dated posts, typically listed in reverse-chronological order)—that have captured the imagination and attention of those seeking medical insight and emotional support. We find that infertility bloggers are, in the main, women; after all, the 'phenomenon of blogging can be seen as an extension of women's earlier forms of narrativizing personal experience' (Lopez 2009, p. 735). And although there remain debates concerning the role of the public and private self, space and body (Striff 2005; Hepworth 2015), online communities have been said to 'not only … alleviate the sense of isolation experienced by many participants but also provide a valuable source of emotional support for individuals going through the highs and lows of fertility treatment' (Malik and Coulson 2008, p. 109). It comes as no surprise then to find that women affected by an infertility diagnosis 'are more active users of the Internet' than the general population (Sohr-Preston et al. 2016, p. 9).

These women 'reported feeling better informed and able to make decisions as a result of online information, which also helped communication with doctors and partners' (Hinton et al. 2010, p. 436). It has been argued that only a small number of women affected by infertility want or request professional psychological services during their infertility treatments. Indeed, LeeAnn Kahlor and Michael Mackert were surprised to find through their research how 'infrequently … women rely on local support groups, counselors, and nurses' (Kahlor and Mackert 2009, p. 88). And yet, we find that women look to the Internet in general and blogs in particular 'in pursuit of medical information and support from other women' (Hinton et al. 2010, p. 436). Indeed, those 'who use the Internet for support paint a picture of a rich environment of emotional sustenance wider, deeper and more personally tailored than was available' to earlier generations (Ibid. p. 438).

Although there are a myriad of family building bloggers, there appears to be a limited set of reasons for keeping such a blog. According to research on the content of and motivation for infertility blogging, the most popular reason for keeping a blog is self-expression and the need to document life experiences (Sohr-Preston et al. 2016). It was also important for bloggers to inform, educate and entertain on the subject of infertility. The authors conclude that 'as a group, participants reported blogging to connect with others to make sense of their own situations while potentially helping others find useful information or amusement while reading about their attempts to do so' (Ibid., p. 18). Either in spite of or because of the willingness to inform others about infertility, bloggers are also using their online voices to take control over a seemingly 'uncontrollable or unspeakable' narrative, using the experience of documenting and sharing to help with their own healing (Wohlmann 2014). The popular Baby Maybe blogger comments that '[w]e have finally reached the top of the waiting list for IVF—a form of assisted conception. I'm blogging about what happens as it happens, as a kind of therapy for me and as an awareness raising exercise of what IVF is all about' (Baby Maybe 2014a).

Although fear is the most common reference point for the family building blogger, these authors speak of a broad and diverse range of emotions, including anxiety, worry, anger, depression, grief and hope (Bronstein and Knoll 2015). Extant literature on the blogging motivations of women affected by an infertility diagnosis explains how they experienced a sense of emotional release through the very act of blogging, in what they term 'purging out, expressing, venting their everyday struggle with infertility' (Ibid.). Such venting routinely focused on the 'emotional effects' that accompany infertility treatments, namely 'the repeated cycle of hope, anticipation and devastation' (Ibid.), or what is better known as the 'infertility merry-go-round' (Miller 2008, p. 83). That said, venting, however cathartic, is only one reason for blogging. It is the social communication that provides a support system for woman affected by infertility and research shows that 'creating a platform for getting feedback, advice, encouragement and support' is a strong extrinsic motivation (Bronstein and Knoll 2015).

Bloggers tend to experience both emotional catharsis and a sense of community from blogging, and yet, each family building blogger has their own specific medical diagnosis and, thus, their own particular pathway through infertility tests, treatments and social environments. Readers are able 'to pick and choose … which blogs [offer] the best fit through blog aggregators, categorized blogrolls, or simply bookmarking' (Sohr-Preston et al. 2016, p. 17). Kahlor and Mackert make the point that infertility blogs dedicated to the topic of secondary infertility are particularly popular because it 'allows participants with children to avoid the potential discomfort of discussing infertility with those who have not yet experienced parenthood' (Kahlor and Mackert 2009, p. 88).

Women undergoing assisted reproductive treatments, and/or taking a bespoke combination of fertility drugs, talk of having few friends or family members who understand their situation. This is not to say that they cannot or do not share these experiences, but rather that it is a one-sided conversation, not a shared dialogue. Moreover, emotional support from family members is 'not always straightforward' because of a basic 'lack of understanding or insensitivity' relating to a particular diagnosis (Hinton et al. 2010, p. 438). Kitten of the Forever Infertile blog makes this point when she tells us that she started writing as 'a way to anonymously vent about things that my family and friends, no matter how supportive they were, just would not understand' (Kitten of Forever Infertile 2015).

Even though friends and family can be 'a major source of support' it is complicated 'if, as often happens, the friend becomes pregnant' (Hinton et al. 2010, p. 438). Some bloggers have gone so far as to put together a list entitled 'Top 10 Things Not To Say To Your Infertile Friend' to save frustration, humiliation and disappointment on both sides of the fertility equation (Megan of Infertile Myrtle 2015). The most hurtful of these comments are, in order, the following:

> 5. Why don't you adopt instead? I'm sure as soon as you do, BAM! You'll get pregnant!
> 4. I know exactly how you feel!
> 3. Go out and get drunk, that's how I got pregnant!
> 2. It will happen when you least expect it.
> 1. JUST RELAX! (Ibid.)

Bloggers routinely espouse online sharing as support when compared with 'their normal social circle' (Hinton et al. 2010, p. 438). We are told that while friends and family 'neither empathise nor understand' (Ibid., p. 438) 'there are millions of other women and couples who are struggling with the same issues' online (Knopman and Talebian cited in Nikol of Not Just a Beauty Blogger 2017). Moreover, we are asked to consider that

> [h]earing what they have to say and how they have dealt with the experience(s) will likely make what you are going through less frightening and make you feel less alienated. And while you may not choose to start a blog, join a Facebook group or start tweeting about infertility, finding someone to talk to, finding someone to 'follow' … or a community to join … will likely make what you are going through a whole lot easier. (Ibid.)

While family building bloggers become online friends and confidants, digital spaces encourage a camaraderie rarely felt beyond the online community.

POSITIVE EXPERIENCES OF INFERTILITY BLOGS: COMMUNITY AND CONTROL

Blogging can 'provide the opportunity to document the minutia of procedures and testing in a forum for those who are likely to understand the vocabulary and nuances' that are involved (Sohr-Preston et al. 2016, p. 17). Susan Seenan, Chief Executive of Infertility Network UK, points out that 'infertility is an emotional rollercoaster, and at times [it] can leave you feeling completely overwhelmed and isolated. Reading about other experiences ... can help you understand that you are not mad, bad, or completely insane, and that others too feel the same as you' (Seenan cited in Selby 2015, p. III). Blogs are sought out for medical guidance and/or emotional support, in part because they look to 'reach out' (Nikol of Not Just a Beauty Blogger 2014) to a shared community and challenge or mitigate the social stigma that comes with a diagnosis. Individuals may be reluctant to disclose to friends and family, or seek support from those uninitiated with the diagnosis, and, as such, blogs are therefore understood as a 'safe space' to connect with others experiencing struggles similar to their own, be they medical, social, sexual or psychological (Sohr-Preston et al. 2016, p. 10). Micro-celebrity Julie, of A Little Pregnant blog fame, writes:

> Several months ago I met a person someone I'd known inside the computer for quite some time ... [w]e hugged, and as I tried to make my squeeze communicate even a fraction of my affection and gratitude, she whispered 'You saved my life.' That's not something I take literally or even personally—every single blogger in our community has been a lifeline, no exaggeration, for others, just by writing, listening, *being*—so I understand it to be a collective truth. But it's also not something I take lightly, because, my God, I mean, *you* all saved *me*. (Julie of A Little Pregnant cited in Friedman 2013, pp. 82–83, emphasis in original)

There is a clear sense of an infertility community, not just in the support available, but in the language used. We are told that as 'with any subculture, the world of infertility blogs can be confusing to outsiders' because infertility 'bloggers have their own lingo, a bewildering array of acronyms and abbreviations that can be intimidating to the uninitiated' (Miller 2008, p. 80). Infertility associations and blogs alike routinely offer a useful list of acronyms, from ACA (anti-cardiolipin antibody) to ZIFT (zygote intra-fallopian transfer), with TTC (trying to conceive), BFN (a big fat negative) and MC (miscarriage) appearing as some of the most commonly used in the blogosphere. One blogger tells us that she 'learned a new language' (April of The Maniscalco Journey 2014a) through her experiences with infertility, a language that she was unfamiliar with at the outset:

> [B]ut as time went on and I took more 'classes' I immersed myself more and more in the language I became a member of the world of infertility acronyms and now I am practically fluent. I can decode a sentence such as 'TTC for 5 yrs, cd14, 2dpo, 1dpiui, BFP on cd24' just as you are reading these words I am typing. (Ibid.)

Her final sentence reminds us of the shared community that she is both part of and writing for. Moreover, this community, or at least the most vocal members of it, comprises women, in part because 'women have traditionally borne the brunt of the medical, social, and cultural burdens' of infertility (Sterling 2013 p. 15) and because of the emotive writing that has its roots in women's journals and diaries (Miller 2008, p. 81). Although readers may not understand or seek to make sense of the acronyms here, those affected by infertility share a common language in a communal safe space.

Family building blogs, although not monolithic in subject or content, routinely share a common language and tone. While Erin Striff refers to bloggers employing a 'cynical, resistant tone' (Striff 2005, p. 190), others go as far as drawing on 'gallows humor' (Ibid., p. 197). Even a cursory glance at the names of the blogs is telling in this regard. While early adopters called themselves Chez Miscarriage, A Little Pregnant, The Naked Ovary, Welcome to the Desert, Barren Mare, The Leery Polyp, I Wasted all that Birth Control and Rotten Eggs, 'the humor in the titles of newer infertility blogs' points to the influence of the early adopters, be it Stirrup Queens, Sperm Palace Jesters, Who Shot My Stork, BabyWanted: ApplyWithin, and On Flunking Applied Biology 101 (Ratliff 2009, p. 131).

Chandra Wells writes that bloggers 'strive to make infertility not only visible but *visceral*' (Wells 2011, p. 208, emphasis in original), and in so doing, draws attention to the 'demographic invisibility of those who cannot procreate' (Ibid., p. 213). Indeed, there is an unnerving degree of personal revelation, be it physical, financial, marital, practical or sexual, in the blogosphere. The revelations can appear unnerving in their brutal honesty, candour and intimacy, and this is due, in the most part, to the anonymity of the form. One blogger suggests that the intimacy that she feels with her readers would not be possible without the anonymity of the Internet, telling us that there is 'this barrier, this kind of protective quality of knowing that we can have these very personal discussions, and I wonder if we'd be as comfortable having those discussions face-to-face' (Tsigdinos of Silent Sorority cited in Miller 2008, p. 84). Perhaps not, but as Scully notes, a single infertility disclosure could lead to other couples coming 'out of the infertility closet' and sharing their stories (Scully 2014, p. 80).

The fact that these communities are available anytime, any day of the week is seen as attractive, considering the time and location restrictions placed on other support mechanisms (Malik and Coulson 2008, p. 106). These online forums have routinely and repeatedly been seen to offer support and a sense of community for those seeking infertility guidance and camaraderie. And there is evidence to suggest that 'many friendships that start online eventually cross into the offline world' (Miller 2008, p. 82). However, both the strength and fragility of these friendships can be understood in the phenomenon of 'cycle buddies', the name given to a group of women tracking similar assisted reproductive treatments (Ibid., p. 84). These friendships 'can quickly become intense, with buddies connecting daily to compare protocols and share feelings' (Ibid., p. 84). Although such support seems entirely positive during what could be an emotionally and physically difficult stage of treatment, the 'tenuousness of these relationships [is] revealed ... when one cycle buddy receives a positive pregnancy test and the other does not' (Ibid., p. 84).

We are told that 'it's difficult when you make friends with someone and their journey is so different to yours. You start off conversing with them, from the same perspective, then find that you are monitoring their pregnancy. It can be hard to see how long it's been for you compared to them' (Malik and Coulson 2008, p. 110). One blogger refers to cycle buddies as 'foul-weather friendships' (Miller 2008, p. 85) because women are there to offer support through treatments and tragedy but rarely remain for conception celebrations or maternal congratulations. This is such a common complaint that babycenter has a community thread devoted to the topic (babycenter 2010). Cycle buddies are seen to be supportive during times of grieving; however, this is said to be less a positive emotional crutch and more a 'disconcerting degree of competitiveness' or what one blogger referred to as the 'Pain Olympics of infertility' (Tertia cited in Miller 2008, p. 85). We are informed that there exists a 'kind of one-upmanship in the effort to disclose the most painful personal story about fertility treatment ... the situation has gotten so bad that one blogger, only half-jokingly, devised a system of "Pain Points" by which aggrieved bloggers could measure their suffering' (Miller 2008, p. 85).

Although blogs, like pathographies, illness narratives, earlier self-help literature and more recent repro-lit, can be understood as a meaningful and safe space for those experiencing infertility, there are words of caution and documented concerns for those who frequent these online diaries, including, but not limited to charges of, real world isolation (Hinton et al. 2010, p. 441), excess (Striff 2005, p. 198), narcissism (Karlsson cited in Hepworth 2015, p. 212), fickle friendships (Miller 2008, p. 85) and inauthenticity (Kritzer 2011; Striff 2005, p. 197).

THE DOWN SIDE OF INFERTILITY BLOGS: ONLINE OBSESSION AND REAL-WORLD ISOLATION

The Internet in general and the blogosphere in particular can 'help people facing infertility by educating, empowering, and diminishing their feelings of depression' (Hinton et al. 2010, p. 436). However, we are informed that online support networks have a habit of encouraging women to withdraw from 'important real-world interactions' (Epstein et al. 2002, p. 507). Those women who are affected by an infertility diagnosis who share online networks without access to 'other outlets are more depressed' than women who access real world networks (Ibid., p. 513). Writing for *The New Atlantis*, Cheryl Miller makes this point when she tells us that although the act of blogging or reading an infertility narrative online 'can serve as an outlet for some, it can trap others in the despair and anger of their condition' (Miller 2008, p. 90). It can, in the words of one user, 'fuel the obsession' (cited in Malik and Coulson 2008, p. 110).

Users have commented that their online community encouraged them to eschew real-world friendships and shun social interactions, resulting in a growing reliance on online platforms. In her infertility memoir, Scully tells us that there 'were many times when I resolved to shut down my Facebook account for good or set myself challenges not to Google anything infertility related for one whole day, but I always failed' (Scully 2014, p. 38). Another user spoke of the 'negative impact' that online message boards had begun to have on aspects of her daily life, telling us that she routinely found that she was 'spending too much time on them and not enough time on other home or work matters' (cited in Malik and Coulson 2008, p. 11). Obsession is not a term used lightly here; it is a term being employed by the users themselves. Such a compulsion is not

58   R. FEASEY

just a problem in terms of support mechanisms, but in terms of the broader lived experience of the women affected by an infertility diagnosis.

Family Building Blogs: Public, Personal But Not Professional

Women are invested in online infertility resources, including infertility blogs and forums, not because they are seeking role models in the shape of women without children, but because they are looking for family-building support and advice from other women affected by an infertility diagnosis. With this in mind, to continue to use the phrase infertility blog is both inaccurate in terms of what is presented in the posts and comments, but also unhelpful in terms of the support on offer in such online diaries. Infertility blogging is said to be a misnomer 'since the label has been applied to blogging about a variety of topics not necessarily discussed within the context of infertility' including pregnancy loss, stillbirth, infant death, adoption and surrogacy (Sohr-Preston et al. 2016, p. 8). Current research employs the term 'family building' in order to 'describe this community since its members, regardless of fertility status or history, all discuss attempts to start, grow, or maintain families' (Ibid., p. 8). The point here then is that even though these blogs are accessible and available to anyone looking for family-building advice and options, the issue of support, role models and representativeness arises for those who are uninterested in third-party or assisted reproductive support, or those looking to end treatment before successfully creating the desired family unit.

The Internet is increasingly being utilised to find health-related information, indeed 'one in 20 searches on Google are health-related' (Gibbs 2015). We find that individuals look to the Internet to research diseases, health problems and treatments in order 'to prepare for doctors' appointments' (Kahlor and Mackert 2009, p. 83). Indeed, those affected by an infertility diagnosis can 'explore an abundance of web sites dedicated to disseminating information about infertility, infertility testing, and infertility treatment options' (Ibid., p. 83). That said, while a number of 'websites offered by fertility clinics are not meeting health information guidelines' (Ibid., p. 83), questions could also be raised as to the medical accuracy of the narratives and treatments presented in online diaries. Although family building blogs are a freely available and accessible source of emotional support and targeted medical information for those affected by an infertility diagnosis, we are reminded that 'information presented is not required to be fact-checked or evidence-based' (Sohr-Preston et al. 2016, p. 19). If one considers that the broader news media routinely fail to 'portray health issues in a way that accurately educates, informs, or empowers the general public' (Sangster and Lawson 2015, p. 1073), one is left to question the ways in which blogs might be seen to support or counter 'the goals of medical professionals' (Ibid., p. 1073).

At a time when pockets of the public and medical community are stating that 'IVF and all other "assisted reproduction techniques" should be a low priority' for the NHS due to budgetary restrictions (Evans 2011; Ross 2016), infertility is 'rarely viewed as a major social concern' (Sterling 2013, p. 4). Part of the issue here might be related to the fact that stories surrounding such treatments are presented as personal narratives, about individuals finding themselves lucky or otherwise in what has been termed the 'postcode lottery' (Matthews-King 2017). We see the stories, hear the narratives and read the testimonials, but they all appear as personal accounts rather than public platforms for change. We find that 'infertility researchers and practitioners have focused primarily on the individual journeys of infertility' (Sterling 2013, p. 4) and my point is that much family building blogging remains consistent with such personalised narratives. The risk here of course is that such stories, tragedies and triumphs can be read as self-serving and ego-driven (Ratliff 2009, p. 142). Chandra Wells tells us that she was 'tempted' into the blogging community 'by what seems on the surface to be an appealing candor but ends up feeling like an inappropriate act of self-exposure, in which she herself is made complicit simply by reading' (Wells 2011, p. 202). Indeed, numerous 'commentators on the blogging trend … view the enactment of self-revelation on the Internet as self-indulgent at best and pathological at worst' (Ibid., p. 202).

The family building blogs are all personal accounts, but that does not necessarily make them authentic. Sherry Turkle suggests that bloggers accounts are 'immaterial and free-floating, divorced from the physical bodies of the real life individuals who invent them' (Turkle cited in Wells 2011, p. 208). However, the bloggers' accounts are not just removed from the physical body but, simultaneously, a step removed from the lived experience of the blogger in question. After all, the writers are all 'self-consciously shaping their blogs as texts, so that their entries are essayistic and rhetorical rather than raw, unfiltered catalogues of daily life' (Wells 2011, p. 208). Bloggers talk about attempting 'to *construct* a persona that nonetheless feels *authentic*, a seeming contradiction in terms' (Karen cited in Wells 2011, p. 208, emphasis in original). In short, the blogger is the author but only a specific version of the author, one that can use the act of blogging to relieve stress, frustration, anger and resentment for an invested and interested readership. Extant literature on film stardom and celebrity culture makes it clear that star images or celebrity brands are constructed identities, even those 'attributed' celebrities, be they reality performers, vloggers, micro-celebrities or influencers whose entire life seems to be played out for the cameras, are careful to create, craft and circulate a very specific identity for public interaction (Rojek 2001; Khamis et al. 2017). And although few performers have gone as far as Katie Price/Jordan or Beyoncé/Sasha Fierce in creating a public alter-ego, the celebrity sector is routinely built on more subtle iterations of this duality. My point is that we do not see the family building bloggers in GP surgeries, waiting rooms, in private bathrooms or office meetings, and we do not, and cannot know the real person behind the *noms de blogs*; we simply read about their constructed selves. This is not to challenge the credibility of the tests, appointments or diagnoses, or to question the validity of their emotional expression, but rather to be reminded that this is a considered version of those thoughts, feelings and events. In short, writing 'becomes a performance for the blogger as much as for the audience' (Striff 2005, p. 198). The Getupgrrl blogger of Chez Miscarriage writes in her biography that

> [t]his is not going to be one of those spiritually uplifting blogs in which I name every fetus ... I've ever lost and then derive comfort from the fact that I have so many little angels looking down on me from heaven. No, this is going to be an angry blog, so please spare me the lectures about my attitude. I get plenty of opportunities to be a smiley-faced trooper in my *real life*. This is the only place where I get to be plain old pissed off at the universe. (Getupgrrl of Chez Miscarriage cited in Pedersen 2010, p. 53, emphasis added)

One blogger goes as far as to highlight not just creative self-expression or inauthenticity in the infertility blogosphere, but outright fabrication as it relates to this self-same online diary, stating that 'I think getupgrrl was a fabricator. Sorry, Grrl, if you're reading this. Too goddamn many red flags' (Kritzer 2011).

There has been some discussion regarding the ways in which computer-mediated communications are able to 'offer an accessible and labile narrative mode for telling stories of personal crisis, stories that can translate into deeper cultural critique and decisive political action' (Wells 2011, p. 203). In her research on infertility blogging, privacy and reproductive rights, Clancy Ratliff makes the point that the act of blogging

> is significant in that it helps enable the formation of positions on the array of social and political issues involved in reproduction, including access to fertility treatment, the discursive construction of women's bodies in medical discourse, selective reduction, prenatal care, adoption, surrogacy, midwifery and home birth, work-life balance, access to services for special needs children, and the choice (or necessity, in many cases) between working outside the home or staying at home with children. (Ratliff 2009, p. 142)

However, much work challenges the power of these online diaries to instil meaningful social, cultural or medical change for the bloggers or their readers, speaking of social passivity over political action. The media and entertainment environment, be it 'plays, novels, television or films … make it hard for the general non-infertile public to relate to the seriousness of infertility' (Sterling 2013, p. 99). One might suggest that bloggers also play a part in society's ambivalence about 'accepting infertility as a legitimate societal problem' (Ibid., p. 4), especially when their very authenticity is in question. Family blogs are charged with inaccuracy, inauthenticity and ego, but it is worth acknowledging the ways in which women who spend time with these blogs make sense of their narratives of hope and despair.

Simone of the Bubbles and Bumps blog tells us that she is aware that for 'every success story there are double the disappointments' and yet she comments that the success stories and the happy endings sign-posted and celebrated in the family building blogs 'make us feel it IS possible' (Simone of Bubbles and Bumps 2015, emphasis in original). And yet although these stories initially offer a source of 'hope and reassurance that treatment could be successful' (Malik and Coulson 2008, p. 110), there is a sense that they can eventually harbour frustration, anger and jealousy if readers have not been so fortunate in their own reproductive attempts. We find that during the course of numerous treatments 'messages reporting positive treatment outcomes appeared to compound the psychological distress [that readers] were experiencing and in some instances resulted in individuals withdrawing active participation from the [online] community' (Ibid., p. 110). This is a cause for concern if one considers the ways in which these blogs were said to be offered as a source of support for women struggling to find sympathetic and empathetic voices elsewhere. Moreover, alongside those shared stories of hope and treatment, there is also a more 'overwhelming sadness and distress' that comes from 'reading stories about other people's grief, particularly as it relates to negative treatment outcomes' (Ibid., p. 110).

Ending Treatment Is Not the Same as Giving Up

There is evidence to suggest that the support on offer in family building blogs is restricted to a very specific audience, namely, those who seek out medical help, and do not stop treatment until a successful birth outcome has been reached. We are told that for those going through a financially, emotionally, mentally and physically difficult cycle of IVF, support through each stage is strong and consistent, but that if a woman seeks to end treatment, irrespective of the number of cycles experienced, the family building blogosphere is less than supportive. Indeed, 'the boundary between support and pressure is sometimes trespassed by the members of the virtual community' because 'the encouragement of others to keep up the fight when in vitro fertilization fails' borders on 'coercion' (Korolczuk 2014, p. 432). Even a cursory glance at the family building posts demonstrates that while support from 'members is often badly needed' the 'strong emphasis put on perseverance and commitment can be perceived as oppressive' (Ibid., p. 438). One woman tells us that

> I am so tired of people judging how families deal with their infertility, from the people telling us to just get over it … to the people pushing us constantly to try again, even though we were told quite forcefully by my doctors that another attempt could kill me. (Cannonball comment on Murdoch 2012)

Carly of the Little Miss-Conception blog tells the rarely heard personal narrative of a near decade-long failed IVF journey, a journey filled with 'nothing but unhappiness and despair' as the blogger makes the difficult decision to end treatment. She writes: 'no more blood tests, appointments, needles, procedures, scans, money, no more drugs, no more IVF cycles and please no more miscarriages. … No more. It's over. We can't do this anymore' (Carly of Little Miss-Conception cited in House 2017). Although it is important to acknowledge Carly's confession as a common, yet seldom heard, infertility narrative, it is the anonymous responses to her decision to end treatment that are most revealing. Commentators were quick to foreground optimism, hope and possible solutions, from losing weight to acupuncture and adoption, at a time when the woman in question was looking to move from actively trying to grieving and closure (comments on House 2017).

From this estimation, much family building blogging can be seen to support the dominant pronatal ideology, making those women who are diagnosed with infertility and who decide to stop treatment before creating a traditional family unit twice shamed: shamed for their original diagnosis and shamed again for what is presented as a lack of perseverance. Although those women who are diagnosed with infertility speak of their sense of shame, these forums are also likely to cast blame, blame for their lack of commitment or dedication to the goal of family building, irrespective of the personal situation, health condition or emotional needs (Korolczuk 2014, p. 439). One blog user writes:

> If someone stops fighting it is interpreted as 'stopping others'. If someone doesn't have the strength anymore, it is interpreted as 'going astray'. If someone says 'I don't have energy for more' … others claim that you just need some time before another attempt. (bloo cited in Korolczuk 2014, p. 439, emphasis in original)

In her seminal work on surrogacy and the reproduction of normative families on the small screen, Lulu Le Vay makes the point that women return, time and again in some cases, to 'the IVF treadmill with the desire to find a resolution through pregnancy' as it perpetuates 'the fantasy of normative family' (Le Vay 2019, pp. 80–81). Indeed, existing literature makes it clear that the 'constant encouragement from others during IVF treatment can make it even more difficult to fight the social stigma attached to being infertile. Such support is based, after all, on the idea that everyone can have a child; that it is just a matter of commitment and will' (Korolczuk 2014, p. 440). New reproductive technologies can and do provide successful birth outcomes for many women, which can make it difficult for others to end treatment before achieving a successful pregnancy. Miller's work on blogging, infertility, family and technology notes that

> [w]hile failing to conceive naturally is devastating … [i]t's compounded by living in a culture that believes (erroneously) that with enough time and

money infertility treatments will produce a baby. Infertility can be isolating, leaving one feeling alienated from the wider fertile community. But failing to conceive even after years of medical intervention can leave one feeling alienated from the infertile world as well. Moreover, those ... unwilling to do whatever it takes to have a child ... can find themselves ... being second-guessed by others, especially by those who used those technologies and feel defensive about their own decisions. (Miller 2008, p. 86)

In a pronatal environment where mature womanhood and appropriate femininity appear intertwined with maternal identity, we are told that refusing to start, or ending treatment prior to a successful pregnancy outcome 'blurs the boundaries between voluntary and involuntary childlessness, leaving the woman vulnerable to the suggestion that she was unwilling and perhaps too selfish, to make the necessary sacrifices to be a mother' (Throsby 2004, pp. 39–40). In her work on seriality, assisted reproductive technologies and celebrity reality television, Heather Osborne-Thompson argues that 'the solutions to the problem of infertility and/or childlessness ... can be found in the ways individuals choose to deal with that problem; namely, the repeated yet strategic deployment of all available technologies for as long as it takes' (Osborne-Thompson 2014, p. 879). In this same way, Sarah Banet-Weiser and Laura Portwood-Stacer have argued that such reality texts provide evidence of the ways in which *any* body, to which I would include a pregnant body 'is possible, if one simply has the desire' (Banet-Weiser and Portwood-Stacer 2006, p. 269). With such work in mind, it is evident that 'normative standards of deserving and undeserving motherhood' exist, which, in turn, create difficulties 'for women for whom treatment is unsuccessful' (Ibid., p. 151).

Today, those affected by an infertility diagnosis 'have access to a suite of medical interventions including IUI, IVF, ICSI, surgical sperm removal, embryo freezing, blastocyst transfer, assisted hatching, egg donation and surrogacy' (Scully 2014, pp. 36–37). And yet, although women 'are willing to go into debt, put ... relationships under strain, jeopardize ... careers, lose friends and push ... bodies to the limit' (Ibid., p. 37), the chance of getting pregnant from an individual IVF cycle remains low (Winston 2018). However, because available treatments are increasing all the time, women are encouraged to try and try again. Infertility clinics and self-help literature both have a tendency to refer to 'giving up' on treatment, be it another round of IVF or trialling a new drug, and this phrase has a pejorative implication which 'renders stopping an act of weakness indicative of a pending downward spiral' (Throsby 2004, p. 15). In her work on female infertility before the development of IVF, Gena Corea notes that

> a woman could, at some point, however painfully, come to terms with her infertility, go on with her life, find a way to live it fully. Now there is no easy way off the medical treadmill. She may now spend a major part of her adult life in debilitating treatment in experimental programs. There is always a promising new program to enrol in, its low success rate played down, it's 'hope' played up. The years roll on. (Corea cited in Le Vay 2019, p. 80)

In short, those women who make the decision to end treatment are presented as 'failures' who lacked commitment, rather than as people capable of making positive choices (Woollett cited in Throsby 2004, p. 15).

It is in the interests of private fertility clinics to encourage women to continue treatments, with unsuccessful cycles being presented less as failures and more as opportunities to better diagnose, with an eye on future treatment rounds. Women undergoing treatment look 'on the bright side' because they can talk about having a cycle 'under [their] belt' (Gallup 2007, p. 113), with each new round offering a chance to adapt treatments according to their specific needs. Simone of the Bubbles and Bumps blog makes this point when she talks about entering her fourth cycle of IVF treatment. Alongside the obvious frustrations and disappointments, she finds hope because the 'more I learned how tailoring medicines to suit your body (not a one size fits all approach) can improve your chances of success the more I understood that maybe we just haven't found the right formula for us yet' (Simone of Bubbles and Bumps 2015).

Drawing on Michael Mulkay's work on the science and politics of reproduction, Rosemary Hepworth explains that the media are keen to foreground successful IVF stories at the expense of those that proved unsuccessful (Hepworth 2015, p. 200). Indeed, we are told that the stories of those women 'for whom the technology had failed, and for whom there may have been more suffering than joy, were almost completely ignored' (Mulkay 2010, p. 73). And such agenda setting 'has had a significant impact on cultural perceptions of IVF treatments' (Hepworth 2015, p. 200) both within and beyond the family building blogosphere. The majority of articles that touch on the theme of infertility 'including personal and celebrity stories' in popular women's magazines 'resulted in a happy ending with a new baby' (Sterling 2013, p. 99) even though

[i]n reality, this is not the case for everyone. Furthermore, details, such as time in treatment, costs, and other pressures were almost always omitted. Overall, these simplistic media representations minimized the infertility experience perhaps making those who actually experienced the harsh realities [of] infertility feel even more isolated and stigmatized. (Ibid., p. 99)

When the medical community and wider society encourage further treatment options for those women affected by an infertility diagnosis, 'the terms of the choice of whether or not to proceed with IVF can hardly be described as neutral' (Throsby 2004, p. 40). Because the success rates of IVF are low, there is a sense that those women who have undergone treatment are both looking to build a family and also proving how much they want to have children. In this way, women can be seen to have engaged with not only the medical procedure, but also an appropriate identity in the pronatal period. In her seminal research on feminism, infertility and the negotiation of normality, Karen Throsby argues that

having engaged with IVF, even when it has failed, serves to validate the participants' claims to normative reproductive values, establishing a distinction between their own childlessness and that of those who have either chosen to live without children, or who would like children but are constructed as not prepared to make the necessary sacrifices to achieve that. (Ibid., p. 107)

A commitment to IVF can therefore be seen to offer the best possible hope for achieving a baby, but also to contribute to 'the production of a legitimised form of childlessness' (Ibid., p. 107) as the woman is able to demonstrate and internalise the fact that she has tried 'everything possible … to have a biological child' (Ibid., p. 171). When IVF treatments fail, women 'have to grieve' (Ibid., p. 12) and yet, while undergoing treatment, or planning future cycles or treatment options, there is always hope, however faint or fleeting. Indeed, the phrases 'pregnant until proven otherwise' (Annabell of IVF One Day at a Time 2013) and 'parents-in-waiting' exist to account for those seeking assisted reproductive treatments (Mamo 2013, p. 227). With this in mind, the decision to stop treatment is a difficult one, because it 'involves confronting a future without much-desired biological children' (Throsby 2004, p. 8) and therefore a life course 'for which there are few role models, maps or guidelines' (Daniluk cited in Throsby 2004, p. 8), and 'for which there is limited social acceptance and understanding' (Throsby 2004, p. 8). In a book-length account of her own infertility and family-building journey, Caroline Gallup makes the point that

> I no longer know what to do in order to get the best outcomes for us. I want to stop, but that means no children—ever. Where would that leave [us]? We've opened up this baby-shaped hole in our lives. We have explored what it should look like, feel like, to be parents. How do we ever close that hole again and carry on as before? (Gallup 2007, p. 162)

Even though the 'experience of infertility can be devastating' it is unsuccessful treatments that 'can leave women feeling sad, anxious and depressed, with a sense of loss and bereavement' (Hinton et al. 2010, p. 436). Add to this the decision to end treatment, and those feelings can be multiplied. Gallup concludes her volume by stating that 'over two years have passed since my last cycle and negative pregnancy test. I'm 43 years old and we've stopped treatment. Drawing a line under the process was one of the hardest decisions we've ever had to make, and to a certain extent I'm still in a state of flux' (Gallup 2007, p. 217). Women who have decided to end treatment, irrespective of the number of cycles attempted, have likened infertility to a 'destructive tornado', with survivors of both having to find a way to rebuild their lives in the aftermath of nature's dark cruelty (Bronstein and Knoll 2015). These women are said to be 'out of synchronization with life's patterns and failing in one's anticipated contribution to society', so much so in fact that they speak of needing to redefine their 'purpose and contribution to the world' (McCarthy 2008, p. 323).

Women have made the point that ending treatment doesn't mean that life goes back to some pretreatment normalcy or routine; rather, the experience of that treatment stays with you and changes you. In this way, you 'survive' infertility, not merely end treatment. In an article on the paradoxical dimensions of loss and opportunity for women who have experienced unsuccessful medical treatment for infertility, Patrice McCarthy explains that

> [t]he heightened awareness of personal strength that emerged from their experience is carried throughout their lives as an ongoing reality. While giving up the hoped-for child constituted a unique and life-defining loss, the infertility also remained as a presence to be considered and remembered, and as a factor influencing the meaning of subsequent life events. (McCarthy 2008)

These are complex emotions and difficult life decisions, and as such, women need to know that support is available. Because of the nature and scope of this chapter, I would like to remind the blogging community of the needs of its routinely loyal readers. After all, it can be difficult to find discursive patterns, or indeed entries of any kind, concerning the end of treatment on family building blogs. Beyond the blogosphere, we need to ask for further skilled, bespoke medical guidance and routine counselling on the decision to end treatment.

Existing family building blogs are peppered with hope, disappointment, optimism, anger, elation, frustration, fear and envy, and they pertain to offer support for other women who are currently experiencing such emotions. However, these blogs spend little time supporting women who look to end treatment, be it for financial, health or age-related reasons. Nor do they offer guidance to women who seek to reimagine their future and their friendships without children. And for all of the distinctions between end of treatment as a 'single definable moment' or a 'long and complex process' (Throsby 2004, p. 16), much of this discussion is absent in the blogosphere due to the fact that the vast majority of family building bloggers, and their broader repro-lit counterparts never get to, or have to make this decision. And this is a cause for concern. After all, while women affected by an infertility diagnosis look to these online diaries for comfort and camaraderie, to find that the sites that are meant to understand them better than their own family and friends cannot offer meaningful support when they need it most must be doubly isolating for women.

I have made the point that bloggers are a diverse group, and that the blogosphere can account for a myriad of different routes through infertility, but what the overwhelming majority of them have in common is their active pursuit of a biological child, through whatever treatment options are deemed appropriate or necessary. Even a cursory glance at the array of family building blogs currently available online makes it clear that the key reason why ending treatments is so rarely addressed in this community is because the format routinely and repeatedly ends with a happy healthy addition to the family unit.

With a wealth of family building blogs online, one might suggest that it is difficult to navigate the options available, or even know where to start. As such, the 'Creating a Family' website tells its readers that they have done the hard work by 'narrowing down the infertility blogger universe to some of the best, and categorised them by diagnosis and treatment … includ[ing] information on where they are in the process if you feel the need to be self protective' (Creating a Family 2018b). And this final disclaimer makes sense when you note just how many of the blogs offer a happy ending in terms of a healthy pregnancy, and/or maternal outcome. We are encouraged to look at blogs such as Stirrup Queens, inConceivable, A Little Pregnant, Hope-Filled Focus, The Hardest Quest, Busted Plumbing, Stealing Baby Kisses, Sunny Day Today Mama, The 2 Week Wait, What the Blog? and Parenthood For Me (Ibid.). Without exception, these writers have, in the words of the website, looked to create a family, on the back of their infertility diagnosis, be it a mother of twins conceived through IUI (Stirrup Queens), a mother of triplets on the back of a polycystic ovary diagnosis (What the Blog?) or a woman who had her child after multiple rounds of IVF (The 2 Week Wait).

For those family building blogs that were recommended to audiences without the accompanying birth or maternal success story in their summary, a brief glance at the titles make it clear that each one in turn speaks of a happy family ending. Candace of Our Misconception blog speaks of the pain, and later the elation, that came with their long and winding infertility journey. Under a blog post entitled 'The Gift of Life', we are told that '[a]fter seven years, it is not very easy to figure out how to start this post. We had our baby seems appropriate enough … or maybe this is better— WE HAD OUR BABY!!!!!!!' (Candace of Our Misconception 2014a, emphasis in original). The couple in question speak with humility, gratitude and joy when they explain their new parenting routine, acknowledging the role of a gestational carrier in their birth journey. We are told that they

> will forever be indebted to our wonder surro and her entire family! Without them, we would not be all blurry eyed and sleep deprived from our daughter … needing to be fed at all hours of the night. … Guess what, we love it. (Ibid.)

The couples' story is said to be inspirational, and the user comments applaud the new parents for their 'perseverance'. Indeed, one might go as far as to suggest that their blog encourages others to keep trying, however difficult their experiences or low their chances of success. The following is an example:

> It gives me so much hope! I had a hysterectomy in April and our carrier just lost our baby in December (he/she was only 3 weeks old). We are as 'stubborn' as you guys were. After 5 surgeries, 4 IUIs, a hysterectomy, and now

a miscarriage we WILL continue trying to have our own 'Jelly Bean'. Thank you for sharing your story! (Ana comment on Candace of Our Misconception 2014a)

Perseverance indeed! Candace experienced '6 failed IUIs involving clomid, ultrasounds, and lots of pain meds' followed by six failed rounds of IVF. Indeed, after her sixth failed IVF attempt, or what was presented as a 'crushing blow to our hopes for a biological child. Shattered to splinters. Cry, drink, eat, repeat' the couple 'picked [them]selves up, decided [they] would not be defeated, and set [their] sights for starting a family in the realm of adoption' (Candace of Our Misconception 2014b). After completing the necessary paperwork, attending relevant classes and passing the required home visits, they were close to being on the waiting list. However, as if to remind us about the hierarchy of appropriate motherhood and society's perception of preferred maternal roles, we find that the couple are presented with the opportunity of using a gestational surrogate, and although they were about to be put on the adoption waiting list, they 'put the brakes on the adoption process and decide[d] to forge ahead with surrogacy' (Ibid.). As is somewhat predictable on the infertility blogroll, the couple

> hear the news [that they] had been waiting for 7 years to hear. WE, I mean SHE, umm this is complicated. … The beta is POSITIVE! … The wait was long, it was unbearable at moments where we wanted to *give up* and just live childfree. But we didn't. … Now, we change diapers and find ways to change the world of infertility by supporting others. Sharing our story, mishaps and how to now parent after infertility. (Ibid., emphasis added)

The post touches on the option of ending treatment, but only tentatively. The topic is soon turned back to the joyous event that is the arrival of their new baby. Likewise, April of The Maniscalco Journey blog writes:

> So I finally can say I have the happy ending to our long journey. We are FINALLY pregnant with TWIN BOYS! … I hope anyone going th[r]ough this long and painful journey finds peace in their decision w[he]ther it's to keep moving forward with treatment *or not*. Throughout my journey, and even to this day, I have couples reaching out to me asking for advice and support and for that I am grateful that I am able to guide them and relate to

their story to help them find hope and peace. (April of The Maniscalco Journey 2014b, emphasis added)

The point here is simply that while some family building bloggers do mention the possibility of ending treatment, it is only ever a fleeting thought or a passing comment that sits within or alongside a pregnancy or birth announcement.

The next blog to be highlighted on the 'Creating a Family' blogroll is Licensed2Love, and although the website summary does not reveal the maternal success, or otherwise of the blogger, a quick click on the site in question presents another happy ending. The blogger experiences a successful pregnancy and reminds readers of the hierarchy of acceptable motherhood when she speaks of both her adopted and birth children:

> A lot has happened in the last year … we finalized the adoption of our two foster children [and] I became pregnant with our first 'birth son'. No, it was not a post adoption miracle as some like to think. … Long story short after receiving some new found hope [and after] several dozen appointments we were able to conceive our 'miracle baby' with the help of science and medicine. I never knew a love like carrying a child and watching them grow. It's indescribable. (Licensed2Love 2017)

Joy and gratitude emanate here in terms of the love that the Licensed2Love blogger has for her children, but with particular reference to her 'miracle baby'. The post reminds readers of the ways in which maternal roles are ranked and qualified with 'birth' children as more acceptable than their adopted counterparts in the current pronatal period. That said, adoption remains preferable to involuntary childlessness. With involuntary childlessness in mind, interested and invested readers might be left questioning the good fortune of the infertile mothers who are presented on the 'Creating a Family' blogroll. After all, if one considers the statistics, namely that 'the chance of getting pregnant from an individual IVF cycle in Britain still only stands at about 21 per cent' (Winston 2018), then logic would assume that these figures would play out in the family building blogosphere. Blog posts should routinely present unsuccessful treatment options, a consideration of how and when to end treatment, and a road map and role models for a life without children. But these are not the personal stories heard or blogging tropes seen.

BLOGGING AS A MATERNAL INFERTILE

Next on the 'Creating a Family' blogroll is the '33 year old married woman living in Scotland' of Baby Maybe renown, whose most recent blog post bemoans her high blood pressure, hospitalisation and the safe arrival of her premature, but otherwise healthy, baby boy. These posts pick up on a theme that runs throughout several book-length studies written by women affected by an infertility diagnosis, who, through the use of the new reproductive technologies, become pregnant. They speak of experiencing guilt and shame, not just in relation to their infertile status, but now in terms of their inability to maintain a serene and selfless demeanour in line with the much-touted 'good' mother (Feasey 2012). Such posts appear divisive in the blogging fraternity. The Baby Maybe blogger speaks candidly about the ways in which a difficult pregnancy is causing her to question her earlier maternal desire:

> I just want him out of me. I believe I am the worst parent ever because I don't want to be pregnant anymore. I know the best thing for Kipling is for me to keep him inside me, but I can't stand being here and I don't have the strength to do this. ... I'm a terrible selfish bitch that can't sit tight and manage a few weeks in hospital. (Baby Maybe 2014a)

The next Baby Maybe blog post is the announcement that 'baby Arran was born safely this morning' (Baby Maybe 2014b), followed soon after with a post that signs out with 'BabyMaybe no longer, BabyDefinitely. Thanks for reading, for commenting, for supporting me. If you would like to follow Arran's journey, you can do so' (Baby Maybe 2014c). Such expressions of anger, frustration, despair and, in the bloggers own words, 'selfishness' are common in the family building blogging community, especially in relation to difficult pregnancies and the experiences of labour. However, such posting is problematic because although it is cathartic, candid and therefore 'worthy' of commentary by the family building bloggers, there is the question of sensitivity here—sensitivity, not in terms of exposing the reality of pregnancy pains or childbirth contractions, but sensitivity to those who are having to or have decided to end treatment. Hearing about friends and family who are pregnant is one thing, having your cycle buddy announce their impending labour is another, and hearing an infertile blogging role model bemoan their pregnancy or birthing experiences on a family building blog could be said to be more difficult again. The Life of an Infertile Myrtle blogger uses the phrase 'Pregnant

Bitchers' to describe infertile women who moan about their pregnancies, because

> bitching about your pregnancy is just a stab in the back for those of us who [would] sell our soul to the devil to get to be pregnant. ... I get it, you want the whole world to know you feel like a whale and that your feet are swollen. But let me speak for the majority of both infertile and fertile myrtles. ... WE DON'T WANT TO HEAR IT! You chose to get pregnant!!! (The Life on an Infertile Myrtle 2015, emphasis in original)

April of The Maniscalco Journey blog echoes this anger, frustration and disappointment when she tells us of a friend who, after trying for 18 months to conceive, became pregnant. She speaks of a shift in sensitivity levels because although this woman began her pregnancy journey thankful for her much-anticipated pregnancy, telling friends and well-wishers that she 'wouldn't take this pregnancy, or anything that comes with it, for granted', this attitude was seen to change as the pregnancy progressed (April of The Maniscalco Journey 2013). We are told that this is not an isolated incident because

> somewhere along the way, everyone who has trouble getting pregnant forgets this promise. Soon after, they are bitching about morning sickness. Or how they 'really wish' they could have just one drink. They are upset when their clothes don't fit anymore ... and cry about not getting any sleep. They send out mass e-mails to their family and friends—with week by week updates on their child—along with at least ten photos of their baby doing pretty much the same thing in each one. (Ibid.)

With this issue of broken promises in mind, Jolene of Infertile Myrtle's Blog shows sensitivity to the family-building community when, after successive 'miracle' pregnancies, she steps down from Infertile Myrtle towards new titles such as Three Boys & a Little Lady. However, on the eve of a hysterectomy, Jolene brings her former infertile *nom de blog* out of retirement. In a post entitled 'Bittersweet Good-bye' Jolene speaks of her infertility journey:

> [I]t truly is a miracle that I've been able to even have one baby, let alone four. I've been able to carry [and deliver] these four healthy babies. ... The idea of going back to that place where I can't have babies is hitting me like a ton of bricks ... thoughts of never again feeling a baby moving within me,

of never again cuddling with a newborn … of never again nursing a baby close to my heart … it's hard to end this chapter of my life. … And so, I bid adieu to my uterus. We've had a love-hate relationship most of my life, but it's a bittersweet good-bye. (Jolene of Infertile Myrtle's Blog 2009)

My point here is that the blogger's earlier sensitivities may have disappeared. After all, she is a self-confessed infertile, now mother of four, bemoaning her hysterectomy and therefore her inability to carry further children, on a family building blog dedicated to an earlier struggle with infertility, for a community itself affected by that diagnosis. Drawing attention not just to her healthy babies, but to the joy of carrying them for months and cuddling them as newborns must be difficult to hear for those who have yet to experience a healthy pregnancy. It seems at best surprising, and at worst, insensitive, to find that the Three Boys & a Little Lady blogger reverted to her former Infertile Myrtle's Blog and its infertile community to make this announcement.

While it seems commonplace for family building bloggers to establish parenting blogs after a birth announcement, the next blogger on the 'Creating a Family' blogroll, Maya, of Don't Count your Eggs, looks to offer both infertility and parenting advice by dividing her blogging time between parenting topics (Momo Monday) and infertility topics (Flashback Friday) (Maya of Don't Count Your Eggs 2014). And although she uses the family building blog to speak of her desire to try for a second child, the author acknowledges the difficulty that some women affected by an infertility diagnosis might have reading a blog that slips between parenting and parent-in-waiting themes (Ibid.).

Lisa Newton from the Amateur Nester blog echoes this sentiment. The blogger understands that 'seeing pictures of our daughter may be difficult for some readers' and therefore, 'out of respect for those of you still in the infertility trenches, we do not post pictures of our daughter here. If you are interested in hearing more about her or my pregnancy, you can head over to my personal blog' (Lisa of Amateur Nester 2018). As a family building blogger, Newton wants to share her infertility story and support those readers who have been affected by a similar diagnosis. The shift from infertile to maternal identity does not change her earlier commitment to the family building blogging community. However, this is a difficult road to navigate. After all, while some readers 'may garner optimism from perusing archived posts to read how a particular blogger progressed from "trying" to "parenting"' (Sohr-Preston et al. 2016, p. 16), others may read the maternal identity as an isolating and alienating addition to a former safe space.

Shirley Shalev and Dafna Lemish make the point that '[a]dvances in medical technology and modern surrogacy enable the infertile female to achieve motherhood even though her body remains infertile. Thus, paradoxically, if a woman selects to avail herself of these medical advances, she becomes an "infertile mother"' (Shalev and Lemish 2013, p. 321). Kitten of the Forever Infertile blog says it best when she states bluntly that '[h]aving a baby cures childlessness; it does NOT cure infertility' (Kitten of Forever Infertile 2015, emphasis in original). In much the same way as someone can carry around an earlier working-class identity, irrespective of their middle-class lifestyle, a mother can continue to carry around her infertile identity long after she has had a successful birth, surrogacy or adoption outcome. And although this is a legitimate thought, feeling and emotional state for those who go on to experience motherhood after being diagnosed with infertility, it can be seen as frustrating for those who have remained forever infertile, not in the name of the blog, but literally. When Kitten of the Forever Infertile blog says that her child 'is all kinds of awesome!' (Kitten of Forever Infertile 2017), it might be difficult to reconcile with her earlier identity for those who have not experienced the transition from 'parent-in-waiting' to mother.

Away from the 'Creating a Family' blogroll, Infertility Diaries, a blog associated with the women's magazine *Redbook* created a stir when one half of the blogging team 'returned from maternity leave after giving birth to twins' after her co-blogger announced her pregnancy (Miller 2008, p. 85). The once-loyal follower who posted 'welcome back. I think I'll be leaving' (cited in Miller 2008, p. 85) spoke for many because 'having TWO mothers blogging about infertility is akin to bringing a baby to [a] reproductive endocrinologist's ... office ... it's just not the courteous or sensitive thing' (Miller 2008, p. 85). One might consider these bloggers to be infertility advocates; indeed, editor-in-chief, Stacey Morrison defended the continued employment of the maternal bloggers on Infertility Diaries, posting that if our 'biggest challenge in maintaining an infertility blog is that our writers keep turning up pregnant, it's a problem we'll be delighted to have' before succumbing to the will of the blogosphere by 'hiring another infertile blogger' (Ibid., p. 85). The sudden about turn here is due to the potential loss of readers; after all, writing on LiveJournal, Naomi Kritzer tells us that she 'quit reading most of the infertility blogs after most of the bloggers I was reading had children' (Kritzer 2011).

If we remind ourselves that nearly four out of five IVF cycles started do not result in a live birth (Throsby 2004, p. 7; Winston 2018), one might assume that the narrative of involuntary childlessness would dominate long-running family building blogs. Readers may well expect to trip over posts relating to life without children or advice on how 'to pursue alternative routes to non-biological parenthood' (Throsby 2004, p. 8). However, rather than open up that line of enquiry, the 'Creating a Family' blogroll speaks about long, protracted and often painful family-building experiences, each of which concludes with a happy maternal ending. And although the website gives us links to a small number of what it terms 'Child Free' blogs, namely, Mrs. Spit and The Next 15,000 Days, they tend to only fleetingly recall or reminisce about their infertility journey, looking instead to blog about a rich and diverse range of well-being subjects. And although it is important for women currently affected by an infertility diagnosis to see that these bloggers have created fulfilling lives without children, the fact that they spend little time talking about how, when and why they stopped treatment or why they decided against alternative family-building options leaves women continuing to search for meaningful support.

Life Without Baby is rare on and beyond this short list as it acknowledges that the blogger did not try all available treatment options on the path to potential motherhood, at a time when protracted efforts are the norm in the family building blogging community. The Life Without Baby author Lisa Manterfield makes the point that even though assisted treatments, third-party reproduction and adoption are all viable family-building avenues, many women 'find that we reach the end of our emotional or financial paths long before we exhaust the list of family building options available to us' (Manterfield 2012). We are informed that even though it is 'hard to walk away from the dream of motherhood ... sometimes it just makes sense' (Ibid.). Manterfield concludes a post entitled 'Don't Ignore ... the Life Without Baby Option' by stating that even though she does not 'want to promote childlessness as an option ... I wish that infertility resources included information about choosing to walk away from motherhood, and how to come to terms with that decision' (Ibid.). But these resources are seldom seen in the blogosphere in favour of support and advice that is said to lead to a more predictable pronatal happy ending. In short, the Life Without Baby blog is the exception that proves the family building blogging rule (Manterfield 2018).

There is evidence to suggest that those affected by an infertility diagnosis turn to the Internet in general and the blogosphere in particular for a number of practical and therapeutic reasons; however, the lack of professional medical expertise, the unrealistic IVF success rates being presented, concerns over social isolation and the unwillingness to support those that look to end treatment lead to questions regarding the seemingly partial support on offer here. However, even when specialist counselling is available, many diagnosed with infertility turn away from the medical professionals in favour of the confessional, and, indeed, visceral modes of address online. GPs in general and infertility specialists in particular might consider providing 'some guidelines for their patients to assess the quality of infertility web sites, perhaps by offering some good starting points that then provide links to other trustworthy resources. This could help lay the foundation for a more symbiotic relationship between specialists and online resources' (Kahlor and Mackert 2009, p. 89). Alternatively, medical practitioners could work more closely alongside existing bloggers, or set up their own blogs to address a need for accurate, anonymous yet candid and confessional online support alongside that offered in more routine surgeries, counselling sessions and group forums. Indeed, in Kahlor and Mackerts' work on the perceptions of infertility information and support services among patients we find that 'respondents had positive opinions of specialists who encouraged Internet usage, considering the specialists more valuable for both infertility information and support' (Ibid., p. 89). With this notion of credible and reliable information in mind, Ann Robinson, director of public awareness for The Information Standard, has been heard commenting that 'it is vital the public be able to differentiate between information that is and isn't trustworthy' (HFEA 2018). Indeed, a recent survey revealed that nearly 80 per cent of respondents thought that 'if you are not a health professional, it's easy to be misled by health information' while nearly half of those who took part in the survey admitted that 'in the past they have believed a piece of health information to be true only to find out later it was inaccurate' (Ibid.). And one wonders how much this is linked to the emergence and development of the blogosphere.

Conclusion

There is a growing volume of confessional life writing on the topic of infertility and the emotional, physical, logistical and financial journey that women go through in order to secure a maternal status, from first-person pathographies to self-help literature and the growing blogosphere. And although one might assume that infertility bloggers document the various ways in which they come to terms with their diagnosis, the number of blogs that take this theme as their starting point makes up a small corner of the larger family building blogosphere. In short, family building blogs are routinely dedicated to sharing the daily experiences of assisted reproductive treatments prior to a long-awaited baby announcement.

When Mary of the Lemonwater blog tells her readers that she worked hard to fulfil a maternal role (Mary of Lemonwater 2015), she is reminding us of the physical, emotional, logistical and financial difficulties commonly associated with assisted reproductive treatments and technologies. By signalling her dedication, determination and single-minded pursuit of motherhood, the blogger can be seen to remind us of the common misconception, routinely played out in the blogosphere, that having a successful pregnancy outcome is 'just a matter of commitment and will' (Korolczuk 2014, p. 440). Such commitment is routine in the blogosphere as family building blogs are archived in favour of parenting journals and mummy diaries. And while Redbook shuffles their bloggers around so as to maintain fresh 'infertiles' to replace the mummy bloggers, authors such as Maya and Newton look to maintain both their infertile and maternal identities.

Although these happy endings might offer hope and comfort to some readers, we need to be reminded that the success rates of assisted reproduction and the representation of such treatment on the family building blogosphere are at odds. This disconnect leaves us to question if those women who write about their experiences have more time, money, support and/or commitment than the wider infertility community. Those long-running blogs that do not offer a predictable pronatal happy ending are few and far between, while those that do not seek treatment are even rarer. In short, the voice of women who 'no longer concentrate on their desire for a technological miracle' but, rather, 'stress their agency even when technology fails' (Ibid., p. 442) appears hard to find in the blogosphere. Further research must decide if that is because they do not seek to blog, or are not sought out in an online experience dominated by treatment plans and birth announcements.

This lack of alternative happy endings, of women finding fulfilment beyond a maternal role, is not unique to the blogging community. In her recent audience study on surrogacy and television, Le Vay speaks of her frustration at the paucity of 'alternative choices outside of motherhood' that are depicted in popular and long-running genre texts such as soap opera and situation comedy (Le Vay 2019, p. 216). She goes on to say that popular television forms a consensus in its representation of infertile women as both failures and not wholly feminine (Ibid., p. 150). One of her respondents noted that

> [i]t's great that these fictional characters can get pregnant, but it's kind of a shame that it can't be left as you can't have kids. …That happens. There really are people who can't have kids and they don't get pregnant even if they try … it would be interesting if someone wrote that into a story instead of doing the nice Hollywood ending. (Laura cited in Le Vay 2019, p. 228)

The overriding message that these women took away from programmes such as *Coronation Street* (1960–) and *Rules of Engagement* (2007–13) was that 'the goal of the narrative for the female characters is to get the baby, no matter what' (Ibid., p. 216). And it is with this pronatal narrative thread in mind that I now turn to look at the ways in which such reproductive treatments and technologies have been presented, not in first-person confessional online diaries and memoirs, but in the documentary tradition, routinely applauded for its objective account of actuality.

REFERENCES

Abbey, Antonia, Frank Andrews, and Jill Halman. 1992. Infertility and Subjective Well-Being: The Mediating Roles of Self-Esteem: Internal Control, and Interpersonal Conflict. *Journal of Marriage and the Family* 54 (2): 408–417.

Abetz, Jenna, and Julia Moore. 2018. Combative Mothering in Mommy Blogs. *Communication, Culture and Critique* 11 (2): 265–281.

Adams, Stephen. 2015. NHS Chief Warns Women Not to Wait until 30 to Have Baby as Country Faces a Fertility Timebomb. *The Mail on Sunday*. Accessed April 12, 2019. http://www.dailymail.co.uk/news/article-3104023/NHS-chief-warns-women-not-wait-30-baby-country-faces-fertility-timebomb.html.

Annabell of IVF One Day at a Time. 2013. PUPO! (Pregnant Until Proven Otherwise). *IVF One Day at a Time*: A Chronicle of the Ups and Downs of Our Infertility Journey. Accessed April 12, 2019. http://ivfonedayatatime. blogspot.co.uk/2013/02/pupo-pregnant-until-proven-otherwise.html.

April of The Maniscalco Journey. 2013. I Am So Done Being Preggo! Maniscalco Journey: Travel, Life and Family. Accessed April 12, 2019. http://aprilmaniscalco.blogspot.com/2013/06/i-am-so-done-being-preggo.html.

———. 2014a. CD22, 9dpo, 8dpiui, Praying for BFP! Maniscalco Journey: Travel, Life and Family. Accessed April 12, 2019. http://aprilmaniscalco. blogspot.com/2014/01/cd22-9dpo-8dpiui-praying-for-bfp.html.

80 R. FEASEY

———. 2014b. BFP!!!!!!!!!!!!!!!!. *Maniscalco Journey: Travel, Life and Family.* Accessed April 12, 2019. http://aprilmaniscalco.blogspot.com/2014/04/.

Baby Maybe. 2014a. Baby Maybe: 32w2d Pregnant. *Baby Maybe.* Accessed April 12, 2019. https://babymaybeinfertility.wordpress.com/2014/05/12/ivf-journey-32w2d-pregnant/.

———. 2014b. Baby Maybe: Birth Announcement! *Baby Maybe.* Accessed April 12, 2019. https://babymaybeinfertility.wordpress.com/2014/05/20/ivf-journey-birth-announcement/.

———. 2014c. Baby Maybe: Epilogue. *Baby Maybe.* Accessed April 12, 2019. https://babymaybeinfertility.wordpress.com/2014/06/21/epilogue/.

babycenter community. 2010. Jealous "Friends"? *babycenter.* Accessed April 12, 2019. https://community.babycenter.com/post/a24041973/jealous_friends.

Banet-Weiser, Sarah, and Laura Portwood-Stacer. 2006. I Just Want to be Me Again!': Beauty Pageants, Reality Television and Post-feminism. *Feminist Theory* 7 (2): 255–272.

British Fertility Society. 2018a. Modern Families Education Project. *British Fertility Society.* Accessed April 12, 2019. https://britishfertilitysociety.org.uk/fei/#link5.

———. 2018b. Fertility Fest—The Modern Families Project. *British Fertility Society.* Accessed April 12, 2019. https://www.fertilityfest.com/the-modern-families-project.

Bronstein, Jenny and Knoll, Maria. 2015. Blogging Motivations of Women Suffering from Infertility. *Information Research* 20 (2). Accessed April 12, 2019. http://www.informationr.net/ir/20-2/paper669.html#.WpAKlmZFnVo.

Bui. 2009. A Few Good Eggs: Two Chicks Dish on Overcoming the Insanity of Infertility: Customer Reviews. *Amazon.* Accessed April 12, 2019. https://www.amazon.com/product-reviews/0060834404/ref=cm_cr_dp_d_cmps_btm?ie=UTF8&reviewerType=all_reviews.

Bullock, Anne-Marie. 2015. Drawing the Line: When IVF Doesn't Work. *BBC Radio 4.* Accessed April 12, 2019. https://www.bbc.co.uk/programmes/b05w85g1.

Candace of Our Misconception. 2014a. The Gift of Life. *Our Misconception:* Chasing Dreams, Babies, and a Mini-human. Accessed April 12, 2019. https://ourmisconception.com/the-gift-of-life/.

———. 2014b. Infertility Timeline. *Our Misconception:* Chasing Dreams, Babies, and a Mini-human. Accessed April 12, 2019. https://ourmisconception.com/infertility-timeline/.

Couser, Thomas. 1997. *Recovering Bodies: Illness, Disability and Life Writing.* Madison: University of Wisconsin Press.

Creating a Family. 2018a. About Us. *Creating a Family.* Accessed April 12, 2019. https://creatingafamily.org/about-us/.

———. 2018b. Infertility Blogroll. *Creating a Family.* Accessed April 12, 2019. https://creatingafamily.org/infertility/blog/.

Edge, Brooke. 2015. Barren or Bountiful? Analysis of Cultural Values in Popular Media Representations of Infertility. PhD diss., University of Colorado. Accessed April 12, 2019. https://scholar.colorado.edu/jour_gradetds/25/.

Epstein, Yakov, Helane Rosenberg, Theresa Grant, and Nancy Hemenway. 2002. Use of the Internet as the Only Outlet for Talking About Infertility. *Fertility and Sterility* 78 (3): 507–514.

Evans, Oliver. 2011. IVF Treatments Not a Priority Amid NHS Budget Cuts. *Oxford Mail.* Accessed April 12, 2019. http://www.oxfordmail.co.uk/news/9144342.IVF_treatments__not_a_priority__amid_NHS_budget_cuts/.

Feasey, Rebecca. 2012. *From Happy Homemaker to Desperate Housewives: Motherhood and Popular Television.* London: Anthem.

Feedspot. 2019. Top 75 Infertility Blogs and Websites On IVF, IUI & ICSI in 2019. *Feedspot.* Accessed April 12, 2019. https://blog.feedspot.com/infertility_blogs/.

Friedman, May. 2013. *MommyBlogs and the Changing Face of Motherhood.* Toronto: University of Toronto Press.

Gallup, Caroline. 2007. *Making Babies the Hard Way: Living with Infertility and Treatment.* London and Philadelphia: Jessica Kingsley Publishers.

Gatrell, Caroline. 2008. *Embodying Women's Work.* Maidenhead: Open University Press.

Gibbs, Samuel. 2015. Google to Put Health Information Directly into Search Results. *The Guardian.* Accessed April 12, 2019. https://www.theguardian.com/technology/2015/feb/10/google-health-information-directly-into-search-results.

Hepburn, Jessica. 2017. Having IVF Eleven Times Made Me Feel Ashamed, Delusional and Lonely. *The Telegraph.* Accessed April 12, 2019. https://www.telegraph.co.uk/women/life/having-ivf-eleven-times-made-me-feel-ashamed-delusional-and-terr/.

Hepworth, Rosemary. 2015. Infertility Blogging, Body, and the Avatar. In *Feminist Erasures: Challenging Backlash Culture*, ed. Kumarini Silva and Kaitlynn Mendes, 198–218. London: Palgrave Macmillan.

HFEA. 2018. Our Health and Care Information has Achieved Certification by The Information Standard. *Human Fertilisation and Embryology Authority.* Accessed April 12, 2019. https://www.hfea.gov.uk/about-us/news-and-press-releases/2017-news-and-press-releases/our-health-and-care-information-has-achieved-certification-by-the-information-standard/.

Hinton, Lisa, Jennifer Kurinczuk, and Sue Ziebland. 2010. Infertility; Isolation and the Internet: A Qualitative Interview Study. *Patient Education and Counselling* 81: 436–441.

House, Laura. 2017. The Rarely Told Story of a Failed IVF Journey: Woman, 29, Shares Heartbreaking Picture of her Prepared Pregnancy Announcement After Trying for a Baby for EIGHT Years with No Luck. *Mail Online.* Accessed April 12, 2019. http://www.dailymail.co.uk/femail/article-4687506/The-rarely-told-story-failed-IVF-journey.html.

INCIID. 2005. Chat Transcript: Julie Vargo and Maureen Regan. *The International Council on Infertility Information Dissemination*. Accessed April 12, 2019. http://www.inciid.org/node/534.

Indichova, Julia. 2001. *Inconceivable: A Woman's Triumph Over Despair and Statistics*. New York: Broadway Books.

———. 2018a. Welcome from Founder Julia Indichova. *fertileheart*. Accessed April 12, 2019. https://www.fertileheart.com/about-fertile-heart/welcome-from-founder-julia-indichova/.

———. 2018b. Fertileheart. *fertileheart*. Accessed April 12, 2019. https://www.fertileheart.com.

Jamie. 2015. A Few Good Eggs: Two Chicks Dish on Overcoming the Insanity of Infertility: Customer Reviews. *Amazon*. Accessed April 12, 2019. https://www.amazon.com/product-reviews/0060834404/ref=cm_cr_dp_d_cmps_btm?ie=UTF8&reviewerType=all_reviews.

Jolene of Infertile Myrtle's Blog. 2009. Bittersweet Good-bye. *Infertile Myrtle's Blog*. Accessed April 12, 2019. http://infertilemyrtlesblog.blogspot.co.uk/2016/08/bittersweet-good-bye.html.

Kahlor, LeeAnn, and Michael Mackert. 2009. Perceptions of Infertility Information and Support Sources Among Female Patients Who Access the Internet. *Fertility and Sterility* 91 (1): 83–90.

Khamis, Susie, Lawrence Ang, and Raymond Welling. 2017. Self-branding, Micro-Celebrity and the Rise of Social Media Influencers. *Celebrity Studies* 8 (2): 191–208.

Khanapure, Amita, and Susan Bewley. 2007. Ageing Motherhood: Private Grief and Public Health Concern. *South African Journal of Obstetrics and Gynaecology* 13 (1): 20–22.

Kitten of Forever Infertile. 2012. Obligatory Introduction. My Journey Through Infertility, Pregnancy, and Parenting. Accessed April 12, 2019. https://yetanotherbitterinfertile.wordpress.com/2012/11/16/hello-world/.

———. 2015. About This Blog: Having a Baby Cures Childlessness; It Does Not Cure Infertility. Forever Infertile: My Journey Through Infertility, Pregnancy, and Parenting. Accessed April 12, 2019. https://yetanotherbitterinfertile.wordpress.com/about/.

———. 2017. The Post That Almost Wasn't. My Journey Through Infertility, Pregnancy, and Parenting. Accessed April 12, 2019. https://yetanotherbitterinfertile.wordpress.com/2017/03/06/the-post-that-almost-wasnt/.

Korolczuk, Elzbieta. 2014. Terms of Engagement: Re-Defining Identity and Infertility On-line. *Culture Unbound* 6: 431–449.

Kritzer, Naomi. 2011. One More Note About Internet Liars. *LiveJournal*. Accessed April 12, 2019. https://naomikritzer.livejournal.com/256974.html.

Le Vay, Lulu. 2019. *Surrogacy and the Reproduction of Normative Family on TV*. London: Palgrave Macmillan.

Licensed2Love. 2017. Long Time No Blog. *Licensed2Love: Life of a Wife, Mom & Nursing Student*. Accessed April 12, 2019. https://licensed2love.wordpress.com/2017/02/19/long-time-no-blog/.

Lisa of Amateur Nester. 2018. About. *Amateur Nester*. Accessed April 12, 2019. https://www.amateurnester.com/about.

Lopez, Lori Kidom. 2009. The Radical Act of Mommy Blogging: Redefining Motherhood Through the Blogosphere. *New Media & Society* 11 (5): 729–747.

Malik, Sumaira, and Neil Coulson. 2008. Computer-mediated Infertility Support Groups: An Exploratory Study of Online Experiences. *Patient Education and Counselling* 73: 103–115.

Mamo, Laura. 2013. Queering the Fertility Clinic. *Journal of Medical Humanities* 34 (2): 227–239.

Manterfield, Lisa. 2012. Don't Ignore ... the Life Without Baby Option. *Life Without Baby*. Accessed April 12, 2019. http://lifewithoutbaby.com/2012/04/23/dont-ignore-the-life-without-baby-option/.

Manterfield, Lisa. 2018. About. *Life Without Baby*. Accessed April 12, 2019. http://lifewithoutbaby.com/about/.

Marsh, Margaret, and Wanda Ronner. 1999. *The Empty Cradle: Infertility in America from Colonial Times to the Present*. London: Johns Hopkins University Press.

Mary of Lemonwater. 2015. When Infertility Affects Your Friendships. *Lemonwater*. Accessed April 12, 2019. https://lemonwaterblog.wordpress.com/2015/05/28/when-infertility-affects-your-friendships/.

Matthews-King, Alex. 2017. IVF Patients Facing Postcode Lottery After NHS Budgets Slashed. *The Independent*. http://www.independent.co.uk/news/health/ivf-nhs-treatment-fertility-lists-wait-patients-lottery-budget-cuts-a8028116.html.

Maya of Don't Count Your Eggs. 2014. About Me. *Don't Count Your Eggs*. Accessed April 12, 2019. http://dontcountyoureggs.typepad.com//about.html.

McCarthy, Patrice. 2008. Women's Lived Experience of Infertility After Unsuccessful Medical Intervention. *Journal of Midwifery Womens Health* 53 (4): 319–324.

Megan of Infertile Myrtle. 2015. Top 10 Things Not To Say To Your Infertile Friend Infertile Myrtle: Life as an Infertile Couple. Accessed April 12, 2019. http://www.infertilemyrtles.com/2015/04/top-10-things-not-to-say-to-your-infertile-friend/.

MFM. 2018. Innovation in Sex Education. *My Fertility Matters Project*. Accessed April 12, 2019. http://www.mfmprojectuk.org.

Miller, Cheryl. 2008. Blogging Infertility. *The New Atlantis: A Journal of Technology & Society Winter* 19: 79–90.

Mulkay, Michael. 2010. *The Embryo Research Debate: Science and the Politics of Reproduction*. Cambridge: Cambridge University Press.

Murdoch, Cassie. 2012. Should You Tell Your Facebook Friends You've Had a Miscarriage? *Jezebel*. Accessed April 12, 2019. https://jezebel.com/5897347/should-you-tell-your-facebook-friends-youve-had-a-miscarriage.

Naomi of Embrace Fertility. 2014. The 46th Month is the Charm. *Embrace Fertility*. Accessed April 12, 2019. http://embracefertility.co.uk/46th-month-charm/.

Natja. 2011. A Few Good Eggs: Two Chicks Dish on Overcoming the Insanity of Infertility: Customer Reviews. *Amazon*. Accessed April 12, 2019. https://www.amazon.co.uk/Few-Good-Eggs-Overcoming-Infertility/dp/0060834404/ref=sr_1_1?s=books&ie=UTF8&qid=1519132433&sr=1-1&keywords=A+Few+Good+Eggs%3A+Two+Chicks+Dish+on+Overcoming+the+Insanity+of+Infertility&dpID=51JI0J4rDdL&preST=_SY291_BO1,204,203,200_QL40_&dpSrc=srch.

NHS. 2018. Overview: Infertility. *NHS*. Accessed April 12, 2019. https://www.nhs.uk/conditions/infertility/.

Nikol aka Not Just a Beauty Blogger. 2014. About Me. *Not Just a Beauty Blogger: My Fashionable Journey Through IVF*. Accessed April 12, 2019. http://www.notjustabeautyblogger.com/about-me/.

———. 2017. The Best Prescription Your Doctor Has Ever Written: Advice from Two Girls in the Know. *Not Just a Beauty Blogger: My Fashionable Journey Through IVF*. Accessed April 12, 2019. http://www.notjustabeautyblogger.com/tag/unexplained-infertility/.

Osborne-Thompson, Heather. 2014. Seriality and Assisted Reproductive Technologies in Celebrity Reality Television. *Feminist Media Studies* 14 (5): 877–880.

Pedersen, Sarah. 2010. *Why Blog? Motivations for Blogging*. Cambridge: Chandos Publishing.

Ratliff, Clancy. 2009. Policing Miscarriage: Infertility Blogging, Rhetorical Enclaves, and the Case of House Bill 1677. *Women's Studies Quarterly* 37 (1–2): 125–145.

Reimer, Vanessa, and Sarah Sahagian. 2016. *The Mother Blame Game*. Toronto: Demeter Press.

Resolve. 2018a. Fast Facts: Who Has Infertility. *Resolve*: The National Infertility Association. Accessed April 12, 2019. https://resolve.org/infertility-101/what-is-infertility/fast-facts/.

———. 2018b. Fast Facts About Resolve: The National Infertility Association. *Resolve*. Accessed April 12, 2019. https://resolve.org/about-us/fast-facts-resolve-national-infertility-association/.

Riley, Sarah; Adrienne Evans, and Emma Anderson. 2019. The Gendered Nature of Self-Help. *Feminism and Psychology*. Accessed April 12, 2019. https://journals.sagepub.com/doi/full/10.1177/0959353519826162.

Rojek, Chris. 2001. *Celebrity*. London: Reaktion Books.

Ross, Ryan. 2016. Third of GPs Back End to NHS IVF Funding. *BioNews*. Accessed April 12, 2019. http://www.bionews.org.uk/page_616283.asp.

Sable, David. 2014. IVF and Infertility By The Numbers. *Forbes*. Accessed April 12, 2019. https://www.forbes.com/sites/davidsable/2014/04/24/ivf-and-infertility-by-the-numbers/#6ca536d85ce0.

Sangster, Sarah, and Karen Lawson. 2015. Is Any Press Good Press? The Impact of Media Portrayals of Infertility on Young Adults' Perceptions of Infertility. *Journal of Obstetrics and Gynaecology, Canada* 37 (12): 1072–1078.

Scully, Anne-Marie. 2014. *Motherhoodwinked: An Infertility Memoir*. CreateSpace Independent Publishing Platform.

Selby, Julie. 2015. *Infertility Insanity: When Sheer Hope (and Google) are the Only Options Left*. Canada: Influence Publishing.

Shalev, Shirley, and Dafna Lemish. 2013. Infertile Motherhood. *Feminist Media Studies* 13 (2): 321–336.

Simone of Bubbles and Bumps. 2015. Take 4 IVF: Reasons to Try Again. *Bubbles and Bumps*. Accessed April 12, 2019. http://www.bubblesandbumps.com/take-4-ivf-7-reasons/.

Sohr-Preston, Sarah, Alyssa Lacour, Tyler Brent, Timothy Dugas, and Lauren Jordan. 2016. Blogging about Family Building (Infertility, Pregnancy Loss, Adoption, Pregnancy, Trying to Conceive): Content and Blogging Motivations. *Studies in Media and Communication* 4 (1): 8–20.

Sterling, Evelina. 2013. From No Hope to Fertile Dreams: Procreative Technologies, Popular Media, and the Culture of Infertility. PhD diss., Georgia State University. Accessed April 12, 2019. https://scholarworks.gsu.edu/cgi/viewcontent.cgi?article=1069&context=sociology_diss.

Striff, Erin. 2005. Infertile Me: The Public Performance of Fertility Treatments in Internet Weblogs. *Women & Performance: A Journal of Feminist Theory* 15 (2): 189–205.

The Life on an Infertile Myrtle. 2015. We're Not Going to Take it! *The Life on an Infertile Myrtle*. Accessed April 12, 2019. https://infertilemyrtlevt.weebly.com.

Throsby, Karen. 2004. *When IVF Fails: Feminism, Infertility and the Negotiation of Normality*. Basingstoke: Palgrave Macmillan.

Tuhus-Dubrow, Rebecca. 2013. I Change, You Change. *The New York Times*. Accessed April 12, 2019. http://www.nytimes.com/2013/01/20/books/review/self-help-memoirs-take-on-everyday-challenges.html.

United Nations, Department of Economic and Social Affairs, Population Division. 2015. World Fertility Patterns 2015—Data Booklet. ST/ESA/SER.A/370. Accessed April 12, 2019. http://www.un.org/en/development/desa/population/publications/pdf/fertility/world-fertility-patterns-2015.pdf.

Vargo, Julie, and Maureen Regan. 2006. *A Few Good Eggs: Two Chicks Dish on Overcoming the Insanity of Infertility*. New York: HarperCollins.

Wells, Chandra. 2011. The Vagina Posse: Confessional Community in Online Infertility Journals. In *Compelling Confessions: The Politics of Personal Disclosure*, ed. Suzanne Diamond, 202–221. Madison: Farleigh Dickinson University Press.

WHO. 2018. Gender and Genetics. *World Health Organisation*. Accessed April 12, 2019. http://www.who.int/genomics/gender/en/index6.html.

Winston, Robert. 2018. Professor Robert Winston: Couple Being Misled Over Chances of IVF Success. *The Yorkshire Post*. Accessed April 12, 2019. https://www.yorkshirepost.co.uk/news/professor-robert-winston-couple-being-misled-over-chances-of-ivf-success-1-9246529.

Wohlmann, Anita. 2014. Illness Narrative and Self-Help Culture—Self-Help Writing on Age-Related Infertility. *European Journal of Life Writing* 3: 19–41. Accessed April 12, 2019. http://ejlw.eu/article/view/90/246.

CHAPTER 3

Assisted Reproduction: Family, Fortunes and Fertility Clinics

INTRODUCTION

Chapter 3 will look at both the media depictions and medical reality of assisted reproductive technologies in factual television, paying particular attention to *Alex Jones: Fertility & Me* (BBC2 2016). It will examine the ways in which such programming can be seen to inform the viewing public about the lived experience of infertility, the much-touted crisis of age-related infertility and the ways in which modern science, medicine and technology can help women affected by an infertility diagnosis to achieve motherhood. However, in their status as non-fiction productions, it is crucially important that such titles not only introduce the various stages of treatment, but that they also present realistic success rates for those participants within and beyond the programme.

ASSISTED REPRODUCTION: LICENSING AND REGULATION

Both the UK and the US offer hope and medical assistance to those seeking alternative forms of reproduction, but there are stark differences between the two countries, not in terms of success rates, costs of private treatment or available advice, but in terms of licensing and regulation.

After the birth of Louise Brown, the UK government formed a committee chaired by Mary Warnock to look into the issues and implications of new reproductive treatments and technologies. Doctors, scientists, health, patient, parental and religious organisations all gave evidence to

© The Author(s) 2019

R. Feasey, *Infertility and Non-Traditional Family Building*,

https://doi.org/10.1007/978-3-030-17787-4_3

87

the committee, culminating in the Warnock report, which in turn informed the Human Fertilisation and Embryology Act (HFEA 1990). The 1990 Act created the Human Fertilisation and Embryology Authority, with the requirement that all clinics need a licence from the HFEA to 'provide fertility treatments, store eggs, sperm and embryos … and carry out embryo testing' (HFEA 2018a). The HFEA maintains a database of all fertility treatments involving a donor since 1991, and, as such, it is in a position to give donor-conceived people and their parents details about their genetic origins and possible siblings (HFEA 2018b). In short, the HFEA looks to reassure those individuals interested in preserving their fertility, those researching a genetic disease in their family, single women, trans- and non-binary individuals, heterosexual and same-sex couples, donors and parents of a donor-conceived person, that they will receive a high quality of care in the UK (HFEA 2017/2020).

In the UK, the NHS offers treatments for fertility problems, be it medicines, surgical procedures or assisted conception. In the case of IVF treatment, NICE updated its fertility guidelines in 2013, making recommendations about who should have access to NHS-funded IVF treatment in England and Wales (NHS 2018a). It suggested that women under the age of 40 'should be offered three cycles of IVF treatment on the NHS if they've been trying to get pregnant through regular unprotected sex for two years, or they've not been able to get pregnant after 12 cycles of artificial insemination' (Ibid.). Clarification is offered for women who turn 40 during treatment, making it clear that 'the current cycle will be completed, but further cycles should not be offered' (Ibid.).

For older women, aged between 40 and 42, just one cycle of IVF will be made available on the NHS if women have 'been trying to get pregnant through regular unprotected sex for two years, or haven't been able to get pregnant after 12 cycles of artificial insemination' but only if these women have 'never had IVF treatment before … show no evidence of low ovarian reserve (where eggs in your ovaries are low in number or quality)' and where they have been informed of the additional implications of IVF and pregnancy for their age group (NHS 2018a). For women above or below the age of 40, we are told that 'if tests show that IVF is the only treatment likely to help you get pregnant, you should be referred for IVF straight away' (Ibid.).

The NHS tells patients that they are working to provide the same levels of service across England and Wales, even though, ultimately, it is the Clinical Commissioning Groups who 'make the final decision about who can have NHS-funded IVF in their local area, leading to some variation across the country' (NHS 2018a). The Clinical Commissioning Groups 'may have additional criteria you need to meet before you can have IVF on the NHS including "not having any children already, from both your current and any previous relationships, being a healthy weight, not smoking and falling into a certain age range"' (Ibid.). After all, some groups only fund treatment for women under 35. Moreover, in 'some cases, only one cycle of IVF may be routinely offered, instead of the three recommended by NICE' (Ibid.).

Such treatment might sound generous in relation to global health-care provision, but there is a disconnect between diagnosing infertility and offering assisted reproductive treatments. After all, '[d]epending on the area you live in, couples eligible for NHS funding can wait between a few months and up to three years to start fertility treatment' with 'NHS waiting times being the main reason why couples opt for private IVF treatment' (Create Fertility 2019). The NHS is aware that women seeking treatment who are either not eligible or ill inclined to wait until treatment becomes available might seek treatment at a private clinic. The NHS offers advice and assistance for those choosing this option, reminding future patients of the differing regulatory standards within and beyond the UK. After all, due to the age restrictions placed on some NHS treatments, the shortage of egg donors and the costs of embarking on licensed private treatment in the UK, many women seek treatment abroad, and thus outside of HFEA regulations (Magee 2015). The NHS is looking to reduce what has come to be termed 'fertility tourism' (Donnelly, L 2017) by telling us that although women routinely consider travelling abroad for treatment, there are a number of issues that they need to think about, including their safety and the standard of care that they will receive (NHS 2018a). The online information also offers links to the HFEA concerning the 'issues and risks associated with fertility treatment abroad' (Ibid.), including, but not limited to, multiple pregnancy rates and lack of counselling support (HFEA 2018c).

The allure of fertility tourism is also its limitation, namely, the ostensibly higher success rates that are boasted by overseas clinics. Prospective patients are urged to be 'cautious' about successful treatment rates because 'they may only be presenting data for women under 35 or their data may relate to pregnancies rather than births' (Ibid.). In short, rates can be 'affected by the types of patients a clinic treats. If a clinic treats a large number of younger women with mild fertility problems, their success rates will inevitably be higher than clinics treating older women or those with more complex diagnoses' (Ibid.). The HFEA tells prospective clients to ask searching questions regarding success rates because

> [t]here are ways clinics can present their statistics that will encourage people to go abroad, but a nine in 10 cumulative pregnancy success rate after four IVF attempts can't be compared with a three in 10 live birth success rate after one cycle—that's comparing apples and oranges. (Magee 2015)

In her work on the 'overly optimistic' presentation of the IVF statistics that circulate in contemporary society, Karin Hammarberg tells us that 'we need to ask if the rate is per started treatment cycle, per egg collection or per woman who reaches the stage of embryo transfer' (Hammarberg 2014). Audiences need to understand the common denominator being used because the 'pregnancy rate is not the same as live birth rate because some pregnancies are lost' (Ibid.). That said, according to the HFEA, the UK provides 'the same success rates for all licensed UK fertility clinics which makes it easy to compare clinics' (HFEA 2018c) in a way that is sometimes difficult to translate to those clinics working outside of the regulatory powers of the HFEA.

In contrast to the UK, the US has what is understood as a 'laissez-faire' assisted fertility regime. Because both research and clinical practice are privatised, the industry is less regulated than that of 'most other capitalist democracies' (Martin 2015, p. 65). The US fertility industry is self-regulated, meaning that many clinics offering assisted reproductive technologies 'are members of professional organizations' such as the Society for Assisted Reproductive Technology (SART) or the American Society for Reproductive Medicine (ASRM) and thus follow the 'clinical and ethical guidelines produced by these organizations' (Riggan 2010). However, it is made clear that while some clinics do follow such guidelines, 'the majority do not' (Ibid.). Indeed, a 'Centers for Disease Control and Prevention study found that only 20% of ART programs follow such guidelines' with 'no legal detriment to clinicians engaging in clinical or ethically dubious practice' (Ibid.). Kirsten Riggan makes the point that any 'technological means, regardless of the medical and ethical consequences, can be utilized in the pursuit of parenthood if the price is right' (Ibid.). She goes on to link the lack of regulation to the increasingly high number of multiple pregnancies and births that now exist in the US, drawing attention to problems associated with this phenomenon. After all, while only 1 per cent of all 'normal' pregnancies in the US are multiple gestations, 31 per cent of pregnancies conceived using IVF are twin gestations and 3 per cent are triplets or higher-order gestations (Ibid.).

Although a woman diagnosed with infertility might be genuinely happy and indeed grateful to have twins or triplets during a single round of treatment, it is important to note that there are increased health-care costs and, more importantly, serious risks to the health of both the mother and child when carrying multiples. Women pregnant with multiples are 'at a higher risk of pregnancy complications' and an increased chance of pregnancy loss:

> While multiple gestations account for only 3% of all live births in the U.S., they are responsible for 23% of early preterm births ... and 26% of very low birth weight infants. ... Multiple pregnancies also have a higher mortality rate ... compared to singletons. ... The mortality rate for twins is seven times greater than singletons, whereas [for] triplet and higher order multiples [it] is twenty times greater. Additionally, children from multiple pregnancies are at a higher risk of long-term medical and developmental problems including cerebral palsy and other neurological complications. (Ibid.)

Back in the UK, research undertaken by the Fetal Medicine Unit at University College London Hospital has made 'a link between higher order multiple pregnancies ... which are linked to dangerous and often life-threatening conditions for mother and baby ... and the numbers of women travelling to ... the US for fertility treatment' (Pritchard 2008). The study highlighted the 'potential dangers to women seeking IVF treatment abroad where there is less regulation of the numbers of embryos transferred into the womb' and costs 'faced by the UK's NHS as it copes with multiple births resulting from IVF patients treated abroad' (Ibid.). Although UK regulatory bodies are able to be 'sidestepped by couples desperate for a baby, such actions are putting a "huge cost burden" of increased ante- and neonatal care associated with multiple births' on the NHS (Ibid.).

Many European countries have recognised these risks and have moved to legally restrict the number of embryos transferred per reproductive cycle. Indeed, existing legislation within the European Union 'sets standards for quality and safety' in the fertility industry across partner countries, and although the standards are not currently being implemented across all European countries, standardised regulation remains the ambition (Fertility Treatment Abroad 2018). The US fertility industry by contrast looks to remain self-regulated, and as such it stands as an outlier compared to the rest of the developed world (Martin 2015, pp. 65–93). We are told that 'both the federal government and the states have given the multi-billion-dollar industry a wide berth' (Ollove 2015a), leaving some to refer to the US as 'the Wild West of the fertility industry' in need of additional regulation at state or federal level (Darnovsky cited in Ollove 2015b). By way of example we are told that

> [s]tates don't regulate how many children may be conceived from one donor, what types of medical information or updates must be supplied by donors, which genetic tests may be performed on embryos [or] how many fertilized eggs may be placed in a woman or how old a donor can be. (Ollove 2015a)

That said, there is disagreement amongst medical staff and lobbyists concerning the matter of self-regulation, because whilst the Law Professors and the Center for Genetics and Society look to question the effectiveness of self-regulation, Sean Tipton, the chief lobbyist for the American Society for Reproductive Medicine, is insistent that '[r]eproductive medicine is one of the most heavily regulated fields of medicine in the U.S.' (Ibid.). As evidence, he informs us that 'the federal government regulates all drugs and medical devices, as well as the reproductive tissue used' in assisted reproductive technologies (Ibid.). And yet, although the ASRM does indeed 'issue lengthy guidelines to its membership, which consists of fertility clinics and sperm banks' critics are quick to note that 'it does not sanction those who are in violation of guidelines' (Ibid.). The charge here is that the ASRM exists, in the words of the John Hopkins Berman Institute of Bioethics, to 'advance the business interests of its members, unfettered by government regulation. It's a field characterized by strong anti-regulatory sentiment because it evolved as a business, not a research enterprise' (Ibid.).

Since 1978, assisted reproduction in general and artificial reproductive technologies in particular have emerged and flourished into a thriving medical sector. By the 1990s it was understood as a 'booming industry' (Sterling 2013, p. 123) and since the late 2000s it has been referred to as 'big business' in the UK, US and globally (Ibid., p. 30). The US fertility business is 'comprised of free-standing and medical center fertility clinics: mostly private sperm and egg banks, surrogate broker services, medical specialties, "donors" selling their eggs and sperm, and a growing population of consumers seeking services' (Mamo 2013, p. 229). The fact that American reproductive medicine often partners with 'large pharmaceutical and medical device companies' in what is referred to as the 'infertility–industrial complex' goes further to remind us of the business model behind much treatment (Sterling 2013, p. 31). However, the UK is not devoid of the charges and challenges of big business. At the time of writing, 77 clinics are licensed by the HFEA to perform IVF (HFEA 2018d) and although the health service is understood as a key provider of assisted reproductive technologies, 60 per cent of all treatment cycles are self-funded by patients, either within NHS clinics or in the private sector (HFEA 2019a, p. 10; Create Fertility 2019) in 'a corporate, mostly for-profit health care system' (Mamo 2013, p. 234). This, as Karen Throsby noted more than a decade earlier, 'constitutes big business' (Throsby 2004, p. 2).

There is of course the argument to be made that it is not solely big business. The fact that IVF and alternative treatments have been made available not just to women affected by an infertility diagnosis, but also to same-sex couples, single 'parents in waiting' and postmenopausal women suggests that IVF is both big business and socially egalitarian. Indeed, the subfield of oncofertility now exists to bridge oncology and reproductive research in order to 'explore and expand options for the reproductive future of cancer survivors' (Ross 2018, p. 235). That said, the fact that fertility clinics 'hired PR agents' and the industry as a whole sought to recruit new patients without addressing issues such as 'same-sex marriage, adoption reform, or cancer prevention' goes some way to suggest that their remit remains 'purely ... economic' (Sterling 2013, p. 75).

ETHICAL AND ECONOMIC ISSUES: EGG AND SPERM DONATION

Although assisted reproduction can be understood as an economic venture in both the UK and the US, as previously stated, there remain stark differences between the two nations, especially in relation to the terms and conditions of egg donation. Although egg donation is legal in both countries, in the former a donor is paid basic expenses while in the latter, significantly higher reimbursements are offered. In the UK, a woman donating her eggs is understood to be doing it for altruistic reasons. The

HFEA tells us that '[e]gg donors can receive compensation of up to £750 per donation "cycle" to cover their costs' but makes it clear that it is 'illegal to pay for egg donation in the UK' (HFEA 2018e). A 'donation cycle is one complete round of treatment, at the end of which the eggs are collected and donated' and although there is the option to claim further expenses to cover the costs of travel, accommodation or childcare, this is understood as compensation rather than payment for services (Ibid.). In order to deter anyone from selling their eggs illegally, we are informed that any 'IVF clinic that suspects a financial incentive has been offered is duty-bound to refuse treatment' (Connell 2009). By contrast, however, in America we find that egg donation is paid at $8000 on average in order to reimburse for 'time, commitment and services' with that figure rising to '$14,000 depending on your qualifications and the number of eggs you produce' (Center for Human Reproduction 2018). We are told that in 'the U.S. where the egg and sperm donation market is a free-for-all, highly desirable donors ... known as "super donors" ... can command fees of up to £25,000' (Connell 2009). Claudia Connell tells us that increasingly lucrative levels of reimbursement are offered to donors, with a 'blonde-haired, blue-eyed egg donor who had graduated from an Ivy League college' being able to 'pretty much name her price' (Ibid.). There is a growing demand for egg donors, and this has coincided with niche targeting, namely to young female students who experience growing student debts while demonstrating a level of intellectual prowess that would be of interest to those looking to create a family (Blyth and Benward 2004, p. 252).

For all of the discussion about egg donation, it is important to remember the role of sperm donors in family building. And for all of the humorous exchanges and awkward fumblings that are presented in situation comedy fare on the theme in question, it is worth considering the regulations and recommendations that are associated with such donations.

The rules on anonymity for donors now allows any child born after 2005 the right to trace their biological father when they turn 18 (the first cases will be seen in 2023), which is putting many previous and potential donors off depositing at a sperm bank. At the same time as the number of donors is decreasing, demand is increasing. There are growing numbers of same-sex couples and older women wanting children, and, as such, The UK National Sperm Bank has been struggling to keep up with the demand. Recent figures from the HFEA 'show an increase of more than 20% in the number of same-sex couples receiving donor insemination. Those figures predate the change in same-sex marriage legislation, which ... had fuelled even more demand ... [i]n some clinics ... one-third of the patients are now same-sex couples' (Elgot 2015; NHS 2018b). And in the same way that fertility tourism encourages those affected by an infertility diagnosis to seek eggs ... abroad (Tuft 2015), so too, 'imported sperm has steadily increased year-on-year to meet the rise in demand and formed almost a third of new registrations, mostly from the USA, followed by Denmark' (Ibid.). The National sperm bank was financed in order to help with the financial and emotional cost of assisted reproductive treatments; however, after it admitted to having 'only nine registered donors' (Ibid.), the bank struggled to secure future funding and closed (Lea 2016). The closure of the bank, a shortage of donor sperm and the cost of those samples that are regulated and available lead growing numbers of women to go abroad or seek out unlicensed donors over the Internet. The screening process for licensed donors is clear and rigorous, with only a small number of those men who present themselves as donors being used in fertility treatments due to age, infectious diseases, genetic abnormalities, sperm quantity, quality and movement (Morton and Bell 2016). Indeed, 'California Cryobank Inc emphasizes in its promotional material that only 5 per cent of the donors applying to its programme are accepted' (Blyth and Benward 2004, p. 259), with that number rising to just 10 per cent in the UK (Elgot 2015). And although using an unlicensed donor is not illegal, 'using unregulated donors puts women at risk of sexual diseases, hereditary disorders and men interested in "no strings" unprotected sex' (Morton and Bell 2016). And while the HFEA limits the number of families created by a single donor father to ten children (based on research relating to the number of half-siblings someone would be comfortable with), unlicensed donors can and do have hundreds of children, creating a multitude of half-siblings (Ibid.). The existence of these as-yet anonymous half-siblings is the reason behind The Donor Sibling Registry, a worldwide organisation including the US and UK that provides support and connection to families which have been developed via donor conception, advocating for the rights of the donor-conceived, and educating the general public about the issues, challenges and rights of the donor-conceived community. However, this registry is only available to those who use regulated rather than unlicensed clinics and donors (Blyth and Benward 2004, p. 258; Kramer and Kramer 2018).

Under the 1990 Act 'a sperm donor will have no parental obligations or rights in respect of any child, so long as the ... consent requirements have been met' (Blyth 2004, p. 229). Consequently, 'a sperm donor could be treated as the child's legal father if his sperm is used other than in accordance with the Act's consent provisions (i.e. when a woman conceives following self- or 'DIY' insemination) *and* the woman receiving his sperm is either unmarried or her husband or partner (if she has one) either did not consent to her insemination or the couple were judicially separated when the woman was inseminated' (Blyth 2004, p. 229, emphasis in original). Children conceived as a result of sperm donation since 2005 will have the right to know the identity of their father; however 'a donor is not the legal parent and is not named on the birth certificate' (Morton and Bell 2016; NHS 2018c). However, 'with an unlicensed donor a woman can ask for child support at any time—and the man could claim paternity' (Ibid.). Laura Witjens, chief executive of the National Gamete Donation Trust, says that 'she appreciates that the cost of [licensed] treatment can be expensive, but goes on to remind us about the hierarchy of appropriate parenting when she concludes that "if you can't afford £1,500 to secure safety for yourself and your child, you should wonder if you're fit for parenthood. It's an expensive job"' (Ibid.).

The differing payment, compensation and/or reimbursement of egg donors are symptomatic of a distinction between UK and US health-care systems. Questions are currently being asked in the UK and the rest of Europe as to whether fertility 'treatments should be considered a basic health "right"' and therefore, 'subsidized by governments or health insurers' (Van Balen and Inhorn 2002, p. 11). We are asked to consider if involuntary childlessness is a medical problem that demands treatment be 'paid or reimbursed by the national health care system' (Ibid., p. 11), or a social problem for which 'society bears no responsibility' (Ibid., p. 12). We are told that

> growing numbers of European politicians, ethicists, and … social scientists have argued [that] the absence of children is a personal issue. … From this perspective, children may just be one of the things in life that an individual may want but cannot necessarily have—like a steady permanent partner, a house, a car, or a full-time job. In other words, childlessness is a matter of fate that one must accept, and it is not something that a society's health care system can be expected to remedy. (Ibid., p. 12)

Meeting a new partner can change your life; so too can the freedom that comes with passing your driving test and owning a car. Owning a property offers you safety and financial certainly against rising property prices. On paper, these may well be things that individuals want but cannot necessarily have, but it feels inconsiderate and insensitive to compare a desire for a child with that of an automobile. Not having a car, or not having the car you desire, means that you rely on alternative modes of transport—the travelling itself is not restricted. Infertility without access to assisted or artificial reproductive services leaves you with very few family-building options in general, and none that allow for the continuation of genetic lineage. By contrast, in the US, there is no such attempted distinction between infertility as a personal desire or a medical condition because, in the privatised free-market system of medical care 'coverage of infertility treatments is neither a government priority nor a priority of most health insurers' (Ibid., p. 11).

DESERVING AND RECEIVING TREATMENT

If one considers that the NHS offers limited treatment options, and that assisted reproductive therapies are out of the financial reach of much of the population, it leads us to ask questions concerning those who deserve, need and receive treatment. After all, even though 'high-tech reproductive medicine is being rapidly exported around the globe, it is often available only to elite segments of the population in developing countries' and remains 'out of reach for disadvantaged ... populations' (Van Balen and Inhorn 2002, p. 11). Evelina Sterling echoes this point when she tells us that 'the infertility-industrial-complex is set up to best meet the needs of a very specific population, white, middle-class married couples creating "reproductive stratification"' (Sterling 2013, p. 106).

As Arthur Greil and Julia McQuillan state in their work on subfecund women, there exists a paradox because '[o]n the one hand, we have a group of women who seem prepared to do "whatever it takes" to become pregnant. On the other hand, there is a large group of women who do not seek treatment at all' (Greil and McQuillan 2004, p. 306). However, this is less a question of choice, and more a consideration of equity of treatment across diverse and minority populations. As Throsby bluntly states, 'IVF is expensive and the poorer sections of society are therefore automatically excluded' (Throsby 2004, p. 6). As evidence we are told that two-thirds of couples in the US who are affected by an infertility diagnosis 'do not seek treatment, and although black women are more likely than white women to have trouble conceiving, this is not reflected among those seeking treatment as a result of higher rates of poverty among those groups' (Ibid., p. 6). We are reminded that 'racist assumptions of hyper-fertility in black women render ... their infertility easily disregardable' (Throsby 2004, p. 3; Sterling 2013, p. 18). A study from the National Survey of Sexual Attitudes and Lifestyles discovered that nearly half of those 'diagnosed with infertility in Britain do not seek out medical assistance' (Surugue 2016). In the UK, 'the decision whether or not to look for medical support appeared to be closely associated with differences in socioeconomic status' (Surugue 2016).

One patient-cum-repro-lit author speaks for many when she states that it 'seems very unfair when you think about it ... that the chance of your having a baby comes down to money in many cases. It starts to become an "elitist" option' (Selby 2015, p. 16). Private fertility clinics have shown little interest in offering affordable or subsidised IVF, making the point that 'society should pay for the diagnosis of the problem' but beyond that, financial responsibility remains on those seeking treatment (Walters cited in Sterling 2013, p. 133). There is a clear disconnect between the promise of assisted reproduction to help a diverse population of potential parents—be they postmenopausal, single or LGBT+ from a myriad of age, class, race and ethnic groups—and the reality of those who seek such assistance. Moreover, there is a clear hierarchy in operation regarding appropriate and inappropriate, deserving and problematised patients. In the same way that the ideology of intensive mothering exists to construct and circulate a hierarchy of idealised and demonised motherhood (Feasey 2012, 2016), so too a hierarchy appears to be operating for those who are deemed worthy of fertility treatment, 'with age, marital status and sexual orientation providing a major basis for the determination of "suitability"' (Douglas cited in Blyth 2004, p. 228).

Medical, ethical and regulatory debate is currently taking place on both sides of the Atlantic to consider the role of assisted reproduction in the birth of high-order multiples, and public readings of such family building is telling in relation to a debate over appropriate and inappropriate motherhood. We find that the 'birth of high-order multiples to married, middle-class couples has typically resulted in warm public reception [leading to] large-scale donations ... and lucrative media opportunities' (Fixmer-Oraiz 2014, p. 243). Alternatively, the reception of Nadya Suleman's octuplets led to charges of pathology, because a 'thirty-three-year old woman of European and Middle-Eastern descent receiving food stamps and disability payments with six young children already at home' (Ibid., p. 231) looked to expand her family.

The traditional stereotype of the white, late 30-something, middle-class parent-in-waiting seems to warrant medical and media attention as well as favourable social reception. Not only are these women depicted as the core consumers of reproductive technologies, but images of 'white babies, usually with blond hair and blue eyes' dominate both media texts and IVF marketing materials (Roberts cited in Le Vay 2019, p. 92). It has been argued that much of the 'concern about infertility focuses almost exclusively on white couples' due to the fact that 'birth rates have fallen below replacement' levels (Sterling 2013, p. 82). Le Vay analyses the short-lived American sitcom *The New Normal* (2012) to draw attention to the paucity of ways in which poor, single, black, minority and lesbian women who are diagnosed with infertility are presented in the media (Le Vay 2019, pp. 103–146).

While those who cannot afford to pay are ignored, overlooked or sidelined for treatment, there is also a sense that, of those who can afford treatment, some are more warmly welcomed than others. A common theme in debates over assisted reproduction in general and artificial reproductive technologies in particular concerns the ways in which such treatments work with, alongside or in opposition to nature. This debate is of interest to postmenopausal women looking to conceive. After all, even though 'the provision of egg donation to postmenopausal women' is offered under the guidance of both the ASRM and HFEA, contemporary commentators suggest that '[i]nfertility should remain the natural characteristic of menopause' and as such 'menopausal pregnancy should be discouraged' irrespective of the age, health or circumstances of the women seeking treatment (ASRM cited in Blyth and Benward 2004, p. 260). Tabloid stories of postmenopausal women conceiving through IVF are said to be 'engaging in unnatural consumption' (Throsby 2004, p. 4) and they are 'a particularly easy target … since they are by definition reproducing outside their … reproductive life span' (Ibid., p. 55). Gayle Letherby has gone as far as to suggest that postmenopausal pregnancy is read as a 'threat to the "ideal" family type and to the dominant image of "ideal" motherhood' (Letherby 1999, p. 368). However, it is not only postmenopausal women who are charged with such 'unnatural' family building; lesbians, gender-queer, same-sex couples and single women are also accused of 'fracturing' conventional family structures (Throsby 2004, p. 4). After all, while IVF has the opportunity to 'shore up traditional "family values", associated technologies are also capable of generating novel family structures' (Ibid., p. 4) and 'social forms that lie beyond the limits of heteronormativity' (Mamo 2013, p. 235).

The Hierarchy of Conception: Egg Freezing, Gestational Carriers and the Biological Child

Society in general and fertility treatment brochures in particular have 'deemed the married heterosexual woman as being the most appropriate to parent' (DiLapi cited in Letherby 1999, p. 368), meaning that, as previously noted, society fails to recognise those 'for whom conception through heterosexual intercourse is not an option' (Throsby 2004, p. 7), irrespective of the non-traditional family-building avenues made possible through assisted reproductive techniques and technologies. What seems to be under discussion here then is less a consideration of conception, pregnancy or mothering whereby middle-class heterosexual married couples employ IUI or IVF techniques to help create 'the longed for biological child' (Davenport 2017), but rather a debate concerning egg and sperm donation as they can be seen to simultaneously engage or circumvent 'natural' reproduction beyond heterosexual family units. Erin Striff suggests that

> egg donation and a multitude of new obstetric techniques has [sic] altered the definition of motherhood into a much more fluid term, implying chosen relationships rather than necessarily biological ones. However, it is often 'natural' motherhood which is viewed as the superior and authentic relationship within our society. (Striff 2005, p. 190)

In her work on anticipated infertility, Lauren Martin reminds us of the medical and societal value placed on biological motherhood. And while Martin picks up on the ways in which the genetic link is presented as the 'reified' or 'gold standard' of mothering (Martin 2010, p. 540), so too the news media presents the biological mother as the maternal ideal. We are told that 'journalists stressed connections with genetics … attained via procreative technologies over other family-building options' with genetically related children being presented 'as the ultimate reward … for persistence with procreative treatments' (Sterling 2013, p. 241).

Like the aforementioned bloggers, journalists look to remind us that 'families should be willing to endure whatever means necessary for however long it takes' to produce a biological child (Ibid., p. 241). And this notion of appropriate family building can be seen to have extended beyond the heteronormative couple to the single mother by choice.

Age-related Infertility and the Single Mother by Choice

Evelina Sterling makes the point that 'as infertility treatments grew in both acceptance and availability' the number of middle-class married heterosexual couples interested in 'fertility care plateaued' (CDC cited in Sterling 2013, p. 70). Therefore 'the infertility field had to appeal to new patients who would also benefit from infertility services but may not fit the traditional definition of infertility', namely, the mature single mother (Sterling 2013, p. 70). Indeed, the 40-something single woman is the 'bread-and-butter' of many fertility clinics on both sides of the Atlantic (Ibid., p. 104). Both the media and medical industries have paid increasing 'attention to this new trend' of family building (Ibid., p. 71) as the number of births among unmarried 30- and 40-year-old women are on the increase (CDC cited in Sterling 2013, p. 71). Although in previous generations 'un-partnered parenting was typically a phenomenon of life circumstances, such as divorce, widowhood, or unplanned pregnancies' (Sterling 2013, p. 17), the early 1980s witnessed the development of more deliberate un-partnered parenting. In 1981, Jane Mattes founded Single Mothers by Choice, a community which now boasts over '30,000 thinkers, tryers, and mothers' (SMC 2018a). The website informs us that the average member is an educated 35-year-old, with vocations ranging from teaching and nursing to the legal profession and banking (SMC 2018b). More specifically we are told that 'about 60 percent of our mothers conceived a child by donor insemination' while '20 percent have become pregnant with either a "known donor" or sex partner, although they are raising their child alone' (Ibid.). And although much assisted reproductive marketing literature depicts white heterosexual families (Sterling 2013, p. 82), Single Mothers by Choice speaks of members from 'all races, religions, ethnic groups, and lifestyles' across Europe and America (SMC 2018b).

In terms of the treatment options and stages available 'much of what applies to couples experiencing infertility is also relevant to single women' (Tomlins 2003, p. 229). The main difference we are told relates to managing the 'practical side of treatment' (Ibid., p. 229). However, this seems to make a number of assumptions about the interest and availability of partners to attend appointments and treatments and assumes a lack of support systems, friends and family members in place for the single mother. There is also evidence of clinical bias even before treatment starts because 'most fertility clinics mandated at least one visit with a mental health professional for un-married women, not something routinely recommended for their married counterparts' in the US (Sterling 2013, p. 182). Fertility clinics are open to the charge of reproductive gatekeeping because while it is important to 'prepare single women emotionally as to what to expect' (Ibid., p. 182) this should not be distinct from their partnered or married counterparts. Moreover, the fact that infertility counsellors boast that 'they could tell within ten minutes if a single woman was ready for donor insemination or just panicking' about her biological clock (Ibid., p. 182) does little to uphold the rigor, responsibility or responsiveness of such support. The disappointment here is that such statements point 'back to specific gender roles and a heteronormative family structure [because] these counselors expected that most women who chose insemination still hoped to meet a man who could share in the parenting' (Ibid., p. 182).

Assisted reproductive treatments offer, as repeatedly stated, a myriad of individuals and couples the opportunities to start or increase their family, but infertility clinics and broader channels of discourse tend to rely on age-related infertility as a focal point for discussion. Current data make it clear that there has been a 'dramatic increase in the age of women at first pregnancy' (Shalev and Lemish 2012, p. 381), with fertility experts reporting that more than 'fifty percent of 37-year-olds will need some sort of procreative assistance in order to have a baby. At age 42, this statistic jumps dramatically to 90 percent of women requiring some type of medical intervention to become pregnant' (CDC cited in Sterling 2013, p. 16). It is unsurprising then that women in their forties make up a large percentage of patients in fertility practices (Sterling 2013, p. 104). Fertility specialists form a consensus in their belief that 'age alone should not be a reason to deny treatment' (Ibid., p. 104), meaning that they give 'many older women hope that they could become mothers ... while hiding the low chances for success' (Ibid., p. 114). It is clear then that those working in the private fertility sector often fail to 'imply a finality in terms of women's procreative capacity since this would only result in fewer people seeking fertility care' (Ibid., p. 70).

A number of fertility specialists interviewed in Sterling's research state that they are candid with patients about their chances of success with and without donor eggs when diagnosed with age-related infertility. However, the specialists tell Sterling that many women rule out the option of using donor eggs, even if that particular procedure offered a better chance of success, due to the desire to maintain a genetic link with their, at this stage, hypothetical child. Practitioners go as far as to suggest that those affected by age-related infertility are 'irrational' in the face of the statistics concerning successful birth outcomes for age-related infertility, because 'they won't have it. Whenever we try to bring up age, women go crazy. They just don't want to know' (Elliott cited in Sterling 2013, p. 104). Irrational or otherwise, fertility specialists are not in the business of turning potential patients away, and as long as they have explained the limited success rates with the woman in question, they are happy to proceed with treatments (Ibid., p. 104).

There is a thriving magazine sector dedicated to conception, pregnancy, birth and motherhood, with titles such as *Fit Pregnancy, Pregnancy & Newborn, The Bump, Today's Parent, The Mother, Mothering, Mother and Baby, Maternity and Infant, Prima Baby & Infant, Your Pregnancy, Mum & Tots, Pregnancy Life & Style* and *Plum* to name but a few recent titles. However, the last title on the list, *Plum*, is the only magazine to have been made and marketed for '35+ mommies to be' (Peoplebabies 2008). The magazine includes topics ranging from infertility, prenatal testing and birth plans to returning to work, fashion and food; however, the magazine failed to appeal to its target demographic and went out of print after only a handful of issues. Although the magazine was committing to raising awareness of the topic of age-related infertility (Parenting 2018; Hallett 2006), there was the sense that women were not willing to acknowledge their age or 'evoke their "infertile" identity' in order to purchase and read an age-related conception and pregnancy title in public view (Sterling 2013, p. 96).

THE SYMBOLIC ANNIHILATION OF WOMEN AND THE LANGUAGE OF PROCREATION

Irrespective of age, sexual preference or life choices, a disconnect exists between the burden of responsibility on women for assisted reproductive treatments—be it socially, culturally, emotionally or medically (Sterling 2013, p. 15; Edge 2015, p. 4)—and the ways in which the treatment, particularly the successful outcome of any treatment, is presented as a medical triumph. When assisted reproductive treatments succeed, 'the achievement is constructed as belonging to medical science and its practitioners' (Ibid., p. 134), and yet it is not just the medical specialists who are foregrounding this discourse, but rather, the new mothers themselves. In the final entry of Leah Wild's IVF diary in *The Guardian* where the new mother discusses her healthy happy newborn twins, she tells the reader that her children were the product of pre-implantation genetic diagnosis (Wild 2001). What was important was the fact that the babies were healthy, without the fatal genetic disorder that Wild carried, but it is also worth drawing attention to the manner in which the new mother spoke about the successful pregnancy and birth:

> My boyfriend and I are the babies' parents ... we are bringing them up. ... We also happen to be their biological parents. Although we'd still be their mum and dad even if we weren't. But our babies have another set of adults responsible for producing them—the PGD medical team. ... You should have seen the cytogeneticist holding my baby boy. ... They were, in a sense, his creation, too. (Ibid.)

The seemingly throwaway comment regarding the genetic link cannot go unnoticed as it confirms and conforms to the long-standing and ubiquitous ideology of appropriate parenting, but what else has been picked up here is the way in which the new mother 'has written herself out' of the process of reproduction (Throsby 2004, p. 134). While the medicalisation of childbirth is indicative of the masculinisation of childbirth (Feasey 2012, pp. 149–151), so too, the medicalisation of reproduction leads to its masculinisation. We find that 'most of the fertility specialists (especially among the "older" and more experienced doctors) were men. As a result, gender inequality can be said to shape the experience of infertility' (Sterling 2013, p. 130). Indeed, there seems to have been a 'shift in our understanding of procreation and motherhood which are no longer seen as automatic and natural. Women are separated from procreation since maternal function can be achieved through technology whether it be through in vitro fertilization, donor eggs, surrogacy or cloning' (Sterling 2013, p. 25; Hanson 2004). It is worth noting that the 'constellation of conception ... refers to *procedures*, with no overt recognition of the predominantly female bodies which are the objects of these interventions' (Throsby 2004, pp. 22–23, emphasis in original). Likewise, we are told that infertility tends to 'depersonalize and dismember women to the point that they are considered only in terms of their procreative parts and their potential' (Sterling 2013, p. 22; Franklin 1990). Extant feminist approaches to IVF echo these concerns when they remind us that

3 ASSISTED REPRODUCTION: FAMILY, FORTUNES AND FERTILITY CLINICS   105

> [i]n the parliamentary debates which established the legislative frame-
> work for fertility treatment in the UK, it was embryos, eggs and sperm,
> and not women, that remained the central focus. ... With the embryo
> firmly positioned at centre stage in the debates against a backdrop of
> promised medical and scientific advances in the fight against disease,
> women are easily instrumentalised as foetal containers for the precocious
> embryo protagonist, or as the suppliers of eggs and embryos. (Throsby
> 2004, pp. 21–22)

The depiction of medical men drawing on scientific advancements to deliver 'miracle babies' appears at odds with much marketing from the fertility clinics themselves, which are less keen to sign-post 'the machinery *in use*' in favour of 'images of white-coated doctors ... interspersed with soft-focused pictures of smiling babies and happy nuclear families' (Ibid., p. 2, emphasis in original). We are reminded that the 'poster family for IVF is the grateful, infertile couple cradling their "miracle baby"' (Ibid., p. 2), which goes some way to presenting IVF and its counterparts as restoring the 'natural order'. However, this appears at odds with the ways in which the medical community in general and the fertility specialists in particular have been seen to present their work.

Six and a half million babies have been born through IVF since Louise Brown (The Infertility Journey 2016), and a growing numbers of babies are the product of assisted reproduction and pre-implantation genetic diagnosis. As such, it is no surprise that the news and entertainment media are committed to reporting on this growing field of study. Indeed, there are some concerns that the 'enthusiastic' coverage of new clinical developments takes place at the expense of the 'randomised controlled trials' that are 'needed to show effectiveness' (Hurley 2013). In short, journalists are keen to hype new clinical developments and promote medical 'miracles' to interested and invested readers. At best, such stories offer false hope to those diagnosed with infertility; at worst, they open up the possibility of exploitation for those seeking reproductive assistance (Ibid.). After all, when 'vulnerable' individuals trying to conceive 'learn of news reports about promising new techniques they may well demand them from their general practitioner or infertility clinics. They may be prepared to pay hundreds of pounds in the *hope* of improving their chances of a pregnancy' with hope rather than promise being the operative word here (Ibid., emphasis added).

SURROGACY

A surrogate is used when a woman who is unable to carry a baby herself uses another woman to carry for her. This situation may occur when a woman 'has no uterus, or because her uterus is damaged, or because carrying a baby may endanger her life' (Tomlins 2003, p. 181). While the gestational or host surrogate, or what has more recently been termed the 'gestational carrier' has no genetic link to the baby being carried because an existing embryo has been transferred, the traditional or straight surrogate 'provides the egg as well as carrying the baby, so the surrogate does have a genetic link to the baby' (Ibid., p. 182). It is worth noting here, however, that although traditional and gestational surrogacy arrangements have been and continue to be made '99 percent of all the world's surrogacies are gestational' (Surrogate Parenting Services 2014).

Eric Blyth uses the term 'third party assisted conception' in order 'to embrace both the ... donor procedure of egg, sperm or embryo donation ... and surrogacy arrangements' (Blyth and Landau 2004, pp. 10–11), and yet, IVF via donor eggs, sperm and gametes and the use of a surrogate appear to be spoken about differently because the very act of surrogacy, of one woman carrying another woman's child to term, confuses and complicates common understandings of motherhood. The very fact that surrogacy arrangements talk about the surrogate mother on the one hand and the commissioning, intended or social parents on the other makes it clear how these arrangements have 'changed the interpretation' of the term mother. We are reminded that the term has expanded so as to include the 'egg mother, birth mother, name mother, surrogate mother, gene mother, biomother, adoptive mother, foster mother, legal mother, organ mother, nurturing mother [and] earth mother' (Lupton cited in Sterling 2013, 21; Hill 2018). Based on a series of interviews with women who looked to explore their social, emotional and medical experiences of infertility and involuntary childlessness (Letherby 1999, p. 359), Gayle Letherby foregrounds a hierarchy of appropriate family building whereby donor insemination is 'more acceptable than egg donation, which in turn is more acceptable than surrogacy' (Letherby 1999, p. 368).

Although all third-party assisted conception procedures navigate similar legal, biological and psychosocial challenges on the way to a successful pregnancy (Blyth and Landau 2004, p. 14) the woman undergoing IVF with donor eggs or sperm looks to have conceived in line with traditional discourses of family building, even if she is not genetically related to the child that she is carrying, whereas a woman using a gestational carrier looks to be challenging conventional notions of family building, irrespective of the fact that she is genetically related to the child. We are reminded that '[t]hird party assisted conception creates the possibility of constructing a family using a combination of social, biological and genetic ties, and consequently provides many of the most challenging social and ethical dilemmas in the field of assisted conception' (Haase 2004, p. 70; Franklin 2013). Because children 'cannot be asked to give prior consent to third party assisted conception' the consideration of the offspring's well-being has become one of the key issues raised by this relatively new model of non-traditional family building (Blyth and Landau 2004, p. 13; Davies 1985). In the UK, the 'key legislative imposition on access to services is that a licensed treatment centre must not provide any treatment to a woman' unless account has been 'taken of the welfare of any child who may be born as a result of the treatment ... and of any other child who may be affected by the birth' (HFEA cited in Blyth 2004, p. 228; HFEA 2018f). However, this has proved difficult to implement. The British Fertility Society claimed that 'a definition of the meaning of the "welfare of the child" has not yet been agreed and in its absence, implementing the assessment is, in practice, the subject of confusion and debate' (The British Fertility Society cited in Blyth 2004, p. 228; British Fertility Society 1999).

Gestational surrogacy has 'only been readily available since the 1980s with the development of the necessary technology and clinical scientific expertise' (Blyth 2004, p. 226). And in the same way that Louise Brown is synonymous with the emergence and development of successful IVF treatments, the birth of Baby Cotton in 1985 is synonymous with discourses relating to surrogacy. Baby Cotton was not the first born through a surrogate, but she was the first to impact 'on the national consciousness' (Ibid., p. 226).

In 1985 Kim Cotton was paid £6500 to act as a traditional surrogate for a Swedish couple, and after giving birth to a baby girl, the surrogate 'was forced to leave her in the care of Victoria Maternity Hospital after the London borough of Barnet imposed a court order' (BBC 1985). Paying for surrogacy was, at the time, permitted by law in the UK, but the Health Minister revealed that Parliament looked to ban it after MPs came under pressure to take urgent action on the back of the Baby Cotton case. With this in mind, The Surrogacy Arrangements Act was 'rushed through Parliament' in 1985, prohibiting commercial surrogacy arrangements (Gamble 2014). The Act made it clear that surrogate mothers could choose to keep the baby if they changed their mind about giving the child to its intended parents. In accordance with current guidance, it is the surrogate mother and, if the woman is married, her husband, who are named on the baby's birth certificate, irrespective of any genetic relationship with the child (Blyth 2004, p. 229). Neither commissioning parent, whatever their genetic relationship to the child, has any legal relationship with the child at birth (Ibid., p. 229). And although the intended, commissioning or social parents can 'apply for a Parental Order' this can take an excess of 6 months to be awarded (Gander 2017). Until the parental order or adoption order is made, the surrogate mother remains the legal mother of the child, irrespective of whether she is in fact genetically related to the child in question.

Although it is beyond the scope of this chapter, it is worth noting that surrogacy laws differ widely from one jurisdiction to another. As such, prospective parents are advised to consider the legal protections in place, be it the transfer of legal parentage, the eligibility criteria, costs, the role of compensation, post-adoption plans and whether surrogacy agreements are enforceable, void or prohibited, before making surrogacy arrangements (Families Through Surrogacy 2019).

Surrogacy Arrangements

As part of the Human Fertilisation and Embryology Act 2008, 'non profit-making surrogacy agencies were officially legalized' in the UK (Gamble 2014) and 'civil partners and couples in an enduring family relationship' were permitted 'to apply for a parental order, in addition to married couples' (Department of Health and Social Care 2010). From '2008, the UK High Court began ratifying international surrogacy cases' (Gamble 2014) while in '2009, the embryo storage rules were changed to remove a longstanding rule that surrogacy patients could not extend storage of embryos' (Ibid.). One year later, 'British nationality law was amended to allow children born abroad to become British automatically on the grant of a parental order' (Ibid.) and in '2012, following a long campaign, the government announced its intention to introduce maternity leave rights for parents through surrogacy,' which came into effect in April 2015 (Ibid.). More recently 'the government told Parliament that … it would change the law to remove discrimination against single parents' (Ibid.).

At the same time as Baby Cotton was being spoken about in the UK media, the US media was inundated with comments and debates surrounding Baby M, the pseudonym used for an infant whose legal parentage was in question. In 1985 Mary Beth Whitehead, a married mother of two living in New Jersey, entered into a traditional surrogacy contract with William Stern for $10,000. Stern's wife, Elizabeth, suffered from multiple sclerosis and therefore, although she was not medically diagnosed with infertility, she 'feared ... severe health problems were she to become pregnant' (Haberman 2014). However, after the birth of the baby girl, Whitehead 'had a change of heart. She chose to forsake the $10,000 and keep the girl' (Ibid.). The Sterns then sued to be recognised as the child's legal parents.

> The New Jersey Supreme Court ... invalidated the surrogacy contract as an affront to public policy, and called the intended payment 'illegal, perhaps criminal, and potentially degrading to women.' Nonetheless, the court gave custody to the Sterns, saying this was in the best interest of the child. (Ibid.)

The father, William Stern was awarded custody, with Whitehead having visitation rights. However, although Baby M is understood as the first American court ruling on the validity of surrogacy, the question of legal parentage had already been asked in Michigan three years earlier, in 1983, when Judy Stiver entered into a surrogacy agreement with Alexander Malahoff. When the baby was born, it had microcephaly and a strep infection:

> Malahoff, claiming that the contract gave him sole custody, refused consent to any treatment for the infection. The hospital obtained a court order to treat the baby. Malahoff then denied any responsibility for custody or support of the baby, but Stiver insisted that he take the baby, claiming that he had a contractual obligation to do so. (Holder 1990, p. 79)

And yet, blood tests, which indicated that it was Stiver's husband and not Malahoff who was the biological father meant that the Stivers 'eventually took the baby they did not want and placed him in a state institution' (Ibid., p. 79). A number of sensationalistic stories of surrogacy have reached the news headlines since the late 1970s: A v C (1978), whereby the surrogate was a prostitute, and Noyes v Turane (1981), where the commissioning mother was a male-to-female transsexual (Freeman 1999, p. 1). We are told that surrogacy 'stories continue to make the headlines, primarily with theories of exploitation, tales of hope, heartbreak, lost and won court battles, and denied citizenship cases' (Le Vay 2019, p. 3). With such themes in mind, the case of baby Gammy reached the front pages in 2014, when an Australian couple who employed a Thai surrogate to carry their twins were seen to take just one of the babies home. The couple returned to Australia with their baby girl, but left the boy who was born with Down's syndrome with the surrogate, who later sought legal custody of the child that she had carried. This final case 'created a powerful narrative which attracted the global spotlight' (Ibid.) because while '[t]he genetic parents were portrayed as unfit' the practice of surrogacy was 'depicted as unethical, immoral and hazardous to children' (Ibid.). We are told, perhaps unsurprisingly, that 'Thailand changed its surrogacy laws in the aftermath of the media outrage' (Ibid.).

While the laws surrounding surrogacy are complex and unstable (Le Vay 2019), the UK looks to offer a consistent ruling on surrogacy arrangements under the Surrogacy Arrangements Act 1985, in that commercial surrogacy is illegal and the birth mother maintains the legal right of determination for the child, irrespective of genetic lineage (Campbell 2013; Surrogacy View 2015). It is slightly different in the US, where 'surrogacy and its attendant legal issues fall under state jurisdiction and the legal situation for surrogacy varies greatly from state to state', be it common law regimes or written legislation (Surrogacy View 2015). While

> [s]ome states facilitate surrogacy and surrogacy contracts, others simply refuse to enforce them, and some penalize commercial surrogacy. Surrogacy friendly states tend to enforce both commercial and altruistic surrogacy contracts and facilitate straightforward ways for the intended parents to be recognized as the child's legal parents. Some relatively surrogacy friendly states only offer support for married heterosexual couples. ... For legal purposes, what matters is where the contract is completed, where the surrogate mother resides, and where the birth takes place. (Ibid.)

Therefore, the key difference between the two countries from the point of view of the intended, social or commissioning parents is that while in the UK 'the Surrogacy Arrangements Act makes it impossible for couples seeking a surrogate to draw up a binding contract recognised by the UK courts' (Doward 2016), the US has in the most part removed 'legal uncertainty over parenthood at the point of birth' by introducing legally binding contracts (Ibid.). The former UK chair of the Families Through Surrogacy Conference says that the US 'provides a global benchmark,

3 ASSISTED REPRODUCTION: FAMILY, FORTUNES AND FERTILITY CLINICS 111

everyone is legally informed, legally protected and empowered to make decisions. In the UK, surrogacy is based on trust as contracts are unenforceable' (Ibid.). Indeed, recent statistics make it clear that because of or in spite of The Surrogacy Arrangements Act,

> [a]lmost two-thirds of all UK parental orders—legal rights conferred on parents who have commissioned a child from a surrogate—are now for a baby born overseas. In the past three years, more than 1,000 UK couples and individuals have secured the services of surrogates abroad, the highest number from any European country. (Ibid.)

While parental orders and payment options are being discussed by lobbying groups, campaigners and governments in both the UK and the US (Horsey et al. 2015), surrogacy is also being discussed and debated in the popular news media. This is perhaps unsurprising as 'the number of babies registered in Britain after being born to a surrogate parent has risen by 255 per cent in the past six years' (Dugan 2014). News and cultural commentators have only recently started to present surrogacy as a viable option for those affected by infertility, be it medical or social, and the ways in which they choose to present this particular form of third-party assisted conception goes some way towards upholding what I have previously termed the hierarchy of appropriate family building. When gestational surrogacy is discussed in the news media, stories reduce the role of the gestational carrier to that of 'intense baby-sitting' while giving voice to the intended, biological parents (cited in Sterling 2013, p. 197). In short, they seek to appropriate gestational surrogacy as an acceptable extension of more traditional family building as it maintains genetic lineage; downplaying the role and responsibilities of the surrogate makes it easier to align this form of third-party assisted conception with more traditional forms of family building.

Le Vay proposes that representations of surrogacy on popular genre television play to a 'winner/loser binary' in that the genetic mother is positioned as the winner and the surrogate as the loser here (Le Vay 2019, p. 4). Through a text-in-action approach we are told that surrogates are silenced and rendered invisible through a combination of framing, editing and mise en scène (Le Vay 2019, pp. 57–102; Skeggs et al. 2008, pp. 5–24). Research participants were said to have taken offence at the representation of surrogates in programmes such as *Giuliana & Bill* (2009–), where the surrogate was said to be 'portrayed as a "prop" in the background, seen as the holding vessel for the genetic child' (Le Vay 2019, p. 86). There is the suggestion that 'surrogate bodies are seen as passive containers for reproduction' so that the maternal subjectivity of the carrier can be 'erased, made invisible' (Ibid.). In the same way that the framing of the surrogate helps to disavow any sense of maternal subjectivity, the framing of the intended mother is said to 'strengthen her role as the genetic' parent (Ibid.). By downplaying or rendering invisible the surrogate mother, the intended mother can more readily be accepted as the biological and hence socially approved maternal figure here.

ASSISTED REPRODUCTION, REPRODUCTIVE TECHNOLOGIES AND THE MEDIA

With all of these legal, ethical and medical themes, debates, statistics and case studies in mind, it is crucially important that we look further at the ways in which assisted reproduction, assisted reproductive technologies and surrogacy arrangements are presented in the media. The topic routinely appears on radio (*Making Babies: The Business of Fertility* 2016, #blessed 2018); serious games (Scott 2018), the Internet (Fertility Network 2017), organised ticketed events (*The Fertility Show* 2017, Fertilityfest 2018) and mainstream Hollywood comedies. In her work on infertility in mainstream romantic comedies, Jennifer Maher tells us that even when films such as *Baby Mama* (2008), *The Switch* (2010) and *Back-Up Plan* (2010) represent post-feminist choices relating to the questions of if, when and how to mother, 'their reification of biological paternity, work to reassure their viewers of the attractiveness of the traditional nuclear family by reinterpreting the very technologies that challenge its dominance' (Maher 2014, p. 854). The concern here is not just related to the continued idealisation of the patriarchal unit, but

> how unrealistic these films are in their treatment of the process of trying to get pregnant … when pregnancy is achieved, in all of the films, there is never a mention of the potential of miscarriage (announcements are made often and early), and all of the inseminations 'take' with the first try. (Ibid., p. 865)

Indeed, the 'accidental wanted' pregnancy now exists as a trope for late 30 and 40-something characters in the genre in question (Maher 2014, p. 866). With the biological nuclear family in mind, it is the married couple Wendy/Elizabeth Banks and Gary/Ben Falcone in the comedic *What to*

3 ASSISTED REPRODUCTION: FAMILY, FORTUNES AND FERTILITY CLINICS   113

Expect When You're Expecting (2012) who have been trying to conceive for two years without any success. Although the couple introduce the options of IVF and adoption, neither route is taken because Wendy gets pregnant after one drunken night. With this scene in mind, family building blogger Charlotte Madsen informs readers that '**it is such a cliché**. In real life that is ***not*** the way infertility works' (Madsen of The Road to Baby Madsen: Our IVF Journey 2014a, emphasis in original). Moreover, we are informed that surrogacy-themed movies routinely make the third-party assisted reproductive process 'look so simple: the doctor takes an embryo and puts it in the surrogate, then she takes a pregnancy test and it's positive … [t]he surrogate never needs any injections or hormone supplements leading up to the embryo transfer and the parents are always so happy and calm' (Madsen of The Road to Baby Madsen: Our IVF Journey 2014b). In order to draw attention to the partial reality being presented here, Madsen states that these media texts

> never show how much the parents go through before deciding to use a surrogate … nor do they mention all the hormone injections and doctor's appointments the couple and surrogate would go through. … These movies also neglect to address the financial investment and emotional implications that … come with using a surrogate. (Ibid.)

By implying that the surrogates 'have some embryos injected into their tummies and then take [a] pregnancy test' these comedies are playing down the lived reality of assisted reproductive technologies in general and the steps and stages of surrogate pregnancy in particular, even if one takes into consideration the genre codes and conventions here. In short, the genre looks to both resolve infertility and foreground what are deemed the most appropriate family-building forms and practices, namely biological kinship in patriarchal units—in line with the now predictable heterosexual imperative (Demory and Pullen 2013, p. 1).

Extant literature exists to account for the melodramatic and telefantastic depictions of infertility by way of long-awaited babies and alien hybrid creatures respectively (Edge 2015). Moreover, television has presented the subject of assisted and third-party reproduction in a broad range of genres spanning soap opera (*Coronation Street* 1960–), sitcoms (*The New Normal* 2012–13, *Rules of Engagement* 2007–13), thrillers (*Mistresses* 2013–16), dramedy (*Gilmore Girls: A Year in the Life* 2016) and drama (*Big Love* 2006–11), but it is to the documentary tradition that I now turn. It is important that we understand the ways in which factual programming and the documentary represent the treatment options, success rates and ethical questions raised as they exist in relation to a discussion of assisted reproductive treatments and technologies. At a time when more women than ever before are looking to have their first baby in their forties, combined with evidence to suggest that young women are naive as to their reproductive capacities, we must interrogate the role of the media in informing and educating women about their fertility reality and the cost and realistic capabilities of contemporary infertility interventions.

INFERTILITY TREATMENTS AND FACTUAL TELEVISION

Patricia Aufderheide informs us that documentaries emerged from early moving picture recordings that were termed educationals, actualities and interest films, and in all cases, they were not simply about real life, but rather 'portraits of real life, using real life as their raw material constructed by artists and technicians who make myriad decisions about what story to tell and to whom, and for what purpose' (Aufderheide 2008, p. 2). From this perspective, the term documentary has been in existence for nearly a century, and although there have been shifts from travelogue films through to newsreels, the propagandist tradition and cinéma vérité, contemporary documentaries, irrespective of whether they are intended for terrestrial or subscription television, theatrical or straight-to-DVD release, are routinely understood as non-fiction films intended to document a specific area of reality with the intent to inform and educate the audience (Beattie 2004; Kahana 2016). Documentary has been understood as the 'creative treatment of actuality' in the sense that these media texts are a meaningful way to interpret the modern world (Kerrigan and McIntyre 2010, p. 111). With this in mind, it is crucial that we look at the ways in which contemporary television documentaries uphold this tradition as they relate to the topic of infertility and assisted reproduction.

There has been a wealth of documentaries and factual television texts that pick up on the topic of fertility, infertility and non-traditional family building since the mid-2000s. *Make Me a Baby* (2007) follows 100 couples as they navigate their journey to parenthood, paying particular attention to those who 'travel down the difficult and often unsuccessful path of fertility treatment'. *The World's Oldest Mums* (2009) meets women who are looking to assisted reproduction to help them conceive after menopause; the autobiographical *Eggs for Later* (2010) looks to anticipated infertility and egg freezing 'as a valuable solution to concerns about age-related infertility' (Van de Wiel 2015, p. 120) and *Too Old to Be a Mum?* (2010) takes age-related infertility as its starting point. *Win a Baby* (2012) follows one woman's attempts to launch an IVF lottery in Britain, whereby a £20 ticket would provide the winner with 'a luxurious all-inclusive fertility treatment package worth £25,000'. *Donor Mum: The Children I've Never Met* (2011) tells the story of one of Britain's first anonymous egg donors, who learns the identity of the recipient of her egg and decides to make contact with *her* children and their intended mother (emphasis added). *Baby Makers: The Fertility Clinic* (2013) follows four couples as they 'pursue their dream of getting pregnant' from the perspective of staff at the busy Hewitt Fertility Centre in Liverpool, one of the largest fertility clinics in Britain, asking them what it is like 'to be involved everyday in the creation of new life'. *Panorama: Inside Britain's Fertility Business* (2016) investigates the ways in which 'some clinics sell add-ons—the extra drugs, tests and treatments offered on top of standard fertility care'. The concern here is that even though such treatments can add several hundreds or even thousands of pounds to existing fertility treatment costs there is 'a worrying lack of good evidence from trials to show these can improve the chances of having a baby'.

In *Future Baby* (2016) 'documentary film-maker Maria Arlamovsky journeys around the world, investigating the state of reproductive treatment' asking the question as to 'how far should we go' to build a family (Griessner 2016). The documentary includes interviews with 'doctors, embryologists, CEOs, journalists, would-be parents, egg donors, a young woman born via IVF, a bioethicist, a biotechnologist and a sociologist' (Bray 2016). This is a documentary that chooses to focus on education and information management for the interested viewer rather than scandal or sensationalism. This is not to say that viewers won't be shocked to hear a father-in-waiting assess the weight and stature of prospective egg donors, or surprised to find a woman without a uterus giving birth and sperm donors from South Africa matched online with surrogate mothers in India; but it is presented with diplomacy rather than judgement here. The programme takes the time to introduce a summary of assisted reproductive technologies and, as such, it 'makes for a solid intro to the contemporary world of IVF' (Ibid.). The Center for Bioethics and Culture has produced a number of documentaries in recent years on the topic of third-party reproductive ethics, namely *Eggsploitation* (2010), *Anonymous Father's Day* (2011) and *Breeders: A Subclass of Women?* (2014). These films are broad in scope, covering the potential health and psychological risks for those who donate their eggs, those who decide to serve as surrogates, those children born via surrogacy and biological fathers (Lahl 2017). I would argue that these films can be seen to be borrowing from John Reith's desire that public service broadcasting should inform, educate and entertain. And although these films are neither British nor public service, they present a strong Reithian principle.

While *Future Baby* and the Center for Bioethics and Culture films are diplomatic and informative, Amanda Micheli's *Vegas Baby* (2016) appears at the other end of the emotional spectrum, giving us an insight into the ways in which a Las Vegas Infertility clinic 'holds a lottery in which childless couples send in videos that make the pitch for ... free treatment' (Keough 2017), and like a scene from *The X Factor* (2004–) or *Britain's Got Talent* (2007–), a 'panel of judges evaluates the pleas from the short list of candidates voted on by social media. It then chooses a handful of compelling finalists before picking one winner' (Keough 2017). The programme hears difficult stories of stillbirth, failed adoptions, relationship strains and financial hardship with IVF pioneer Geoffrey Sher as the master of ceremonies presiding over the family-building fate of the entrants.

There are a myriad of medical facts, conception figures, ethical questions and personal narratives being presented in these texts, but I would like to pay particular attention to a documentary that can be said to combine medical expertise, personal testimony, celebrity culture and the Reithian principles of the BBC, namely *Alex Jones: Fertility & Me*.

Fertility, Infertility and the Documentary Tradition

Charlotte Alexandra "Alex" Jones, a Welsh television presenter, best known for co-presenting the BBC magazine programme *The One Show* (2006–), fronted a one-off documentary for the BBC on the topic of fertility, infertility and assisted reproductive treatments and technologies. The programme summary makes it clear that the newly married, late 30-something presenter was keen to try for a baby, but was concerned, on the back of recent news headlines related to the topic of age-related infertility, about her own chances of conception and pregnancy:

> Alex was always reading headlines urging women not to delay motherhood and, at 38, she was worried she might be one of the 3.5 million people in the UK who struggle to conceive. So she decided to find out more about the

fertility issues so many people face, and this is her story. She investigates what pioneering science is doing to help people struggling to become pregnant, and she travels the world to see the cutting-edge techniques that could revolutionise fertility treatment in the future and give people new hope of having children. (BBC2 2016)

The programme is ostensibly filmed in accordance with Reithian principles, enriching the lives of its audience through information, education and entertainment. The show takes the time to balance the voices of those affected by an infertility diagnosis and those seeking treatment against a backdrop of fertility facts, figures and cutting-edge medical advances.

It is, however, the closing credits that leave audiences uneasy, for it seems to demonstrate a lack of consideration and judgement on the part of the producer and presenter. On the back of being told about the reality of infertility in general and age-related infertility in particular, and on hearing from individuals and couples who have sacrificed so much in the hope of creating or extending their family, we close with the news that 38-year-old Jones was fortunate enough to experience a 'straightforward' pregnancy. I am not looking to diminish the good fortune of the presenter, challenge her interest in making this programme or question her desire to play out her fertility journey to an invested public. My point is simply that this conclusion seems at odds with the tone and content of the production. It does little to address the seriousness of the topic under discussion or promote the very real medical problem of age-related infertility, which was in itself said to be the starting point for the personal journey and the programme's narrative.

It reads as if Jones is happy to offer a dramatic plot and create drama out of her own medical investigations, but only with the proviso that she herself is, at final closure, not diagnosed with age-related infertility. As she herself says, 'I have always had a pretty healthy diet and enjoyed exercise' and in the same way that she is happy to present her physically fit physique and youthful complexion, as is common in the entertainment arena, so too she seeks public approval regarding the health of her ovaries. It does leave the audience wondering how different this documentary would look if the final closure had been different. The presenter speaks to women who have been struggling to conceive for several years and yet after less than a year of marriage, this woman conceives naturally and goes on to have a healthy baby in her late thirties, without intervention.

The programme begins with a statistic that draws attention to the extent of infertility in the UK, before outlining the presenter's relationship status (recently married) and family-building plans (wants to start trying for a baby as soon as possible). We are asked to note the decreasing numbers of younger mothers and the growing numbers of 40-something mothers in the UK, and we are encouraged to fill in the gaps when we realise that the late 30-something presenter looking to start a family will, if successful, result in another first-time geriatric primigravida:

> Around 3.5 million people in the UK have difficulty conceiving a child and, as I'm 38, I'm concerned that I might, too. My main fear is realising too far down the line that it's actually not working. So I'm on a mission to find out more about fertility. It can be an issue for people of all ages, but these days, more women over 40 are having babies than those under 20. And that's possible because the science of fertility is keeping pace.

However, as soon as we are reminded about the very real risk of age-related infertility, the audience is encouraged to relax, because, in a sentence that one might consider to be misleading, we are asked to consider 'how cutting-edge techniques are giving *everyone* new hope of having children … even … for those born without a womb'.

We are informed that the documentary will give the audience advice on keeping 'our eggs and sperm healthy' before adding the frisson of personal revelation in that Jones herself is going to 'get some tests done … to find out how fertile I am'. On the first step to exploring her fertility status she is seen speaking to her mother and sister, and this intergenerational discussion reminds the audience about changing maternal expectations. While the presenter is looking to join the growing numbers of first-time late 30 and 40-something mothers, her own mother made it clear that 25 was considered old for a first-time mother a mere generation ago. Jones' mother puts her daughter's childfree status down to her lack of the right partner, because 'obviously you can't do anything until you meet the right man, can you' but rather than counter or redress this on the back of the medical teams and experts interviewed in the programme, or a discussion of NHS guidelines for single and/or lesbian mothers for example, Jones concludes: 'No, and it just took me absolutely ages.' In the context of a different show or interview situation, this might go unnoticed, but in a programme that has already addressed the ways in which *everyone* is given hope in their desire to start a family, it seems a missed opportunity.

3 ASSISTED REPRODUCTION: FAMILY, FORTUNES AND FERTILITY CLINICS 119

Jones' mother tells us that she 'started the menopause at 44', to which Jones replies: '[T]hat's really young, that is young, gosh ... I mean, that's six years away. ... I had no idea my mother was so young "when she went through the menopause"'. The programme then misses the opportunity to talk about early menopause beyond the single case of Jones' own mother, or even the routine facts and age statistics as they relate to that stage in a woman's life. After all, the menopause 'is a natural part of ageing that usually occurs between 45 and 55 years of age', with the average age for a woman to reach the menopause in the UK being 51 (NHS 2018d). Approximately '1 in 100 women experience the menopause before 40 years of age' (Ibid.). My point here then is that mid-forties can be considered younger than the average, but not too far removed from the routine time frame given by the NHS. Within the context and genre conventions of the documentary, it is clear that the narrative would foreground Jones herself, her family unit and personal experiences, but again, it seems difficult to overlook the missed opportunity to better inform the audience here.

When Jones states that 'if I take after her, it could mean that I have just six years to have a family of my own. For some reason, I just thought I was invincible, really, and didn't think that there was a cut-off point, but that really hit home', it may speak for many women, themselves naive to the reality of age-related infertility. After all, we live in a society preoccupied with appearance and selflessness as key indicators of appropriate motherhood over and above more pragmatic concerns relating to ovaries and egg stocks.

Jones meets with Professor Tim Child, a consultant in reproductive medicine, to discover 'exactly how age affects my chances of having a baby' and the meeting begins with Jones seeking reassurance from the consultant because 'somebody told me, and it scared the living daylights out of me, they said, "Alex, do you know that your fertility will literally fall off a cliff after 35?" ... Tell me it's not true. It's not true'. Child reassures Jones, telling her 'it's not true' before citing the following statistics:

> During someone's 20s, about 90%, 95% of people will get pregnant after a year of trying, during early 30s, 85% to 90%, late 30s, 75% to 80% chance of getting pregnant ... but the risk of miscarriage does go up. Early 40s, you may be heading down towards a 50% chance of getting pregnant over a year.

I am not sure what definition of a cliff either Jones or Child is working with here, but a decline from 95 per cent to 50 per cent, with an increased chance of miscarriage, could, I propose, be understood as a dramatic change in the likelihood of a healthy pregnancy. To have a jokingly concerned Jones plead with a reproductive medical specialist, who then seeks to reassure her as to the much-maligned reality of age-related infertility, is surprising at best and disappointing at worst. After all, the programme spoke of wanting to inform its audience at a time when women were said to be ill informed about the reality of age-related infertility. In her work on women's health, Danielle Mazza argues that women are ill informed about the reality of age-related infertility, because '88% of women overestimated by 5–10 years the age at which fertility begins to decline' (Mazza 2011, p. 140; Madsen 2003). More surprising perhaps is the fact that '18 percent of women aged over 35 seeking assisted reproductive' support were also unaware of the impact of age on infertility (Mazza 2011, p. 140; Hammarberg and Clarke 2005, Nargund cited in Adams 2015).

The findings from a recent survey based on women who had spoken to their medical provider about fertility discovered that 'fewer than 50 percent of participants could correctly answer seven out of ten basic questions' relating to their fertility. The findings suggested that women were 'wrong most often about … how much fertility declines at various ages' (Shapiro 2012). We are reminded of the difference between medical fact and common misconception when we are told that

> [a]t age 30, a healthy woman has about a 20 percent chance of conceiving per month and by the time she reaches 40, her odds drop to about 5 percent. Yet the women surveyed thought that a 30 year old woman would have a 70 percent chance of conceiving and that a 40 year old's chances could approach 60 percent! (Ibid.)

Moreover, 'women are misinformed about the efficacy of [Assisted Reproductive Technology], overestimating their chance of having a baby using these techniques' (Mazza 2011, p. 140; Hammarberg et al. 2001). It is difficult for women to make sense of competing discourses concerning age-related infertility because while an overestimation of the risks of age-related infertility 'creates an unnecessary worry', underestimation 'may result in serious disappointments if it becomes difficult to become pregnant' (Lampi 2008, p. 21). What remains clear is that for women to be able 'to plan the timing of births together with other important life decisions such as education' they need to be aware of the fact that the risk of infertility increases with age (Ibid., p. 3). And for the majority of women surveyed, 'the media is the most common information channel' on the topic in question (Ibid., p. 14).

With such fertility naivety and the role of the media to inform and educate in mind, Jones has an appointment with Geoffrey Trew, a consultant in Reproductive Medicine at Hammersmith Hospital in order to 'find out how healthy my ovaries are' and to help 'reveal my chances of becoming pregnant'. Basic blood tests assess ovarian health and an ultrasound scan examines the gynaecological health of the pelvis, paying particular attention to ovarian cysts, fibroids and the antral follicle count, and it is this latter check that 'tells us if the reserve of eggs is good'. Jones embarks on these tests, reminding the audience that they are 'available to anyone, no matter what your age—just ask your GP for them if you're having problems conceiving'. This is a helpful reminder about the role and responsibilities of the NHS in Britain, but there is little information here about when to seek such assistance and waiting times, even though the NHS encourages women over 35 who are struggling to conceive to come for earlier testing and treatment than their younger counterparts.

We are provided with statistics relating to fibroids, benign growths in the womb (more than 1 in 3 women in the UK) and polycystic ovary syndrome, a normal condition which affects how the ovaries produce eggs (1 in 7 women in the UK), and are told that although 'conditions like these can make getting pregnant more difficult or impossible, we are reassured that they can respond to treatment'. Again, the message here is positive, in the sense that tests are available to pick up concerns that can routinely be treated in line with a successful pregnancy outcome.

Jones wants to see what else she can do to increase her chances of conception so she visits a private practice and speaks to Zita West, a midwife who specialises in advising couples in their thirties and forties about their fertility. The midwife does not shy away from the fact that 'age is the biggest factor' in contemporary infertility before going on to talk about sex, vitamin deficiency, key nutrients, stress and energy levels. The initial consultation at West's clinic costs around £240, and although we are ensured that the office was 'very nice' and the consultation itself was 'thorough' the programme makes a point of stating that 'this kind of information is also available through your GP'. That said, GP appointments are, according to the NHS, currently between 10 and 12 minutes long (Lacobucci 2016; NHS 2018e), which would not give the patient in question the same level of depth and detail offered in the private consultation here. The fact that Jones visits a private clinic and then reminds us of the responsibilities of the NHS might seek to reassure audiences of the equity of services on offer, but the effort to do so just goes further to foreground the role of private treatment providers in family building, especially when age is a factor.

After assuring us that she already lives an active, healthy life, with a good diet and a lifelong love of exercise, Jones tells us that she needs to learn more about male fertility, and wants to 'get the lowdown on sperm', starting with questions about age-related male factor infertility, diet and exercise. During an interview with Professor Allan Pacey we are told that

> [a]ge does affect male fertility, but not quite in the same way that it does in women ... men above the age of 40 are about half as fertile as men under the age of 25. They may have the same numbers of sperm, but the quality of the sperm in the 40-or-above-year-olds may be less good at the genetic level, compared to the younger chap. ... We do detect more miscarriages in women who become pregnant through older men's sperm, in comparison to younger men's sperm.

Jones' response here is interesting because it reminds us of a culture that associates infertility with the female body and the responsibility for infertility as belonging to women. She might be seen to speak for the wider culture when she states that 'we tend to think of a miscarriage as being the female's problem' and when Pacey reiterates that there is 'a lot of evidence now to show that the quality of the sperm has a bearing on how likely a miscarriage is to happen' she states that it was 'the first time' that she, an educated, articulate, 38-year-old married woman looking to start a family, had heard of such a correlation. My point here is simply that if she was unaware of the risks associated with age-related male infertility, then one might assume that others too remain unaware, irrespective of whether the women in question are conceiving naturally, turning to IVF or looking to use a gestational surrogate.

We are informed that the size of a man's testicles relates to the sperm production rate. However, although the sizing is predetermined by genes, there are risk factors associated with lifestyle that can be altered to increase sperm quality, because exposure to 'certain chemicals, wearing tight underwear sitting down a lot or working in a hot environment can have a detrimental effect on sperm because they raise the temperature of testicles'. We are told that there are simple things that both men and women can do to increase their fertility, but that for those who are affected by an infertil-

3 ASSISTED REPRODUCTION: FAMILY, FORTUNES AND FERTILITY CLINICS   123

ity diagnosis, they can and should 'turn to science for help'. What is important here is the time that the specialist takes to demonstrate not just the scientific advances that are leading to more successful IVF rates, but the reality of age-related infertility. We are told that

> [i]n the early '80s, IVF success rates averaged 10%. Today, it's well over 30% for women under 35, although rates fall as you get older to about one in ten for women in their early 40s. As you age, it's not just the egg quantity that drops—it's also the egg quality. Some eggs collapse as soon as the sperm is injected, because their membrane is too soft, while others develop a tougher membrane over time, making it difficult to be fertilised, as it's harder for the sperm to get in.

Jones is shown how eggs from a woman her age are 'less likely to fertilise and less likely to lead on to a baby' than eggs taken from a younger woman, which leaves the presenter telling us that 'it's hit home how fragile our little eggs are and how they do age'. Jones refers to the contemporary 'trend' of having children later in life, meaning that, in her words, 'more women are leaving it too late, their eggs are just unable to be fertilized' and for others again 'their eggs have virtually run out' before introducing the audience to a personal account of a couple who used donor eggs to conceive and carry a baby to term. The professional couple met in their forties and, after being told of their 2 per cent chance of having their own biological baby, looked to use the donor eggs of a younger woman, giving them a 60 per cent chance of a successful pregnancy. We meet the family, and are told about the process of creating an embryo and implantation, at which point Jones asks if 'it feels strange at all to be carrying an embryo, a baby, essentially, that genetically wasn't created by yourself' irrespective of the fact that the baby is genetically linked to her husband and carried by the woman in question. And although the mother is clear that she is both 'amazed' and 'delighted' that at the time of her 50th birthday science enabled her to carry *her* baby, the question itself tends to remind us of the long-standing and ubiquitous link between biological motherhood and appropriate maternal practices, irrespective of the father or husband in question here. Jones reminds us that the NHS does on occasion and in specific regions pay for egg donation, before acknowledging that 'going private means adding around £2,000 per IVF cycle' with only a 40 per cent chance of success, depending on the age of the egg donor. However, no further details or data are provided as they relate to the age ranges in question here. But if one considers, as previously mentioned, that 'the chance of getting pregnant from an individual IVF cycle in Britain stands at about 21 per cent if you're under the age 35—and that your chances are even lower if you're older', then the age of the egg donor is of crucial importance (Winston 2018).

Again, Jones might be seen to speak for many women of her and subsequent generations when she tells us that

> it's been an eye-opener, really, because my friends and I used to say, 'well, if nothing works, we'll just do IVF'. We thought it was just a quick-fix solution, really. But what I've learned is that it's really difficult, both emotionally and physically. And, actually, the odds are really stacked against you. The success of IVF, with your own or a donor egg, depends heavily upon choosing a healthy embryo to transfer into the womb. If the embryo isn't healthy, it won't implant successfully.

We are introduced to further cutting-edge research, as Child trials preimplantation genetic screening and next-generation sequencing. Child 'screens embryos to check they are genetically healthy' and to check that they 'carry the correct number of chromosomes', which could help reduce the risk of miscarriage. But, at the same time as we are reminded of the availability and success rates of such currently privately run tests, we are told of the cost, which is 'at least £2,000 on top of the IVF cycle'. What is important to note here is that 'even if doctors select a genetically viable embryo to transfer, there is still over a 30% chance that it won't implant successfully in the womb' because 'there are many other things that could affect why embryos implant or not'. With this figure in mind, we are then introduced to a research team working in the Spanish city of Valencia under Dr Carlos Simon which is looking to 'transform implantation success rates' by more accurately assessing the right time for embryo transfer according to each patient. That said, the statistics presented here refer to conception rather than live births, meaning they have chosen to overlook the age-related reality of pregnancy loss.

The programme is playing with its audience and their fertility awareness because of all the realistic discussion and medical insight, for all the facts, figures, data and statistics relating to male and female infertility, subfertility, the risks of miscarriage and IVF success rates, we are routinely reminded that, if one can afford it, there are a myriad of tests, screenings, medical treatments and thus hope for those looking to build a family with the use

3 ASSISTED REPRODUCTION: FAMILY, FORTUNES AND FERTILITY CLINICS 125

of reproductive technologies. The fact that we are introduced to a number of cutting-edge treatments which are 'currently only available in a handful of clinics around the world' reminds us of the inequality of opportunities for women currently affected by a diagnosis. These tests may 'one day be available to everyone, improving the chances of having a baby for women of all ages' but that day is not today. We are routinely reminded that 'science is constantly pushing the boundaries of what is possible' as it relates to conception, which lessens the impacts of the aforementioned facts, figures and statistics while maintaining a sense of hope and optimism for invested audiences.

Even when we are introduced to women who were born without a womb, we are informed that science can help, because if these women were born with ovaries and eggs, they can still have their own biological children, they just cannot carry that child to term ... that is, until Swedish surgeon Mats Brannstrom 'became the first person in the world to successfully transplant a womb from one woman to another'. These are small but important steps in what Brannstrom thinks is 'going to be a routine procedure in five to ten years in many, many countries around the world ... including the UK'. More progress, more hope, more disappointment perhaps for those who cannot afford the treatment or for those for whom it is already too late.

As the programme nears closure, Jones looks back over her fertility journey and tells us that

> carrying a child is still not something anyone can take for granted, despite the extraordinary research happening right across the globe. It occurred to me that I never considered the possibility that I wouldn't have children one day, which is really naive, especially knowing what we know now. But that's changed. I do now realise it's something I might have to face. Today, I'm going to hear the results of my fertility tests, to find out how my ovaries are doing and whether I've got a healthy reserve of eggs left.

Jones gets her results back and, in short, she is fertile, and there should be no problems with a natural conception, irrespective of the fact that she is nearly 40. In relation to her ultrasound, Jones is told that there are

> no significant cysts in the ovaries at all, which, straight away, is very reassuring. We then come onto the fertility aspect. So the ultrasound measurement, the antral follicle count, that came out to be a total of 12. That means that

about 12 eggs were maturing in my ovaries when I had the scan. So, *for your age*, that is absolutely fine, with no concerns at all. We then look at the blood test—yours has come out at 14.8. You're in the very healthy range, there. I'd be reassured, not worried, about the health of the ovaries. (Emphasis added)

So although Jones was 'unnerved' to be faced with the reality of her own fertility, her tests results are very encouraging, indeed positive, and she tells us that she hopes that she and her husband will start their own family soon. However, being reassured that her fertility is 'fine … *for your age*' is not the same as being told that her fertility and thus chance of conception is good. It is as if she has just been told that the chances of a successful pregnancy outcome at 38 is high, not low, as the programme has more than hinted at here. Moreover, when Jones informs the audience that she has 'got every sympathy with any couple or individual who are having a difficult time of it' it seems a little hollow, especially given the epilogue:

It just so happens that my husband and I … are having a baby (cheering and applause). Lots and lots of you had guessed, and I was trying to breathe in and eventually, I can breathe out, which is just lovely. When I started filming this documentary, I had no idea how things would turn out for us but, luckily, it was a *straightforward process* and of course, we are thrilled to be having a baby. (Emphasis added)

A straightforward process speaks of a natural conception and biological connection deemed worthy of applause, which may very well be the case, but it seemed at best unnecessary and at worst insensitive to mention in a programme committed to understanding the problems associated with conception. *Alex Jones: Fertility & Me* made it clear, repeatedly, that 'humans … are fairly inefficient, actually, at making healthy embryos [and] there are no guarantees when it comes to getting pregnant [because] there are so many things at play' and yet we finish the programme with a pregnant, smiling, slim and serene Jones performing in line with the good mother myth. The presenter adheres to appropriate family-building practices in the pronatal period, removed from the risks associated with age-related infertility as they were described in the programme. We are routinely reminded that '[f]ertility problems do not align with the "good" mother … because she is supposed to be a natural one, in control of her body and her children' (Edge 2015, p. 146). Jones is presented as both here. In short, the programme seems to introduce, while simultaneously disavow, the lived reality of age-related infertility.

At the time of editing this volume, Jones has been heard telling *The Sunday Telegraph's Stella* magazine that she suffered a missed miscarriage back in 2017, a year after the birth of the baby that she announced in the final minutes of her fertility documentary. Jones tells the journalist that she doesn't want to become 'a poster girl for how fertility can go wrong', but rather looks to share the news of her current pregnancy as it reaches its final trimester. Rather than remind readers of the infertility and miscarriage risks for women looking to conceive in their forties, as she herself presented them to an invested audience in 2016, Jones is now 'adamant that your early 40s are not too old to have a baby' (Sturgis 2019). She is quoted as saying: '[a]s long as you keep yourself healthy, that's all you can do. As a society we are changing. People are living a lot longer and are more aware of taking care of themselves' (Jones cited in Sturgis 2019), before moving on to the topic of balancing work, marriage, motherhood and a second pregnancy. Jones was happy to talk about her fertility and natural pregnancy as it was in keeping with the ideology of the good mother, and she only briefly touches on a miscarriage announcement as part of an interview that applauds her current maternal efforts and celebrates her impending new arrival. It is no coincidence that the interview picks up on Jones' slim appearance, serene demeanour, her desire to breastfeed and her ability to manage motherhood, marriage and work 'on little sleep' because her toddler was 'up at four, five and six this morning' (Sturgis 2019). In short, Jones is presented to us as the much-touted maternal ideal (Feasey 2012). However, this seems to be at best disingenuous and at worst damaging as it sets 40-something women up for false fertility hope—false hope that Jones herself looked to quash.

HOLLYWOOD'S BEST-KEPT SECRET: AGE-RELATED INFERTILITY

As Jones introduces what is termed the 'trend' for older motherhood, the presenter suggests that 'we all feel ten years younger. You know, 40 is the new 25 or the new 30. But, inside, we're all still the same as we were 100 years ago' (BBC2 2016). We may be, but clearly Jones herself is not. This sense that famous film, television and entertainment personalities experience a different fertility timeline from the rest of the adult population is neither original nor new; rather it must be understood as a recurring trope in the entertainment landscape in general and the women's gossip sector in particular.

Fashion-forward celebrities are looking to defy the ageing process in terms of both their physical appearance and sartorial choices while the cosmetics industry appears committed to making mature skin more radiant than ever before. And yet, even though 40 may well be the new 30, or indeed, the new 20 in terms of physical appearance and surface attractiveness, statistics are clear in that fertility declines with age, however age-defying ones appearances are (Feasey 2014). Indeed, fertility is a social leveller because although celebrities may be different from you and me, one thing they are not is more fertile (Ibid.).

Many of the 40-something women who the mass media applaud for their youthful physiques, on trend fashions and smooth visages, are those self-same celebrities who have been affected by an infertility diagnosis. While stars such as Sarah Jessica Parker, Marcia Cross and Nicole Kidman are championed in the beauty and fashion sector for looking 'youthful [...] despite having passed the dreaded "middle-age" milestone' (Celeb News 2013), it is worth thinking about the ways in which these women might be understood as both fashion and fertility role models. After all, although a celebrity's willingness to share her diagnosis and treatment with the public might be understood as a calculated self-exposure exercise, such candid confessional discourses can bring this topic into the public consciousness, and, in this sense, be beneficial for other women affected by infertility.

Indeed, an exhaustive number of contributions to newspaper blogs and postings congratulate these women for speaking publicly about their infertility. This outpouring of appreciation is understandable and indeed to be expected if one considers where and how this information is available. Celebrity infertility stories are routinely found in the women's gossip and tabloid sector, alongside a range of blogs and celebdocs, and these media forms have historically relied on the celebrity confessional. My point here is that while celebrities have long been relaying intimate stories of romance, family and heartache, they have more recently begun to share their most candid infertility and non-traditional family building narratives. Rather than deride these women for trivialising their infertility stories for financial or fame reward, it is worth noting that these stories are of significance to those female readers and women in the audience who are themselves diagnosed. Time and again, blogs thank performers for being open and ostensibly candid about their infertility and pregnancy loss stories (Wertman 2013; Donato 2016). Indeed, Giuliana and Bill Rancic became RESOLVE's celebrity spokes-couple of the year on the back of their candour about and commitment to infertility awareness (Edge 2014, p. 876; Edge 2015, p. 138).

At the time of writing, Michelle Obama is speaking about her own IVF experiences and the reality of age-related infertility (Obama cited in Riley-Smith 2018; Smith 2018; Obama 2018). IVF is a viable fertility option, with obvious success stories, and, in one sense then, the ways in which recognisable women such as the former First Lady share their non-traditional family building stories can help educate other women about their own fertility options. However, these women tend only to announce their infertility once they have secured a successful pregnancy outcome, which in itself sends out a rather misleading finale to the infertility narrative. Erin Striff makes this point when she tells us that

> [p]ublic fertility stories are often structured as a 'near-miss,' in that we know of a celebrity's previous failed rounds of IVF only when they may at the same time perform their successful achievement of pregnancy ... the struggle with infertility only becomes acceptable to discuss in the public eye if it has been overcome in some way, reiterating the feeling that infertility is something to be ashamed of. (Striff 2005, p. 195)

In short, celebrity infertility has become, to some degree, accepted, but only on the back of a successful maternal celebration. The overwhelming majority of these public narratives have a happy ending, which could be said to 'minimize the infertility experience' while making those who do not go on to experience a successful pregnancy 'feel even more isolated and stigmatized' (Sterling 2013, p. 99). Even though Sharon Begley of *Newsweek* reported that 'getting a baby' through assisted reproductive technologies was almost as easy as getting a tattoo (Begley cited in Sterling 2013, p. 124), the truth is that these procedures fail more often than they succeed, and this reality is rarely spoken of as part of the celebrity infertility narrative. There have been numerous technical advances relating to assisted conception in recent years, and yet 'IVF remains, at best, a hopeful art driven by the best of intentions and less than complete knowledge' (Hall 2005, p. 71).

Fertility declines with age. Indeed, a growing number of fertility clinics refuse to admit 45-year-old women for treatment because of their very slim chance of success (Gatrell 2008, p. 48). And yet, since 2000 the tabloid and women's magazine sector has routinely covered stories and presented photo shoots with a growing number of older celebrity mothers from the film, literary and political arenas. To name but a few, Marcia Cross (44) Cherie Blair (45), Mimi Rodgers (45), Marcia Gay Harden (45), Iman/Zara Mohamed Abdulmajid (45), Susan Sarandon (46), Arlene Phillips (47), Angela Bassett (47), Kelly Preston (47), Holly Hunter (47), Geena Davis (48), Wendy Wasserstein (48), Helen Fielding (48), Elizabeth Edwards (48) and (50) and Beverly D'Angelo and Laura Linney (49). Suzanne Schlosberg tells us that Marcia Cross is unique on the celebrity motherhood circuit for openly discussing the option of donor eggs. That said, 'even then she only says it's common knowledge how difficult it is for women in their forties to get pregnant with their own eggs. She always stops short of admitting to using them herself' (Schlosberg cited in Neporent 2011). Brooke Edge states that

> [c]elebrities rarely 'come out' as infertile or as having employed Assisted Reproductive Technologies. While Halle Berry expressed 'surprise' at being pregnant at forty-six, her publicist felt compelled to tell *Us Weekly* that the pregnancy was 'natural'. This celebrity revelation is notable for what it says about the need to foreclose speculation that this A-list celebrity, famed in part for her youthful beauty and body, required medical intervention to reproduce. ... These celebrity pregnancies risk skewing public opinion of fertility and age forecasts, as well as cultural expectations of fertility and femininity, often linked as one and the same. (Edge 2014, p. 873)

Doctors have been heard commentating that 'the probability of conceiving and delivering a child with a woman's own eggs at forty-five is virtually zero' (Sterling 2013, p. 99), and as such, older mothers who themselves struggled with fertility lambast 'nameless celebrities for not sharing the truth about infertility and for making mature motherhood seem so effortless' (cited in Sterling 2013, p. 67). Henry Bodkin informs us that '[m]iddle-aged celebrities who give birth without acknowledging they underwent IVF are fuelling "highly damaging" misconceptions about the chances of getting pregnant in later life' (Bodkin 2017). An analysis of interviews with celebrity mothers in over 400 issues of *Cosmopolitan*, *People Magazine* and *US Weekly* found that they 'routinely "glamourized" pregnancy at advanced ages and downplayed the impact of delaying trying for a baby' (Ibid.). We are told that the 'reluctance to show the challenges that often go along with trying to conceive and have children at older ages is a form of misinformation that can affect the beliefs and decisions of their audience for the worse' (Ibid.). Reproductive specialists speak of their disappointment at each new 40-something celebrity pregnancy story because they see that these

> miracle celebrity pregnancies give women ridiculous expectations. I'm yet to see a patient who had viable eggs in her mid-forties. Even with IVF, we've never had a pregnancy after age 45. … Every time it's announced that a celebrity like Laura Linney has had a baby around the age most women's bodies are preparing for menopause, it sparks a wave of publicity and a tsunami of hope and delusion among the wider population who believe they too can conceive at 49. (Freedman 2014)

Bloggers and clinicians alike can be heard stating 'wouldn't it be lovely if just one 40 or 50-something celebrity would come forward, be vulnerable and say "I am a mother via egg donation and I am proud"' (Global IVF cited in pvedadmin 2013). I am not of course suggesting that these women have used assisted reproductive technologies; indeed, most have not admitted reproductive help of any kind. I am merely pointing out that the exceptional nature of their celebrity birth stories might mislead a generation of women as to the reality of their own fertility options. My concern is simply that the successful celebrity infertility narrative masks statistical facts relating to fertility, pregnancy and new motherhood. And although there is a growing trend towards delaying motherhood, as women in their late thirties and beyond are seen to have children, it is worth noting the rise in what is understood as 'reproductive complacency' (Ibid.). After all, a 'survey of educated young professional women found that 90 per cent thought that they could wait until age 45 to start having their own biological children, even though next to none over 44 are able to, despite advanced technology' (Bonifazi cited in Feasey 2012, p. 132). After all, the 'live birth rate for women using assistive reproductive technology … with fresh, nondonor eggs or embryos is 15% at age 40, 5% at 43, and 2% after 43' (Ibid., p. 132).

The average age of a first-time mother in the UK is increasing (ONS 2013); more women than ever before are having children when they are in their late thirties, early forties and beyond (Ibid.); assisted reproductive technologies are advancing; the number of women taking advantage of such treatments is increasing and more celebrities than ever before are presenting their infertility stories in the women's tabloid and gossip sector.

Although one might suggest that the celebrity infertility confessional can offer hope through identification, by defying the privacy of infertility treatment, the partial account on offer here could perhaps lead to reproductive complacency, false hope or further reinforce the sense of stigma and failure that many infertile women yet to experience their own successful pregnancy are said to be undergoing (Whiteford and Gonzalez 1995), none of which are helpful to individuals or beneficial to society (Feasey 2014).

CONCLUSION

This chapter has introduced medical, ethical, financial and legal debates as they relate to assisted reproductive treatments and technologies in general, and IVF, egg and sperm donations and surrogacy arrangements in particular, drawing attention to the possibility of non-traditional family building for postmenopausal women and women born without wombs, as well as for cancer patients, single parents and gay and lesbian families. Although a myriad of factual programmes and television documentaries have introduced the topic of infertility, sub-fertility and age-related infertility, I would suggest that the ways in which many of these texts include celebrity confessionals and infertility profiles prior to a happy ending diminish important messages about age-related infertility and the current success rates of assisted reproductive technologies. My point here then is not so much that these programmes are not being honest with their audiences—indeed, they can be seen to offer 'facts that could enable women to make better choices' about their fertility (Sterling 2013, p. 70)—but rather that they weave an unrealistic optimism through their infertility findings. Factual programming tends to anchor optimism and hope-fuelled messages to the otherwise realistic depiction of age-related infertility, offering a limited, fractional or partial account of infecundity. Such optimism is perhaps unsurprising given that we live in a pronatal period where women are not only encouraged to take on a maternal role, but encouraged to do so in line with the ideology of appropriate motherhood.

One might suggest that the pronatal period maintains social inequality and the status quo because it speaks to 'patriarchy, male dominance and control over women's bodies' (Miller 2005, p. 50). In short, patriarchal society remains the chief beneficiary of the pronatal period in general and the 'good' mother myth in particular because it 'presents mothers as effective consumers whilst giving them the sole responsibility of childcare without financial recompense for their labours' (Feasey 2012, p. 6). And although the aforementioned celebrity-fronted television documentary was presented, directed and produced by women, the BBC is, at the time of writing, being challenged by MPs for 'failing to acknowledge the "structural problem that exists regarding equal pay" in the corporation' (BBC 2019). In short, the programme and medium are not removed from wider debates about sex, gender, discrimination and patriarchy that dominate the contemporary entertainment landscape.

However, in terms of the focus here, the concern is that these programmes are encouraging rather than countering infertility ignorance. And while a generation of women are said to be naive as to the reality of infertility in general and age-related infertility in particular (Madsen 2003; Mazza 2011; Shapiro 2012), so too, they remain ill informed about the commonality of miscarriage and pregnancy loss. And it is to the representation of these successful conceptions yet unsuccessful pregnancies that I now turn.

REFERENCES

Adams, Stephen. 2015. NHS Chief Warns Women Not to Wait Until 30 to Have Baby as Country Faces a Fertility Timebomb. *The Mail on Sunday.* Accessed April 12, 2019. http://www.dailymail.co.uk/news/article-3104023/NHS-chief-warns-women-not-wait-30-baby-country-faces-fertility-timebomb.html.

Aufderheide, Patricia. 2008. *Documentary Film: A Very Short Introduction.* Oxford: Oxford University Press.

BBC. 1985. 1985: Inquiry Over "Baby-for-Cash" Deal. *BBC Home:* On This Day. Accessed April 12, 2019. http://news.bbc.co.uk/onthisday/hi/dates/stories/january/4/newsid_2495000/2495857.stm.

———. 2019. Equal Pay: BBC Criticised by MPs Again. *BBC News.* Accessed April 12, 2019. https://www.bbc.co.uk/news/entertainment-arts-46965303.

BBC2. 2016. Alex Jones: Fertility & Me. *BBC TWO.* Accessed April 12, 2019. https://www.bbc.co.uk/programmes/b07wshm4.

Beattie, Keith. 2004. *Documentary Screens: Nonfiction Film and Television.* London: Palgrave Macmillan.

Blyth, Eric. 2004. The United Kingdom: Evolution of a Statutory Regulatory Approach. In *Third Party Assisted Conception across Cultures: Social, Legal and Ethical Perspectives*, ed. Eric Blyth and Ruth Landau, 226–245. London: Jessica Kingsley Publishers.

Blyth, Eric, and Jean Benward. 2004. The United States of America: Regulation, Technology and the Marketplace. In *Third Party Assisted Conception across Cultures: Social, Legal and Ethical Perspectives*, ed. Eric Blyth and Ruth Landau, 246–265. London: Jessica Kingsley Publishers.

Blyth, Eric, and Ruth Landau. 2004. Introduction. In *Third Party Assisted Conception Across Cultures: Social, Legal and Ethical Perspectives*, ed. Eric Blyth and Ruth Landau, 7–20. London: Jessica Kingsley Publishers.

Bodkin, Henry. 2017. Older Celebrities Who Deny IVF Treatment are Fuelling Misconceptions About Conceiving in Later Life, Doctors Warn. *The Telegraph*. Accessed April 12, 2019. https://www.telegraph.co.uk/news/2017/10/30/older-celebrities-deny-ivf-treatment-fuelling-misconceptions/.

Bray, Catherine. 2016. Film Review: Future Baby. *Variety*. Accessed April 12, 2019. http://variety.com/2016/film/reviews/future-baby-review-1201771150/.

British Fertility Society. 1999. Recommendations for Good Practice—Welfare of the Child: British Fertility Society 1999. *Human Fertility* 2 (2): 85. Accessed April 12, 2019. http://www.tandfonline.com/doi/abs/10.1080/14647279 92000198401?journalCode=ihuf20.

Campbell, Angela. 2013. *Sister Wives, Surrogates and Sex Workers: Outlaws by Choice?* London: Routledge.

Celeb News. 2013. Why Forty Really is the New Thirty. *Daily Mail*. Accessed April 12, 2019. https://www.iol.co.za/entertainment/celebrity-news/why-forty-really-is-the-new-thirty-1498868#.UzAgd40nS70.%20(March%20 24%202014).

Center for Human Reproduction. 2018. For Egg Donors FAQ: How Much will I Get Paid to Donate My Eggs. *Center for Human Reproduction*. Accessed April 12, 2019. https://www.centerforhumanreprod.com/egg-donation/donors/faqs.

Connell, Claudia. 2009. I'm Beautiful, Clever, and I'll Sell You My Eggs for £12,000. *Daily Mail*. Accessed April 12, 2019. http://www.dailymail.co.uk/femail/article-1206660/Im-beautiful-clever-Ill-sell-eggs-12-000.html.

Create Fertility. 2019. Waiting Lists for IVF Treatment. *Create Fertility*. Accessed April 12, 2019. https://www.createfertility.co.uk/blog/waiting-lists-for-ivf-treatment.

Davenport, Dawn. 2017. So You're Infertile, Why Not Just Adopt? *Creating a Family*. Accessed April 12, 2019. https://creatingafamily.org/infertility-category/why-not-just-adopt/.

Davies, Iwan. 1985. Contracts to Bear Children. *Journal of Medical Ethics* 11: 61–65. Accessed April 12, 2019. https://www.ncbi.nlm.nih.gov/pmc/articles/PMC1375145/pdf/jmedeth00253-0007.pdf.

Demory, Pamela, and Christopher Pullen. 2013. Introduction. In *Queer Love in Film and Television: Critical Essays*, ed. Pamela Demory and Christopher Pullen, 1–12. London: Palgrave Macmillan.

Department of Health and Social Care. 2010. The Human Fertilisation and Embryology (Parental Orders) Regulations 2010: Impact Assessment. *GOV. UK*. Accessed April 12, 2019. https://www.gov.uk/government/publications/the-human-fertilisation-and-embryology-parental-orders-regulations-2010-impact-assessment.

Di Donato, Jill. 2016. Encouraging Words from 13 Celebrities Who had Miscarriages. *Romper.* Accessed April 12, 2019. https://www.romper.com/p/encouraging-words-from-13-celebrities-who-had-miscarriages-9718.

Donnelly, Laura. 2017. Fertility Tourism being Driven by Sweeping NHS IVF Cutbacks. *The Telegraph.* Accessed April 12, 2019. https://www.telegraph.co.uk/news/2017/07/02/fertility-tourism-fuelled-sweeping-nhs-ivf-cutbacks/.

Doward, Jamie. 2016. Childless UK Couples Forced Abroad to Find Surrogates: Lack of Clarity in UK Laws Causes Anguish for Prospective Parents. *The Observer.* Accessed April 12, 2019. https://www.theguardian.com/lifeandstyle/2016/feb/20/childless-uk-couples-forced-abroad-surrogates.

Dugan, Emily. 2014. Revealed: Surrogate Births Hit Record High as Couples Flock Abroad. *Independent.* Accessed April 12, 2019. http://www.independent.co.uk/news/uk/home-news/revealed-surrogate-births-hit-record-high-as-couples-flock-abroad-9162834.html.

Edge, Brooke. 2014. Infertility On E!: Assisted Reproductive Technologies and Reality Television. *Feminist Media Studies* 14 (5): 873–876.

———. 2015. Barren or Bountiful? Analysis of Cultural Values in Popular Media Representations of Infertility. PhD diss., University of Colorado. Accessed April 12, 2019. https://scholar.colorado.edu/jour_gradetds/25/.

Elgot, Jessica. 2015. UK Sperm Bank has Just Nine Registered Donors, Boss Reveals. *The Guardian.* Accessed April 12, 2019. https://www.theguardian.com/science/2015/aug/31/britains-national-sperm-bank-wants-men-to-prove-their-manhood.

Families Through Surrogacy. 2019. Surrogacy by Country. *Families Through Surrogacy.* Accessed April 20, 2019. https://www.familiesthrusurrogacy.com/surrogacy-by-country/.

Feasey, Rebecca. 2012. *From Happy Homemaker to Desperate Housewives: Motherhood and Popular Television.* London: Anthem.

———. 2014. From Heartache to Happiness: The Codes, Conventions and Clichés of the 40-something Celebrity Infertility Story. *MaMSIE.* Accessed April 12, 2019. http://mamsie.org/2014/11/10/from-heartache-to-happiness-the-codes-conventions-and-cliches-of-the-40-something-celebrity-infertility-story/.

———. 2016. *Mothers on Mothers: Maternal Readings of Popular Television.* Oxford: Peter Lang.

Fertility Treatment Abroad. 2018. International Organisations Relevant to Infertility Treatment. *Fertility Treatment Abroad.* Accessed April 12, 2019. http://fertility.treatmentabroad.com/about-infertility/international-organisations.

Fixmer-Oraiz, Natalie. 2014. (In)Conceivable: Risky Reproduction and the Rhetorical Labor of Octomom. *Communication and Critical/Cultural Studies* 11 (3): 231–249.

Franklin, Sarah. 1990. Deconstructing Desperateness: The Social Construction of Infertility in Popular Representations of New Reproductive Technologies. In *The New Reproductive Technologies*, ed. Maureen McNeilm, Ian Varcoe, and Steven Yearly, 200–229. London: Palgrave Macmillan.

———. 2013. *Biological Relatives: IVF, Stem Cells, and the Future of Kinship*. Durham: Duke University Press.

Freedman, Mia. 2014. This Celebrity Just Gave Birth at 49, But Don't Assume You Can Too. *HuffPost*. Accessed April 12, 2019. http://www.huffingtonpost.co.uk/mia-freedman/laura-linney-baby_b_4635390.html.

Freeman, Michael. 1999. Does Surrogacy Have a Future after Brazier? *Medical Law Review*. 7 (1): 1–20.

Gamble, Natalie. 2014. History of UK Surrogacy Law. *nga law*. Accessed April 12, 2019. http://www.nataliegambleassociates.co.uk/knowledge-centre/history-of-uk-surrogacy-law.

Gander, Kashmira. 2017. UK's First Surrogate Mother on Carrying Someone Else's Baby and How the Law Must Change. *The Independent*. Accessed April 12, 2019. http://www.independent.co.uk/life-style/health-and-families/uk-first-surrogate-mother-kim-cotton-carry-someone-else-baby-law-change-a7645831.html.

Gatrell, Caroline. 2008. *Embodying Women's Work*. Maidenhead: Open University Press.

Greil, Arthur, and Julia McQuillan. 2004. Help-seeking Patterns among Subfecund Women. *Journal of Reproductive and Infant Psychology* 22 (4): 305–319.

Griessner, Lanay. 2016. Film Review: Future Baby. *BioNews*. Accessed April 12, 2019. http://www.bionews.org.uk/page_646604.asp.

Haase, Jean. 2004. Canada: The Long Road to Regulation. In *Third Party Assisted Conception Across Cultures: Social, Legal and Ethical Perspectives*, ed. Eric Blyth and Ruth Landau, 55–72. London: Jessica Kingsley Publishers.

Haberman, Clyde. 2014. Baby M and the Question of Surrogate Motherhood. *The New York Times*. Accessed April 12, 2019. https://www.nytimes.com/2014/03/24/us/baby-m-and-the-question-of-surrogate-motherhood.htm.

Hall, Stephen. 2005. The Good Egg. In *Cells: An Anthology of Current Thought*, ed. Jillian Lokere, 46–72. New York: Rosen Central.

Hallett, Alicia. 2006. Plum Magazine. *Alicia Hallett Design*. Accessed April 12, 2019. http://hallettdesign.com/portfolio/plum-magazine/.

Hammarberg, Karin. 2014. If IVF Success is Judged on the Number of Live Births, the Figures Don't Look so Good. *The Conversation*. Accessed April 12, 2019. http://theconversation.com/if-ivf-success-is-judged-on-the-number-of-live-births-the-figures-dont-look-so-good-29412.

Hammarberg, Karin, Jill Astbury, and Baker H.W. Gordon. 2001. Women's Experience of IVF: A Follow-up Study. *Human Reproduction* 16 (2): 374–383.

Hammarberg, Karin, and V.E. Clarke. 2005. Reasons for Delaying Childbearing—A Survey of Women Aged Over 35 Years Seeking Assisted Reproductive Technology. *Australian Family Physician* 34 (3): 187–188.

Hanson, Clare. 2004. *A Cultural History of Pregnancy: Pregnancy, Medicine and Culture (1750–2000)*. New York: Palgrave Macmillan.

HFEA. 1990. Human Fertilisation and Embryology Act 1990. *Legislation.gov.uk*. http://www.legislation.gov.uk/ukpga/1990/37/contents.

———. 2017/2020. Our Strategy 2017–2010. *Human Fertilisation and Embryology Authority*. Accessed April 12, 2019. https://ifqlive.blob.core.windows.net/umbraco-website/1346/hfea_strategy-2017_aw.pdf.

———. 2018a. Applying for a Clinic Licence. *Human Fertilisation and Embryology Authority*. Accessed April 12, 2019. https://www.hfea.gov.uk/about-us/applying-for-a-clinic-licence/.

———. 2018b. Donor Conceived People and their Parents. *Human Fertilisation and Embryology Authority*. Accessed April 12, 2019. https://www.hfea.gov.uk/donation/donor-conceived-people-and-their-parents/.

———. 2018c. Fertility Treatment Abroad. *Human Fertilisation and Embryology Authority*. Accessed April 12, 2019. https://www.hfea.gov.uk/treatments/explore-all-treatments/fertility-treatment-abroad/.

———. 2018d. All UK Clinics: Your Search Results. *Human Fertilisation and Embryology Authority*. Accessed April 12, 2019. https://www.hfea.gov.uk/choose-a-clinic/clinic-search/results/?distance=25.

———. 2018e. Donating Your Eggs. *Human Fertilisation and Embryology Authority*. Accessed April 12, 2019. https://www.hfea.gov.uk/donation/donors/donating-your-eggs/.

———. 2018f. Code of Practice: Welfare of the Child. *Human Fertilisation and Embryology Authority*. Accessed April 12, 2019. https://www.hfea.gov.uk/code-of-practice/8.

———. 2019a. The State of the Fertility Sector 2017–18. *Human Fertilisation and Embryology Authority*. Accessed April 12, 2019. https://www.hfea.gov.uk/media/2716/the-state-of-the-fertility-sector-2017-2018-final-accessibility-checked.pdf.

Hill, M.A. 2018. Assisted Reproductive Technology: 18 Ways to Make a Baby. *UNSW Embryology*. Accessed April 12, 2019. https://embryology.med.unsw.edu.au/embryology/index.php/Assisted_Reproductive_Technology#Some_Recent_Findings.

Holder, Angela. 1990. Surrogate Motherhood and the Best Interests of the Children. In *Surrogate Motherhood: Politics and Privacy*, ed. Lawrence Gostin, 77–87. Bloomington: Indiana University Press.

Horsey, Kirsty, Natalie Smith, Sarah Norcross, Louisa Ghevaert, and Sarah Jones. 2015. Surrogacy in the UK: Myth Busting and Reform. Report of the Surrogacy UK Working Group on Surrogacy Law Reform. Accessed April 12, 2019.

https://kar.kent.ac.uk/59740/1/Surrogacy%20in%20the%20UK%20 Report%20FINAL.pdf.

Hurley, Richard, ed. 2013. Are New Technologies in Infertility Treatment Always Good News? *BMJ* 347: 1–2.

Kahana, Jonathan, ed. 2016. *The Documentary Film Reader: History, Theory, Criticism.* Oxford: Oxford University Press.

Keough, Peter. 2017. Gambling with Lives in *Vegas Baby. The Boston Globe.* Accessed April 12, 2019. https://www.bostonglobe.com/arts/movies/2017/ 06/22/gambling-with-lives-vegas-baby/8i5anJlgvHbXo2nyGkHRuJ/ story.html.

Kerrigan, Susan, and Phillip McIntyre. 2010. The Creative Treatment of Actuality: Rationalizing and Reconceptualizing the Notion of Creativity for Documentary Practice. *Journal of Media Practice* 11 (2): 111–130.

Kramer, Wendy and Kramer, Ryan. 2018. Home. *The Donor Sibling Registry.* Accessed April 12, 2019. https://www.donorsiblingregistry.com.

Lacobucci, Gareth. 2016. GP Appointments should be 15 Minutes Long, Says BMA. *BMJ* 354 (8071): 4709.

Lahl, Jennifer. 2017. Surrogacy, *The Handmaid's Tale,* and Reproductive Ethics: Egg Donation, Sperm Donation and Surrogacy. *Issues in Law & Medicine* 32 (2): 241–243.

Lampi, Elina. 2008. What do Friends and the Media Tell Us? How Different Information Channels Affect Women's Risk Perceptions of Age-related Infertility. Working Papers in Economics, School of Business, Economic and Law, University of Gothenburg, 246, 1–24.

Le Vay, Lulu. 2019. *Surrogacy and the Reproduction of Normative Family on TV.* London: Palgrave Macmillan.

Lea, Laura. 2016. UK's National Sperm Bank Stops Recruiting Donors. *BBC News.* Accessed April 12, 2019. http://www.bbc.co.uk/news/uk-37786576.

Letherby, Gayle. 1999. Other Than Mother and Mothers as Others: The Experience of Motherhood and Non-Motherhood in Relation to Infertility and Involuntary Childlessness. *Women's Studies International Forum* 22 (3): 359–372.

Madsen, Charlotte. 2014a. Infertility on Film and Television—Part 1: The Movies. *The Road to Baby Madsen: Our IVF Journey.* Accessed April 12, 2019. http:// roadtobabymadsen.blogspot.com/2014/06/infertility-in-movies-and-tele- vision.html.

———. 2014b. Infertility on Film and Television—Part 2: Rules, Housewives and Friends. *The Road to Baby Madsen: Our IVF Journey.* Accessed April 12, 2019. http://roadtobabymadsen.blogspot.com/2014/06/infertility-on-film-and- television-part.html.

Madsen, Pamela. 2003. Just the Facts, Ma'am: Coming Clean about Fertility. *Fertility and Sterility* 80 (4): 27–29.

Magee, Anna. 2015. Why are so Many British Women Travelling Abroad for Fertility Treatment? *The Telegraph*. Accessed April 12, 2019. http://www.telegraph.co.uk/women/mother-tongue/11482483/Fertility-treatment-Why-British-women-are-travelling-abroad.html.

Maher, Jennifer. 2014. Something Else Besides a Father. *Feminist Media Studies* 14 (5): 853–867.

Mamo, Laura. 2013. Queering the Fertility Clinic. *Journal of Medical Humanities* 34 (2): 227–239.

Martin, Lauren. 2010. Anticipating Infertility: Egg Freezing, Genetic Preservation, and Risk. *Gender & Society* 24 (4): 526–545.

———. 2015. *Reproductive Tourism in the United States: Creating Family in the Mother Country*. London: Routledge.

Mazza, Danielle. 2011. *Women's Health in General Practice*. 2nd ed. Chatswood: Churchill Livingstone.

Miller, Tina. 2005. *Making Sense of Motherhood: A Narrative Approach*. Cambridge: Cambridge University Press.

Morton, Natalie, and Sarah Bell. 2016. I Fathered 800 Children, Claims Sperm Donor. *BBC News*. Health. Accessed April 12, 2019. http://www.bbc.co.uk/news/health-35262535.

Neporent, Liz. 2011. Nicole Kidman Dishes on Fertility Woes. *ABC NEWS*. Accessed April 12, 2019. http://abcnews.go.com/Health/WomensHealth/nicole-kidman-talks-openly-infertility/story?id=12968754.

NHS. 2018a. Availability: IVF. *NHS*. Accessed April 12, 2019. https://www.nhs.uk/conditions/ivf/availability/.

———. 2018b. LGBT Paths to Parenthood. *NHS*. Accessed April 12, 2019. https://www.nhs.uk/Livewell/LGBhealth/Pages/Havingchildren.aspx.

———. 2018c. Treatment: Infertility. *NHS*. Accessed April 12, 2019. https://www.nhs.uk/conditions/infertility/treatment/.

———. 2018d. Overview: Menopause. *NHS*. Accessed April 12, 2019. https://www.nhs.uk/conditions/menopause/.

———. 2018e. GP Appointments and Bookings. *NHS*. Accessed April 12, 2019. https://www.nhs.uk/using-the-nhs/nhs-services/gps/gp-appointments-and-bookings/.

Obama, Michelle. 2018. *Becoming*. London: Viking.

Ollove, Michael. 2015a. Lightly Regulated In Vitro Fertilization Yields Thousands of Babies Annually. *The Washington Post*. Accessed April 12, 2019. https://www.washingtonpost.com/national/health-science/lightly-regulated-in-vitro-fertilization-yields-thousands-of-babies-annually/2015/04/13/f1f3fa36-d8a2-11e4-8103-fa84725dbf9d_story.html?utm_term=.2952577087f4.

———. 2015b. States Not Eager to Regulate Fertility Industry. *The Pew Charitable Trusts*. Accessed April 12, 2019. http://www.pewtrusts.org/en/research-and-analysis/blogs/stateline/2015/3/18/states-not-eager-to-regulate-fertility-industry.

ONS. 2013. Live Births in England and Wales by Characteristics of Mother: Statistical Bulletin. *Office for National Statistics.* Accessed April 12, 2019. http://webarchive.nationalarchives.gov.uk/20160107145922/http://www.ons.gov.uk/ons/dcp171778_296157.pdf.

Parenting. 2018. 11 Best Pregnancy Magazines for New Moms. *Parenting: Healthy Babies.* Accessed April 12, 2019. https://parentinghealthybabies.com/best-pregnancy-magazines-for-new-moms/.

Peoplebabies. 2008. Pregnancy Magazines are Plentiful. *Peoplebabies.* Accessed April 12, 2019. http://celebritybabies.people.com/2008/01/23/pregnancy-magaz/.

Pritchard, Sarah. 2008. NHS Suffers Under the Strain of Multiple Births Resulting from Fertility Tourism. *BioNews.* Accessed April 12, 2019. https://www.bionews.org.uk/page_90812.

pvedadmin. 2013. Celebrity Infertility Secrets? *Parents Via Egg Donation.* Accessed April 12, 2019. https://blog.pved.org/2013/06/13/celebrity-infertility-secrets/.

Riggan, Kirsten. 2010. Regulation (or Lack Thereof) of Assisted Reproductive Technologies in the U.S. and Abroad. *Dignitas* 17: 1/2. Accessed April 12, 2019. https://cbhd.org/content/regulation-or-lack-thereof-assisted-reproductive-technologies-us-and-abroad.

Riley-Smith, Ben. 2018. I Felt Like I Had Failed: Michelle Obama Reveals She Had Miscarriage and Used IVF to Conceive Daughters. *The Telegraph.* Accessed April 12, 2019. https://www.telegraph.co.uk/news/2018/11/09/michelle-obama-had-miscarriage-used-ivf-conceive-girls/.

Ross, Sherry. 2018. *She-Ology: The Definitive Guide to Women's Intimate Health. Period.* Savio Republic.

Scott, Lee. 2018. *Infertility, The Media & Me.* Game.

Selby, Julie. 2015. *Infertility Insanity: When Sheer Hope (and Google) are the Only Options Left.* Canada: Influence Publishing.

Shalev, Shirley, and Dafna Lemish. 2012. Dynamic Infertility: The Contribution of News Coverage of Reproductive Technologies to Gender Politics. *Feminist Media Studies* 12 (3): 371–388.

Shapiro, Connie. 2012. Eventual Mons-to-be: Heads Up! *Hopefully Yours, Connie.* Accessed April 12, 2019. http://connieshapiro13.blogspot.com.

Skeggs, Beverley, Helen Wood, and Nancy Thumin. 2008. Oh Goodness, I am Watching 'Reality' Television: How Methods Make Class in Audience Research. *European Journal of Cultural Studies* 11 (1): 5–24.

SMC. 2018a. Thinking? Trying? Mothering? *Single Mothers by Choice.* Accessed April 12, 2019. https://www.singlemothersbychoice.org.

————. 2018b. Frequently Asked Questions. *Single Mothers by Choice*. Accessed April 12, 2019. https://www.singlemothersbychoice.org/about/faq/.

Smith, David. 2018. Michelle Obama Reveals Miscarriage and Condemns Reckless Trump in New Book. *The Guardian*. Accessed April 12, 2019. https://www.theguardian.com/us-news/2018/nov/09/michelle-obama-book-miscarriage-ivf-treatment-trump.

Sterling, Evelina. 2013. From No Hope to Fertile Dreams: Procreative Technologies, Popular Media, and the Culture of Infertility. PhD diss., Georgia State University. Accessed April 12, 2019. https://scholarworks.gsu.edu/cgi/viewcontent.cgi?article=1069&context=sociology_diss.

Striff, Erin. 2005. Infertile Me: The Public Performance of Fertility Treatments in Internet Weblogs. *Women & Performance: A Journal of Feminist Theory* 15 (2): 189–205.

Sturgis, India. 2019. Alex Jones: I was Back on TV an Hour after Doctors Told Me I'd Miscarried. Accessed April 23, 2019. https://www.telegraph.co.uk/women/life/alex-jones-back-tv-hour-doctors-told-miscarried/.

Surrogacy View. 2015. Surrogacy Laws. *Surrogacy View*: A Fertility Council Network Sie. Accessed April 12, 2019. http://www.surrogacyview.com/surrogacy-laws/.

Surrogate Parenting Services. 2014. Gestational Surrogacy or Traditional Surrogacy? That is the Question. *Surrogate Parenting Services*. Accessed April 12, 2019. http://surrogateparenting.com/gestational-surrogacy-traditional-surrogacy-question/.

Surugue, Léa. 2016. Nearly Half of Infertile Couples in the UK Don't Look for Medical Help. *International Business Times*. Accessed April 12, 2019. http://www.ibtimes.co.uk/infertility-half-british-people-diagnosed-do-not-seek-medical-help-1568339.

The Infertility Journey. 2016. 6.5 Million IVF Babies since Louise Brown. *The Infertility Journey*. Accessed April 12, 2019. https://www.theinfertilityjourney.com/single-post/2016/07/21/65-Million-IVF-Babies-Born-Worldwide-Since-Louise-Brown.

Throsby, Karen. 2004. *When IVF Fails: Feminism, Infertility and the Negotiation of Normality*. Basingstoke: Palgrave Macmillan.

Tomlins, Jacqueline. 2003. *The Infertility Handbook: A Guide to Making Babies*. Sydney: Allen & Unwin.

Tuft, Ben. 2015. UK Citizens are the Most Likely in Europe to go Abroad to Find a Surrogate Mother. *The Independent*. Accessed April 12, 2019. https://www.independent.co.uk/news/science/uk-citizens-are-the-likeliest-in-europe-to-go-abroad-to-find-a-surrogate-mother-10109448.html.

Van Balen, Frank, and Marcia Inhorn. 2002. Introduction: Interpreting Infertility: A View from the Social Sciences. In *Infertility Around the Globe: New Thinking* on *Childlessness, Gender and Reproductive Technologies*, ed. Marcia Inhorn and Frank Van Balen, 3–32. London: University of California Press.

Van de Wiel, Lucy. 2015. Frozen in Anticipation: Eggs for Later. *Women's Studies International Forum* 53: 119–128.

Wertman, Tonya. 2013. Infertility and the Media. *SheKnowsParenting*. Accessed April 12, 2019. http://www.sheknows.com/parenting/articles/991979/infertility-celebrities-and-the-media.

Whiteford, Linda, and Lois Gonzalez. 1995. Stigma: The Hidden Burden of Infertility. *Social Science and Medicine* 40 (1): 27–36.

Wild, Leah. 2001. Leah Wild: The Final IVF Diary Entry Sees the Twins Surrounded by People in White Coats. *The Guardian*. https://www.theguardian.com/lifeandstyle/2001/apr/18/familyandrelationships.features102.

Winston, Robert. 2018. Professor Robert Winston: Couple Being Misled Over Chances of IVF Success. *The Yorkshire Post*. Accessed April 12, 2019. https://www.yorkshirepost.co.uk/news/professor-robert-winston-couple-being-misled-over-chances-of-ivf-success-1-9246529.

CHAPTER 4

Pregnancy Loss: Shame and Silence over a Shared Experience

INTRODUCTION

Recent statistics tell us that one in four women in the UK 'will lose a baby during pregnancy and birth' and this is as true for women using assisted reproductive treatments and technologies as it is for those who conceive naturally (Tommy's 2018a). Furthermore, while one in 36 women will experience two miscarriages due to nothing more than chance (Campbell et al. 2004, p. 147), it is not possible to save the ectopic or molar pregnancies that affect approximately one in 100 and one in 600 conceptions respectively (Miscarriage Association 2018a). Moreover, one in every 225 births ends in a stillbirth, equivalent to 9 babies being stillborn every day in the UK (Tommy's 2019a; NHS 2018a), with the CDC foregrounding similar statistics for women in the US (CDC 2018a). With this in mind, this chapter will examine the ways in which miscarriage, missed miscarriages, miscarriage due to ectopic or molar pregnancy and stillbirth are presented within and beyond the social media environment. It will introduce Facebook postings, twitter announcements, YouTube vlogs and surrounding channels of popular news and media discourse, considering the ways in which such experiences can be used in order to educate, inform or offer camaraderie in relation to the sensitive subject of pregnancy loss.

While miscarriage is a very common experience, ectopic and molar pregnancies are less so, and although there are clear distinctions between the statistics and stages of these different experiences, I will follow the

© The Author(s) 2019
R. Feasey, *Infertility and Non-Traditional Family Building*,
https://doi.org/10.1007/978-3-030-17787-4_4

Miscarriage Association guidelines and use the term pregnancy loss 'to include miscarriage, ectopic and molar pregnancy' (Miscarriage Association 2018b). After all, '[e]motionally ... there is little difference between the experience of an ectopic pregnancy and a miscarriage—the disappointment and the sense of loss are similar' (Tomlins 2003, p. 144; Miscarriage Association 2017a). Each loss can, in turn, be devastating for women, partners and families alike (Collins et al. 2014, pp. 44–50).

THE LANGUAGE OF REPRODUCTIVE DISRUPTION: FROM NATURAL PREGNANCY LOSS TO SPONTANEOUS ABORTION

Through this chapter and the book as a whole, I am using the term pregnancy *loss*, but I am mindful of the frustration and anger that is associated with that notion. Writing a guest post for *The Hollywood Reporter*, the screen actress Kiele Sanchez persuasively and passionately argues:

> Lost implies I misplaced him. That I was careless. Maybe that's why we women feel such shame. We didn't *lose* them. They were ripped from our clutched hands. Minds numbed quiet by horror. Voices stuck in our throats. Rage with nowhere to go but inward. If anyone is lost it is me, wondering how this is my reality. Worrying about my weight. What is this sad, misshapen body? The hits don't stop. (Sanchez 2016, emphasis in original)

However, although I am mindful of the pain and problematics associated with this term, to speak of reproductive disruption is too broad because, as noted briefly in the introduction, it refers to a myriad of ways in which 'the standard linear narrative of conception, birth, and the progress of the next generation is interrupted' (Van Balen and Inhorn 2002, p. 4). Such disruptions include

> various sexually transmitted diseases ... births of children with congenital health problems and disabilities; lactational difficulties ... maternal deaths from pre- and postpartum complications; chronic, debilitating complications of childbirth ... unwanted pregnancies ... life-threatening reproductive diseases ... endocrinological disorders ... and premature menopause. (Ibid., p. 4)

While reproductive disruption is too broad a term, we cannot expect members of the public without clinical or medical expertise to negotiate the language of anembryonic yolk sacs, embryonic miscarriages or spontaneous abortion failure breakdown (Kolte et al. 2015, pp. 495–498). Although 'spontaneous abortion' can be used to describe the natural death of an embryo or foetus before it is able to survive independently (Petrucelli 2015b), the term abortion is more routinely used to refer to the elective ending of a pregnancy and, as such, it can be frustrating or painful when used in relation to the 'loss of a wanted pregnancy' (Danielsson 2018a). Thus, this work will continue to use the language of pregnancy loss because it is the term routinely used in both medical literature and first-person accounts of miscarriage (Roston et al. 2015). This is not to say that it does not bring its own upset or heartache, but it is the term commonly referred to throughout recent writing, writing I look to draw on here.

Moreover, concerns also exist over the term miscarriage because the word seems to put blame on the pregnant woman for her loss. The word is comprised of *mis*, meaning 'mistakenly, wrongly or badly', and *carriage*, meaning 'a means of conveyance'; and yet 'there is nothing within this healthy physiological event that would justify the prefix mis-. Rather, miscarriage is more often a healthy body recognizing a pregnancy that is incompatible with life' (Gorfinkel 2018). Another screen actress, this time, Melissa Rauch, tells us that the term miscarriage 'deserves to be ranked as one of the worst, most blame-inducing medical terms ever [because] it immediately conjures up an implication that it was the woman's fault, like she somehow mishandled the carrying of this baby' (Rauch 2017). In short, existing terminology 'falls short in offering more enlightened alternatives' (Gorfinkel 2018). In order to find an appropriate, sensitive and meaningful replacement, women's health practitioner Iris Gorfinkel suggests the term 'natural pregnancy loss' because it is said to 'reduce the blame implicit in the word miscarriage and help to engender a sense of empowerment and well-being' (Ibid.). However, this alternative merely shifts the focus from one problematic term, miscarriage, to another, loss.

STATISTICS, SILENCE AND ISOLATION

Statistics relating to pregnancy loss in general and miscarriage in particular are not hard to find; however, there is a tendency not to seek out those statistics unless you are one of those statistics. This is self-perpetuating because women who have themselves experienced miscarriage speak of loneliness and isolation as they themselves self-censor (Sifferlin 2015). We are reminded of the following:

The statistic says 1 in 4:
1 in 4 yet most of us who experience it still suffer in silence.
1 in 4 yet it's not something that is openly discussed.
1 in 4 of us go through it at least once yet when someone, in casual conversation, mentions that we should start thinking about expanding our family we don't divulge that we are struggling, or have suffered a loss. We smile and nod instead of talking about our experience, avoiding the pity, preferring to keep our vulnerability to ourselves. (Romero 2016)

With this 'conspiracy of silence' (Kohn and Moffitt 2000, p. 133) in mind, it is perhaps unsurprising to find that over half of all respondents in a recent survey relating to miscarriage and its causes 'believed that miscarriage occurred in 5% or less of all pregnancies' (Bardos et al. 2015). What is striking here then is the 'significant information gap between the medical diagnosis of miscarriage and the patient's personal experience' (Ibid.). Gorfinkel tells us that after nearly three decades 'of practising women's health' she is 'continually taken aback by ongoing erroneous beliefs surrounding miscarriage' (Gorfinkel 2018) because even though we have access to a wealth of health and medical information, those who have experienced pregnancy loss tend to assume that they themselves are to blame. A recent survey

found that respondents most commonly cited a stressful event (76 per cent), long-standing stress (74 per cent) and lifting a heavy object (64 per cent) as causes for miscarriage. The study ... showed that respondents inaccurately thought the following could [also cause] miscarriage: a sexually transmitted disease (41 per cent), an abortion (31 per cent) or use of implanted long-term birth control (28 per cent). Nearly 23 per cent of respondents erroneously believed a miscarriage could be caused solely by the woman not wanting the pregnancy. (Gorfinkel 2018)

Contemporary society remains ill-informed about the commonality of pregnancy loss, leaving many women who experience it feeling scared, ashamed, guilty or lonely. One woman highlights the disappointment, frustration and indignation felt by many at the shroud of secrecy that continues to surround miscarriage when she posted on Facebook that '[I] felt alone until I realized there is this big, secret miscarriage club—one that nobody wants to be a member of—and when I realized it existed, I felt angry that no one told me they had active membership' (anon cited in Hobson 2015). Another club member commented that she 'didn't realise that these things happened to healthy women who were ready for a family' and that how 'hearing about it more in the media could have prepared [her] or made [her] aware of just how common it was' (Emma cited in

Holman 2015). To hear women ask for greater media awareness is important here, and with this in mind, this chapter will look at the ways in which online platforms from national health resources to social networking sites encourage women to share their stories and/or inform them about the physical and emotional reality of loss.

The point here then is that while health resources such as the NHS website do well to document important symptoms, causes and diagnoses, there is little in the way of emotional support past helpful contact details. However, at the other extreme, social media appears peppered with personal narratives relating to miscarriage that might be said to counter loneliness and isolation for women experiencing pregnancy loss, but they do little to inform or educate about the wider medical environment in which women experience that loss. Access to both areas is crucial, but while the former only tends to be searched for once a pregnancy loss, or a fear of a diagnosis, is experienced, the latter can be easily dismissed as a small part of an otherwise more upbeat, entertaining or escapist online presence. While medical advice about pregnancy loss lacks emotional connection, personal accounts rarely educate us, and women are missing out on vital medical and/or emotional support as a result.

INFORMATION ABOUT PREGNANCY LOSS: MISCARRIAGE, FAILED PREGNANCY AND STILLBIRTH

In the UK miscarriage is the term used to describe the loss of a pregnancy during the first 23 weeks (NHS 2018b), while in the US the term is routinely defined as the loss of a baby before the 20th week of pregnancy (CDC 2018b). The key indicators are vaginal bleeding, cramping and pain in the lower abdomen and a discharge of tissue. Although miscarriages are common in the first three months of pregnancy with 'around one in five confirmed pregnancies end[ing] this way' (NHS 2017), recurrent miscarriages, ectopic pregnancies, molar pregnancies, missed miscarriages and stillbirths are less so. With this in mind, I will introduce the causes and diagnoses of pregnancy loss before outlining advice concerning prevention as it is outlined by the freely available NHS Choices website. The world-leading website boasts 20,000 regularly updated articles and 43 million visits per month, encouraging 'patients and the public to take control of their health' (NHS 2014, 2015a). In the same way that the NHS provides information relating to symptoms, causes, diagnosis and prevention, so too the American Pregnancy Association gives details relating to the signs, symptoms, treatment and prevention of miscarriage (American Pregnancy Association 2018). The NHS website is, like the NHS itself, free at the point of use for all UK residents because it is funded from general taxation and National Insurance contributions; likewise, its non-profit American counterpart includes the details of obstetric and gynaecologic resources as part of its mission to promote reproductive and pregnancy wellness through education, support, advocacy and community awareness.

There are a myriad of reasons as to why a miscarriage happens during pregnancy, but in the majority of cases the exact cause is unidentified. We are told very clearly and in no uncertain terms that 'the majority aren't caused by anything the mother has done'; rather, most first trimester (between 1 and 12 weeks) 'miscarriages are caused by abnormal chromosomes in the baby' (NHS 2018b). Irrespective of the thoughts or actions of the pregnant woman, a baby that has too many or not enough chromosomes can't and won't develop properly. Indeed, health providers look to debunk common misconceptions about miscarriage when they tell us that a failed pregnancy is not linked to a woman's emotional state, shock, exercise, sex, air travel, spicy food or work environment (NHS 2018c). The Miscarriage Association goes as far as stating, in bold, on their homepage, that **'it's important to know that your miscarriage is very unlikely to have happened because of anything you did or didn't do'** (Miscarriage Association 2018c, emphasis in original), and then reiterates this point under their Frequently Asked Questions, with further emphasis. We are reminded that it is 'usually difficult to know why any pregnancy loss happens, though it's *highly* unlikely to be because of anything you did or didn't do' (Miscarriage Association 2018d, emphasis in original).

We are reminded that '[a]lmost all miscarriages happen in the first trimester, and many in the first few weeks after conception' and that '[e]arly miscarriage often occurs because there is something wrong with the embryo; it is no more than nature's way of screening out embryos that are not going to produce healthy babies' (Tomlins 2003, p. 139). The NHS states that 'in women under 30, 1 in 10 pregnancies will end in miscarriage, in women aged 35–39, up to 2 in 10 pregnancies will end in miscarriage; in women over 45, more than half of all pregnancies will end in miscarriage' (NHS Direct Wales 2017a, NHS 2018c). However, although early miscarriages are common, there are a number of things that are known to increase the risk, including obesity, smoking and drug use during pregnancy, drinking more than 200 mg of caffeine a day, drinking more than two units of alcohol a week and age of the pregnant woman (Ibid.).

Moreover, if a miscarriage occurs between 14 and 26 weeks, during what is understood as the second trimester of pregnancy, it is 'sometimes the result of an underlying [chronic] health condition in the mother' such as 'diabetes ... severe high blood pressure; lupus; kidney disease; an overactive thyroid gland or an underactive thyroid gland' (NHS Direct Wales 2017a; NHS 2018c). A number of infections such as 'rubella, cytomegalovirus, bacterial vaginosis, HIV, chlamydia, gonorrhoea, syphilis [and] malaria' (Ibid.) may also increase a woman's risk of miscarriage (Ibid.). In its exhaustive overview, the NHS also mentions the role that food poisoning, specific medications (misoprostol, retinoids, methotrexate and nonsteroidal anti-inflammatory drugs), problems and abnormalities with the womb (fibroids and abnormal shaping), a weakened cervix (cervical incompetence) and polycystic ovary syndrome (where the ovaries are larger than normal, which can lower the production of eggs) can play in pregnancy loss (Ibid.).

If a woman suspects that she is miscarrying then she will be immediately referred to either an early pregnancy unit at a local hospital or a maternity ward, depending on the stage of pregnancy. A transvaginal ultrasound will confirm if the woman is experiencing a miscarriage, and if so, if it is a complete or incomplete (also known as a delayed) miscarriage depending on whether the '*products of conception*' (Tomlins 2003, p. 142, emphasis in original) remain in the womb. If the miscarriage is delayed then a woman will have to discuss options for end-of-pregnancy management with medical staff. In most miscarriages 'the pregnancy tissue will pass out naturally in a week or two' (NHS 2018d), but if pregnancy tissue remains in the womb, a woman will be asked to choose between expectant (wait for the tissue to pass naturally out of your womb), medical (take medication that causes the tissue to pass out of your womb) or surgical (have the tissue surgically removed) management (Ibid.). These end-of-pregnancy techniques are medically safe yet emotionally difficult, especially when asked to take a home pregnancy test, just to make sure that you are no longer carrying pregnancy tissue (Ibid.). However, in those situations where a miscarriage cannot be confirmed using an ultrasound, perhaps due to the very early stages of a pregnancy, a woman may be 'offered blood tests to measure hormones associated with pregnancy' (NHS 2018e) and then advised to have a further ultrasound or pregnancy test a week later (Ibid.).

Most miscarriages are a 'one-off event' (NHS 2018b); however, if a woman has experienced recurrent miscarriages then 'further tests are often used to check for any underlying causes' (NHS 2018e). Transvaginal and 3D ultrasounds scans look at the structure of the womb, lower abdomen and pelvis; blood tests check for 'high levels of the antiphospholipid (aPL) antibody and lupus anticoagulant', which are 'known to increase the chance of blood clots and alter the way the placenta attaches' (Ibid.); while karyotyping tests the foetus for abnormalities in the chromosomes. Genetic problems can be referred to a clinical geneticist who will 'explain your chances of a successful pregnancy in the future and whether there are any fertility treatments' that might be appropriate (NHS 2018e). In broad terms, the known causes are anatomical, chromosomal, hormonal and related to immune disorders. Although most miscarriages are isolated events, 'the risk of another loss is around 20 percent after one previous miscarriage, 28 percent after two previous miscarriages, and 35 percent after three previous miscarriages' (Tommy's 2019b; Tommy's 2018b; Mayo Clinic 2018).

While those experiencing miscarriage symptoms seek advice and support from medical staff, for some women, it is only when they attend antenatal appointments that they realise that they have experienced a miscarriage. We are told that a missed, delayed or silent miscarriage can be diagnosed during a routine scan, revealing that the baby has no heartbeat or that the baby is too small for the date of the pregnancy. Pregnancy hormones remain high with a missed miscarriage so a woman 'may have had no idea that anything was wrong, still feel pregnant and have a positive pregnancy test' (Miscarriage Association 2018d). The missed miscarriage is less common than a routine miscarriage, but the end-of-pregnancy management options are the same. Like the missed miscarriage, ectopic and molar pregnancies do not always produce symptoms, so they are routinely picked up during routine ultrasound scans during the first trimester.

We are reminded that it is not possible to save an ectopic pregnancy, so an ectopic pregnancy is understood as a miscarriage due to an ectopic pregnancy which affects around one out of 90 pregnancies in the UK each year (NHS 2018f), or according to the Miscarriage Association, one in 100 conceptions respectively (Miscarriage Association 2018a). This figure rises to one in 50 conceptions in the US (Danielsson 2018b). These pregnancies are 'potentially serious' because of the risks associated with 'internal bleeding' (NHS 2018g) and treatment options are 'expectant management (you're carefully monitored), medication (an injection of a powerful medicine called methotrexate is used to stop the pregnancy growing) or ... keyhole surgery (to remove the fertilised egg, usually along with the affected fallopian tube)' (NHS 2018f). As with miscarriage and missed miscarriages, there are no clear or definitive reasons why a woman experiences an ectopic pregnancy. Indeed, we are informed that 'many women who have an ectopic pregnancy have no known risk factors and no obvious cause' (Miscarriage Association 2018e). That said, previous ectopic pregnancies, pelvic inflammatory disease, earlier surgery on the fallopian tubes, fertility treatments whereby medications stimulate ovulation, becoming pregnant while wearing an intrauterine device, smoking and age have all been associated with an increased risk of a miscarriage due to an ectopic pregnancy (NHS 2018f).

While the UK records 250,000 cases of miscarriage each year, it also experiences 11,000 ectopic pregnancies and 1500 molar pregnancies. A molar pregnancy is where a 'lump of abnormal cells grows in the womb instead of a healthy foetus' (Ibid.). The growth is known as a 'hydatidiform mole' and can be either 'a complete mole, where there's a mass of abnormal cells in the womb and no foetus develops' or 'a partial mole, where an abnormal foetus starts to form, but it can't survive or develop into a baby' (NHS 2018h). We are told that a molar pregnancy 'happens if the amount of genetic material in a fertilised egg isn't right—for example, if an egg containing no genetic information is fertilised by a sperm, or a normal egg is fertilised by two sperm' (Ibid.). And like with miscarriage and miscarriage due to ectopic pregnancy, there is no single reason why this happens. We are reminded that a molar pregnancy is 'a chance event' (Miscarriage Association 2018f) and that even though '[d]octors understand **how** it happens ... there are no obvious underlying causes or risk factor ... [i]t just happens' (Miscarriage Association 2018f, emphasis in original). However, the risk of a molar pregnancy is increased according to the following:

> Age (teenage women and women over 45), Ethnicity (twice as common in women of Asian origin) [and] Previous molar pregnancy (if you've had a molar pregnancy before, your chance of having another one is about 1 in 80, compared with 1 in 600 for women who haven't had one before. If you've had two or more molar pregnancies, your risk of having another is around 1 in 5). (NHS 2018h)

Expectant management or letting the body take its natural course is not an end-of-pregnancy option for a molar pregnancy; rather, the main treatments are 'suction removal (the abnormal cells are sucked out using a thin tube passed into your womb through your vagina), medication (if the growth is too large to be sucked out, you may be given medication to make it pass out of your vagina) or surgery to remove the womb (this may be an option if you don't want to have any more children in the future)' (Ibid.).

Legal definitions draw clear distinctions between miscarriage, stillbirth and neonatal death, and although these can differ by country, in the UK we are informed that

> miscarriage is when a baby (or fetus or embryo) dies in the uterus during pregnancy. In the UK, that definition applies to pregnancies up to 23 weeks and 6 days, and any loss from 24 weeks is called a stillbirth. If the baby is born alive, even before 24 weeks, and lives even for a matter of minutes, that is considered a live birth and a neonatal death. (Miscarriage Association 2018c)

While there are more than 3000 stillbirths every year in the UK, a further 1515 babies died during the first seven days after birth in 2016, 'resulting in a perinatal mortality rate of 6.6 deaths per 1000 total births' (ONS 2018). One in every 225 births ends in a stillbirth and one in approximately every 400 births ends in neonatal death (Tommy's 2019a; NHS 2018a). We find that

> half of all stillbirths are linked to placental complications ... 10% of stillborn babies have some kind of birth defect that contributed to their death [and a] small percentage of stillbirths are caused by problems with the mother's health, for example pre-eclampsia, or other problems, including cord accidents and infections. (NHS Direct Wales 2017b)

Moreover, we are told that

> there are also a number of things that may increase your risk of having a stillborn baby, including: having twins or a multiple pregnancy, having a baby who doesn't reach his or her growth potential in the womb, being over 35 years of age, smoking, drinking alcohol or misusing drugs while pregnant, having a body mass index over 30 [and] having a pre-existing physical health condition such as epilepsy. (NHS 2018i)

That said, like miscarriages, it is not always possible to find a cause for stillbirths or neonatal deaths. Indeed, a 'large proportion of stillbirths seem to happen in otherwise healthy babies' (NHS Direct Wales 2017b). Furthermore, in the same way that women who have experienced recurrent miscarriages are at a higher risk of a future miscarriage, women who have had a previous stillbirth are more likely to have another when compared to the general population (NHS 2015b).

The key difference between a miscarriage and a stillbirth is in the end-of-pregnancy management. Even though they may, on occasion, be only days or hours apart, miscarriage is concerned with pregnancy tissue passing out of the womb, while the mother of a stillborn baby experiences labour, has the opportunity to hold her newborn, collect mementos, makes decisions related to genetic testing and formally register the birth (NHS 2018j).

If a woman suspects that she has experienced a stillbirth, an ultrasound scan will check for a heartbeat, and if no heartbeat is present, choices exist for how to proceed, be it waiting for labour to begin naturally or inducing labour with medication. Only if the mother's health is at immediate risk would a stillborn baby be delivered by caesarean section (NHS 2018k).

Miscarriage, missed miscarriage, miscarriage due to ectopic or molar pregnancies and stillbirth make varying physical demands on the female body, but it can be difficult to make sense of their impact on future pregnancy outcomes. The NHS tells us that 'for *most* women, a miscarriage is a one-off event and they go on to have a successful pregnancy in the future' (NHS 2018b, emphasis added), going further to reassure readers that '*most* women are able to have a healthy pregnancy after a miscarriage, even in cases of recurrent miscarriages' (NHS 2018b, emphasis added). And by healthy pregnancy there is an assumption here of a successful pregnancy outcome. However, when we look at the reassurances related to miscarriage due to ectopic and molar pregnancies, the wording is a little different. Here we are told that women will be successful in getting pregnant, but the wording does not foreground a 'healthy' pregnancy. For example, after a miscarriage due to ectopic pregnancy, where some of the associated treatments are known to reduce a woman's chances of a natural conception, we are told that '*most* women ... will be able to get pregnant again, even if they've had a fallopian tube removed' (NHS 2018f). Likewise, with the rarer miscarriage due to a molar pregnancy, the NHS informs us that 'you can *usually* get pregnant ... if you wish' although it recommends waiting for one year after treatment before trying (NHS 2018h). Being told that a woman who has had a molar pregnancy has 'an excellent chance' of having 'a perfectly normal pregnancy next time' (Miscarriage Association 2016) is unclear because it leaves the question of whether a normal pregnancy means a successful pregnancy outcome, or simply a normal risk of pregnancy loss.

Most women who miscarry may well go on to have successful, uneventful pregnancies, but this seems to downplay the fact that one in four women will experience miscarriage and that the risk of further miscarriages increases with each loss (Tommy's 2019b; Mayo Clinic 2018). The NHS tells us that even where recurrent miscarriages occur '[m]ore than 60% of these women go on to have a successful pregnancy' with specialist support and medication (Tommy's 2018c), with that number growing to 65 per cent for women who have previously experienced an ectopic pregnancy (NHS 2018f). My point here is that 60 and 65 per cent respectively might appear comforting, reassuring or promising, but they can look low for the remaining 40 and 35 per cent of women who have already experienced pregnancy loss and are committed to family building.

We are reminded that women 'can try for another baby as soon as [their] symptoms have settled' (NHS 2018b), be that a few short weeks after a miscarriage or up to one year after a molar pregnancy. Either way, women are strongly encouraged to ensure that they are 'emotionally and physically ready' before trying (Ibid.). Being physically ready to try for a baby may demand waiting a few weeks or months, but being emotionally ready may take much longer, even continuing past a successful pregnancy outcome. After all, the NHS and a myriad of campaigning, charity and support groups make it clear that irrespective of the duration of the pregnancy, the diagnosed pregnancy disruption, the end-of-pregnancy management option chosen or decisions made relating to a stillbirth, a pregnancy loss 'can be an emotionally and physically draining experience' (NHS 2018b). Such experiences tend to incite 'feelings of guilt, shock and anger' which can have 'a profound emotional impact, not only on the woman herself, but also on her partner, friends and family' (Ibid.). This emotional impact can be experienced as a bereavement, relating to anxiety and depression (Ibid.), recently compounded by revelations that the 'bodies of more than 15,000 unborn foetuses have been incinerated in the UK … with some treated as "clinical waste" and others burned to heat hospitals' (Withnall 2014). And although the NHS has since banned the incineration of foetal remains in all its hospitals (Knapton 2014) there is now a generation of women who 'look back now and feel [that they] have let [their] child down' (Miscarriage Association 2018g).

The NHS foregrounds advice and support from hospital counselling services to local and national charity groups, but it is a health provider first and foremost. It is groups such as The Miscarriage Association, Tommy's, The Ectopic Pregnancy Trust, The Ectopic Pregnancy Foundation, The

Molar Pregnancy Support and Information site, Cruse Bereavement Care, the Mumsnet's Miscarriage Care Campaign, Stillbirth and Neonatal Death Society (SANDS) and Pregnancy After Loss Support (PALS) that offer emotional support to those affected by loss. Under a banner entitled 'A Range of Emotions', The Miscarriage Association highlights the point that there is no single way to deal with or move on from pregnancy loss, and that how you 'feel will depend on your circumstances, your experience and what the pregnancy meant to you' (Miscarriage Association 2018b). It states that the 'loss of a baby in pregnancy can be an unhappy, frightening and lonely experience' and that although the experience is not necessarily 'a major event for everyone ... feelings of shock, grief and loss are common' (Ibid.). Pregnancy loss can be a difficult, distressing and isolating experience (Miscarriage Association 2018c), and yet, women are reminded that they are not alone in feeling some or all of the following, during different stages of their grieving process: 'sad and tearful ... shocked and confused ... numb ... angry ... jealous ... guilty ... empty [and] lonely' (Miscarriage Association 2018b).

These emotions are common, and in many ways they echo a more traditional grieving process that takes individuals from denial through anger, bargaining and depression to acceptance (Kübler-Ross and Kessler 2007). What is surprising here is the seeming contradiction between pregnancy loss statistics and the feelings of loneliness that can be said to follow such a loss. Pregnancy loss is a common occurrence and a myriad of official and unofficial, medical and personal resources exist to support those who have experienced a miscarriage. Indeed, there exists a 'Babyloss Awareness Week', which seeks to remember the brief lives of babies lost while calling for better bereavement care (Miscarriage Association 2017b). And yet it is isolation that is routinely highlighted in first-person accounts of loss (Tommy's 2018d).

Talking About Miscarriage: From Silence to Sharing

Writing about loneliness on a social media forum seems to be counterintuitive. After all, social media is routinely touted as a way to build meaningful communities, a place in which to share and connect families, groups and beyond (Zuckerberg cited in Sulleyman 2017). However, there is the suggestion that online spaces are doing little to negotiate those feelings of loneliness that are commonly experienced after pregnancy loss. Loneliness is a recurrent and routine trope in the aforementioned narratives as they appear in private online forums, more openly available social media message boards and a myriad of blogs that dedicate posts to miscarriage. We are reminded that 'for most women, at the time when you desperately need love and support, the taboo, secrecy and shame surrounding miscarriage makes it the loneliest place on earth' (Pritchard 2015). Jodi Abbott and Eugene Declercq make the point that although '[m]illennials have become accustomed to posting their lives online ... they are discovering that few experiences are as isolating as losing a desired pregnancy' (Abbott and Declercq 2015). However, although loneliness is a common trope in social media posts on miscarriage, finding these posts in the first place is harder than finding those associated with infertility and family building. Recent content analysis and survey findings tell us that miscarriage and stillbirth 'emerged as less common topics than trying to become pregnant or being pregnant' in family building, and, as such, women 'seeking information or support ... may feel isolated when visiting such blogs and their accompanying resources' (Sohr-Preston et al. 2016, p. 17).

The recent Mumsnet Miscarriage Care campaign made the point that the 'treatment and support women receive following a miscarriage fails to meet the official national guidelines' in the UK (Mumsnet 2016). It offered some stark statistics including the fact that

> [a]round a quarter of a million women miscarry in the UK each year; [h]alf of all women who miscarry are treated alongside women with ongoing pregnancies; [h]alf of women wait for over 24 hours for a scan to find out if their baby is still alive; 58% of women wanted counselling after miscarrying [but only] 12% were offered it [while] [o]nly 15% of women who miscarried at home felt they had the right support, information and pain relief. (Ibid.)

However, what is most surprising about their findings, and what chimes with the work presented by the NHS and the Miscarriage Association is that 'only 23% of women who had miscarried spoke about their experiences with a friend' (Ibid.). Public health researchers Elaine Nsoesie and Nina Cesare echo this point when they tell us that pregnancy loss 'can be a difficult and painful experience, one that people often don't talk about even among friends and family. Women who suffer miscarriages can feel shame and isolation' because although 'many women experience miscarriage, few talk about it openly' (Nsoesie and Cesare 2017). Outside of health research, a feminist writer for *Stylist* magazine echoed these comments when she stated that for many women, through the heartbreak and the guilt and the endless internal questions, the only option is to put on a brave face. To pitch tomorrow's presentation like nothing has happened, to coo over a friend's new baby with a smile. Because while losing a friend or relative activates an immediate support network of sympathy and understanding, losing a baby can bring a lonely silence. (Stylist 2011)

This is not to suggest that medical advice or emotional support is unavailable; far from it, women who have experienced pregnancy loss have access to a myriad of campaigning voices offering not just practical advice, but emotional guidance in the form of shared stories, be they in prose, videos or poetry. However, being able to search for facts, statistics, personal stories and common narratives does little in the first instance to quash loneliness. It is sharing rather than searching or researching the subject that can be seen to quell the sense of isolation. Alongside health researchers and feminist writers, wellness and lifestyle bloggers encourage women to share their miscarriage experiences. We are told that even though sharing can be difficult in the short term, it will help individuals and society in the longer term. Julia of the Lemon Stripes blog reveals:

I wasn't sure who to tell or how to feel. … I told close friends and family about our loss but no one really knew what to say or how to act … my miscarriage story made people uncomfortable … because so few people actually talk about it. … I wanted to share my story so far in [the] hope that it teaches women to speak up about their experiences, to change the discourse and not feel ashamed of their bodies or their paths to pregnancy. (Julia of Lemon Stripes 2016a)

This post speaks of a need for women to share their candid stories in order to stop the loneliness and dissipate the sense of shame that often accompanies pregnancy loss, concluding with guidance on how to help a friend through miscarriage, be it with 'thoughtful miscarriage cards' or by sending 'sweet quotes'(Ibid.). The blogger rouses a community of women to unite, stating that

[i]f you've survived a miscarriage yourself, I encourage you to share your story even with just a close friend. … You never know, that person may have gone through the same thing. I know that once I started opening up about it, friends that have healthy babies finally shared their stories with me as well.

I was shocked at how many times that happened and those conversations brought me back to life. (Ibid.)

However, rather than extend the discussion of loss or offer further posts on her experience, Julia ends her miscarriage post, on a site otherwise dedicated to wellness, fashion and decor (Julia of Lemon Stripes 2016b) by making it clear that 'I don't plan to talk about this journey again … until I have a healthy pregnancy' (Julia of Lemon Stripes 2016a). One might read this solitary post as having a meaningful impact by encouraging a discussion or as a limited effort to engage debate in an otherwise upbeat lifestyle blog. Either way, the blog post, like a myriad of family building blogs before it, ends with hope, optimism and, soon after, the revelation of what she terms her rainbow baby (a baby born subsequent to a miscarriage, stillbirth or the death of an infant from natural causes), with the lifestyle blog now covering motherhood, life and wellness (Julia of Lemon Stripes 2017). The original blog post about her miscarriage and subsequent mommy blogging could be seen to give hope to women about family building, post pregnancy loss.

The fact that Julia encourages women to share their stories and support one another through loss goes further to remind us that such dialogue is currently lacking. Privacy, silence and isolation are common experiences post miscarriage and stillbirth, which is self-fulfilling as women continue to feel the loneliness that can accompany a loss, even when they encourage us to speak, share and connect. After a miscarriage at 11 weeks, Selfish Mother blogger, Rebecca Parfitt was told by her doctor that 'you've had a miscarriage, it's very common, it's just nobody talks about it' and the frustration here is that 'its commonality makes it a small thing: just one of those things' (Parfitt 2017). Looking beyond the blogosphere, Sanchez is hurt and frustrated because

[p]eople keep saying, 'He's with you always. You carry him with you, in your heart.' I smile kindly and don't say, 'But I want to carry him in my belly. In my arms. Babies are big and my heart is small, tender and beaten.' People don't know what to say and they're trying their best, but I feel so alone that it's almost crippling. … I feel like I should be sent to the desert … there is some tribe of women waiting for me. … We pull out our hair and bleed and know that there is no pleasure in this world. (Sanchez 2016)

Bloggers, repro-lit authors, online commentators, anonymous interview subjects, health journalists, contemporary celebrities and clinical researchers can be seen to form a consensus as they speak of the isolation that can stem from pregnancy loss. Irrespective of the popularity or professionalism of the writing, whether they are speaking to a niche demographic or a broad readership, beyond questions of editorial control or agenda setting, the theme is consistent.

Repro-lit author Jacqueline Tomlins tells us that after a miscarriage women 'may find friends and family have no idea about what you are really going through, and you will inevitably have to deal with those well-meant, but unhelpful platitudes, "better luck next time", and "it wasn't meant to be"' (Tomlins 2003, p. 146). The platitudes come from a desire to 'eliminate the pain and undo' the pregnancy loss (Purdie 2017). And yet, although phrases such as 'at least you know you can get pregnant … it happens for a reason' and 'you can always try again' might be well intentioned, for some women, the loss is so great that they find such comments insensitive, hurtful and dismissive (anon cited in Hobson 2015). According to a recent twitter netnography, women who had experienced pregnancy loss were seen to express feelings of isolation, to speak of a desire for support and to bemoan insensitive comments: namely, the suggestion that there will be future opportunities to have a baby or that it was not the appropriate time to have a child (Hobson 2015). On the back of repeated platitudes about future pregnancies, one woman cries: 'I don't want another baby, I want THIS baby, the one I thought I would have, the one I started planning for, hoping for, dreaming about, talking to' (cited in Hobson 2015, emphasis in original). Andrew Moscrop, a clinical researcher in primary care, explains that 'the loss is not simply, perhaps not even, a fetus: it is a loss of anticipated motherhood, loss of a child imagined, and loss of apparent certainties', and he concludes by stating that these feelings and emotions can 'be understood only through conversation with women who have experienced' them (Moscrop 2011, p. 2). So if Sanchez is to be sent to the desert, she will not be there alone. The tribe of women waiting to meet her will be vast, and growing. But as recent research continues to remind us, even though '[t]wenty five percent of women will miscarry … none of us ever talk about it' (Stylist 2011). After an early miscarriage, Allison Gibson echoes this point when she states that

> [t]hroughout the days that followed, I found myself saying the same thing over and over again: 'Nobody talks about … it.' My online searches for information unearthed clinical articles that described in almost comically toned-down terms what symptoms I might be encountering. Searches for commiseration found personal essays that were focused on moving on with

life after a miscarriage. I was left feeling isolated and unprepared for the physical [and] emotional ... side effects. (Gibson, A 2016a)

Nobody talks about it. The question continues as to why women routinely self-censor, and the answer comes in three parts: the 12-week rule, gender discrimination in the workplace and near 'universal feelings of shame, embarrassment and guilt' (Stylist 2011).

Although miscarriage has always been a common event, the emergence and development of obstetric ultrasonography has more recently changed how women feel about pregnancy and, in turn, how they feel about making a pregnancy announcement. The 12-week rule is a relatively recent social phenomenon, linked to the fact that 'most women have an ultrasound scan at 12 weeks', which has 'become the benchmark for women to feel like the pregnancy is real' (Willis 2018). Although a miscarriage or stillbirth can happen at any stage of the pregnancy, 'the odds are highest in the first trimester' (Ibid.). In short, at 12 weeks, after their ultrasound and on the back of 'seeing' their baby, many women 'believe with some confidence that their pregnancy will be ongoing' (Ibid.) and make their pregnancy announcement accordingly. Moreover, '[m]edically speaking, the risk of miscarriage isn't the only reason why some women and couples choose to keep news of their pregnancy private in the first trimester' (Ibid.). After all, the ultrasound may reveal a genetic condition, leaving women to make 'life-changing decisions about how they are going to proceed' (Ibid.). By waiting until the ultrasound to announce a pregnancy, a woman is able to avoid difficult questions and revelations as they relate to miscarriage and termination. However, by avoiding difficult questions, they are also shutting off support. We are reminded that

> [e]very baby book and doctor says you shouldn't tell people you're pregnant before your 12-week scan '[i]n case something happens'. But that infers that you're also not supposed to tell people that something did happen. It reinforces the idea that miscarriage is something that you should feel guilty about and keep secret. (Alison cited in Stylist 2011)

In a blog post dedicated to her own miscarriage, Parfitt talks about the 12-week rule as a way to 'silence ... newly pregnant women' (Parfitt 2017), making the point that

> we are advised to 'keep quiet' about our pregnancy for the first three months, 'just in case', until we reach the 'safe' time ... we mustn't let on, we

4 PREGNANCY LOSS: SHAME AND SILENCE OVER A SHARED EXPERIENCE   161

mustn't talk about it. We must carry on as normal. Women have done this since time began. But this silence feels more like a gag on womankind, not a saving grace. (Ibid.)

This simultaneous silence and frustration continues in the discussion comments attributed to Cassie Murdoch's article in the liberal feminist blog *Jezebel*, entitled 'Should You Tell Your Facebook Friends You've Had a Miscarriage?' One woman speaks of adhering to the 12-week rule, even though, at 7 weeks pregnant, she finds it emotionally and physically difficult to do so. The irony here though is the fact that the commentator wished that society was able to more freely discuss pregnancy and miscarriage:

I wish I could tell the world. ... But because of society's taboo regarding talking about pregnancies that are less than 12 weeks, I feel pressured to say nothing (and suffer even more stress alone, in silence) ... miscarriage, sad as it is, is natural and normal and nothing to be ashamed of/stigmatized. I can only imagine we would have a healthier attitude towards it if people talked about it more openly! (Not here anymore comment on Murdoch 2012)

Moving away from discussion comments to a health story for *The Telegraph*, Rebecca Holman states, albeit with jest and light-heartedness in the first instance, that she cannot understand how a woman could keep something as important as a pregnancy a secret for an entire trimester. However, she goes on to echo the earlier commentators when she talks about women self-silencing, isolation and the 12-week rule:

I do get it. Why tempt fate by choosing to talk about a pregnancy when you don't know what the outcome will be? Sadly, one in four doesn't make it to the 12-week mark. But then what? If you miscarry before telling friends and colleagues, do you just keep your head down and stay quiet about the whole thing? For many, this does seem to be the case—how else do you account for the fact that miscarriage is such a rarely discussed topic, given how regularly it occurs? (Holman 2015)

What we witness here then is a desire to speak more openly about pregnancy loss from those who themselves remain silent about their own experiences, and this contradiction is self-fulfilling. These women routinely speak of their frustration at adhering to the 12-week rule and yet struggle to break it, in part because of the fear of social awkwardness. Even for those who have not experienced pregnancy loss first-hand, they 'do get' why women stay quiet and isolate themselves for fear of challenging friends and colleagues with a miscarriage update. However, it is clear that for some women, the fear of social awkwardness is compounded by the very real possibility of workplace discrimination. After all,

> [d]espite the advancement of equality laws in the UK, many women fear that telling superiors about a miscarriage may risk marginalisation or being overlooked for promotion or training opportunities as, once the news is out, they'll inevitably be seen as a mum in waiting who will soon be on maternity. (Stylist 2011)

In a news article dedicated to the topic of miscarriage in the workplace, Julia Carpenter echoes this point when she tells readers that women routinely stay silent about their miscarriages, even if they happen during work hours, for fear of discrimination. We are told that 'motherhood penalties' at work silence women, because pregnancy, and indeed a pregnancy loss, can be enough to put women on the 'mommy track' whereby women are assumed to put motherhood over career and thus close off future advancement opportunities (Carpenter 2019). The article concludes by reminding us that further 'awareness of the prevalence of miscarriage, coupled with a greater understanding for women and their bodies, could help women navigate this issue at work' (Siler cited in Carpenter 2019).

At the same time as women are struggling with the social awkwardness of pregnancy loss and the very real possibility of workplace discrimination, many also speak of 'shame, embarrassment and guilt' over what they describe as their 'imperfect' and 'malfunctioning' bodies (Stylist 2011). After all, contemporary society equates appropriate womanhood with motherhood, and motherhood in our current pronatal climate is judged in line with an ideology of intensive mothering that begins during pregnancy. In short, to speak of miscarriage or pregnancy loss is to position yourself outside of, or as counter to, perceived ideas of acceptable femininity and womanhood. Recent survey findings from the field of obstetrics and gynaecology inform us that women who have experienced miscarriage routinely feel guilty (47 per cent), feel that they are somehow to blame (41 per cent), feel alone (41 per cent) and feel ashamed (28 per cent) (Bardos et al. 2015). However, while we remain silent and/or silenced there is little chance of changing the dialogue surrounding pregnancy loss.

4 PREGNANCY LOSS: SHAME AND SILENCE OVER A SHARED EXPERIENCE 163

Miscarriage has been understood as 'the last taboo' of the contemporary period (Stylist 2011), and yet in an enlightening book entitled *Centuries of Solace: Expressions of Maternal Grief in Popular Literature* (1992) we are reminded that there has been frequent writing about pregnancy loss for over two centuries. The authors examine the myriad ways in which women from different generations have written about pregnancy disruption, specifically miscarriage and the death of a child, from sentimental nineteenth-century poetry published in women's magazines to twentieth-century confessional stories in 'pulp' journals. The work offers a nuanced consideration of class, race, religion and generation as it pertains to an understanding of both maternal grief and the social meanings of motherhood. But what is more relevant to a discussion of pregnancy loss, isolation and loneliness is the fact that we are encouraged to read these writings as a 'precursor of contemporary help groups' (Taylor 1993, p. 239). We are told that because women have moved from the domestic to the public arena, the 'submerged culture that supported women through pregnancy loss and [the] death of a child has been replaced by ... grassroots activism' (Ibid., p. 239). In short, there has been a marked increase in the visibility of women's discourses relating to pregnancy loss in popular gendered publishing. But while we are asked to consider the ways in which such 'narratives challenge and redefine the silence that shrouds the topic of maternal grief ... and address the grieving mother's isolation through encouraging women to join self-help groups' (Ibid., p. 239), contemporary women still speak of a secrecy that surrounds the 'physical, emotional, and logistical side effects of miscarriage' (Gibson, M 2016b).

Self-help groups are said to offer 'emotional catharsis' and grant 'permission to grieve' (Simonds and Katz Rothman 1992, p. 158), which is important when we understand that '[m]iscarriage—like infertility generally—is one of those things that most people who have never experienced it don't really understand' (Tomlins 2003, p. 146). And yet, one in four women will experience pregnancy loss. A disconnect exists between the number of women who have experienced loss and the number of these women who are prepared to share their stories. I do not mean sharing anonymously on family building blogs, online chat rooms, message boards or self-help groups, but with those family and friends closest to them.

Wendy Simonds and Barbara Katz Rothman acknowledge the ways in which women's writing through poetry, stories and essays all acknowledge and legitimise women's experiences of maternal grief (Simonds and Katz Rothman 1992); similarly, blogging and repro-lit foreground the experience of miscarriage and stillbirth to this same end. Such writing reminds us of the emotions that are attached to individual experiences and personal narratives of miscarriage and loss.

In her infertility memoir, Anne Marie Scully reminds the reader of the impact that miscarriage or the fear of pregnancy loss has on women as she recalls a follow-up scan after discovering that her baby was 'measuring too small for the dates' (Scully 2014, p. 129):

> One by one the happy couples emerged looking happier than before they went in. Although I felt terrible about it, I thought that if one other couple in that room had a miscarriage then statistically we might not. When I saw their smiling faces walk through the door my fear intensified. ... He turned to me then said, with as much compassion as someone who deals with this a couple of times a week can, 'it's gone, I'm sorry'. (Ibid., pp. 130–131)

Although women can and do deal with miscarriages in diverse ways depending on a myriad of relationship, fertility, economic or age factors, Scully's experience might be seen to speak for many, picking up as it does on the feelings of sadness, guilt and failure:

> Although I was desperately sad for us, I was also incredibly sad for the baby. I felt I had let him down, that I had given up on him somehow. ... I told him how sorry I was that we would never get to give him all the kisses and cuddles that he deserved. Thinking your child is out there somewhere, in heaven or otherwise, all alone without you is heartbreaking. (Ibid., pp. 132–135)

It is worth noting that even though pregnancy loss is common, 'it doesn't make it an easy thing to experience, and it doesn't mean that it won't have a significant effect upon you emotionally' because 'miscarriage always brings with it an enormous sense of loss' (Tomlins 2003, pp. 139–140). We are reminded that pregnancy loss can be devastating, irrespective of experience or circumstance, because, according to Tomlins,

> [e]ven in the very early stages of pregnancy ... you may feel bonded with your baby; even though it is only days or weeks old, you may love it already. ... For you, the loss is real and tangible, a potential life inside you that dies, a much wanted son or daughter who couldn't stay. (Ibid., p. 140)

Moreover, this sense of loss might be magnified for women if they have had to wait a long time for pregnancy, or if it was difficult to achieve or if the loss was experienced more than once. Speaking about her experiences of recurrent miscarriages, the writer explains how she went from feeling unlucky to needing intervention after her third miscarriage. The language of the 'recurrent miscarriage' as opposed to another unfortunate accident is meaningful in this regard. She explains the feelings associated with multiple miscarriages as being

> especially tough. You may feel you've just got over the last one—whether it was two months or two years ago—and now you are thrown back into all that sadness and grief; the huge disappointment, the feelings of failure, the erosion of self-esteem, the sense of despair. On top of all that, you have to cope with the physical effects of the miscarriage. (Tomlins 2003, p. 145)

Miscarriage after assisted reproductive treatment is said to be 'enormously difficult because of all the emotional and physical energy that has been invested in achieving the pregnancy' in the first instance. We are told that '[m]iscarriage after IVF also means facing another round of treatment, just when you thought you would be leaving all that behind' you (Tomlins 2003, pp. 140–141). The sense of disappointment is clear, but the words are revealing in what they tell us about the difficulty of ending treatment. Picking up on the themes of the earlier chapters, the wording here suggests that IVF leading to pregnancy disruption can only be followed by 'another round of treatment' rather than a future without children, or the desired number of children.

Extant literature on the depiction of assisted reproductive treatments in contemporary news and magazine media makes it clear that although in reality 'an estimated 31 percent of all implanted embryos later miscarry' there is 'very little mention of miscarriage, especially as a component of infertility' in the reporting of such stories (Sterling 2013, p. 123). The suggestion here then is that in 'many cases, journalists portray pregnancy as the end-goal of infertility treatments', not necessarily a healthy live birth. Indeed, 'miscarriages might have just been part of the expected [conception] collateral when attempting to get pregnant through procreative technologies' (Ibid.). And in women who experience a stillbirth or neonatal death we find that their grief can be compounded in one sad yet ostensibly facetious comment: 'I'm 30 pounds heavier than my normal weight. Apparently my body hasn't gotten the memo that we lost the baby' (Sanchez 2016).

Stillbirth and neonatal death are considered rare, and perhaps they are in relation to the experience of miscarriage, but 1 in 225 and 1 in 400 do not indicate rare incidences. Indeed, in relation to the European drug regulatory agency's definitions for words relating to frequency of side effects, we find that while the term 'very common' (more than 1 in 10 people are affected) would be used to describe a miscarriage, the term 'uncommon' (between 1 in 100 and 1 in 1000 people are affected) is used to describe a stillbirth or neonatal death rather than 'rare' (between 1 in 1000 and 1 in 10,000 people are affected) (NHS 2018m). And although I am not suggesting that pregnancy loss is akin to an adverse reaction, the terminology used here is meaningful. Personal and professional accounts of pregnancy loss routinely downgrade the commonality of the experience, and only when we are able to talk candidly about the statistics and the personal stories will we as a society be able to better support women who experience pregnancy loss or the death of a baby. Writing for *The New York Times*, Megan Scott makes this point on the back of her own stillbirth experience when she speaks of her desire to reach out and help other women grieving for their lost babies:

> Ever since losing my daughter when I was just 24 weeks pregnant, I've dreamed of becoming a superhero. When I read or hear about another family that's experienced a stillbirth, I want to don a disguise and fly to the mother's side. I want to guard her front door, answer her phone, manage her Facebook account, intercept her text messages, anything that can shield her from the well-meaning, yet often thoughtless behavior of people. I want to tell her … that there are other women out there who know what it's like, who can offer the support … who can show you that you can and will survive. (Scott 2010/2015)

She concludes her article by reminding us, in line with the earlier figures, that '[s]tillbirths are not rare' before asking readers to share their stories, their heartbreak and their survival because it is 'the only way to move forward, remember our lost children, and honor our experience' (Scott 2010/2015). While miscarriage is very common and stillbirth and neonatal death remain an uncommon experience, the depiction of pregnancy loss is not routinely seen in the contemporary media landscape. That is not to say that the experience does not exist in a wide array of popular texts that span medium, format and demographics, but rather that its visual presence does not match the frequency of the lived experience.

In recent mainstream cinema we have seen pregnancy loss depicted on and off-screen, presented as both a marginal point of reference and a fundamental life experience in children's animation (*Up* 2009), family films (*Marley and Me* 2008), romantic comedies (*What to Expect When You're Expecting* 2012), crime (*The Girl on the Train* 2016), romance (*The Light Between Oceans* 2016), fantasy (*The Time Traveller's Wife* 2009), drama (*The Help* 2011) and horror titles (*Grace* 2009). Likewise, the small screen has presented audiences with the depiction of loss in a range of genre texts that span soap opera (*Coronation Street* 1960–), sitcom (*Girlfriends* 2000–08), dramedy (*Six Feet Under* 2001–05, *This is Us* 2016–), mystery (*Desperate Housewives* 2004–12), drama (*Kingdom* 2014–), teen (*90210* 2008–13), hospital (*Grey's Anatomy* 2005–) and reality programming (*19 Kids and Counting* 2008–15, *Giuliana & Bill* 2009–) (Woods and Winderman 2018).

Pregnancy Loss on Social Media

Popular and long-running television shows have a habit of using miscarriage as a convenient 'reset button' (TV Tropes 2018) that enables characters to present a dramatic narrative arc before returning quickly to a pre-pregnant physique and plot, because in genre television in general and serial television in particular 'reverting to a status quo is more important than advancing' the narrative (Ibid.). However, outside of the fictional screen space, for those women who passed the 12-week scan, or for those more rebellious individuals who decided to make an earlier pregnancy announcement (Fogle 2015; Jones 2016; Goldberg 2016), the difficulty comes with not having a reset button. What I mean by this is that pregnancy loss post pregnancy announcement leaves women having to tell and retell their experience of miscarriage or stillbirth to invested friends and family members. Hence, one might question whether having a miscarriage in the age of social media is helpful in as much as a single message, penned and posted once, is all that is needed in order to share such difficult news. However, it could also be argued that posting a miscarriage announcement on social media leads to isolation and alienation on a platform that is more routinely saturated with outlandish pregnancy stories, maternal musings and smug mums oversharing (Horton 2016). In order to understand how women can benefit from, or otherwise, sharing their stories of loss online, it is important that we look at social media miscarriage announcements and the ways in which these brief media texts are picked up in wider channels of discourse.

In an article for *Broadly* entitled 'The Public Pain of Announcing Your Miscarriage on Facebook', Jennifer Purdie quips that 'pregnancy announcements, whether elaborately planned or quick and spontaneous, have ... become a genre on social media' (Purdie 2017), and although 'some status updates are simply ultrasound photos and excitement, Pinterest offers more than 1,000 ideas on how to publish pregnancy announcements' (Purdie 2017). In an article entitled 'Congrats, You're Pregnant! Now Keep It to Yourself' in the *Huff Post* Life blog, Mike Julianelle asks if women could limit their pregnancy announcement to immediate friends and family and keep it away from social media (Julianelle 2017). On the back of the couple who used the '#ShareaCoke' campaign to make their pregnancy announcement online, the blogger asks:

> Did you see this HILARIOUS video that went viral over the summer? ... Kudos to this couple for their originality and inventiveness and artistic vision and free time and narcissism, but can this over-the-top pregnancy announcement trend stop now? First of all, who wants to sit through two long minutes of lip-syncing just to find out someone they know (let alone *don't* know) is having a kid? (Ibid., emphasis in original)

In short, parents-to-be invest time and creative brain power when sharing such notable news on social media (Purdie 2017). And yet, irrespective of how elaborate, creative or outlandish the announcements are, many of these would-be parents 'struggle with what to say when those pregnancies end in miscarriage' and loss (Ibid.). However, although some women find it difficult to post when their pregnancies end in miscarriage (Ibid.), Asher Fogle is unwavering in her decision to announce not just her pregnancy, but also her miscarriage to 'friends, family and Facebook' (Fogle 2015). Writing for *Good Housekeeping*, Fogle argues that social media sharing can stave off loneliness:

> We'd done all the genetic tests and passed the first trimester, so we thought we were in the 'safe zone.' After the news broke, we received an unbelievable amount of well-wishes and congratulations. But when I miscarried ... there was no hiding. None. I felt like a social media cautionary tale. But we opted to take the same route. We told everyone about our loss just as publicly as we announced our joy—and it was the best thing that could have happened. ... I was inundated with support. (Fogle 2015)

Fogle makes it clear that online support helped her to 'push through' the pain of miscarriage because social media was in a position to present her with a wealth of condolences and support that she would not have received had she kept her pregnancy, and subsequent loss, private. So too, writing for *Upworthy*, Rebecca Swift explains how her social media miscarriage announcement presented her with a much-needed wave of support beyond close friends and family. Swift informs her readers that although she thought she was 'in the clear at 12 weeks [her] little one didn't make it' (Swift 2016). On the back of her post, she discovers an outpouring of support, and this goes some way to remind her and us that '**You are not alone**' (Ibid., emphasis in original).

Both writers waited until they had passed their first trimester before making their pregnancy announcements for fear of an early miscarriage, and their stories of pregnancy loss go some way to remind us that there is no guaranteed 'safe zone' during pregnancy, and announcements, at any time, should be made with that knowledge in mind. However, their announcements, although heartbreaking, led to camaraderie, support and comfort. Their stories are not unique. Rather, many women speak of finding solace and solidarity on the back of their social media miscarriage announcements (babycenter community 2015). The personal pregnancy loss posting on a shared media platform opens up an avenue for condolences, sympathy, empathy and advice in a way that can be ignored, glanced at, gazed at or devoured depending on the day, time, practical questions or emotional needs of the woman in question.

ARE WORDS ENOUGH? BLOGGING, VLOGGING, FACEBOOK AND TWITTER

Much theoretical work from media to sociology, and business to gender studies considers the emergence and development of blogging as it relates to marketing and promotion (García-Rapp 2017), the rise of social media influencers (Khamis et al. 2017), the changing nature of celebrity (Berryman and Kavka 2017), community building (Rotman and Preece 2010) and emotional exchange (Gibson, M 2016b). Moreover, extant literature considers the ways in which vlogging can be understood as a platform for health and well-being advice, support, information and instruction, ranging from nursing practice (Murphy et al. 2017), inclusive masculinity (Morris and Anderson 2015), lesbian and gay identity

(Lovelock 2017), health and body image (Parnell 2017), anxiety treatment (Primack cited in Codrea-Rado 2016), mental health support (Betton and Tomlinson 2013) and chronic illness management (Liu et al. 2013). To date, little work exists to account for the ways in which vloggers help or hinder, educate or create confusion for women who have experienced pregnancy loss, or friends, family members or future generations of young women who would like to understand this very common experience.

While a blog is understood as 'a personal way of expressing your thoughts, observations, opinions and passions' in the form of an Internet diary, the vlogger takes a similar personal journey, albeit filmed and distributed over the Internet (Kouri et al. 2016, p. 185). Nathalie Soelmark's research considers the representation of infertility and assisted reproduction in digital media and installation art, with vlogging as one of a number of areas of consideration as it relates to the intersection between media and biotechnology. Soelmark argues that art, including vlogging, has the 'capacity to structure feelings' (Soelmark 2014a, p. 181; Soelmark 2014b) while simultaneously 'question[ing], and critically address[ing] dominant norms, ideals and values of body, technology and kinship' (Ibid., p. 182). The research looks at the ways in which vlogs connect performers to themselves and their viewers, reminding us of the ways in which 'the aesthetic-affective dimension of media cultural productions have ramifications for how we relate to ourselves, others, and the world' with 'small, mundane, ambivalent, and ugly feelings play[ing] a crucial role' (Ibid., p. 182).

When Holman asked the question 'Would You Talk About Your Miscarriage on Social Media', she foregrounds the 12-week rule before suggesting that the rule 'could be about to change' (Holman 2015). Holman introduces the postings of YouTube vloggers Sam and Nia Rader, a Texan couple with two small children who made a video of their 'shocking' pregnancy announcement (Jones 2015) before a follow-up video just a few days later detailing their pregnancy loss (Murphy 2015). In the 'Our Baby Had a Heartbeat' channel on their blog, Radar spoke about her early miscarriage to her subscribers:

> To those of you who have experienced miscarriage before, I can relate now. I have felt my womb empty out. I never, ever, ever knew that women felt that way. … I just want to say, too, that maybe there's someone out there that's going through this with us. … I am mourning with those of you who are feeling this. (Radar cited in Murphy 2015)

4 PREGNANCY LOSS: SHAME AND SILENCE OVER A SHARED EXPERIENCE   171

There was an outpouring of sympathy and empathy for the couple, but it was tinged with incredulity as many who watched, or even just heard about, the videos questioned the authenticity of both announcements. In the pregnancy announcement, millions of viewers watched Radar telling 'his wife she was pregnant after sneaking into the bathroom after her for a urine sample' but 'soon after came under fire from medical experts and internet critics who suggested that they had faked the entire incident in order to gain publicity for their YouTube channel' (Stern and Lankston 2015). Those bloggers, vloggers and cultural commentators who accused the couple of staging both videos made the point that fabricating a pregnancy only to announce a miscarriage was distasteful and disrespectful to those who had themselves experienced a loss. On the back of the miscarriage entry 'viewers felt free to let loose with real vitriol, calling the couple whores and scammers' (Miller 2015). Moreover, it wasn't just media consumers but popular entertainment outlets ranging from *The Daily Beast*, *BuzzFeed*, *Slate* and *E! News* to *The Washington Post* who picked up on the story.

Writing about the videos in *Refinery29*, Kelsey Miller speaks of the 'collective eye-roll at [the] vlogger couple's "shocking" all-caps pregnancy announcement', reminding us that the childhood sweethearts 'have been vlogging for more than a year, openly aiming for viral stardom' (Miller 2015). What is of note here, however, isn't the eye-roll *per se*, but the animosity that swept through the review comments. The top comment on the blog post on *Gawker* quietly signals the 12-week rule when it says '[s]weet, can't wait to see the viral video showing her devastation if she should miscarry in a few days or weeks' (Gawkers Post cited in Miller 2015). Both the theme and tone continue when we are told that '[t]here's a fucking reason people don't announce pregnancies to everyone at that point, Sam! I'm glad that, God forbid, the worst should happen, millions of people will be able to intrude on your wife's terrible grief' (cited in Miller 2015).

And they did, both miscarry and share that experience with their subscribers. This routinely private event garnered millions of views. The couple tweeted that 'our tiny baby brought 10M views to her video and 100,000 new people into our lives. She turned our life around and brought us closer together' (cited in Mills 2015). Irrespective of whether Radar thought she was or was not pregnant or did or did not experience a miscarriage, the vloggers succeeded in putting 'miscarriage back on the agenda and sh[one] a spotlight on the number of bloggers, vloggers and social media users who are now openly discussing topics around fertility' before welcoming their third and fourth child soon after (Holman 2015).

And at the same time as the Radars were sharing their miscarriage with millions of viewers, Facebook CEO Mark Zuckerberg announced that his wife Priscilla was pregnant, having previously suffered three miscarriages. Both used digital communities to speak to online audiences, both acknowledged the isolation that can stem from the experience and both looked to quash the self-silencing that often follows pregnancy loss. Zuckerberg's post suggests that

> you feel so hopeful when you learn you're going to have a child ... and then they're gone. It's a lonely experience. Most people don't discuss miscarriages because you worry your problems will distance you or reflect upon you—as if you're defective or did something to cause this. In today's open and connected world, discussing these issues doesn't distance us; it brings us together. It creates understanding and tolerance, and it gives us hope. (Zuckerberg 2015)

Louisa Pritchard, the features director of *Grazia* magazine, states that it is 'perhaps unsurprising that the founder of Facebook, the man who has done the most to encourage the current era of over-sharing, should tackle one of the few remaining taboos of our age. But he's right to do so' (Pritchard 2015). Zuckerberg ended his post by saying that

> [w]hen we started talking to our friends we realised how frequently this happened—that many people we knew had similar issues and that *nearly* all had healthy children after all. We hope that sharing our experience will give more people the same hope we felt and will help people feel comfortable sharing their stories as well. (Zuckerberg 2015, emphasis added)

Pritchard picked up on Zuckerberg's announcement in her own writing on the subject of miscarriage, giving further hope to those who have experienced pregnancy loss by telling her readers that she herself has 'happily gone on to have two gorgeous little boys' after her miscarriage. The author is encouraging 'the secret club of women [to] break the taboo' because 'the more we talk about miscarriage, hopefully the fewer women will find themselves crying alone in the office loos, as all their hopes and dreams for the little life they were carrying disappear' (Pritchard 2015).

Writing for CNN, Jodi Abbott and Eugene Declercq echo this point, stating that 'Zuckerberg's frank admission of his wife's three miscarriages

4 PREGNANCY LOSS: SHAME AND SILENCE OVER A SHARED EXPERIENCE 173

led to a vast outpouring of stories from women and families who have faced a similar situation' (Abbott and Declercq 2015). The authors comment that 'there is a certain stigma associated with miscarriages, as though it's the fault of the parents. But it isn't, and the stigma will be removed only if we talk about it more—openly and honestly. There is no shame in having a miscarriage' (Ibid.). The news and entertainment media were quick to offer praise to the CEO for seeking to 'break the taboo' associated with pregnancy loss and for challenging the ubiquitous and longstanding myths that surround miscarriage, as they are related to cause, blame, impact and prevention (Sanghani 2015).

Although there is no question that Zuckerberg's words have been seen by millions, it may give false hope or unrealistic reassurance to women who have not yet experienced miscarriage, or who are trying to open up a dialogue about the subject. Indeed, some women who have experienced a miscarriage find themselves to be a little less congratulatory in their reception of Zuckerberg's announcement and the ensuing accolades and approvals. The social media post was not received as a miscarriage announcement *per se*, but rather as a pregnancy announcement with a recurrent pregnancy loss backstory, which, perhaps like the Radars and Pritchard, or more recently Zara Tindall (BBC News 2018a), James Van Der Beek (BBC News 2018b), Michelle Obama (Obama 2018) or Alex Jones (Sturgis 2019), could be deemed unhelpful in debunking the secrecy and silence that surround pregnancy loss and the reality of that experience.

According to Elizabeth Petrucelli, an educator and advocate for families experiencing pregnancy loss, Zuckerberg didn't help to lessen the stigma of miscarriage. Rather, his announcement, like the aforementioned blog posts and repro-lit authors, suggested that it is only appropriate to announce your pregnancy after the first trimester. In so doing, the announcement was read less as supporting women to discuss their pregnancy and miscarriages early and often, but rather as further fuelling the 'stigmatization that we shouldn't announce a pregnancy right away' (Petrucelli 2015a). Petrucelli also goes on to challenge his optimistic tone, by reminding us that not every miscarriage story has a happy ending (Ibid.). The number of women who go on to have a successful pregnancy after miscarriage, even after recurrent miscarriages, is high, but it does not happen for everyone, and the suggestion is that Zuckerberg's popular post should have made this point more clearly for interested readers.

Social media announcements relating to pregnancy loss are not restricted to those social media founders or to women who went on to have a successful pregnancy. Lillia, cited in Holman's article on social media and miscarriage, like Zuckerberg before her, decided to speak about her miscarriage and subsequent missed miscarriage on Facebook. The key difference here is that the latter author is speaking after two failed pregnancies rather than during a successful third pregnancy. She says:

> I couldn't cope with pretending I was fine this time, so I posted what had happened to me on Facebook. ... I've received amazing support, and messages and huge emotional help. Telling all my friends was the right thing to do. ... I think, if I am ever lucky enough to be pregnant again, I will tell people early, so they are ready to support me if the worst happens. ... I still need to talk, and that is where the taboo needs to be broken down. (Lillia cited in Holman 2015)

Like Zuckerberg, the author is clear that sharing her pregnancy loss on social media was the right thing to do as it opened up a support network when she most needed it. However, she is more honest than Zuckerberg in the sense that there are no assurances or guarantees about a future successful pregnancy. Luck, as she calls it, is a pretty apt term for the possibility of a successful outcome, but she is happy to be part of a dialogue that looks to debunk the taboo of talking about pregnancy loss and voicing the lived experience of involuntary childlessness.

On the back of such social media announcements, Cassie Murdoch's article on the liberal feminist blog *Jezebel* tells us that she is 'firmly in the age group where my friends are popping children from their loins at an alarming rate' and as such it is 'interesting to watch how they've all handled their pregnancy announcements—and for some of them, sadly, their subsequent miscarriage updates', leaving the blogger to question, like the Zuckerbergs and Radars before her, 'just how good an idea it is to share the details of your uterine happenings with the world' (Murdoch 2012). And in order to provide us with an answer she concludes that although 'it is no doubt painful to take to your Facebook profile and announce you're no longer pregnant, it's worth remembering that sharing your bad news publicly can have good consequences too' (Ibid.). After all, posting your pregnancy loss is one important step in seeing 'the walls of privacy continue to break down' (Ibid.). Murdoch makes the point that the 'more people will feel comfortable sharing the intricacies of their health and fertility issues', the more society is likely to 'eliminate a lot of the unnecessary shame and guilt that women can feel over losing a baby' (Ibid.).

Ruth Bender Atik, National Director of the Miscarriage Association, suggests that 'there are huge positives in the development of blogging and vlogging on the topic of miscarriage' because we hear the voices of 'ordinary' people sharing 'genuine feelings' (Bender Atik cited in Holman 2015). We are asked to consider the ways in which 'conversation and honesty around miscarriage' should be understood as a meaningful and empowering step because 'anything that raises awareness of the issue is a positive' thing (Ibid.). Indeed, with the growing numbers of women, partners, family and friends sharing their pregnancy disruptions on social media, there is a sense of optimism in that 'greater public discourse will help reduce stigma and the sense of isolation that some women feel' (Nsoesie and Cesare 2017). Psychologists have argued 'that the opportunity for women to share their experiences of miscarriage can be invaluable' because it goes some way towards 'accepting that they are not responsible for what happened' (Holman 2015). Since you are sharing online 'with a large community, you receive responses from people who had similar experiences' and this community, commonality and camaraderie is key to societal and personal acceptance.

There exists rigorous qualitative and quantitative research to remind us that pregnancy loss in general and miscarriage narratives in particular are becoming more frequent within and beyond social media, be it blogging (Richards 2018), vlogging (Saccone 2016), video diaries (Conway 2017) or personal documentaries uploaded to support groups (Miscarriage Association 2018h), celebrity stories in the gossip sector (Bologna 2015), novels (Roy 2011), poetry (Mosquera 2017), Instagram accounts (#IHadAMiscarriage 2017), music (Jay Z 2012), memoirs (Kimball 2017), news blogs (Romero 2016) or news reporting (Cockerell 2018). There is a tendency to assume that this increased visibility leads to an increased awareness and a potential change to the ways in which we understand, make sense of and support those who have experienced miscarriage.

On the back of these statistics, netnographies whereby researchers can interrogate existing public conversations as they exist on social media in general, and twitter in particular, are useful to examine in this regard. Public health researchers gathered tweets from a 12-month period 'that mentioned the term "miscarriage" in reference to pregnancy loss' (Nsoesie and Cesare 2017). They then categorised nearly 60,000 tweets into four topics: 'celebrity miscarriage news; [opinion-editorial] articles and politicized discussions; potential causes; and personal or familial experiences' (Ibid.). They noticed that 'the number of daily tweets about miscarriage during the week after a celebrity's disclosure was, on average, higher when compared with other weeks' (Ibid.). Their findings supported an earlier survey which 'indicated that disclosures of miscarriage by public figures as well as family and friends could lessen feelings of isolation for those who have had a miscarriage' (Ibid.). Indeed, the earlier survey found that while 28 per cent of respondents who had themselves miscarried said that they felt less alone when celebrities announced their pregnancy losses, this figure rose to 46 per cent when their own friends talked about their miscarriages (Bardos et al. 2015).

However, we are reminded that even though people are 'comfortable sharing almost any kind of news on Facebook these days', pregnancy loss remains 'difficult to navigate' (Murdoch 2012). As my own recent collaboration with practice-based researchers can testify, audience studies on topics such as infertility, miscarriage and pregnancy disruption 'tend to be small, because it can be difficult to find women willing to participate' (Nsoesie and Cesare 2017; Levy and Farrar 2018). Lillia comments that 'it's taken me three weeks to feel I want to talk about it, but I think some of my friends are still wary about bringing it up because it's seen as such a sensitive topic' (Lillia cited in Holman 2015). Therefore, although the author has received what she refers to as 'amazing support and messages' from her online network, there remains a difference between online outpourings of sympathy and support, and real-world interactions. She makes the point that 'our widespread reticence to discuss miscarriage has put people off discussing it with her, despite her public declaration' (Lillia cited in Holman 2015).

Removing the shroud of secrecy surrounding pregnancy loss can be said to alleviate shame, disavow guilt, encourage awareness and take a step towards relieving feelings of loneliness. However, there are clear distinctions between social media postings and more intimate communications. At the same time as personal and professional voices tell us that social media can help break the taboo around pregnancy loss, it is important to also acknowledge those who believe such moments should only 'be privately shared with family and close friends and not posted publicly' (Emma cited in Holman 2015). Holman concludes her article by stating that it feels 'deeply intrusive' to watch or read personal narratives about miscarriage on social media, so although she hopes that vloggers such as the Radars 'will help us talk about miscarriage more, I wouldn't want it to become an online trend' (Holman 2015). There is a fine line to be drawn here then between sharing and exposing, between having privacy and sharing publicly. The suggestion is that the Radars' announcement was part personal confession, part publicity campaign. Only time will tell if future miscarriage announcements online will help women heal or lead to further fame-seeking accusations.

Although the question of intrusion might be the deciding factor in making a pregnancy loss announcement online, one also needs to consider the fact that the author of such an announcement, blog or vlog, cannot control public reaction, as evidenced with the case of the Radars and Zuckerbergs respectively. Indeed, psychiatrists have recommended not posting such details precisely because

> [i]t's possible someone will say something as good as they can say, but it will still feel hurtful … so … rather than posting online … tell others about it in person, which will allow them to show compassion through body language and not just words [because] when communicating on an individual level, you can be touched and see facial expressions; it can make you feel more supported. (Saltz cited in Purdie 2017)

One woman who experienced pregnancy loss seems to speak for many when she comments that while 'I'm definitely still healing emotionally, I would be happy to talk more about it. So many people grieve silently, but I've found that talking really helps the most' (cited in Hobson 2015)—real-world talking, not just online sharing.

Conclusion

This chapter introduced the statistics, steps and stages as they relate to miscarriage and loss—be it miscarriage, missed miscarriage, ectopic and molar pregnancies or stillbirth—before considering the ways in which pregnancy loss announcements on social media can help debunk miscarriage myths and offer a support network. Pregnancy loss is very common, with as many as one in four pregnancies ending in miscarriage, but women continue to refer to this experience as unknown and unexpected. Given the prevalence of news and information, and the potential for communication and shared experiences on social media, it is important to see what medical information and emotional support about pregnancy loss is being seen and heard online. Realising what information is available and where gaps exist between the medical information and the personal narratives might go some way towards helping health-care professionals to better prepare and support patients about the true causes and cases of miscarriage and thus to lessen feelings of guilt and shame said to be often experienced. This is crucial now as we find that people are increasingly 'turning to the digital world to find out about their health, find a doctor, engage on forums and use apps rather than visit traditional practices' because they find them 'unresponsive' (Miah and Rich 2018). For those women who have experienced pregnancy loss, be it a single or recurrent event, the desire to build or extend their family does not disappear, and, as such, alternative family-building options might be considered. And it is to existing and potential adoptive families that I now turn.

REFERENCES

#ihadamiscarriage. 2017. #ihadamiscarriage. *Twitter*. Accessed April 12, 2019. https://twitter.com/hashtag/ihadamiscarriage?ref_src=twsrc%5Egoogle%7Ctwcamp%5Eserp%7Ctwgr%5Ehashta.

Abbott, Jodi, and Eugene Declercq. 2015. Zuckerberg's Important Message on Miscarriage. *CNN*. Accessed April 12, 2019. https://edition.cnn.com/2015/0805/opinions/abbott-declercq-pregnancy-loss/index.html.

American Pregnancy Association. 2018. Miscarriage: Signs, Symptoms, Treatment, and Prevention. *American Pregnancy Association*: Promoting Pregnancy Wellness. Accessed April 12, 2019. http://americanpregnancy.org/pregnancy-complications/miscarriage/.

babycenter community. 2015. Telling People You had a Miscarriage. *babycenter*. Accessed April 12, 2019. https://community.babycenter.com/post/a58428586/telling_people_you_had_a_miscarriage.

Bardos, Jonah, Daniel Hercz, Jenna Friedenthal, Missmer Stacey, and Zev Williams. 2015. A National Survey on Public Perceptions of Miscarriage. *Obstetrics and Gynecology* 125 (6): 1313–1320.

BBC News. 2018a. Queen's Granddaughter Zara Tindall Reveals Second Miscarriage. *BBC*. Accessed April 12, 2019. https://www.bbc.co.uk/news/uk-44997019.

———. 2018b. James Van Der Beek Shares Message about Miscarriage Heartbreak. *BBC*. Accessed April 12, 2019. https://www.bbc.co.uk/news/entertainment-arts-45487825.

Berryman, Rachel, and Misha Kavka. 2017. I Guess A Lot of People See Me as a Big Sister or a Friend: The Role of Intimacy in the Celebrification of Beauty Vloggers. *Journal of Gender Studies* 26 (3): 307–320.

Betton, Victoria, and Victoria Tomlinson. 2013. Social Media Can Help in Recovery—But Are Mental Health Practitioners up to Speed? *Mental Health and Social Inclusion* 17 (4): 215–219.

Bologna, Caroline. 2015. 21 Celebrities Who Opened Up About Their Miscarriages to Support Other Women. *HuffPost*. Accessed April 12, 2019. https://www.huffingtonpost.co.uk/entry/21-celebrities-who-opened-up-about-their-miscarriages-to-support-other-women_us_563104aee4b0c66bae5a817d.

Campbell, Pam, Gill Wakley, Ruth Chambers, and Julian Jenkins. 2004. *Demonstrating Your Clinical Competence in Women's Health*. Oxford: Radcliffe.

Carpenter, Julia. 2019. Miscarriages are Common. But at Work, a Culture of Silence Keeps Women Quiet. *CNN Business*. Accessed April 21, 2019. https://edition.cnn.com/2019/01/09/success/miscarriage-work-women/index.html.

CDC. 2018a. Facts About Stillbirth. *Centers for Disease Control and Prevention*. Accessed April 12, 2019. https://www.cdc.gov/ncbddd/stillbirth/facts.html.

———. 2018b. Pregnancy and Infant Loss. *Centers for Disease Control and Prevention*. Accessed April 12, 2019. https://www.cdc.gov/features/pregnancy-infant-loss-day/index.html.

Cockerell, Jennifer. 2018. Health Secretary Jeremy Hunt Orders Review of Parents. Registering Rights after Miscarriage. *The Independent*. Accessed April 12, 2019. http://www.independent.co.uk/news/uk/home-news/health-secretary-jeremy-hunt-review-register-baby-name-miscarriage-parents-a8190261.html.

Codrea-Rado, Anna. 2016. Can you Treat Anxiety with YouTube Videos? *The Guardian*. Accessed April 12, 2019. https://www.theguardian.com/lifeandstyle/2016/aug/30/treat-anxiety-youtube-videos-mental-health.

Collins, Catherine, Damien Riggs, and Clemence Due. 2014. The Impact of Pregnancy Loss on Women's Adult Relationships. *Grief Matters: The Australian Journal of Grief & Bereavement* 17 (2): 44–50.

Conway, Kerry. 2017. Pregnancy After Miscarriage: My Mental Health Diary. *Channel Mum*. Accessed April 12, 2019. https://www.channelmum.com/video/pregnancy-after-miscarriage-my-mental-health-diary-kerry-conway/.

Danielsson, Krissi. 2018a. Some Doctors Use the Word Abortion for Miscarriages. *verywellfamily*. Accessed April 12, 2019. https://www.verywellfamily.com/why-did-my-doctor-say-my-miscarriage-was-an-abortion-2371319.

———. 2018b. Ectopic Pregnancy Statistics. *verywellfamily*. Accessed April 12, 2019. https://www.verywellfamily.com/what-do-statistics-look-like-for-ectopic-pregnancy-2371730.

Fogle, Asher. 2015. The Best Advice I Received after My Miscarriage. *Good Housekeeping*. Accessed April 12, 2019. http://www.goodhousekeeping.com/life/inspirational-stories/a33933/advice-and-support-after-miscarriage/.

García-Rapp, Florencia. 2017. Popularity Markers on YouTube's Attention Economy: the Case of Bubzbeauty. *Celebrity Studies* 8 (2): 228–245.

Gibson, Allison. 2016a. What No-one Tells You About Having a Miscarriage'
Evening Standard. Accessed April 12, 2019. https://www.standard.co.uk/lifestyle/health/what-noone-tells-you-about-having-a-miscarriage-a3250071.html.

Gibson, Margaret. 2016b. YouTube and Bereavement Vlogging: Emotional Exchange Between Strangers. *Journal of Sociology* 52 (4): 631–645.

Goldberg, Haley. 2016. This Blogger Defied Social Expectations with Her Early Pregnancy Announcement, Self. Accessed April 12, 2019. https://www.self.com/story/this-blogger-defied-social-expectations-with-her-early-pregnancy-announcement.

Gorfinkel, Iris. 2018. It's Time to Stop Calling Pregnancy Loss Miscarriage. *The Globe and Mail*. Accessed April 12, 2019. https://www.theglobeandmail.com/life/health-and-fitness/health/its-time-to-stop-calling-pregnancy-loss-miscarriage/article26823539/.

Hobson, Katherine. 2015. People Have Misconceptions about Miscarriage, and That Can Hurt. *NPR*. Accessed April 12, 2019. https://www.npr.org/sections/health-shots/2015/05/08/404913568/people-have-misconceptions-about-miscarriage-and-that-hurts.

Holman, Rebecca. 2015. Would You Talk About Your Miscarriage on Social Media? *The Telegraph*. Accessed April 12, 2019. http://www.telegraph.co.uk/health-fitness/body/would-you-talk-about-your-miscarriage-on-social-media/.

Horton, Helena. 2016. Facebook Motherhood Challenge Sweeps Social Media—But Faces Hilarious Backlash. *The Telegraph*. Accessed April 12, 2019. https://www.telegraph.co.uk/news/newstopics/howaboutthat/12139649/facebook-motherhood-challenge-faces-hilarious-backlash.html.

Jay Z. 2012. Glory. Produced by The Neptunes.

Jones, Allie. 2015. All is Lost—Nightmare Man Surprises Wife with Her Own Pregnancy. *Gawker*. Accessed April 12, 2019. https://gawker.com/all-is-lost-nightmare-man-surprises-wife-with-her-ow-1722515765.

Jones, Samantha. 2016. Breaking the 12 Week Pregnancy Announcement Rule. *Storms and Rainbows*. Accessed April 12, 2019. http://www.stormsandrainbows.co.uk/blog/breaking-12-week-rule/.

Julia of Lemon Stripes. 2016a. Surviving Miscarriage. *Lemon Stripes*. Accessed April 12, 2019. https://lemonstripes.com/lifestyle/surviving-miscarriage/.

———. 2016b. About. *Lemon Stripes*. Accessed April 12, 2019. https://lemonstripes.com/about/.

———. 2017. Rainbow Baby. *Lemon Stripes*. Accessed April 12, 2019. https://lemonstripes.com/motherhood/rainbow-baby/.

Julianelle, Mike. 2017. Congrats, You're Pregnant! Now Keep It to Yourself. *Huffpost: The Blog*. Accessed April 12, 2019. https://www.huffingtonpost.com/mike-julianelle/congrats-youre-pregnant-now-keep-it-to-yourself_b_5922112.html.

Khamis, Susie, Lawrence Ang, and Raymond Welling. 2017. Self-branding, Micro-Celebrity and the Rise of Social Media Influencers. *Celebrity Studies* 8 (2): 191–208.

Kimball, Alexandra. 2017. Unpregnant: The Silent, Secret Grief of Miscarriage. *The Globe and Mail.* Accessed April 12, 2019. https://www.theglobeandmail.com/life/parenting/unpregnant-the-silent-secret-grief-of-miscarriage/article27576775/.

Knapton, Sarah. 2014. Aborted Babies Incinerated to Heat UK Hospitals. *Telegraph Science.* Accessed April 12, 2019. http://www.telegraph.co.uk/science/2016/03/15/aborted-babies-incinerated-to-heat-uk-hospitals/.

Kohn, Ingrid, and Perry-Lynn Moffitt. 2000. *A Silent Sorrow: Pregnancy Loss: Guidance and Support for You and Your Family.* London: Routledge.

Kolte, A.M., L.A. Bernardi, O.B. Christiansen, S. Quenby, R.G. Farquharson, M. Goddijn, and M.D. Stephenson. 2015. Terminology for Pregnancy Loss Prior to Viability: A Consensus Statement from the ESHRE Early Pregnancy Special Interest Group. *Human Reproduction* 30 (3): 495–498. Accessed April 12, 2019. https://academic.oup.com/humrep/article/30/3/495/659554.

Kouri, Prikko, Marja-Liisa Rissanen, Patrick Weber, and Hyeoun-Ae Park. 2016. Competences in Social Media Use in the Area of Health and Healthcare. *Forecasting Informatics Competencies for Nurses in the Future of Connected Health: Proceedings of the Nursing Informatics Post Conference*, 183–193.

Kübler-Ross, Elisabeth, and David Kessler. 2007. *On Grief and Grieving: Finding the Meaning of Grief Through the Five Stages of Loss.* London and New York: Scribner.

Levy, Claire, and Ruth Farrar. 2018. *Infertility, The Media & Me.* Film.

Liu, Leslie, Jina Huh, Tina Neogi, Kori Inkpen, and Wanda Pratt.2013. Health Vlogger-viewer Interaction in Chronic Illness Management. In *Proceedings of the SIGCHI Conference on Human Factors in Computing Systems CHI Conference*, 49–58.

Lovelock, Michael. 2017. Is Every YouTuber Going to Make a Coming out Video Eventually?: YouTube Celebrity Video Bloggers and Lesbian and Gay Identity. *Celebrity Studies* 8 (1): 87–103.

Mayo Clinic. 2018. Pregnancy After Miscarriage: What You Need to Know' Mayo Clinic. Accessed April 12, 2019. https://www.mayoclinic.org/healthy-lifestyle/getting-pregnant/in-depth/pregnancy-after-miscarriage/art-20044134?pg=1.

Miah, Andy, and Emma Rich. 2018. Insights Into the Digital Health Generation. *Meet Up.* Accessed April 12, 2019. https://www.meetup.com/GlobalNet21/events/247147257/.

Miller, Kelsey. 2015. Even If Sam & Nia Did Fake It, What Does Our Reaction Say About Us? *Refinery 29.* Accessed April 12, 2019. http://www.refinery29.com/2015/08/92311/sam-nia-pregnancy-miscarriage-hoax-bias.

Mills, Emma. 2015. YouTube Couple Announce Miscarriage After Surprise Pregnancy Video. *The Telegraph*. Accessed April 12, 2019. https://www.telegraph.co.uk/news/worldnews/northamerica/usa/11798727/YouTube-couple-announce-miscarriage-after-surprise-pregnancy-video.html.

Miscarriage Association. 2016. Information Leaflet: Molar Pregnancy (Hydatidiform Mole). *Miscarriage Association*. Accessed April 12, 2019. https://www.miscarriageassociation.org.uk/wp-content/uploads/2017/12/Molar-Pregnancy-Nov-2016.pdf.

———. 2017a. Your Feelings After Miscarriage? *Miscarriage Association*. Accessed April 12, 2019. https://www.miscarriageassociation.org.uk/wp-content/uploads/2016/10/Your-feelings-after-miscarriage-June-2014.pdf.

———. 2017b. Babyloss Awareness Week. *Miscarriage Association*. Accessed April 12, 2019. https://www.miscarriageassociation.org.uk/2017/10/babyloss-awareness-week/.

———. 2018a. Worried About Pregnancy Loss? *Miscarriage Association*. Accessed April 12, 2019. https://www.miscarriageassociation.org.uk/information/worried-about-pregnancy-loss/.

———. 2018b. A Range of Emotions. *Miscarriage Association*. Accessed April 12, 2019. https://www.miscarriageassociation.org.uk/your-feelings/common-feelings/.

———. 2018c. Miscarriage. *Miscarriage Association*. Accessed April 12, 2019. https://www.miscarriageassociation.org.uk/information/miscarriage/.

———. 2018d. Frequently Asked Questions. *Miscarriage Association*. Accessed April 12, 2019. https://www.miscarriageassociation.org.uk/information/frequently-asked-questions/.

———. 2018e. Ectopic Pregnancy. *Miscarriage Association*. Accessed April 12, 2019. https://www.miscarriageassociation.org.uk/information/ectopic-pregnancy/.

———. 2018f. Molar Pregnancy. *Miscarriage Association*. Accessed April 12, 2019. https://www.miscarriageassociation.org.uk/information/molar-pregnancy/.

———. 2018g. Talking About the Sensitive Disposal of Pregnancy Remains. *Miscarriage Association*. Accessed April 12, 2019. https://www.miscarriageassociation.org.uk/information/for-health-professionals/films-and-good-practice-guides/talking-sensitive-disposal-pregnancy-remains/.

———. 2018h. News: The Latest News from the Miscarriage Association. *Miscarriage Association*. Accessed April 12, 2019. https://www.miscarriageassociation.org.uk/story_type/02-videos/.

Morris, Max, and Eric Anderson. 2015. Charlie Is So Cool Like: Authenticity, Popularity and Inclusive Masculinity on YouTube. *Sociology* 49 (6): 1200–1217.

Moscrop, Andrew. 2011. Scans, Misogyny, and Miscarriage: Media Pictures of Late Gestation Fetuses Provoke Scaremongering Over Early Pregnancy Ultrasonography. *BMJ* 343: 1–2.

Mosquera, Susan. 2017. My Forever Child. *My Forever Child.* Accessed April 12, 2019. https://myforeverchild.com/blogs/memorial-poems/my-forever-child-poem.

Mumsnet. 2016. Miscarriage Care: The Background. *Mumsnet.* Accessed April 12, 2019. https://www.mumsnet.com/campaigns/miscarriage-care-campaign-press-release.

Murdoch, Cassie. 2012. Should You Tell Your Facebook Friends You've Had a Miscarriage? *Jezebel.* Accessed April 12, 2019. https://jezebel.com/5897347/should-you-tell-your-facebook-friends-youve-had-a-miscarriage.

Murphy, Patricia. 2015. Youtube Couple Suffers Miscarriage After Their Pregnancy Announcement Goes Viral Online. *Independent.ie.* Accessed April 12, 2019. https://www.independent.ie/life/family/youtube-couple-suffers-miscarriage-after-their-pregnancy-announcement-goes-viral-online-31440207.html.

Murphy, Judy, William Goossen, and Patrick Weber, eds. 2017. *Forecasting Informatics Competencies for Nurses in the Future of Connected Health: Proceedings of the Nursing Informatics Post Conference 2016.* Amsterdam: IOS Press.

NHS. 2014. One Billion Visits to NHS Choices Website. *NHS.* Accessed April 12, 2019. http://content.digital.nhs.uk/article/5161/One-billion-visits-to-NHS-Choices-website.

———. 2015a. About the NHS Choices Website. *NHS.* Accessed April 12, 2019. https://www.nhs.uk/about-us/about-the-nhs-website/.

———. 2015b. Women with History of Stillbirth at High Risk of Another. *NHS.* Accessed April 12, 2019. https://www.nhs.uk/news/pregnancy-and-child/women-with-history-of-stillbirth-at-high-risk-of-another/.

———. 2017. Miscarriage. Brighton and Sussex University Hospitals: NHS Trust. Accessed April 12, 2019. https://www.bsuh.nhs.uk/wp-content/uploads/sites/5/2016/09/Miscarriage.pdf.

———. 2018a. Overview: Stillbirth. *NHS.* Accessed April 12, 2019. https://www.nhs.uk/conditions/stillbirth/.

———. 2018b. Overview: Miscarriage. *NHS.* Accessed April 12, 2019. https://www.nhs.uk/conditions/miscarriage/.

———. 2018c. Causes: Miscarriage. *NHS.* Accessed April 12, 2019. https://www.nhs.uk/conditions/miscarriage/causes/.

———. 2018d. What Happens: Miscarriage. *NHS.* Accessed April 12, 2019. https://www.nhs.uk/conditions/miscarriage/what-happens/.

———. 2018e. Diagnosis: Miscarriage. *NHS.* Accessed April 12, 2019. https://www.nhs.uk/conditions/miscarriage/diagnosis/.

———. 2018f. Overview: Ectopic Pregnancy. *NHS.* Accessed April 12, 2019. https://www.nhs.uk/conditions/ectopic-pregnancy/.

———. 2018g. Symptoms: Miscarriage. *NHS.* Accessed April 12, 2019. https://www.nhs.uk/conditions/miscarriage/symptoms/.

184   R. FEASEY

————. 2018h. Molar Pregnancy. *NHS*. Accessed April 12, 2019. https://www.nhs.uk/conditions/Molar-pregnancy/.

————. 2018i. Causes: Stillbirth. *NHS*. Accessed April 12, 2019. https://www.nhs.uk/conditions/stillbirth/causes/.

————. 2018j. Coping with Stillbirth. *NHS*. Accessed April 12, 2019. https://www.nhs.uk/conditions/pregnancy-and-baby/coping-with-stillbirth/.

————. 2018k. Overview: Stillbirth. *NHS*. Accessed April 12, 2019. https://www.nhs.uk/conditions/stillbirth/.

————. 2018l. Afterwards: Miscarriage. *NHS*. Accessed April 12, 2019. https://www.nhs.uk/conditions/miscarriage/afterwards/.

————. 2018m. What are Side Effects? *NHS*. Accessed April 12, 2019. https://www.nhs.uk/common-health-questions/medicines/what-are-side-effects/.

NHS Direct Wales. 2017a. Pregnancy Guide: Miscarriage. *NHS Direct Wales*. Accessed April 12, 2019. https://www.nhsdirect.wales.nhs.uk/livewell/pregnancy/miscarriage/.

————. 2017b. Stillbirth. *NHS Direct Wales*. Accessed May 1, 2019. https://www.nhsdirect.wales.nhs.uk/livewell/pregnancy/LosingBaby/.

Nsoesie, Elaine and Cesare, Nina. 2017. What the Public is Saying About Miscarriage in 140 Characters. *NPR*. Accessed April 12, 2019. https://www.npr.org/sections/health-shots/2017/08/27/542809414/what-the-public-is-saying-about-miscarriage-in-140-characters.

Obama, Michelle. 2018. *Becoming*. London: Viking.

ONS. 2018. Child Mortality in England and Wales: 2016. *Office for National Statistics*. Accessed April 12, 2019. https://www.ons.gov.uk/peoplepopulationandcommunity/birthsdeathsandmarriages/deaths/bulletins/childhoodinfantandperinatalmortalityinenglandandwales/2016.

Parfitt, Rebecca. 2017. Miscarriage in White. *Selfish Mother*. Accessed April 12, 2019. http://www.selfishmother.com/miscarriage-in-white/.

Parnell, Jade. 2017. Vlogging: A New Phenomenon, but is it a Concern for People's Health? *Journal of Aesthetic Nursing* 6 (4). Accessed April 12, 2019. http://www.magonlinelibrary.com/doi/abs/10.12968/joan.2017.6.4.196?journalCode=joan.

Petrucelli, Elizabeth. 2015a. Why I am Not Applauding Zuckerberg's Miscarriage Announcement. *ElizabethPetrucelli.com*. Accessed April 12, 2019. http://elizabethpetrucelli.com/zuckerbergs-miscarriage-announcement/.

————. 2015b. My Wanted Pregnancy—Aborted. *ElizabethPetrucelli.com*. Accessed April 12, 2019. http://elizabethpetrucelli.com/my-wanted-pregnancy-aborted/.

Pritchard, Louisa. 2015. Miscarriage: It's Time for This Secret Club of Women to Break the Taboo. *The Telegraph*. Accessed April 12, 2019. http://www.telegraph.co.uk/women/womens-health/11785240/Miscarriage-This-secret-club-of-women-must-break-the-taboo.html.

4 PREGNANCY LOSS: SHAME AND SILENCE OVER A SHARED EXPERIENCE 185

Purdie, Jennifer. 2017. The Public Pain of Announcing Your Miscarriage on Facebook. *Broadly.* Accessed April 12, 2019. https://broadly.vice.com/en_us/article/3k8b8k/the-public-pain-of-announcing-your-miscarriage-on-facebook.

Rauch, Melissa. 2017. Actress Melissa Rauch Announces Her Pregnancy and Reflects on the Heartache of Miscarriage. *Glamour.* Accessed April 12, 2019. https://www.glamour.com/story/actress-melissa-rauch-announces-pregnancy-and-reflects-on-miscarriage.

Richards, Mandi. 2018. A Blog About Miscarriage. *A Blog About Miscarriage.* Accessed April 12, 2019. http://ablogaboutmiscarriage.blogspot.co.uk.

Romero, Natalie. 2016. Let's Open Up About Miscarriage. *HuffPost: The Blog.* Accessed April 12, 2019. https://www.huffingtonpost.com/natalie-romero/lets-open-up-about-miscarriage_b_7973930.html.

Roston, Michael; Rogers, Angelica and Duner, Alex. 2015. Stillbirth: Your Stories. *The New York Times.* Accessed April 12, 2019. https://www.nytimes.com/interactive/2015/health/stillbirth-reader-stories.html.

Rotman, Dana, and Jennifer Preece. 2010. The 'WeTube' in YouTube—Creating an Online Community Through Video Sharing. *International Journal of Web Based Communities* 6 (3): 317–333.

Roy, Deanna. 2011. *Baby Dust: A Novel about Miscarriage and Pregnancy Loss.* Texas: Casey Shay Press.

Saccone, Anna. 2016. Miscarriage at 11 Weeks. *Anna Saccone Joly.* Accessed April 12, 2019. https://www.youtube.com/user/TheStyleDiet/search?query=miscarriage.

Sanchez, Kiele. 2016. Kiele Sanchez Opens Up About How *Kingdom* Helped Her Heal After Miscarriage. *The Hollywood Reporter.* Accessed April 12, 2019. https://www.hollywoodreporter.com/live-feed/kiele-sanchez-how-miscarriage-influenced-910313.

Sanghani, Radhika. 2015. Mark Zuckerberg Facebook Admission: 7 Myths About Miscarriage Busted. *The Telegraph.* Accessed April 12, 2019. http://www.telegraph.co.uk/women/womens-health/11780013/Mark-Zuckerberg-miscarriage-Facebook-post-7-myths-busted.html.

Scott, Megan. 2010/2015. Stillbirth: Your Stories. *The New York Times.* Accessed April 12, 2019. https://www.nytimes.com/interactive/2015/health/stillbirth-reader-stories.htm.

Scully, Anne-Marie. 2014. *Motherhoodwinked: An Infertility Memoir.* CreateSpace Independent Publishing Platform.

Sifferlin, Alexandra. 2015. Most Americans Don't Know the First Thing About Miscarriages. *Time.* Accessed April 12, 2019. http://time.com/3849280/pregnancy-miscarriage/.

Simonds, Wendy, and Barbara Katz Rothman. 1992. *Centuries of Solace: Expressions of Maternal Grief in Popular Literature.* Philadelphia: Temple University Press.

Soelmark, Nathalie. 2014a. Relational (Trans)formations: On the Aesthetics of Mediated Experiences with Infertility and Assisted Reproduction in Video Blogs, TV and Film Documentaries, and Installation Art. PhD diss., University of Southern Denmark. Accessed April 12, 2019. http://www.forskningsdatabasen.dk/en/catalog/2305627165.

———. 2014b. Atmospheric Video Blogs on Infertility. *Body, Space & Technology* 13: 1–12. Accessed April 12, 2019. https://www.bstjournal.com/articles/49/.

Sohr-Preston, Sarah, Alyssa Lacour, Tyler Brent, Timothy Dugas, and Lauren Jordan. 2016. Blogging about Family Building (Infertility, Pregnancy Loss, Adoption, Pregnancy, Trying to Conceive): Content and Blogging Motivations. *Studies in Media and Communication* 4 (1): 8–20.

Sterling, Evelina. 2013. From No Hope to Fertile Dreams: Procreative Technologies, Popular Media, and the Culture of Infertility. PhD diss., Georgia State University. Accessed April 12, 2019. https://scholarworks.gsu.edu/cgi/viewcontent.cgi?article=1069&context=sociology_diss.

Stern, Carly and Lankston, Charlie. 2015. Couple Who Broadcast Details About Their Miscarriage on YouTube Hit Back at Critics and Haters. *Daily Mail.* Accessed April 12, 2019. http://www.dailymail.co.uk/femail/article-3203602/Couple-broadcast-details-miscarriage-YouTube-hit-critics-haters-claim-persecuted-Christian-faith.html.

Sturgis, India. 2019. Alex Jones: I was Back on TV an Hour after Doctors Told me I'd Miscarried. Accessed April 23, 2019. https://www.telegraph.co.uk/women/life/alex-jones-back-tv-hour-doctors-told-miscarried/.

Stylist. 2011. Miscarriage. *Stylist.* Accessed April 12, 2019. https://www.stylist.co.uk/life/miscarriage/46588.

Sulleyman, Aatif. 2017. Mark Zuckerberg Wants Facebook Users to be Like Church Pastors. *The Independent.* Accessed April 12, 2019. https://www.independent.co.uk/life-style/gadgets-and-tech/news/facebook-mark-zuckerberg-social-network-users-church-pastors-morality-responsibility-divided-society-a7810296.html.

Swift, Rebecca. 2016. What it's Like to Have a Miscarriage in the Social Media Age. *Upworthy.* Accessed April 12, 2019. http://www.upworthy.com/what-its-like-to-have-a-miscarriage-in-the-social-media-age.

Taylor, Verta. 1993. Book Review: *Centuries of Solace: Expressions of Maternal Grief in Popular Literature. American Journal of Sociology* 99 (1): 238–240.

Tomlins, Jacqueline. 2003. *The Infertility Handbook: A Guide to Making Babies.* Sydney: Allen & Unwin.

Tommy's. 2018a. Statistics About Pregnancy Loss. *Tommy's.* https://www.tommys.org/our-organisation/charity-research/pregnancy-statistics.

———. 2018b. Recurrent Miscarriage. *Tommy's.* Accessed April 12, 2019. https://www.tommys.org/pregnancy-information/pregnancy-complications/pregnancy-loss/miscarriage/types-miscarriage/recurrent-miscarriage.

―――. 2018c. Miscarriage Statistics. *Tommy's.* Accessed April 12, 2019. https://www.tommys.org/our-organisation/charity-research/pregnancy-statistics/miscarriage.

―――. 2018d. Miscarriage—Information and Support. *Tommy's.* Accessed April 12, 2019. https://www.tommys.org/pregnancy-information/pregnancy-complications/pregnancy-loss/miscarriage-information-and-support.

―――. 2019a. Statistics About Stillbirth. *Tommy's.* Accessed April 12, 2019. https://www.tommys.org/our-organisation/charity-research/pregnancy-statistics/stillbirth.

―――. 2019b. Trying Again After a Miscarriage. *Tommy's.* Accessed April 12, 2019. https://www.tommys.org/pregnancy-information/pregnancy-complications/baby-loss/miscarriage/miscarriage-support/trying-again-after-miscarriage.

TV Tropes. 2018. Convenient Miscarriage. *TV Tropes.* Accessed April 12, 2019. http://tvtropes.org/pmwiki/pmwiki.php/Main/ConvenientMiscarriage.

Van Balen, Frank, and Marcia Inhorn. 2002. Introduction: Interpreting Infertility: A View from the Social Sciences. In *Infertility Around the Globe: New Thinking on Childlessness, Gender and Reproductive Technologies,* ed. Marcia Inhorn and Frank Van Balen, 3–32. London: University of California Press.

Willis, Olivia. 2018. The 12-week Pregnancy Rule: Why is the First Trimester Shrouded in Secrecy? *ABC News.* Accessed April 21, 2019. https://www.abc.net.au/news/health/2018-05-12/is-it-time-to-re-think-the-12-week-pregnancy-rule/9751468.

Withnall, Adam. 2014. Thousands of Unborn Foetuses Incinerated to Heat UK Hospitals. *The Independent.* Accessed April 12, 2019. http://www.independent.co.uk/life-style/health-and-families/health-news/thousands-of-unborn-foetuses-incinerated-to-heat-uk-hospitals-9212863.html.

Woods, Heather, and Emily Winderman. 2018. The Quiver is Full: Metonymy and Affiliation in *19 Kids and Counting's* Depiction of Pregnancy Loss in Advanced Maternal Age. *Feminist Media Studies* 18 (1): 108–121.

Zuckerberg, Mark 2015. Priscilla and I Have Some Exciting News: We're Expecting a Baby Girl! *Facebook.* Accessed April 12, 2019. https://www.facebook.com/zuck/posts/1010227657605014.

CHAPTER 5

Adoption: Eligibility, Assessment and Selection

INTRODUCTION

America 'adopts more children than the rest of the world *combined*, internationally as well as domestically' (Fogle 2015, emphasis in original; Adoption Network 2018), with approximately 135,000 children being adopted 'from the foster care system, private domestic agencies, family members, and other countries' every year (Ibid.). Although there has been a fall in international adoptions, David Crary notes that the number of domestic adoptions in the US has remained relatively stable in recent years (Crary 2017). However, in the UK, the number of children in need of adoption has doubled in the past five years while the number of children adopted has fallen for a second year, down from a peak of 5360 in 2015 to 4350 in 2017 (Department for Education 2017). With this in mind it is crucial that we understand the ways in which adoption is depicted in documentaries such as *Catwalk Kids* (2011), *Finding Mum and Dad* (2014), *Wanted: A Family of My Own* (2014) and *15,000 Kids and Counting* (2014) (with the last title referring to the number of children in need of forever families in the UK each year) and *Finding Me a Family* (2017). After all, public service and commercial programming is in a position to inform audiences about child protection, the adoption process and the role and responsibility of prospective adopters. These programmes make it clear why children are taken into care: they do well to foreground those older, ethnic minority, additional support needs children and sibling groups awaiting adoption, and highlight what the stages are for those

© The Author(s) 2019

R. Feasey, *Infertility and Non-Traditional Family Building*,
https://doi.org/10.1007/978-3-030-17787-4_5

189

considering family building via this route. However, there is the suggestion that these texts and the wider social context are less vocal about the support needed by both children and families as they move beyond the matching and adoption process.

The reality of adoption has changed over recent generations. Gloria Hochman, Director of Communications at the National Adoption Center, makes the point that up until the 1970s, adoption was primarily of babies by married couples who could not produce children biologically (Fogle 2015). Although the feminist, civil rights and LGBT+ movements have helped to transform ideas about who can and should adopt, there is the sense that this message is not reaching a mainstream public. Recent research published by the UK government has suggested that although up to 650,000 people have considered adoption, 'many are put off because of myths and misconceptions about the process' (Pemberton 2018). This number is in the millions in the US. We are told that while '81.5 million Americans have considered adoption' only 1 in 500 of these adults would be needed to provide 'every waiting child in foster care' with a permanent family (Fogle 2015; Fixsen 2011). The difference between consideration and commitment to adoption is often down to misconceptions and misinformation because, according to Adam Pertman, President and Founder of the National Center on Adoption and Permanency, people's 'notions about adoptions, how it works, and who the people in it are, are still not well-informed' (Fogle 2015; Dave Thomas Foundation 2018a).

Reliable and accessible, candid rather than sensational stories become crucially important if we consider the need for future adoptive families. Especially if one considers that in America alone '23,000 children age out of foster care [every year] without finding a permanent family' and while only '2% of children who age out … will go on to get a college education … 80% of the prison population comprises adults who were in the foster care system at some point in their childhood' (Fogle 2015). In short, both the UK and the US are in need of adoptive parents, either to increase or merely maintain their current levels of family building for those infants and children who find themselves in care. It is crucial that we understand the role that the media in general, and adoption documentaries in particular could play in helping raise awareness of this form of family building, for those affected by an infertility diagnosis and beyond. However, before we consider the representation of adoption in the media, we need to make sense of the lived experience of adoption, from policies to practices.

Adoption in the UK

Recent statistics tell us that 'very few babies are "given up" for adoption in the UK' (Adoption UK 2018a). However, 'each year in England alone, there are around 4000 children waiting in foster care, unable to live with their birth families' and of these 4000 children, the 'majority are older children, sibling groups who need to be placed together or children with disabilities' (Ibid.).

The ubiquitous and long-standing perception of adoption is of unmarried single teenagers giving up a newborn in the hope of that child having a better start in life with a respectable, professional, middle-class family, in the manner of a storyline from the popular and long-running *Friends* (1994–2004). However, the reality is that it tends to be children rather than babies who are in need of adoptive families, and while the media depiction of happy healthy newborns fill our screens, removed from the romanticised fictions, those children awaiting adoption may have experienced loss or trauma 'even if they were adopted shortly after birth' (NHS 2018a). Moreover '[m]any have also sadly experienced abuse and/or neglect' (Adoption UK 2018a). It may be unpalatable but unsurprising then to be reminded that at a time when the number of children looking for adoptive families is rising, the number of individuals and families looking to adopt has fallen (Adoption UK 2018b). Sue Armstrong Brown, Chief Executive of Adoption UK, makes it clear that we need 'to do more to recruit potential adopters' (Ibid.). We need to understand the role that the media can and does play in informing potential adopters about the need for families and the reality of family building for children, sibling groups and potential parents.

Adoption agencies in England are all either part of a local authority or independent voluntary adoption agencies. At the time of writing there are close to 50 regional and national independent adoption agencies. First4Adoption, the national information service for those interested in adopting a child in England, tells us that local authorities and independent agencies are similar in the sense that they are both regulated by Ofsted, they both 'search for prospective adopters' and they both 'prepare and support people to become adoptive parents' (First4Adoption 2018a). They differ because while the local authorities have children in their care, the independent organisations do not (Ibid.). However, it is important to note that while neither of the agencies 'charge prospective parents for their services within the UK … there are some charges for those who wish to adopt children from abroad' (Ibid.).

Prospective parents are rigorously assessed in all aspects of life, from finances, work routines and domestic arrangements to relationships. Prospective adopters are asked about their own childhood and how they were parented. These assessments are so thorough that one potential adopter noted that 'our social worker knows us better than our family. She knows everything, even our ups and our downs, and stuff that you normally don't share with your family, but she knows' (*Wanted: A Family of My Own* E1). In her family-building memoir, Julie Selby tells readers that the more she learned about adoption assessments, the more the process 'seemed stressful and just as big an emotional rollercoaster as the IVF journey. In some ways, it can be harder [because] with IVF no one really assesses whether you are a "good" potential parent' (Selby 2015, p. 30).

In what sounds like a relatively straightforward, but routinely experienced as a time-consuming, emotionally difficult and lengthy, process of assessment, an approved prospective adopter 'enter[s] the matching stage of the adoption process' with the social workers liaising to 'identify possible matches' with children and parents (Adoption UK 2018a). We are told that social workers 'take care to consider the needs of the child(ren) with what the type of family and care prospective adopters can provide' (Ibid.). We are informed that although on occasion 'they have a child for adopters in mind early on … sometimes social workers need to look to other areas of the UK for a match' (Ibid.).

When looking for a match, social workers working with approved adopters and children awaiting adoption search The Adoption Register which holds all records of both parties. Likewise, family-finding services such as Children Who Wait are also available to assist in this process. These systems provide 'profiles of children waiting for adoption including information on the children's backgrounds and needs as well as photographs and, in some cases, online video content' (Adoption UK 2018a). When 'a possible match has been found, prospective adopters are given further information and can discuss with their social worker whether they feel they can provide the family and type of care the child(ren) needs' (Ibid.). Prospective 'adopters can then decide whether to proceed to matching panel, where an independent team will formally decide on the match. Once a panel has approved the match, introductions can commence' (Ibid.). For potential adopters interested in intercountry adoption, adoption agencies are asked to follow the guidelines set out by the Department for Education and work with the Intercountry Adoption Casework Team who will process all such cases, with the reminder that 'The Children and

Adoption Act 2006 requires [that] the Secretary of State for Education ... publish the list of countries on which [they] have placed adoption restrictions': namely Cambodia, Guatemala, Nepal and Haiti (Department for Education 2018a; International Adoption Guide 2018; IAC 2018). Such restrictions include, but are not limited to, those countries which are deemed to have insufficient safeguards to 'prevent children being adopted without proper consents being given and improper financial gain being made by individuals in the adoption process' (Department for Education 2018b). We are told that

> there is a trade in babies being sold for overseas adoption; and mothers being paid, or otherwise encouraged, to give up children for adoption. Such practices are contrary to the principles of the Hague Convention on Protection of Children and Co-operation in Respect of Intercountry Adoption and the United Nations Convention on the Rights of the Child. (Ibid.)

We are reminded that these babies and children 'have had unsettled starts in life and all will have experienced some form of loss by being taken into care' (Adoption UK 2018a). And because some babies and children 'may have additional needs resulting from physical, mental or emotional problems or disabilities' (NHS 2018a), it is important to get a detailed health history and a full understanding of the physical, mental, emotional and educational needs of the child 'so that if you decide to go ahead with the match, you will be as well informed as possible' (Ibid.). After all, we are told that 'realistic expectations will increase the chances of a successful adoption' (Ibid.).

Adoption as a Cure for Childlessness but not Infertility

As a routine part of the adoption process 'potential adopters are required to have a comprehensive health assessment' (NHS 2018b) in order to check for physical or mental concerns 'that might affect your ability to provide a safe, stable and loving home until a child reaches adulthood and, ideally, beyond' (Ibid.). The assessment will look at your health history, lifestyle and family medical history before a thorough physical examination (Ibid.).

It is perhaps unsurprising that the NHS points to the health and medical history of potential adoptive parents and the children awaiting adoption on their website, but it is worth noting that under the page entitled 'Adopting a child: your health and wellbeing', the first sentence tells us that your

> decision to adopt may be affected or influenced by your medical history, including any *attempts* to start a family. Any adoption agency will take into account your health and needs when it considers whether you are suitable to be approved as an adoptive parent. (NHS 2018b, emphasis added)

The word 'attempts' is significant here in that it seems to point to adoption after miscarriage, infertility or unsuccessful assisted reproductive treatments. This link is made even clearer when, in the next section, we are informed that '[m]any couples come to adoption because they have been unable to conceive a baby. Trying to conceive a child over a long period of time, unsuccessfully, has a big emotional impact. In this situation, it's important for you to come to terms with the fact that you cannot conceive before starting the adoption process' (NHS 2018b); not just 'come to terms with the fact that you cannot conceive' but actually end fertility treatment before you apply to adopt (Ibid.). Indeed '[m]ost agencies prefer you to wait several months between your treatment ending and formally applying to be approved as adopters' (Ibid.). Although the page is dedicated to health and well-being, it is significant to note that the only case study included, alongside a myriad of helpful factsheets and forums, is of a couple who adopted after a failed round of IVF (Ibid., NHS 2018c).

Away from the NHS website, on a page entitled 'How do I decide if it's right for me', the national adoption information service informs us that whether you are 'married or single, divorced or living with a partner, gay or straight, unemployed or disabled, and whatever your cultural background ... adoption may be for you' (First4Adoption 2018b). What is interesting here, however, is how the service echoes the NHS pages when it states that 'you have a wish to be a parent but fertility issues mean that you cannot have a birth child' (Ibid.). The link makes it clear that adoption is 'one of a range of alternatives that you may be considering if you cannot conceive and give birth to a child' (First4Adoption 2018c).

When starting on the adoption process, an adoption agency will ask 'that you don't attempt to conceive once you are being assessed to adopt'

(Ibid.). Moreover, you will be advised to take a break of 'at least six months … after your last treatment or after a miscarriage' (Ibid.) before starting an adoption assessment. For a woman who has undergone fertility interventions and who may have spent several months or years having assisted reproductive tests and treatments, having to wait several months before she can begin the adoption process might feel excruciating; however, medical and adoption services form a consensus in terms of their advice when they tell women in this situation to 'use this time to prepare. For example, you can read up on adoption issues[,] hear from other adopters in different stages of the process' (NHS 2018b), look at those children who are waiting to be adopted 'and start considering how you would parent children with various needs' (Ibid.).

A website dedicated to 'Older Parent Adoption' reminds us that although there are a myriad of reasons why 'singles and couples arrive at the decision to adopt in their 40s and later' they foreground what they term 'many years of infertility treatments' as one such reason (adoption. com 2018). Although adopters need to be over 21, there is no upper age limit in the UK. Rather, '[a]gencies will expect you to have the health and vitality to see your children through to an age of independence' (First4Adoption 2018d). Likewise, very few American 'states have laws that state a maximum age for adoptive parents. When it comes to finding adoptive parents for a child, the thing that matters most is the ability to provide a loving, nurturing, and safe home' (American Adoptions News 2018). That said, '[p]rospective birth mothers often choose to place their babies with younger parents' in open adoption (Ibid.). However, rather than be deterred from the adoption process, older women interested in adopting are encouraged to foster first, to look to international adoption or consider independent adoption (adoption.com 2018). With notions of foster-for-adoption and independent adoption in mind, I will now turn to the differences in UK and US adoption processes and practices.

ADOPTION IN THE US

Although adoption 'laws vary widely from state to state' (Dinwoodie 2017), what the American states and the UK have in common is 'the need for foster and adoptive parents … especially … for older children, groups of siblings and disabled children' (Nelson 2017). Moreover, we are informed that the 'licensure process for adoption … is much the same in both countries, with orientations, applications, initial background checks and references, trainings and assessments all taking place over the course of about six months, before prospective parents can move forward with being matched with a child' (Ibid.). In the US, adoption agencies must be licensed by the state in which they operate, with the government's Child Welfare Information Gateway website listing each licensed agency (Child Welfare Information Gateway 2004, 2015). And, like The Adoption Register in the UK, the US government-affiliated website AdoptUSKids. org and charitable organisations such as the National Adoption Center assist in sharing information about children with potential adoptive parents (AdoptusKids 2018a; National Adoption Center 2018).

While in the UK the stages of adoption move through what is termed a pre-stage exploration, initial checks and registration, training and assessment and matching with the right child before moving in (First4Adoption 2018e), in the US they similarly move from exploring your adoption options, understanding the laws, selecting an adoption services provider, completing a home study, engaging in the placement process and filing necessary legal documents before parenting your child (Child Welfare Information Gateway 2015).

Yet although the need for adoptive parents exists in both countries, there are distinctions in how the adoption process works. A key difference between countries is that while adoption in the UK is via a local agency or voluntary independent adoption agency, there are currently a number of different 'types of agencies or service providers you may work with in a domestic adoption' in the US, namely 'a public agency, a licensed private agency, an attorney ("independent adoption") … an adoption facilitator [if allowed by State laws] or [an] unlicensed agency' (Child Welfare Information Gateway 2015; McDermott 2018). The differences are outlined thus:

> public agency adoption … locate and prepare adoptive families to adopt children from foster care. … In a licensed private agency adoption, birth parents relinquish their parental rights to an agency, and adoptive parents work with an agency to adopt. … In an Independent Adoption, attorneys assist prospective adoptive parents and birth parents with the adoption process, which usually involves the adoption of an infant. Families adopting independently identify the expectant parents (or pregnant woman) without an agency's help. … Adoptive placements by facilitators and unlicensed agencies offer the least amount of supervision and oversight. A facilitator is any person who links prospective adoptive parents with expectant birth mothers for a fee. (Child Welfare Information Gateway 2015)

Furthermore, we find that although 'public and licensed private agencies are required to meet State standards ... [u]nlicensed agencies and facilitators often do not have the same State oversight; consequently, there may be more financial, emotional, and legal risk for adoptive and birth families using unlicensed services' (Child Welfare Information Gateway 2015). State-funded public agency adoptions from foster care, much like the UK system, are routinely for those families who want to 'adopt older children, sibling groups, or children with special physical or psychological needs' (parents.com 2019), whereas the more expensive private agencies are routinely employed by those families who want to adopt a newborn, and thus match with a pregnant woman outside of the foster care system (Ibid.). While public agency 'adoptions through the state in the US ... much like UK adoptions ... are almost entirely without cost, a private agency adoption can cost anywhere between $20,000 and $40,000' (Nelson 2017).

On a site dedicated to weighing up the options of public and private adoption, we are reminded that 'the ultimate goal of the foster care system is to reunite biological parents with their children' and as such it can take 'anywhere from 1–5 years ... to adopt a child this way' (AdoptHelp 2019). Routinely, this happens with an older child. Indeed, it is unusual to adopt a newborn through public adoption (Ibid.). The site makes it clear that although 'adopting through the foster system may cost significantly less than adopting privately, it may take significantly more time' and present you with older children in need of permanence (Ibid.). As such, prospective adopters are asked to consider if the age of the child, 'the time it takes to adopt or the cost to adopt is more important' (Ibid.).

April Dinwoodie, Chief Executive of The Donaldson Adoption Institute and co-founder of Fostering Change for Children, echoes the point that experiences of adoption in the US depend on 'how much money you have because the private and public adoption systems are worlds apart' (Dinwoodie 2017). Dinwoodie goes on to demand reform that would see the country 'move away from a fractured and transactional adoption process to a more uniform and transformational process where everyone—expectant parents, first/birth parents, adopted persons and adoptive families—are better prepared and supported' (Ibid.). In terms of being better prepared, there is evidence to suggest that fostering for adoption, also known as 'dual approval' or 'early permanence', might be useful in this regard. Fostering for adoption, although still in its infancy in the UK, is commonplace in the US (Nelson 2017).

Fostering for Adoption

In the US today, a little 'more than half of children who go into foster care return to their birth families' (AdoptUsKids 2018b). We are told that '[a]dopting from foster care is similar to other types of adoption in that after all of the decision making, paperwork, and preparation are completed, a dream of family is fulfilled' (Ibid.). However, there are some differences: namely that the 'children in foster care have experienced some form of trauma' and, as such, the 'parents who adopt from foster care undergo specific training to understand the effects of trauma and help children heal' (Ibid.).

Embarking on foster parent training and experiencing life as a foster parent prior to adoption is said to help prepare potential parents for future family building. Beyond the training, we are asked to consider the benefits of fostering before adoption (AdoptUsKids 2018b). After all, a woman who longs to love and care for a child can take on a parenting role earlier than if awaiting adoption, she can get important insight and experience into caring for different age ranges and need levels and she can see if she feels a meaningful connection or bond with the children in her care. The children in question also benefit because there is a chance that they could bond with and potentially be adopted by their foster parent, meaning fewer moves and earlier family stability (Ibid.). And although 'foster parents must always be prepared for the very real possibility that [the] children they hoped to adopt are returned to their birth parents or placed with other relatives' (Ibid.), recent statistics remind us that 'approximately 40% of American adoptions are from the U.S. foster care system' (Fogle 2015; Child Welfare Information Gateway 2011).

If or When: Adoption After Infertility

The UK or the US, local authority or private agency, irrespective of the route or country in question, both medical and family services suggest that adoption is a meaningful next step on the path to family building for women who have been affected by an infertility diagnosis. Over three quarters of adoptive parents choose this family-building path because of infertility, pregnancy-related health concerns or following miscarriages (Selwyn et al. 2014, p. 120). It has been suggested that women who have embarked on fertility treatment are ten times more likely to build a family via adoption than those who have not been affected by infertility (Fogle 2015). That said, we are reminded that

5 ADOPTION: ELIGIBILITY, ASSESSMENT AND SELECTION   199

[y]ou don't have to try fertility treatments first. Adoption can be a positive first choice if you are unable to conceive. Some people have moral or religious objections to assisted conception, some would rather avoid any unpleasant symptoms and side effects of treatment, some consider the prospects of success too slim, and some find their motivation to love and parent a child or children that need a family is stronger than the biological drive to produce a child that shares their genes. (First4Adoption 2018c)

Although the national information service for people interested in adopting a child in England acknowledges that adoption might lead on from an infertility diagnosis, they remind interested parties that even though adoption 'is a great way to become a parent [it is] not a direct alternative to conception' (Ibid.). After all, 'it is a very different kind of parenting' (NHS 2018b).

However, outside of the infertility, pregnancy loss or adoptive community, there seems to be a misconception that IVF is a 'cure' for infertility, and, likewise, that adoption is a 'cure' for failed assisted reproductive treatments. In the comments section of a news article dedicated to the rarely told story of a near-decade-long unsuccessful IVF journey, the couple who had tried for eight years to conceive were told in compassionate and sympathetic tones in the readers' comments to 'please adopt. You're both young, you both have a huge amount of love to give and there are so many babies and young children needing parents like you' (Ann comment on House 2017), and likewise 'there's a child or two, or more, out there who need a good home. Just adopt or take in a foster child. Once [you have] a child to care for, [you will] forget all about the IVF' (MineOpine comment on House 2017). The adoption theme continues, but in a more judgemental tone when we are told 'why not adopt a baby, there are many that need homes' (kitesurfercarly comment on House 2017) and likewise that 'if you wanted one that badly you should have adopted' (Samglo comment on House 2017).

One traumatised father whose child is taken into care in *15,000 Kids and Counting* makes the leap from infertility to adoption when he states: 'I know, fair enough there is people out there that can't have children but why take fucking our children off of us, that are their rightful parent and give 'em to somebody else?' (*15,000 Kids and Counting*: E1). Furthermore, comments on a *New York Times* post entitled 'Too Many Ways to Have a Baby' (Belkin 2009) present adoption as a simple, straightforward and logical next maternal step for women affected by an infertility diagnosis:

To me the answer is quite simple. If you can't have children the natural way, adopt. There are SOOOO many children already out there, just wanting to be loved. (yip comment on Belkin 2009)

Why fight biology so hard? There are so many adults who want to be parents, there are so many children who want to be loved. It amazes me that more people don't jump into adoption immediately like we did. (Sarah comment on Belkin 2009)

Adopt. If you can't love a child who isn't perfect, or who isn't a DNA carbon copy of you, maybe you shouldn't be a parent. (ACW comment on Belkin 2009)

While I cannot begin to understand how wrenching it must be for women who want to have babies but can't, I'm also puzzled by why they go to such lengths to conceive when they could adopt. There are thousands upon thousands of babies in this country—and many others—waiting for a loving home. So why all the obsession with being pregnant and having your own baby? (Question comment on Belkin 2009)

Although some women will transfer their attention and maternal efforts from assisted reproductive treatments and technologies to the adoption process, for others, these are entirely separate and distinct paths. Although one might be greatly desired and aggressively pursued, the other may not be a viable or desirable option; and this decision should be removed from judgement. In response to the posts from the *New York Times*, Dawn Davenport, from The National Infertility and Adoption Education non-profit organisation comments:

[W]hy not just adopt? Well, first of all, while it may be true that there are 'thousands upon thousands of children … waiting for a loving home,' not all of them are available for adoption, and few of them are babies. … Most people who want to adopt will be able to, but it is far from easy or quick. But more important than the general misunderstanding of the realities of adoption, these comments reflect a basic misunderstanding of infertility and adoption. Adoption is not a cure for infertility, and an adopted child is not a generic replacement for the longed for biological child. Adoption is a 'cure' for childlessness, but not for infertility. (Davenport 2017)

Davenport goes on to say that some women who have been affected by an infertility diagnosis are happy and fulfilled as adoptive mothers, while others feel a need to conceive and breastfeed. They want a genetic connection with a baby, rather than the experience of parenting an adopted child. The journalist tells us not to judge these women because 'they simply want what comes so easy for most of us' (Davenport 2017). After all, even though adoption is 'a great—no, really a phenomenal—way to create a family ... it is not for everyone' (Ibid.). To assume that a woman looking to reproductive treatments can or will shift her maternal attentions to the adoption process is unfair to the infertile woman and the prospective adopted child (Ibid.).

In an article for CNN Parents entitled 'When Adoption Is not an Option', Justine Brooks Froelker begins by pointing out that her 'infertility journey ... has not resulted in that adorable picture of the "complete" family, baby and all' before suggesting that this situation makes those around her feel both 'uncomfortable and sad' (Froelker cited in Wallace 2016; Froelker 2017). After two rounds of unsuccessful IVF, Froelker decided to end assisted reproductive treatments. She says that if and when she lets people know that she is unable to conceive and is no longer looking for further treatment options, 'they immediately move into problem-solving mode', which routinely means being asked 'why don't you just adopt?' Froelker suggests that they 'want to take care of my pain. They sure as heck don't want to sit in pain with me, because it's so uncomfortable, so they'd rather have sympathy for me and fix it' (Ibid.). While many others speak of their frustration, anger or irritation from this line of questioning, Froelker draws on her experiences as a mental health therapist and 'shifts into educator mode' by trying 'to help people understand that adoption is an "awesome option" for many families, but it wasn't on the table for her and her husband' (Ibid.). Froelker writes that it 'is OK to say adoption isn't for you. ... It is OK to own that decision' (Ibid.) because

> [i]t takes a lot more courage for me to stand up and say, 'I know adoption is not right for my family,' but the only thing harder than that would be to not listen to my truth and my husband's truth and what I know is right for our family and to just adopt because that is what we are supposed to do. (Ibid.)

While Froelker offers insight into getting off the assisted reproductive treadmill and navigating a path through infertility that does not result in a maternal role, other voices can be seen and heard that remind us of the long-standing and near ubiquitous link between womanhood and motherhood. By way of an example, Truly-MD.com co-founders and fertility doctors Jaime Knopman and Sheeva Talebian tell us, either irresponsibly or insensitively that

> there is almost always light at the end of the tunnel. Parenthood can be achieved in many different ways. It can happen naturally; it can happen after an IVF cycle with your own eggs or IVF with donor eggs. It can happen using a surrogate. And last but not least, it can also happen after adoption. And while we totally understand that the journey may take on several unexpected turns, peaks and valleys, if you stay on course you will reach your destination. (cited in Nikol aka Not Just a Beauty Blogger 2017)

In short, women affected by an infertility diagnosis are routinely and repeatedly judged: judged for their initial infertility diagnosis; judged for not seeking assisted reproductive treatments, judged for seeking and later stopping treatments before a successful pregnancy outcome; later again judged for either not looking to adopt, or for adopting. After all, according to Marcia Sandelowski and Frank de Lacey,

> [a]doption is still generally regarded in the West as a second-best solution to infertility. It requires would-be adoptive parents to accept a biologically unrelated child as their own in a social milieu that favours biology as the proper basis for parental ties and birth mothers to choose relinquishment over abortion as the resolution to an unintended or otherwise 'problem' pregnancy. (Sandelowski and de Lacey 2002, p. 40)

Gayle Letherby has produced extensive research on the social, emotional and medical experience of motherhood and non-motherhood in relation to infertility and involuntary childlessness. On the back of a semi-structured interview and written correspondence with 65 women who defined themselves as infertile and/or involuntarily childless, she found that 'nonmothers often feel stigmatised and perceive that others view them as less than whole, pitiable and "desperate"' (Letherby 1999, p. 359). Moreover, she discovered that '[w]omen who achieve motherhood following "infertility/involuntary childlessness" (particularly social rather than biological motherhood) still feel that they do not meet the ideal' (Ibid., p. 359). Her respondents noted that even after adoption, they had a 'longing' or felt a void on the back of their non-biological maternal role (Ibid., p. 367). This feeling was due in part to the fact that 'biological motherhood is more highly valued than social motherhood' (Ibid., p. 367). In short, biological motherhood is understood as 'true' motherhood (Letherby 2003, p. 60). Letherby continues:

> [A]doption as an option was often regarded as a last resort after medical treatment had failed. The higher value placed on biological motherhood was supported by women who became social parents and mothered children to whom they are biologically/genetically unrelated. (Ibid., p. 367)

However, as mentioned previously, in relation to the hierarchy of appropriate motherhood in a pronatal period committed to the ideology of intensive mothering, adoption is seen to be more acceptable than voluntary or involuntary childlessness (Letherby 1999).

Judgement is also said to occur for those women who look to adopt even though they have not been diagnosed with infertility, and already have their own biological children. A recent mumsnet thread on the topic of adoption began with one mother of two young biological children considering adopting a third child:

> My husband and I are considering adopting our third child. We have 2 biological children aged 4 and 2 who are wonderful, and we love very much. We really enjoy being parents and thought we could provide a loving home to a child who really needs it. However, are we being naive? What is looking after a child with developmental delay/attachment issues/behavioural issues like in that context? I would love to hear the thoughts of people who have experience of adopting. We would only be able to be matched with quite a young baby given our youngest child's age. (Butterflymum79 2016)

The naivety here is less to do with her limited knowledge of developmental delay, for example, and more to do with the reality of adoption as it relates to the age of the children seeking families. In short, babies rarely come up for adoption and those that do are not short of potential forever homes. One might expect that the mumsnet thread would look to foreground the realities associated with adoption; after all, many of the thread commentators either work within adoption services or are themselves adoptive or potential adoptive parents. What is unexpected, however, is the challenging tone. Several comments pick up on the misunderstanding and misinformation being presented in the original post, before going on to question the woman's reason for extending her family. The first reply, from an existing adoptive mother, makes it clear that there is no shortage of potential adopters for babies, and that in this instance, her maternal services would not be needed. We are told that it would be a

[d]ifferent story if you could take on an older child, a sibling group or a high needs child but as you point out that's unlikely to be a possibility in your situation. ... The only really good reason to adopt is that you desperately want a child and for some reason adoption is the best way forward—please don't do it in order to 'provide a loving home', no child deserves to be a charity project. (Kewcumber 2016)

The thread continues with stories from existing adoptive mothers, with what are shorthand references to experiences of caring for ACs (adoptive children) as opposed to BCs (biological children), before the aforementioned commentator returns to say that

it really isn't the case just now that for a young low apparent needs child you will be providing them with any more loving a home than anyone else who will be waiting for a child at the same time. And whilst it is certainly true that any child comes with a risk, you are in denial if you don't accept that the risks of issues with an adopted child are significantly higher than with a birth child. (Ibid.)

This theme is then echoed through several voices as we are reminded that

[t]he children in care who really need a loving home are children of school age with special needs and sibling groups and younger children with significant special needs. ... As others have said, if you apply to adopt a child under two without significant need, all you are doing is taking such a child away from another adoptive family, *many of whom may be childless*. There is no 'need' for such adopters, there's too much demand and not enough supply. (Kr1stina 2016, emphasis added)

There is a kind of a new mommy war emerging here in the sense that, removed from debates concerning the animosity that is said to exist between stay-at-home and working mothers (Akass 2011), there seems to be frictions between those who look to adopt as a way of family building on the back of an infertility diagnosis or pregnancy loss and those who look to adopt as a way of extending their own biological units. The thread continues:

And to the comment that you are taking a child away from another family who may be childless, while not wanting to diminish the pain of childlessness, that comment is unnecessarily cruel and extremely offensive to us who have adopted when already having a bc. We did the pre adoption training with many couples who had fertility issues and often felt that we were viewed as a couple who shouldn't be considering adoption as we already had a bc, however that is something to be challenged. ... There is NOT a one child policy and nor should there be. The love we feel to and from our beautiful dd [dear daughter] confirms to us that we are a happy family and she loves her 'big sister' if she had gone to a couple with no children she wouldn't have had that experience. (meandyouplustwo 2016)

When the mother who originated this thread notes, on the back of an enlightening but challenging online dialogue, that there is 'lots to think about—perhaps waiting is something to consider. It gives us more possibilities in who we could take and allows us to give our attention to our bcs whilst they are still little' (Ibid.), it might irk those who are looking to adoption as a route to family building on the back of an infertility diagnosis rather than biological family extension.

Mumsnet, the UK parenting website that encourages users to share parenting advice and information (boasting a network of 10,000 bloggers, vloggers and social media influencers), is peppered with numerous threads dedicated to the topic of adoption, ranging from 'Just Started the Adoption Process' and 'Difference between LA and Voluntary Agencies' to 'Getting Cold Feet' and 'Really Struggling', and some of the posts in the later threads are frank and candid about the reality of adopting children with additional needs in terms of the impact that it has on friendships, relationships and wider family harmony. Talk of strains and struggles, turmoil and tragedy are common on these message boards, but although these posts are numerous, they are not the only voices here. When one mumsnet reader asked '[c]ould I hear your adoption success stories?' we are told that

DH [dear husband] and I are just starting the process of looking into adopting a child. I feel really nervous on so many levels. Would really appreciate just learning about adopted children & families, how it happened, how you feel, how you bonded. Anything really!! You name it I want to hear about it. Thanks. (longtermfamilyplanning 2009)

To which another prospective adoptive mother added:

Oh I'd love this too! There must be some positive stories out there? We're still waiting to start the whole process ... but we're almost there. I can sense there are millions of pitfalls and challenges which I'm glad to know about, but we seem to rarely hear of anything more positive and this would be good to know too to get some more personal experiences if poss[ible]. (looseleaf 2009)

A myriad of successful adoption stories followed: some spoke of difficult first years and late bonding, while others spoke of immediate love and connections with little in the way of additional support needs. Women who have been affected by infertility speak about their much-longed-for, and now finally realised, children. One adoptive mother tells us that she is penning her first-ever mumsnet post because

> I know how much I wanted to hear success stories when I was going through [the] process and I've got one! After years of failed ivf and losing a pregnancy we adopted two beautiful girls. ... It was not easy ... they came from a background of neglect and had issues of attachment but ... [t]hey are clever beautiful funny little girls who love us totally and completely ... hard to sum it up in a quick post except to say I'm a mammy and I never ever thought I would say that. Wishing you the same xx. (goodenoughmam 2014)

And likewise:

> We went through years of awful awful disappointing frustrating depressing unexplained infertility. When DD [dear daughter] came home I realised I would have willingly chosen to go through it all again if I had known she was the little pot of gold at the end of the rainbow. (ktbeau 2010)

One adoptive mother says 'a lot of people, when they find out the children are adopted ... say that they would never have "guessed". But I suspect that is the case for so many families—we often only see/hear about the disasters so the hundreds and thousands of success stories go unnoticed because no one has "guessed"' (neverjamtoday 2009). These existing and potential adoptive parents speak candidly within their families and on these anonymous message boards, but the issue of openness comes into question when we consider the relationship between adopted babies, infants, children and their biological families.

OPEN ADOPTION

At the age of 18, individuals in the UK are entitled to their birth certificates and are free to access their adoption records, while in America, nearly all states allow the adoptee, upon reaching adulthood, access to non-identifying information about themselves and their relatives. Moreover, nearly all states permit the release of identifying information when the person whose information is sought has consented to the release. However, the notion of open adoption goes further than being granted access to either identifying or non-identifying information. In the same way that the US is leading on fostering for adoption, so too they are forerunners in what are termed open adoptions, where contact takes place between a child's birth and adoptive families, be it 'occasional or frequent, in person or remote' (Child Welfare Information Gateway 2015; OPA 2018). Existing research shows that such contact is beneficial for all parties—children, birth families and adoptive families alike—because

> [c]hildren learn about their birth families in a gradual ... comfortable way, and they observe their birth and adoptive families interacting with each other. Birth parents know that their children have a loving home, and adoptive parents are not burdened with secrets to keep from their children. (Child Welfare Information Gateway 2015)

Although most adopted children in England 'never meet their birth family' (Ratcliffe 2017), we are told that 'over 85% of adoptions in the US are either semi or completely open' (Grant 2013), with contact between adoptive and birth parents considered to be best practice for all parties involved (Siegel 2008; Neil 2007, 2009; Young and Neil 2009). Guidance on open adoption in America comments that there is no one correct or right way to enter into the adoption process, and yet, those considering an adoption plan for their child are encouraged to ask themselves:

> Do I want to have a say in who will raise my child?
> Does it matter to me if I won't know if my child is safe and healthy?
> Do I want to watch my child grow up through photos, phone calls, letters, or visits?
> Do I want to be able to tell my child about his or her family background or other important information in the future?
> Do I want my child to know, for example, if he or she looks or acts like someone else in the family? (OPA 2018)

The Office of Population Affairs makes it clear that 'if your answer to any of these questions is "yes," open adoption may be the best choice for you and your baby' because it 'can give you peace of mind by knowing your child will have information about his or her family history, identity, and background' (Ibid.).

Although one might look to challenge the leading nature of the questions and the bias presented in the line of enquiry, much of the research on open adoption appears compelling for both adoptive and birth mothers, with both families having a say as to the level of openness they seek, be it fully open or semi-open, as it relates to levels of communication and exchange (Ibid.). We are told that open adoption allows children to 'understand how they came to be adopted' and 'ask questions about their family backgrounds as these questions come to mind throughout their lives' (Ibid.). Both fully open and semi-open adoptions differ from a confidential or closed adoption where no contact takes place and no identifying information is passed on. For those who want an insight into the lived experience of, and theories relating to, open adoption, it is worth noting that extant research exists within and beyond the social work sector for interested and invested readers (Siegel 2008, 2012, 2013; Scott et al. 2011; Neil et al. 2015; Robinson 2017).

Although the process of open adoption is not the same in each American state, The Office of Population Affairs gives an exhaustive list of the benefits for both biological parents and the children in question, with full details and supplementary resources to help anyone looking to understand or commit to this mode of placement (OPA 2018).

While the US moves closer to open adoptions, most babies, infants or children do not stay in contact with their birth family post adoption in England (Ratcliffe 2017). However, there is a sense that, on the back of recent research with adopted children, adoptive parents, their birth families and social workers, the UK may be moving towards greater openness in adoption with the creation of the Contact After Adoption website. The site is dedicated to helping practitioners working on post-adoption contact plans and to supporting birth relatives and adopters through contact planning for their child (Contact After Adoption 2018).

The Contact After Adoption website is based on longitudinal research that looks to explore people's experiences of contact and its impact on children and adults (Neil et al. 2015). Elspeth Neil, Mary Beek and Emma Ward tell us that the 'findings are of particular importance due to the study's duration—the children, all placed under the age of four, have been followed through preschool, middle childhood and into late adolescence' (Ibid.). Based on the fact that the researchers were able to follow the same family groups over an extended period of time, and when experimentation with more open adoption arrangements were taking place, 'a strong body of evidence has been collected about the impact of open adoption on all those involved, and on how children's experiences of and need for contact change as they grow and develop' (Ibid.).

In short, we are told that 'face-to-face contact should be considered in more adoption cases' (Neil cited in Ratcliffe 2017) because adopted 'young people experienced benefits from contact which included gaining information about their birth family, building an open atmosphere with their adoptive parents and enjoying relationships with birth family members' (Neil et al. 2013). Hugh Thornberry, chief executive of Adoption UK comments that

> the risks of direct contact, such as disrupting a placement or retraumatising a child, could be carefully managed by professionals and families. A more open approach to adoption can avoid another risk, which is that lots of children can build up an idealised version of their birth family despite what might be said to them. (Thornberry cited in Ratcliffe 2017)

Much contemporary social care research foregrounds the notion that '[o]pen adoption can have positive effects on the psychological well-being of adopted children' (Robinson 2017, p. 167). However, there is of course a clear distinction between an open adoption and unsolicited social media contact (Ratcliffe 2017); after all, '[c]ontact is only really beneficial to children when everyone who is involved is doing it willingly and with an open heart'. The authors make the point that

> [w]e need to do more to help adoptive parents think through the potential benefits of contact for their child, as well as assessing risks and difficulties. But we also need to do more to help them think through the potential difficulties if they refuse reasonable requests to promote contact. (Neil cited in Ratcliffe 2017)

Adoption is presented in medical and family services, mumsnet threads and government reports as both a rewarding yet demanding form of family building. With prospective and birth parents, social workers and foster carers all having to demonstrate emotional resilience in their desire to provide a successful outcome for children in need of forever families (Wallwork 2017), it is interesting to see what adoption stories are heard, faces seen, needs overlooked or groups ignored in popular media culture as they can help inform, educate and communicate the lived reality of this form of family building.

ADOPTION IN THE MEDIA

Adoption storylines are evident in a diverse array of media texts spanning genres, mediums and demographics, and such representations have the power, according to one mumsnet post, to 'challenge what people mean by family, rights, responsibilities and identities' (thomassmuggit 2018). Turning then to the stories that make it beyond the self-selecting readers of the mumsnet adoption thread to the mainstream entertainment media environment, we discover that this particular route to family building has been subject to recent interest in a diverse range of film genres: family films (*Free Willy* 2003, *Hotel for Dogs* 2009, *Annie* 2014, *A Wrinkle in Time* 2018), animated adventures with or without anthropomorphic families (*Meet the Robinsons* 2007, *Despicable Me* 2010, *Kung Fu Panda 2* 2011), superhero and heroic narratives (*Superman* 1978, *The Legend of Tarzan* 2016), biographies (*The Blind Side* 2009, *Lion* 2016), drama (*Paper Dream* 2012, *Clarity* 2015) and romance and comedy (*Mother and Child* 2009). Family building blogger Charlotte Madsen makes the point that screen depictions of women affected by an infertility diagnosis routinely look to adoption as the next step in family building after unsuccessfully trying IVF. When one character in the comedic *What to Expect When You're Expecting* (2012) tells her husband that 'we'll do three rounds of IVF. And if that doesn't work, we'll just adopt', not only is it presented as a predictable cliché, but it goes some way to helping explain 'why we infertiles get so many people asking "why don't you just adopt?"' (Madsen of The Road to Baby Madsen: Our IVF Journey 2014). Adoption also appears in a number of documentaries (*Adopt Me I'm a Teenager* 2005, *The Dark Matter of Love* 2012, *Closure* 2013, *Stuck* 2013, *Twinsters* 2015) and the horror genre where infertile women find themselves nurturing 'homicidal, even demonic' children (*The Omen* 1972/2006, *The Ring* 2002, *Orphan* 2009) (Edge 2015, p. 116).

Over on the small screen, the theme of adoption has been presented in television comedy in general (*Brooklyn Nine-Nine* 2013–) and television situation comedy in particular (*30 Rock* 2006–13, *Modern Family* 2009–, *Mom* 2013–). A BBC sitcom pilot entitled *The Coopers vs The Rest* (2016) seemed to offer a promising take on the tried and tested family format, with an interracial couple and three adopted children taking over from the white, middle-class, traditional, biological, nuclear family unit of earlier genre texts. However, the promise was short-lived because the programme was never picked up from the pilot, with reviewers making the point that although the 'script certainly was grounded in an emotional truth' the adoptive mother and her 'hostile cervix' were lacking in maternal warmth (Mohan 2016). We are told that it was as if the woman's 'hostile cervix ... seemed to be affecting her whole personality—after a while, all that severity was grating' (Ibid.). The link between infertility and adoption is clear from the outset, but what is equally interesting here, looking back to the mumsnet thread as it threw scorn on the 'saviour' instinct, is the way in which the pilot was described on the public service website:

> The Cooper family share a small house, and absolutely no DNA. Mum Tess wanted to *save* as many kids as she could from the sort of childhood she had. So, along with her husband Toby, she now divides just about enough money and nowhere near enough time between their three adopted children Frankie, Alisha and Charlie. Written by award-winning writer (and adoptee) Andy Wolton. (BBC2 2016, emphasis added)

The notion of saving children is reminiscent of what is taken to be a problematic rather than positive reason for adopting. The adoptive parents on the mumsnet message board make the point that

> [w]e have ... had many many conversations over the years about how much it irritates us when people assume we 'rescued' our children for altruistic reasons ... adoptions for altruistic reasons rarely end well either at the assessment stage or more sadly with the child's experience of having to feel grateful. No need to take my word for it—you can read the adult adoptee threads and find plenty of evidence. (Kewcumber 2016)

The pilot is routinely praised for the originality of its premise but then poorly reviewed. Rather than looking to the trials and tribulations of a struggling yet well-meaning family unit, as is typical of the genre (Mills 2009), with adoption being of note but not the driving force of the show, we are told that the theme of adoption is 'rather laboured' and indeed 'hammer[ed] home' here at the expense of humour (Chen et al. 2016).

Adoption as a plot point also exists in American film and television drama (*Sex and the City* 1998–2004, 2008, 2010; *Grey's Anatomy* 2005–) where 'natural' pregnancy has a habit of following on from an adoption storyline. Brooke Edge tells readers that '[a]dopting a child would assist in moving these women who had pursued professional and sexual freedom closer to the Cult of True Womanhood, in the self-sacrificing mother vein of melodrama' (Edge 2015, p. 89). The fact that characters such as Charlotte

York/Kristin Davis and Meredith Grey/Ellen Pompeo become 'pregnant post-adoption with "miracle" babies' (Ibid., p. 89) is said to be 'emblematic of [a] longstanding (but scientifically unfounded) belief that infertile couples who adopt are more likely to subsequently conceive naturally' as it could be said to 'represent to audiences that these women proved themselves worthy of biological children once they gave themselves over to another's child' (Ibid., p. 89). These are not isolated instances; rather, there has been a rise in the depiction of post-adoption pregnancy storylines in the media, with adoption being presented as 'a cure for infertility' (Marsh and Ronner 1999). These representations hark back to an earlier period of 'psychogenic infertility' whereby psychological factors were said to interfere with the body's ability to make pregnancy possible (Sandelowski 1990; Boivin et al. 2011; Jensen 2016, p. 128). Edge reminds us that the representation of 'post-adoption surprise pregnancies in popular culture ... help bolster the presumed psychological unsuitability to mother as an underlying factor behind infertility' (Edge 2015, p. 89).

Moreover, adoptive families have become popular on factual television. Rupert Hawksley makes the point that '[f]actual television tends to follow cyclical trends. There will suddenly be a cluster of shows about, say, baking or benefit claimants. The new big topic is adoption' (Hogan 2014). With this trend in mind, we find televisual documentaries such as *Wanted: A Family of My Own*, *15,000 Kids and Counting*, *Exposure: Don't Take my Child* (2014), *Britain's Adoption Scandal* (2016), *Finding Mum and Dad* and *Finding Me a Family* in the UK, with titles such as *Family Addition with Leigh Anne Tuohy* (2013–) and *Catwalk Kids* on screen in the US.

And although these programmes tend to focus on different aspects of the adoption process, be it biological parents struggling to keep their children, the role and responsibilities, policies and practices of the social workers, those same social workers looking for new adoptive families, the potential adoptive parents themselves and those short- and longer-term foster families who bridge the transition, they routinely draw attention to the role of activity days and broader promotional events that bring children in need of adoptive families to the attention of prospective adopters.

It is worth noting that the working title of Channel 4s *Finding Mum and Dad* was *The Adoption Party*, and even though the title was changed, the programmes hashtag offered useful signposting for the audience. After all, the show presents 'the story of a handful of adoption activity days, events in which prospective parents looking to adopt, mingle, play and chat with children looking for permanent families' (Dean 2014). Moreover,

Catwalk Kids shows us how America's public adoption system has moved beyond activity days to more aggressive marketing strategies in order to present those children in need of what is termed 'permanence' to prospective families. And it is to the representation of these adoption parties and the adoption process on both sides of the Atlantic that I will now turn.

In previous generations, adoption was routinely about finding homes for illegitimate newborn babies with couples who wanted to either start or increase their family, with the assumption that by adopting babies they could form early bonds, nurture these infants throughout their formative years and pass them off as their own biological children (Fogle 2015). Today, however, only 2 per cent of the children adopted in England are under one (Henderson 2012). Most children, 71 per cent, are aged one to four and 24 per cent are aged between five and nine (Action for Children 2011/12). The British Association for Adoption and Fostering makes the difference between generations of adoption practices clear when it tells us that children available for adoption today

> have often been removed from parents who have mental health, drug and alcohol problems. They have most likely been left with those parents until the bitter end because the state believes that children do better with their own parents. By the time these children are removed, they are already damaged by years of neglect and abuse. (Henderson 2012)

Action for Children makes the point that children in foster care routinely present with angry and/or aggressive behaviours, attachment difficulties, disability, a history of trauma and abuse, offending behaviours, placement issues, risk-taking behaviours, sexualised behaviour, significant health and school issues. Indeed, only 3 per cent of those children in care present with none of the above (Action for Children 2011/12).

The point here is that with the under four-year-olds accounting for nearly three quarters of all adoptions, children as young as five and six are already considered hard to place, because, much like in previous generations, families are looking to adopt babies and infants. For those sibling groups with children spread across the desired and less desirable age ranges, this then leads to difficult moral and ethical questions about if and when sibling groups should be split up in order to allow the younger siblings to be adopted at the expense of their older brothers and sisters.

In the words of one social worker, 'adopters have a range of children to choose from' (*15,000 Kids and Counting* E2) or, in the blunt but honest

214   R. FEASEY

words of another, 'it's a buyers market [and] the majority of adopters will opt to have a child as young as they possibly can' (*Finding Mum and Dad* E1)—and not just babies and children, but 'straightforward or less complicated' babies and children (Ibid.). The fundamental problem is that there are not enough adopters in the UK or in the US, so if a potential adopter states a preference for age, gender or skin tone, then that is taken on board in the matching process. Even access to the family home is taken into consideration when prospective adopters consider the child that they would like to adopt (*Wanted: A Family of My Own*: E4).

Programmes such as *Finding Mum and Dad* and *Catwalk Kids* demonstrate that physically and mentally healthy babies rarely struggle to find new families, but that for those children considered harder to place, new marketing efforts have been employed in order to help secure homes. These programmes inform us that children with additional needs, children with disabilities, children aged over five years, single boys, those children from black and minority ethnic groups or single-sex sibling groups that are yet to be separated are hardest to place, especially from written profiles. In one particularly eye-opening sequence we watch as an approved adoptive couple complete a pro forma for matching in which they are asked to answer if they would accept, would not accept, or would be prepared to discuss a child with the following history: 'experience of neglect … parents with severe learning difficulties … parents with history of drugs or alcohol misuse … down's syndrome … AIDS or HIV … autistic spectrum disorder … foetal alcohol syndrome' (*Wanted: A Family of My Own*: E1). Likewise, another social worker is flicking through files, noting that one set of potential adopters 'doesn't feel able to consider … challenging behaviour, sexual abuse [or] cerebral palsy' (*15,000 Kids and Counting* E2). In short 'the children coming through the care system have high needs. They have very disruptive family backgrounds, they have had already traumatising experiences' (*Wanted: A Family of My Own*: E1) and potential families must understand what it means and what support is going to be needed if they were to consider adopting these children.

Although these programmes include a diverse array of potential adoptive families, be they single women, gay and lesbian couples, couples looking to extend their families as their own biological children have grown up and those seeking to add to their adopted families, the majority of potential adoptive families depicted are those affected by infertility and/or loss. Many of the women shown have experienced recurrent miscarriages, stillbirth, unsuccessful surrogate pregnancies and failed IVF treatments. For some, they are looking to adopt because of social infertility, but most are looking to adopt because of a medical diagnosis.

In *Wanted: A Family of My Own* we are introduced to Jones and Sandra who, we are told, attempted IVF before they decided 'OK, we can sit and lament about the situation and be sad, or we can see what we can do in starting our family', which in their case meant adoption (*Wanted: A Family of My Own*: E3). We are also introduced to Andy and Alison who started trying for a family nearly a decade earlier, and who, 'having gone through three unsuccessful IVF attempts ... decided to try and adopt siblings' (Ibid.). Likewise, Diane and Grant speak of 'missing out on having [their] own ... baby' after Diane was diagnosed with cancer and underwent a hysterectomy before the couple had a stillborn baby boy via a surrogate (Ibid.). Hearing prospective adopters Dan and Ania tell us that 'after the second miscarriage we thought, we just want a family, it doesn't matter whether it's adoption, we want a child' (*Wanted: A Family of My Own* E1) might make audiences as yet unfamiliar with the lived reality of infertility question the desire for a family for those who seek babies via IVF but stop short of searching for an older child or children through adoption.

Likewise, in *Finding Mum and Dad* we are introduced to James and Karen who are about to be approved as adopters when they tell us that they have 'never been able to have children of our own' (*Finding Mum and Dad* E1). In *Finding Me a Family*, we are introduced to Simon and his wife Julie who, after ten years together and several failed IVF attempts, are now looking to adopt (*Finding Me a Family* E2). So too, we meet Ronnie who 'lost' a baby over two decades ago when she was married and has since tried but been unsuccessful using IVF as a Single Mother by Choice (Ibid.). In *Wanted: A Family of My Own* we are told that David and Leanne have been 'desperate to become parents' for over eight years, and after 'quite a lot of time' spent on IVF they have decided to adopt, because, in the words of David, 'every time we've gone round a treatment of IVF, [Leanne] always had such disappointment and hurt and sorrow'. Indeed, the narrator makes the link clear when they state that 'like David and Leanne, many people decide to adopt after years of trying for children of their own' (*Wanted: A Family of My Own* E2). Commenting on her caseload, one social worker speaks about a baby in need of an adoptive family, telling the audience that 'he's the age of a baby that someone wants who doesn't have their own children' (*15,000 Kids and Counting* E1), when he may also of course be the perfect child for a family with existing biological children.

In *Finding me a Family*, Shakeel and his wife Nasreen do not reveal details about their path to adoption; however, one is encouraged to read an infertility narrative as they speak of their years together as a married couple, their desire for a family and the support that they are receiving from future grandparents as it relates to their adoption plans (*Finding Me a Family* E2). Likewise, in *15,000 Kids and Counting* we meet Carl and Sharon, and although they do not refer to infertility or failed assisted reproductive treatments *per se*, the implication here is that they have come to adopt as they were not successful in getting or staying pregnant. They mention that they 'tried for four years' but that 'nothing happened' before informing audiences that 'we always said that if it didn't happen, then we'd go down the route of adoption' (*15,000 Kids and Counting* E3). We are told that

> 18 months ago, we had no children, 18 months on, we've got three children. You just don't know what's round the corner. You can have this perfect family in your head, and you could think it's never going to happen, but it's happened for us and I can't imagine life without the three children now. (Ibid.)

The programme follows Carl and Sharon increasing their family from two to three children as the biological parents of their adopted boys have had a daughter who was also removed from their care. This seems a warm and welcome ending for baby Destiny as she is placed with her biological siblings in what is presented as a warm and welcoming forever family; however, there is a note of caution introduced but not elaborated on here. Carl and Sharon are presented as considerate, kind and nurturing parents; indeed, they are presented as the perfect adoptive parents for the sibling group in question. That said, they are neither naive nor idealistic about the lived experience of adoption. They make it clear that although they care for their new daughter and are desperate for her to join their family, they did not experience love at first sight. We are told 'it's horrible to say you don't love her straight away, but if you did say you did love her, you'd be fooling yourself. But we definitely care for her ... love will just take time to develop'. And although one might look to commend Sharon for her honesty and candour here, much like with those women in Ann Oakley's seminal work who speak of having no instant bond with their own biological children on first contact (Oakley 1979/81, p. 117), the more concerning announcement is that the 'birth mum will most probably continue to have children and there's only so many children that we'll be able to give a home to'. So, at the same time that the couple are welcoming their daughter to their family in part because they could not imagine having to explain to their young boys when they are older that 'you had a sister, but we said no', they are already concerned for the day when that will happen with future siblings (*15,000 Kids and Counting* E3).

Although Sharon is open about the need to allow time for genuine love to develop on meeting her new addition to the family, elsewhere, for children for whom finding permanence is more difficult, we are told that activity days are useful in encouraging what has been termed 'chemistry' (*Wanted: A Family of My Own* E1), a 'bond' (*Finding Mum and Dad* E1) or a 'connection' (*Finding Me a Family* E1). And likewise in the US, we are told that fashion shows encourage adoptive parents to picture themselves with some of the older children, with adoptive families being heard saying that 'the minute they looked into that child's eyes they couldn't walk away, and that's when they knew that was the child that they were supposed to adopt' (*Catwalk Kids*).

Either way, what is interesting in these programmes is the frequency with which adoption is presented as the next, indeed the final, stage in family building for involuntarily childless women who have been unsuccessful in their assisted reproductive efforts. However, the reality of parenting a 'harder to place' child makes for a very different family unit than the one imagined through IVF treatments, and for many women, there is no clear or logical progression from one form of family building to the next. For those seeking assisted reproductive treatments, they want what many others around them already have, to be an 'ordinary' family with a healthy newborn baby, and yet we are reminded that some of the children approved for adoption 'are already damaged by years of neglect and abuse. They are no longer children in need of an ordinary family; in fact often that is the last thing they can cope with, and they are the last thing an *ordinary* family can cope with' (Henderson 2012, emphasis added). Although these programmes tend to present adoption as the final step in family building, the reality is that seeking reproductive assistance is not the same as adoption, the families on offer and the roles and responsibilities within those families are different, and to present them as part of the same maternal drive might be rather misleading here.

For families who have in many cases never experienced a successful pregnancy, it might be understandable that they seek to emulate the early bonding that is routinely spoken about within and beyond popular media culture, irrespective of the reality of that particular situation. However, while couples such as Diane and Grant in *Wanted: A Family of My Own* are undeterred by the protracted waiting times for their desired siblings under the age of 24 months, there remain growing numbers of five-, six- and seven-year-olds still waiting for adoption. The couple have 'set their hearts on adopting siblings under two' (*Wanted: A Family of My Own* E3), and after ruling out learning difficulties or difficult needs, it is made clear that they have given the adoption team 'quite a narrow remit' to work with (Ibid.). We are told towards the end of the programme that it has been 'five months since they were approved and they're still waiting for news' and when the social worker suggests that they 'have a number of single children' (Ibid.) that they could be matched with, the couple remain undeterred from their original preference. When asked what might happen if in the longer term the preferred match cannot be found, Diane answers that 'it will happen. ... I mean, we've been approved. All the hard work is behind us. ... I'm still extremely positive. No worries whatsoever' (Ibid.). What is clear here is that for some prospective parents, even older prospective parents, the idea of a family means caring for babies and toddlers, but that the chance of adopting individual toddlers, let alone toddler siblings without additional needs, is small.

The statistics are very clear in that less than a quarter of children adopted in England are aged between five and nine (Action for Children 2011/12), and the foster parents, social workers and indeed the children themselves all wish to educate potential adopters about the benefits of adopting older children. One prospective adoptive mother invited to an adoption activity day notes that

> it's really hard for the older ones to compete with the little cute ones. I mean, that little girl [pointing to a six-year-old riding merrily on a small go-cart], how could she be hard to place? Everyone wants babies and toddlers and the older ones don't seem to have that little chance and they deserve that. You get out what you put into a child, and it doesn't have to be a baby, it doesn't have to be a toddler. (*Finding Mum and Dad* E1)

Moreover, when one foster carer is speaking to the social worker helping to secure an adoptive family for the brothers in her care, she mentions that 'everyone's she's spoken to all want younger or girls' rather than the boys that she is seeking to place with families (Ibid.). And elsewhere, when another social worker speaks about needing to find homes for her older children we are told that 'a lot of families want babies without problems'

(*15,000 Kids and Counting* E3), and then that 'there's young children like these two [siblings, three and seven] that are desperate, they're actually asking for parents' (*15,000 Kids and Counting* E2). Adoption is routinely taken to mean adopting a baby, infant or very young siblings, so that when women or couples speak of their desire, and in some cases, their desperation for a family, they mean a very narrow version of that term. With this rigid, traditional family unit in mind, social workers are heard commenting that they would 'like more work to be done with adopters to help them understand that babies aren't the be-all and end-all' (Ibid.). In short, what is needed here is not just information, but education.

Wanted: A Family of My Own makes its aims clear as it talks about 'going behind the scenes of the adoption process from both the child and the prospective parents'' point of view, while also 'exploding some of the myths and stereotypes about who can and cannot adopt' (BOB 2014). In this same way, *15,000 Kids and Counting* is looking to shed light not just on those who can adopt, but on the loving, nurturing families made up of older children, boys, siblings, those with special needs and minority groups. What many of these documentaries hope to show is that family building does not have to meet a traditional ideal and that prospective parents should consider seeking approval to adopt older children even if it sits outside of their initial comfort zone. And this is where these documentaries and the marketing of children seeking forever families play a role. This is not about judging, ranking or shaming prospective parents who seek to adopt a newborn or infant, but rather to inform and educate all prospective adopters about the possible advantages of adopting older children, especially older boys who are routinely overlooked. This is not about individual children in need of permanence or specific adoptive parents, but a more general comment about the reality of contemporary adoption, and a need for future adopters to consider the needs of the children alongside their own wishes in both Britain and America ... and this is where the activity days and catwalk shows come in.

MARKETING CHILDREN IN THE UK: FROM EXCHANGE EVENTS TO ACTIVITY DAYS

Adoption activity days, commonly referred to as adoption parties, were first employed in America before being introduced in the UK. In previous years, prospective adopters who were looking to be matched with a child

220   R. FEASEY

had written details, a photo and, more recently, short videos of the children to read, watch and make decisions about. Prospective adopters were given only the details of those children that they had requested to be matched with, be that based on age, gender or background. Adoption Exchange events existed so that local authorities could 'come together to show would-be adopters some of the children waiting for families' (*Wanted: A Family of My Own*: E4). These events looked to 'bring the children to life—what they will be like to live with, what they are interested in, what they are good at. So it's a lot of information about how the children are doing now in their foster placement … just a way of bringing them to life and showing them what they are really like' (Ibid.). But the children were not themselves present.

Organisers asked audiences not to 'think of it as advertising and selling children' but rather, to understand it as 'promoting children in a way that we can find the right family for them' at the same time as we hear one social worker stating that she has 'tried *selling*' her older children at the event with limited success (*15,000 Kids and Counting* E2, emphasis added). My point here is simply that charges or accusations of marketing children existed before activity days, fashion shows and television appeals. There was a limit to what exchange events were able to offer to approved adopters looking to start or extend their family. The suggestion is that by giving a set of would-be adopters yet to be matched the opportunity to not only read about or see short videos, but to actually interact with these children, you are opening up the possibility of matches beyond a potential adoptive family's original criteria. Indeed, during these activity days, the children's dates of birth are routinely omitted, so as to avoid the trap of only looking at a rigid age profile before actually interacting with the children (*Finding Mum and Dad* E1). Social workers make the argument for activity days when they note that the events

> are a good way of opening the minds of prospective families, because they come to a day and they might have had an idea that they want to have a child who's under three years of age and then they meet a four- or five-year-old and they fall in love with them. (*Finding Me a Family* E2)

Moreover, we find that

> traditionally, adopters and kids are either matched by social workers, or parents can search for children in specialist magazines. They don't usually meet

their child until the moment they are introduced as a new mummy or daddy. They walk in, they're expected to be a family. It's a big ask. I mean, I wouldn't even choose a sofa from DFS online without going to sit on it. I think the value of these days is adopters have the opportunity to meet children first. As real children. (*Finding Mum and Dad* E1)

We hear an approved adopter mention that

[i]n my head, we were always looking for a little girl. Just thought that was, you know, what I wanted. But today, it's kind of flipped my thinking a little bit towards maybe a little boy. (*Finding Me a Family* E1)

And likewise:

In our heads we thought about adopting maybe a girl. Yeah, a little girl. But it was nice to have the experience of boys. It's opened my mind. It has opened mine. Before it was, No, no just a little girl, but now it's, Hmm. (*Wanted: A Family of My Own* E1)

And on the back of an activity day, we are informed that 'you can't get what we've had today from two paragraphs and a photo … you just can't' (*Finding Me a Family* E1).

In his review of the documentaries in question here, Sam Wollaston notes that the idea of adoption activity days sounds 'unbearable … a kind of shop window for kids, or a matchmaking event'. He jokingly suggests that social workers and adoption charities could take the idea 'a step further and do an app? Kinder (rhymes with Tinder), swipe right for the ones you like. Or a talent contest, The A Factor' (Wollaston 2017). However, inappropriate jokes aside, he comments that activity days are 'clearly a good idea, because approved adopters get a much better idea of children from meeting them than from a picture and a couple of paragraphs … and [b]ecause it works' (Ibid.). In short, activity days 'are successful because adopters get to meet children they might not have selected from their written profiles' (*Finding Me a Family* E1).

There is much to praise in these closed events, not just the engaging staff or the entertainment provided for the children, but the manner in which these days are run and the number of successful matches that take place on the back of them, which, it is worth noting, are only attended by the harder-to-place children. We find that 'for many of our children coming to these days, it's their last shot. We're talking about a group of children here for whom we have already exhausted the traditional ways of trying to find them a family' (*Finding Mum and Dad* E1). Moreover, in many cases, these events are the final chance for sibling groups to be adopted together before social workers have to start considering separation as a more viable option for one or all children in terms of future adoption prospects.

During the trial period of five adoption activity days, 42 children were placed out of 251 that attended, and 'considering these are the most difficult to place children, that's quite a high percentage' (*Finding Mum and Dad* E1). We are informed that 'coming to a party could double a child's chance of being adopted' (Ibid.). Adoption activity days have since been 'rolled out nationwide' (Ibid.). Today, 400 children seeking forever families through adoption are invited to activity days held around the UK, giving them the opportunity to see, meet and play with approved adopters in events run fortnightly by children's charity Coram (Stanford 2017; CoramBAAF 2019). Out of the older children, those with additional needs, sibling groups and those children from black and minority ethnic groups that are considered harder to place, we are told that '[o]ne in four of those children who attend find their new parents there' (Ibid.).

However, these events, then and now, are not without criticism, and the documentaries in question do a good job of presenting both sides of a sensitive argument here. There is no suggestion that these days are nothing if not controversial, with compelling arguments on both sides. In the documentary tradition and indeed the broader public service remit, audiences are informed rather than instructed here. In the same way that activity days are applauded by social workers and approved adopters for showcasing the children in a fun and thoughtfully coordinated environment with the option of interaction, they have also attracted criticism for their likeness to 'beauty pageants' (Stanford 2017) and for their proximity to a 'cattle market' for children (*Wanted: A Family of My Own* E1).

Although foster parents are informed about the day and advised on how they will be run, the activities available and the role of foster and potential adoptive parents, the social workers and event organisers; some seem initially 'horrified' at the thought of the event while others have a similar reaction after the experience (Ibid.). Much of this negativity comes from the fact that the children in their care have not been played with or picked out. One foster carer expressed her concern by telling the event organisers that she 'felt like I was supposed to be selling an unwanted product' before her husband jokes that next time 'I'll drag adopters in. I shall drag them in, tie them up and [tell them that] you will spend time with these two boys. And you will take them home!' (*Finding Mum and Dad* E1). And on the other side of the adoption equation, from the foster carer to prospective adopter, we are told that 'this is the first time it's felt like we are actually rejecting children, rather than choosing children, so it was quite … yeah … difficult' (Ibid.). However, social workers make a point of reminding us that although these concerns are valid, they are actually adult concerns and anxieties relating to how children will feel if they are not picked on the back of an activity day. Because the language of cherry-picking, choosing or rejecting is not how these events are introduced to the children, they are free to enjoy the myriad of entertainment activities, the party food and the playful atmosphere without sharing the concerns of their foster carers. Social workers make the point that 'the challenge is managing the emotional wobbles of the adults that come', be they nervous adopters or protective foster carers, rather than any sense of disappointment from the children themselves (Ibid.). After all, the infants do not fully understand the full significance of the day as it unfolds, and for the older ones, social workers have gently explained the nature of the event through the language of looking for not just any family, but the right family. They are told that these days are 'a chance to find the right family for you and if we haven't found the right family [on] this day that you're going to go to, then we will look at another family. We'll keep on and keep on' (*Finding Me a Family* E1).

Although the UK has been relatively conservative in its efforts to find and match potential adopters, it has, in the form of activity days, gentle marketing techniques and media attention on celebrity figures with adoption stories to share, started to borrow from techniques used in the US. For those already uncomfortable or ill at ease with the gentle marketing strategies employed in adoption exchange events and activity days in the UK, they might be openly hostile to the strategies used to market children, tweens and teenagers in America as they are presented in contemporary adoption documentaries. However, there are two sides to the discussion being presented in these texts as adoption agencies work closely with media agencies and corporate businesses to promote, publicise and advertise children in need of adoption. American adoption agencies pride themselves on being the country that adopts more babies, children and young people than all other countries combined, and this is perhaps in no small part due to the strategies being employed here, with a literal fashion show being one of the more divisive events on offer for approved adopters to attend.

Recent figures make it clear that 1500 kids were waiting to be adopted last year in the UK, and while we have been watching *One Born Every Minute* (2010–) for nearly a decade, we are less familiar with the fact that one child is being taken into care every 20 minutes (*15,000 Kids and Counting* E1). Less catchy, perhaps less palatable media fare, but an incredibly powerful statistic that warrants more media interest and audience awareness, especially as this figure has doubled in the last five years (Ibid.). Moreover, of the '400,000 children currently in foster care in the USA, more than 100,000 of them are waiting to be adopted' (AdoptUSKids 2018a). It may come as no surprise then that Americans are employing more direct sales and marketing strategies in their bid to secure potential adopters.

The language of marketing, advertising, promotion and publicity is peppered throughout these adoption-themed documentaries and the wider debates as they relate to finding prospective adopters and raising awareness for children in the foster care system, and although they have specific meanings relating to public relations efforts, long-term strategies, brand messages or hype, they seem to be used somewhat interchangeably in a discussion about adoption, where the nuances are not needed.

In *Catwalk Kids*, audiences are asked to consider why 'Americans stage fashion shows for children awaiting adoption' before asking 'should we try it in Europe?' (Padi Productions 2011). Audiences are taken to middle America to see some of the 'aggressive marketing' strategies currently employed by public adoption agencies in the search for adoptive families for those children deemed most difficult to place, namely teenagers, sibling groups and those with special needs (Ibid.). The point here is that although children routinely find permanent homes on the back of 'fashion shows, weekly TV spots, adoption conferences, online videos and photographic exhibitions featuring children for adoption', both the techniques employed and the feelings of those children who are not placed with adoptive parents after the staging of such events are a cause for broader concern (Ibid.).

In the UK, the emergence and development of adoption exchange events and more recently of adoption activity days face charges of marketing infants and young children, and yet we are asked to look at these strategies as positive because the 'promotion' in question is about finding 'the right family' for each child in foster care (*15,000 Kids and Counting* E2). Moreover, the long-standing work between children's charities and *The Sun* newspaper are understood as both an acceptable and, indeed, an admirable form of awareness raising for children in need of adoption.

In a recent news feature, *The Sun*'s 1.5 million 'army of caring readers' are asked 'could you be a "forever family" for these kids?' (Sloan et al. 2016). As part of National Adoption Week we are shown smiling photographs of disabled and ethnic minority children and sibling groups accompanied by a few brief details about the needs of the child(ren) presented; be it a need for routine, regular medical check-ups, an understanding of autism or a strong support network. Indeed, David Holmes, then chief executive of the British Association For Adoption And Fostering, comments that '[w]e need more adoptive families particularly for children over three, disabled children and brothers and sisters who need to stay together' before stating that he is 'grateful to *The Sun* for their fantastic support of National Adoption Week over so many years' (Ibid.). And it is not only *The Sun* that brings attention to individual children, specific sibling groups and the need for future adopters, in their coverage during National Adoption Week.

Indeed, the middle market tabloid newspaper, the *Daily Mail*, features some of the children and sibling groups that were included in the recent *Finding Me a Family* with the headline announcing 'a six-year-old girl living in limbo has made an emotional appeal for a new mummy and daddy for herself and her three brothers' (Thornton and Lovell 2017). The *Daily Mail* was allowed to share the children's story with their 1.4 million readers as part of National Adoption Week 'in an attempt to get the cute quartet a home, as social services are desperate to keep the siblings together' (Ibid.). However, it is clear that although one particular sibling group is featured, there remain others also in need of a permanent family. We are told that while they are 'four of nearly 100 children in the Yorkshire area who need an adoptive family' they are also 'one of seven sets of four brothers and sisters from across the country who desperately need a new permanent home together' (Ibid.). The accompanying text makes it clear that, in the words of their foster carer, to 'take them on you've got to have the organisational skills of a sergeant major and the patience of a saint. They need really clear boundaries. I believe they have lived in chaos and so they find comfort in the rules', before adding that 'they would bring so much joy to a family' (Ibid.).

Likewise, the *Daily Mirror* shares the 'tale of five-year-old Alfie, who was taken into foster care because his birth parents were unable to look after him' (Myall and McKelvie 2016) with its half a million readers in a feature entitled 'Will you be my Forever Parents?'. The article includes numerous photographs of a happy-looking boy, while the text alludes to developmental delay, the need for routines and a stay-at-home parent who has time to commit to him as he is not in mainstream education. As if echoing the earlier stories, his foster carer reminds us that 'looking after him is so rewarding … I'm confident that with the right help and support he will thrive—and make a family very happy' (Ibid.).

Each of these and a myriad of similar tabloid stories over the past decade have showcased content, happy-looking children in artfully posed photographs and less professional snaps with a note highlighting the warmth and affection that they have brought to their foster families. They also include candid details about their likes and dislikes, current and medium-term educational, behavioural and medical needs, the ideal prospective family and contact details for anyone interested in adopting. In short, for the duration of National Adoption Week in the UK, the need for adoptive families is highlighted alongside the desires of individual children and sibling groups.

Statistics do not exist to account for the success or otherwise of these front-page adoption pleas; rather, the tabloid coverage can be understood as an extension of the adoption activity days, public service and commercial documentaries, social media stories and broader children's charity promotions that take place during and beyond National Adoption Week.

Marketing Children in the US: From Television Spots to Fashion Shows

While the UK looks to the daily tabloids to raise awareness of children available for adoption nationally, the Heart Gallery in the US looks to introduce the American public to smiling photographs of children in need of forever homes. The main difference here is that while the UK tabloids are circulated amongst millions of readers, the US Heart Gallery, a photographic and audio exhibit, travels around the states, with the children's portraits being displayed in a myriad of public spaces including government agencies and community centres. The first Heart Gallery was created in Santa Fe by New Mexico's Children, Youth and Families Department back in 2001, with the portraits being used as a way to draw attention to those harder-to-place children who were in need of adoption. We are told that since its emergence '120 Heart Galleries have been unveiled across the United States, with unprecedented national exposure and unparalleled increase in the number [of] adoption consummations' (Lubbock Interagency Adoption Council 2018). Professional photographers volunteer their time, talent and materials to the exhibitions, looking to 'utilize the power of photography to capture the individuality and dignity of children living in foster care, in order to advocate for their permanency, raise public awareness about their needs, and obtain support to help meet those needs' (Heart Gallery of America 2018).

After seeing the Heart Gallery in America, the British photographer Cambridge Jones, himself adopted, looked to replicate the Gallery in the UK, and on the back of this idea, put on an exhibition in the Getty Gallery in London entitled 'Home Time', whereby 'celebrities were paired with kids needing adoption' (Jones 2018). Talking about his exhibition Jones stated that

> the real issue here is the press coverage. In the USA up to 40% of kids photographed (and they are deliberately the hardest to place) found homes. The reason is the media coverage … the message penetrates far beyond the normal eyes and ears of those who have already considered adoption. (Jones 2007)

We are told that the goals of his exhibition were to 'raise general awareness' about the need for adoptive families, to 'bring a wider range' of potential adopters to the matching process and to 'increase the chances of finding homes for some of the kids featured' (Jones 2007). He makes it clear that the success of his exhibition 'will not be judged by the pictures, the people who attend the gallery or the opening party. IT WILL BE ALL ABOUT HOW MUCH PRESS INTEREST WE CAN MANAGE TO GENERATE. This is what has made such a huge impact in the states' (Jones 2007, emphasis in original). Indeed, the final success of the exhibition lay in the fact that 'all the children [photographed] found homes, every single one is now in a permanent home for the rest of their life' (*Catwalk Kids*).

From the single artistic vision to the far-reaching non-profit child welfare organisation, these media texts look to secure adoptions for children currently in foster care; however, they 'raise serious concerns about children's right to privacy and just as importantly their safety' (Phillips 2016), even before we look to the challenges associated with the more aggressive marketing techniques used in the States.

There are clear similarities between the ways in which the UK and the US seek to raise awareness for children seeking adoptive families, be it through National Adoption Week in the UK (Awareness Days UK 2018) or National Adoption Day in the States (National Adoption Day 2018), UK photographic exhibitions or US photographic galleries. Exhibitions and galleries both raise the profile of children seeking permanent families, but in the US they go a stage further than photographic portraits with the development of television segments showcasing the children in question. The Adoption Exchange partners with a local news station to feature a child or existing sibling group that is in need of adoption in what is termed the 'Wednesday's Child' segment (The Adoption Exchange 2018).

Every week, harder-to-place children, be they older children, sibling groups or those with health and developmental needs in foster care who are available for adoption, are featured on the local evening news as part of the Wednesday's Child programme. Although the segment started in 1992 through a partnership with NBC-4 and the Washington Metropolitan Council of Governments, its success in finding adoptive families for difficult-to-place children led to a nationwide expansion (Freddie Mac 2013). Because these children were understood to be harder to place it has been noted that, like the attendance of some of the older children and sibling groups on activity days in the UK, this is 'their last chance to find a permanent home and a family' (Ibid.).

Catwalk Kids highlights not just the importance of Wednesday's Child for these children, but the process of putting together the segments. We see Kenyon, 13, and Kayla, 11, invited to a day of snow and sledging fun, with favourite foods and presents given by the Wednesday's Child coordinator before they are asked about their likes and dislikes, their experiences of foster care and their desire for a permanent family in a filmed interview. The children are told what to expect from the event, making it clear that the segment will always be 'positive, we are going to show you in your best light, we take the best pieces of the whole day and we put it together to form what we call a package' (*Catwalk Kids*). However, although one *might* understand the need for hair and make-up, it is the leading questions that leave the audience ill at ease here. Moreover, when the siblings shrug or shake their heads to questions, the producer answers for them. Being told that the interview was 'painless, right' leaves little room for negotiation. We are told from the outset that Kenyon in particular is resistant to take part: he feels uncomfortable with the word adoption, has experienced neglect and abuse and has moved between 20 foster homes; and yet here he is being asked on camera about his experiences of the foster system and his desires for a forever family. He looks and sounds awkward. This is not to say that the final 'package' doesn't offer a meaningful way of making contact with prospective adopters, but the behind-the-scenes filming is difficult to watch, however well-intentioned the people and purpose behind it. The social worker on the day sums it up best when she suggests that they are 'marketing our kids but in a sense it's kind of a necessary evil' (Ibid.).

Recent statistics make it clear that '2,500 children have been adopted, giving them a chance for a brighter future. And more than 42,000 viewer inquiries have been generated from people interested in becoming foster and adoptive parents' on the back of these local news segments (Freddie Mac 2013; Dave Thomas Foundation for Adoption 2018b). Indeed, in the same way that tabloid coverage is praised for its efforts in raising the profile of particular children and the need for adoptive families more generally in the UK, so too 'CBS4 KCNC's Director, Tim Wieland, received an Award for Excellence by the United States Children's Bureau' (The Adoption Exchange 2016). The award was for his 'outstanding accomplishments in achieving permanency for America's children waiting in foster care' (Ibid.). We are told that Wieland has 'played an enormous role' in finding permanent homes for '66% of children featured' in the television segments (Ibid.).

While the British tabloids and subsequent adoption exhibitions feature photos and stories of children in need of permanent families, as echoed in the American Hearts Gallery, Wednesday's Child demands more commitment from and thus awareness on behalf of the children being showcased. However, even these television segments seem low-key when compared to the adoption catwalks that have emerged in recent years.

While both the UK and the US offer closed adoption activity days whereby children are able to interact with approved adopters, the ways in which each country approaches this are where the differences can be found. Adoption activity days in the UK are set up to allow children to play and be entertained while potential families gently observe and interact with the children, their social workers and foster parents; alternatively, children in the US are encouraged to be more proactive in finding their forever families by taking part in fashion shows in order to appeal to prospective adopters. These events are not open to members of the public, just to those already approved for adoption, but the similarity ends there. Some of the older children who take part in adoption activity days in the UK are aware of the purpose of the day—to find them and children like them an adoptive family, but this is spoken of quietly, gently, almost as an afterthought to the entertainment of the day, whereas the aggressive marketing strategies evident in the American fashion catwalks offer a less subtle directive to the children seeking adoption.

Children are heard talking about pressure, stage fright and embarrassment, and the adoption fashion show coordinator explains that 'there have been several kids who told us they didn't want to do it. Even though they want to find permanence, they're scared' (*Catwalk Kids*). However, with 28 children appearing on stage, numerous more with their Heart Gallery photo behind the stage and over 50 approved adoptive families at the event, the very real possibility that these harder-to-place older children could find matches gives organisers a reason to put on these events, and for some vulnerable children, a reason to take part, year on year. We are asked to consider whether it is a reasonable 'short-term sacrifice if they then find a family?' (Padi Productions 2011). In short, we are left with the dilemma of whether the risk of public rejection for the many is worth finding permanent homes for the few. We are reminded that the 'innovative recruitment efforts employed by both private and public adoption agencies … prevent the tragic "aging out" of some 28,000 young people each year' in America. And by doing so, it goes some way towards helping them avoid homelessness, mental illness and entering the criminal justice system (Ibid.). We hear from Adam Pertman, Director of the Evan B Donaldson Institute of Adoption, that 'kids who genuinely need homes get them more frequently and more easily and more regularly in our system than in other systems' (*Catwalk Kids*), and as a response to accusations of marketing their children, he continues by stating that 'if you don't do something instead of nothing, the kid is going to age out and not have any real chance in life, who is that good for, is that better than marketing' (Ibid.). We are reminded of the success of these events, in terms of finding places for children who are considered harder to adopt, but the documentary also asks us to consider the cost. The film does a good job of presenting the good, the bad and the ugly of American adoption, with the overarching point being that 'it may be uncomfortable for people, but they need to be uncomfortable' because unless these children are seen they are not adopted (Ibid.). In short, 'recruitment marketing is very important to these kids [because] otherwise they are just children in a file' (Ibid.).

The documentary talks about the success stories as they stem from America's more aggressive marketing techniques, and yet this overlooks the fact that some local adoption officials have been persuaded to stop such events in part due to 'the low number of children placed' and in part because the routine rejection of those children not selected for adoption 'ends up being just another form of abuse' (Murphy cited in The Washington Times 2001). American teenagers in need of adoption who have attended a number of catwalk shows just outside of Nashville tell us that although they didn't want to appear on stage, they made the decision to 'grin and bear it' (The Washington Times 2001). We are told that '[i]t feels like these people are going to the zoo and looking at the animals. I'm not embarrassed about needing to be adopted. I just don't like making public what's between me and my family' (Ibid.). The concern here then is that these 'events publicly humiliate the most vulnerable children, building up and then dashing their hopes' (Ibid.).

Either way, there is little suggestion that the UK will follow in the footsteps of these fashion shows, because while Holmes was heard distinguishing the UK's adoption activity days from what he sees as America's adoption 'beauty parades' (*Catwalk Kids*), Jonathan Ewen, Director of Barnardo's, is heard making the point that 'I don't agree that it's a sign of people not caring if [the UK] don't adopt an approach which may have been very successful in the States. The important thing is that you do something that is actually appropriate and works in the culture that you are actually working in', with the suggestion here being that it isn't appropriate and/or doesn't work (Ibid.). He continues saying that 'I'd want to see the evidence that it wasn't harmful for those young people who weren't chosen. Now, show me the evidence and I'll believe the practice' (Ibid.). The Researching Reform author, Natasha Phillips, echoes Ewen's concerns when she enquires about

> the damage this is doing to [the children's] self-esteem, or general development. At best, these children may grow up thinking that in order to be loved they must be fun, glamorous and engaging. At worst, those children who are not 'chosen', may develop mental health difficulties that will linger on into adulthood. (Phillips 2016)

Looking to make sense of the emergence and development of such adoption fashion shows in the US, Phillips states that such strategies are less about the children and more about 'the State … desperately trying to rid itself of a massive financial burden' (Ibid., Alvarez 2017). While national and local authorities spent £1.70 billion on foster care during 2016–17 in the UK (Narey and Owers 2018), America's 'State and federal expenditures for foster care administrative costs (placing and monitoring children in foster care) totaled $4.3 billion' (Zill 2011). Phillips concludes with the notion that '[m]aking a sale is not equal to a happy ending' (Phillips 2016). And with the ostensibly happy ending in mind, it is important to draw attention to the lived reality of adoption breakdown in the UK and in the US, drawing attention to what happens after the gallery photos have been taken down, the fashion shows have ended and those children in need of forever homes find permanency, albeit temporarily. Adoption disruption is not uncommon, but it is seldom spoken about within these documentaries or beyond.

Missing Representations: Adoption Breakdown and Families in Crisis

These documentaries routinely show the difficult job of social workers, foster carers and adoption charities as they balance the 'success and the controversy' of adoption events (Wollaston 2017), but what they fail to do is offer a follow-up to the first days, weeks, months and years of those families created through adoption, because if they did, they might make for even more controversial viewing. In *Finding Me a Family* a passing comment is made by one social worker about wanting to avoid adoption breakdown (*Finding Me a Family* E2), but the idea is passed over quickly, leaving viewers no time to ask themselves what it is, how often it occurs and what happens when it does. However, even if one did have the time to unpack this passing comment, it is difficult to find a clear definition of adoption disruption and, as a consequence, hard to find robust statistics. In what is understood to be the most comprehensive research study ever to be carried out into adoption in England, Julie Selwyn, Dinithi Wijedasa and Sarah Meakings analysed national data on 37,335 adoptions over a 12-year period to find that

> the term 'disruption' or 'breakdown' has been defined in many different ways. In some studies, adoption disruption refers to when the child is

returned to the agency between placement and legal finalisation, other studies separate disruptions pre and post order, while others use a wider definition based upon whether the child is living in the adoptive home at the time of data collection. This distinction between pre and post disruption has not been made consistently in the UK literature and so by conflating new placements with those that had been stable for some time the relative risks have been difficult to ascertain. (Selwyn et al. 2014, p. 16)

We are told that the 'UK does not have terms that differentiate between pre and post order disruptions and UK studies often use disruption and breakdown interchangeably' (Selwyn et al. 2014, p. 16). In America, however, 'distinctions are usually made between breakdowns that occur before the Adoption Order (disruption) and those that breakdown post order (dissolution)', although more recently the term 'dissolution' seems to have been replaced by the term 'displacement' (Ibid.). Selwyn argues that the term displacement has been employed in the US

to indicate three possible outcomes after a disruption: 1) the adoption is legally dissolved 2) children remain adopted but stay in care and 3) children return to their adoptive home after spending some time in care. (Ibid., p. 16)

What this means then is that it is difficult to locate rigorous figures with the rates of disruption having been quoted as 'ranging between 2% and 50%' with the suggestion 'that adoptions disrupt frequently' (Selwyn et al. 2014, p. 16). We are told that local authorities and adoption agencies are not always candid about the numbers of adoption breakdowns, with some 'hav[ing] been forced to admit to a rate of 20%' (Henderson 2012). A report from the mid-1980s discovered

breakdown rates rising from 16% for children placed at age five, to 60% at nine and over—that's six out of 10 children adopted going back into care. And that report counted three years as a successful adoption, which doesn't take into account the fact [that] breakdowns also happen later than that. The author of the report, Sandy Jamieson, former assistant director of social work in charge of childcare, reviewed the figures twice in the early 90s and found the situation had not improved, and indeed had possibly got worse. (Ibid.)

Since that time, it has been 'estimated that one in five adoptions fall apart before the adoption order is granted' in the UK (Freer 2011), while 'the charity Adoption UK estimated that as many as one third of adoptions break down after the adoption order has been granted' (Ibid.) due in part to a lack of clear information about their child's needs and long-term support for the family post adoption (Mapes 2016). In a recent survey of almost 3000 subscribers to Adoption UK's newsletter, we find that

> [m]ore than a quarter of families, when asked to describe their adoption, said they were facing serious challenges that had an impact on the wider family, were at risk of breakdown or disruption, or had already been disrupted. Almost half said their adoption was 'challenging but stable' and just over a quarter described it as 'fulfilling and stable'. (Harte and Drinkwater 2017)

Furthermore, '[m]ore than half of those surveyed reported living with a child who was violent ... serious incidents included hospital visits and sexual assault' (Harte and Drinkwater 2017). There were case studies of adoptive parents sending their children back into the care system because they were simply unprepared for the behaviour of these growing children. We are told that they took on infants with developmental delays so that it was not until they were around four years of age that the 'severe behaviour started to come out' and by the time the child was six or seven, aggressive self-harming meant that the child, their child, 'had become unparentable' (Ibid.).

Sue Armstrong Brown from Adoption UK makes the point that adoption 'is not a silver bullet. These children's problems don't just disappear overnight. Both adoptive parents and adopted children need skilled help and support' (Harte and Drinkwater 2017). And where that support should be targeted is a key focus of Selwyn, Wijedasa and Meakings' research. The study, funded by the Department of Education, noted that although much support exists to help adoptive families in the early years of their placements, it is routinely in the teenage years that disruption occurs, particularly for adolescents who were experiencing mental health problems on the back of a history of neglect, abuse and exposure to domestic violence prior to adoption (Selwyn cited in Hilpern 2015). We are informed that

> [o]f those children whose adoption placements had broken down, 91 per cent had witnessed domestic violence and 34 per cent had been sexually abused before they were adopted. Mental-health problems were also preva-

lent in the children who had left home, with 97 per cent scoring in the clinical range of mental-health problems (compared with 10 per cent in the general population). (Ibid.)

Although these statistics appear stark, the research did offer some slightly more optimistic details as they relate to adoption disruption in the sense that leaving the family home does not always 'signal the end of the relationship' between adoptive parents and their children. After all

> [i]n *many* cases, parenting continues at a distance—with adoptive parents acting as financial guarantors for a flat, having them round for Sunday dinner, doing their washing or listening on the end of a phone, with the relationships improving all the time. And even when this doesn't happen, we found that *many* young people came back to their families later on. (Ibid., emphasis added)

Although stories of adoption disruption are sad for all parties concerned, this seminal research makes it clear that even in a worst-case scenario, in a case of adoption disruption, there can be and, in many cases, does continue to be a meaningful relationship between both parties, irrespective of the domestic arrangements. However, we cannot remain naive as to the reality of those adoption disruptions that break down irretrievably, and although these are of concern for those children who return to foster care or age out of the system, *The New York Times* recently reported on an even more harrowing version of adoption breakdown in the US, namely the notion of unwanted adopted children being traded on the Internet. Nicholas Kristof described the practice as 'private re-homing', which is

> something that once meant finding a new home for a dog that barked too much. Now it refers to families recycling their adopted children, often through Internet postings. There are commonly no courts involved, no lawyers, no social service agencies and no vetting of the new parents. There's less formality than the transfer of a car. (Kristof 2013)

The stories are of families adopting children from abroad who present with all of the issues and difficulties outlined earlier, namely angry and/or aggressive behaviours, attachment difficulties, disability, history of trauma and abuse, offending behaviours, placement issues, risk-taking behaviours, sexualised behaviour and significant health and school issues (Action for Children 2011/12). It has been suggested that between '10 percent [and] 25 percent of adoptions don't work out. That could mean 24,000 foreign-born children are no longer with the families that adopted them' (Kristof 2013). We are told that 'state foster care systems are more reluctant to take custody of children from international adoptions, and giving a child to the authorities may entail an investigation for abuse or paying for the child's care until new parents are found' (Ibid.). In short, vulnerable children are being rehomed over the Internet, leaving them exposed to further physical, emotional and mental abuse. The journalist informs us that the 'first step to address this issue would be to make adoption agencies responsible for children they bring to America, including finding new homes when adoptions fail', going on to make a seemingly facetious but noteworthy point that '[i]f we have rules about recycling bottles, we should prevent children from being abandoned and recycled' (Ibid.).

On the back of her own experience of adoption disruption, Claire Patterson has set up a support group in the UK, with a desire to increase 'overall openness' from local authorities, social workers and, in turn, parents themselves. After all, 'the stigma and sense of isolation many Adoptive Parents feel is currently encouraged by a society and government that does little to support them Post Adoption Disruption' (Patterson 2018). The adoption-themed documentaries do well to raise the profile of foster families, social workers, adoption charities and individual children in need of adoption, but on the back of Patterson's plea for openness and education, public service providers could shine a spotlight on some of the case studies, policies and practices on both sides of the Atlantic that leave forever families to return or re-home their children. Not in the manner of sordid, scandalous or sensationalistic viewing, but in a candid, honest and realistic narrative that encourages discussion, debate and draws attention to the welfare and needs of these children and their adoptive parents.

On the topic of disruption, we are reminded of the long-standing link between adoption and infertility. After all, there is the suggestion that women who have been affected by an infertility diagnosis and who have attempted but failed to start a family through assisted reproductive treatments become so committed to the idea of family building via adoption that, even when informed by social workers about a myriad of problematic behaviours and attachment difficulties presenting in their future children, they will overlook the medium- and long-term demands in favour of the short-term desire for a maternal role. Selwyn asks us to

[p]ut yourself in adoptive parents' shoes, many of whom have had infertility problems. They can have all the warnings in the world, but when there's the chance of this lovely little person coming into their lives, they don't think about it all going wrong. (Selwyn cited in Hilpern 2015; Patterson 2018)

Earlier issues relating to judgement, blame and womanhood as motherhood all reappear in this last statement. Judgement, because those women affected by an infertility diagnosis are making ill-informed decisions about adoption; blame, because the adoption process is routinely driven by a woman's desire to mother rather than a husband's or partner's need to parent; and the long-standing link between womanhood and motherhood that dominates the pronatal period because societal pressure encourages women to conform to a maternal role rather than look to alternative life paths or avenues that do not include children.

CONCLUSION

The reality is that there are more children in need of adoption than there are families looking to adopt. With this in mind we have a situation whereby the most vulnerable children, adolescents and teenagers remain in long-term foster care or routinely move between foster placements. As for those babies, infants and children under four who are more routinely adopted, they may have delayed behavioural problems which become difficult for adoptive parents to manage without long-term support. In short, there is a concern both for children in the care system and for those who are living with their much-touted forever families. This chapter has looked at the similarities and differences in adoption processes and practices in the UK and the US, paying particular attention to the marketing strategies used in both countries as they look to recruit adoptive parents for their harder-to-place children, be they older, disabled, sibling groups or from ethnic minority backgrounds. It has considered the ways in which popular media texts ranging from the tabloid press to documentaries have helped to raise the profile of adoption, but not without controversy, especially in relation to the more aggressive efforts employed in the US in recent years. On the back of these discussions I would encourage future work to look at the representation of couples and single women who have had their children taken into care, for hearing them talk about their addictions, lack of education and bleak futures makes it clear that it is not just the infants and children who need support, but the biological mothers and fathers as

238   R. FEASEY

well in many cases. Hearing one young woman state that she hopes that her daughter 'gets to go with a good family … and she gets better GCSEs than I got. Two Fs, English and Maths, Wow! Never had a job. My life's just rubbish' (*15,000 Kids and Counting* E1) makes it clear that the ostensibly happy ever after for her daughter leaves the potential of an unhappy ever after for the biological parents. Further research should also consider the role, representation and responsibility of short- and longer-term foster parents as they are only touched on briefly here, in order to both understand and raise the profile of these carers both in terms of respecting the valuable work that they do but also in order to encourage families into the profession (Andersson 2001).

REFERENCES

Action for Children. 2011/12. At a Glance: A Year of Working with Action for Children Fostering, Adoption and Short Breaks. *Action for Children.* Accessed April 12, 2019. https://www.actionforchildren.org.uk/media/3474/fostering_report_2011-12.pdf.

AdoptHelp. 2019 Public vs. Private Adoption. *AdoptHelp.* Accessed April 25, 2019. https://www.adopthelp.com/public-vs-private-adoption/.

Adoption Network. 2018. Adoption Statistics. *Adoption Network*: Law Center. Accessed April 12, 2019. https://adoptionnetwork.com/adoption-statistics.

Adoption UK. 2018a. Finding a Child? *Adoption UK*: For Every Adoptive Family. Accessed April 12, 2019. https://www.adoptionuk.org/faqs/finding-a-child.

———. 2018b. Adoption UK Responds to Department for Education Figures. *Adoption UK*: For Every Adoptive Family. Accessed April 12, 2019. https://www.adoptionuk.org/news/adoption-uk-responds-to-department-for-education-figures.

Adoption.com. 2018. Older Parent Adoption. *adoption.com.* Accessed April 12, 2019. https://adoption.com/older-parent-adoption.

AdoptUSKids. 2018a. About the Children. *AdoptUSKids.* Accessed April 12, 2019. https://www.adoptuskids.org/meet-the-children/children-in-foster-care/about-the-children.

———. 2018b. About Adoption From Foster Care: Thousands of Children in Foster Care Need Permanent Families. *AdoptUSKids.* Accessed April 12, 2019. https://www.adoptuskids.org/adoption-and-foster-care/overview/adoption-from-foster-care.

Akass, Kim. 2011. Motherhood and Myth-making: Despatches from the Frontline of the US Mommy War. *Feminist Media Studies* 12 (1): 137–141.

Alvarez, Frank. 2017. Foster Care Costs: What Happens When Children Aren't Adopted? *News From Our Heart.* Accessed April 12, 2019. http://foster-care-newsletter.com/foster-care-costs-children-not-adopted/#. Wxj4sS%2D%2DLVo.

American Adoptions News. 2018. Am I too Old to Adopt? *American Adoptions News: America's Adoption Agency.* Accessed April 12, 2019. https://www.americanadoptions.com/blog/am-i-too-old-to-adopt/.

Andersson, Gunvor. 2001. The Motives of Foster Parents, Their Family and Work Circumstances. *British Journal of Social Work* 31: 235–248.

Awareness Days. 2018. National Adoption Week 2018. *Awareness Days.* Accessed April 12, 2019. https://www.awarenessdays.com/awareness-days-calendar/national-adoption-week-2018/.

BBC2. 2016. The Coopers vs The Rest. *BBC2.* Accessed April 12, 2019. https://www.bbc.co.uk/programmes/b07tczch.

Belkin, Lisa. 2009. Too Many Ways to Have a Baby? *The New York Times: Motherlode—Adventures in Parenting.* Accessed April 12, 2019. https://parenting.blogs.nytimes.com/2009/04/29/too-many-ways-to-have-a-baby/.

BOB. 2014. Wanted: A Family of My Own. *BOB: Box of Broadcasts—On Demand TV and Radio for Education.* Accessed April 12, 2019. https://learningonscreen.ac.uk/ondemand/index.php/prog/06F18102?bcast=109776432#.

Boivin, Jacky, Griffiths E., and Venetis C.. 2011. Emotional Distress in Infertile Women and Failure of Assisted Reproductive Technologies: Meta-analysis of Prospective Psychosocial Studies. *BMJ* 342. Accessed April 12, 2019. http://www.bmj.com/content/342/bmj.d223.

Butterflymum79. 2016. Adopting Our 3rd Child. *Mumsnet.* Accessed April 12, 2019. https://www.mumsnet.com/Talk/adoptions/2616226-Adopting-our-3rd-child.

Chen, Laurie, Phil Harrison, David Stubbs, Ben Arnold, Mark Gibbings-Jones, Grace Rahman, and Paul Howlett. 2016. Monday's Best TV: *Great British Menu; All Aboard! The Country Bus; The Coopers vs the Rest. The Guardian.* Accessed April 12, 2019. https://www.theguardian.com/tv-and-radio/2016/aug/29/mondays-best-tv-great-british-menu-all-aboard-the-country-bus-the-coopers-vs-the-rest.

Child Welfare Information Gateway. 2004. How to Assess the Reputation of Licensed, Private Adoption Agencies. *Child Welfare Information Gateway* website. Accessed April 12, 2019. https://www.childwelfare.gov/pubs/twenty/.

———. 2011. *How Many Children Were Adopted in 2007 and 2008?* Washington, DC: U.S. Department of Health and Human Services, Children's Bureau. Accessed April 12, 2019. https://www.childwelfare.gov/pubs/adopted0708/.

———. 2015. Adoption Options: Where Do I Start? *Child Welfare Information Gateway* website. Accessed April 12, 2019. https://www.childwelfare.gov/pubPDFs/f_adoptoption.pdf.

Contact After Adoption. 2018. Welcome. *Contact After Adoption.* Accessed April 12, 2019. https://www.uea.ac.uk/contact-after-adoption.

CoramBAAF. 2019. Supporting Agencies and Professionals who Work with Children and Young People. *CoramBAAF*. Accessed April 12, 2019. https://corambaaf.org.uk.

Crary, David. 2017. As Number of Adoptions Drops, Many US Agencies Face Strains. *US News*. Accessed April 12, 2019. https://www.usnews.com/news/best-states/new-york/articles/2017-04-30/as-number-of-adoptions-drops-many-us-agencies-face-strains.

Dave Thomas Foundation for Adoption. 2018a. About Us. *Dave Thomas Foundation for Adoption*. Accessed April 12, 2019. https://www.davethomasfoundation.org/about-us/.

———. 2018b. Research. *Dave Thomas Foundation for Adoption*. Accessed April 12, 2019. https://www.davethomasfoundation.org/our-programs/our-research/.

Davenport, Dawn. 2017. So You're Infertile, Why Not Just Adopt? *Creating a Family*. Accessed April 12, 2019. https://creatingafamily.org/infertility-category/why-not-just-adopt/.

Dean, Will. 2014. *Finding Mum & Dad*: TV Review—Channel 4's Sensitive Documentary Shows that Finding a Family is far from Child's Play. *The Independent*. Accessed April 12, 2019. https://www.independent.co.uk/arts-entertainment/tv/reviews/finding-mum-dad-tv-review-channel-4s-sensitive-documentary-shows-that-finding-a-family-is-far-from-9062531.html.

Department for Education. 2017. Children Looked After in England (including adoption), Year Ending 31 March 2017. *Department for Education*. Accessed April 12, 2019. https://assets.publishing.service.gov.uk/government/uploads/system/uploads/attachment_data/file/664995/SFR50_2017-Children_looked_after_in_England.pdf.

———. 2018a Intercountry Adoption: Information for Adoption Agencies. *Department for Education*. Accessed November 9, 2018. https://www.gov.uk/guidance/intercountry-adoption-information-for-adoption-agencies.

———. 2018b. Adoptions: Restricted List. *Department for Education*. Accessed April 12, 2019. https://assets.publishing.service.gov.uk/government/uploads/system/uploads/attachment_data/file/288019/Adoptions_restricted_list_2010.pdf.

Dinwoodie, April. 2017. Adoption in America: The Good, The Bad, and a Path to Reform. *HuffPost: The Blog*. Accessed April 12, 2019. https://www.huffingtonpost.com/april-dinwoodie/adoption-in-america-the-g_b_11111576.html.

Edge, Brooke. 2015. Barren or Bountiful? Analysis of Cultural Values in Popular Media Representations of Infertility. PhD diss., University of Colorado. Accessed April 12, 2019. https://scholar.colorado.edu/jour_gradetds/25/.

First4Adoption. 2018a. Voluntary Adoption or Local Authority? *First4Adoption*. Accessed April 12, 2019. http://www.first4adoption.org.uk/find-an-adoption-agency/vaa-or-la/.

—. 2018b. How Do I Decide If it's Right for Me. *First4Adoption*. Accessed April 12, 2019. http://www.first4adoption.org.uk/who-can-adopt-a-child/how-do-i-decide/.

—. 2018c. Fertility Issues and Thinking about Adoption. *First4Adoption*. Accessed April 12, 2019. http://www.first4adoption.org.uk/who-can-adopt-a-child/how-do-i-decide/fertility-issues/.

—. 2018d. 10 Common Misconceptions Quashed. *First4Adoption*. Accessed April 12, 2019. https://www.first4adoption.org.uk/who-can-adopt-a-child/10-common-misconceptions-squashed/.

—. 2018e. The Adoption Process. *First4Adoption*. Accessed April 12, 2019. http://www.first4adoption.org.uk/the-adoption-process/.

Fixsen, Amanda. 2011. Children in Foster Care: Societal and Financial Costs. *A Family for Every Child*. Accessed April 12, 2019. https://www.afamilyforeverychild.org/wp-content/uploads/2018/04/children_in_foster_care.pdf.

Fogle, Asher. 2015. Surprising Facts You May Not Know About Adoption as the Country Changes, So Does this Ever-evolving Institution. *Good Housekeeping*. Accessed April 12, 2019. https://www.goodhousekeeping.com/life/parenting/a35860/adoption-statistics/.

Freddie Mac. 2013. Dave Thomas Foundation for Adoption to Lead Freddie Mac Foundation Wednesday's Child Effort. *MarketWired*. Accessed April 12, 2019. http://www.marketwired.com/press-release/dave-thomas-foundation-adoption-lead-freddie-mac-foundation-wednesdays-child-effort-1862675.htm.

Freer, Bridget. 2011. When Adoptions Go Wrong. *The Telegraph*. Accessed April 12, 2019. https://www.telegraph.co.uk/women/mother-tongue/8283942/When-adoptions-go-wrong.html.

Froelker, Justine Brooks. 2017. *Ever Upward: Overcoming the Lifelong Losses of Infertility to Define Your Own Happy Ending*. Mason Rising.

goodenoughmam. 2014. Could I Hear Your Adoption Success Stories? *Mumsnet*. Accessed April 12, 2019. https://www.mumsnet.com/Talk/adoptions/821001-Could-I-hear-your-adoption-success-stories.

Grant, Amanda. 2013. Why You Should Consider Adoption. *Adopting*. Accessed April 12, 2019. https://www.adoptimist.com/adoption-blog/why-you-should-consider-open-adoption#.WusOeS%2D%2DLVp.

Harte, Alys and Drinkwater, Jane. 2017. Over a Quarter of Adoptive Families in Crisis, Survey Shows. *BBC News*. Accessed April 12, 2019. http://www.bbc.co.uk/news/uk-41379424.

Heart Gallery of America. 2018. Heart Gallery Mission. *Heart Gallery of America*. Accessed April 12, 2019. https://www.heartgalleryofamerica.org/About_Heart_Gallery/Mission.html.

Henderson, Meg. 2012. Adoption: Why the System is Ruining Lives. *The Guardian*. Accessed April 12, 2019. https://www.theguardian.com/society/2012/oct/31/adoption-why-system-ruining-lives.

Hilpern, Kate. 2015. A Woman Who Handed Back Her Adopted Three-Year-Old Son Says: I Didn't Abandon Him. *The Independent*. Accessed April 12, 2019. https://www.independent.co.uk/life-style/health-and-families/features/a-woman-who-handed-back-her-adopted-disabled-three-year-old-son-says-i-didnt-abandon-him-10111992.html.

Hogan, Michael. 2014. *Wanted: A Family of My Own*, ITV, Review: Empathetic and Sensitive. *The Telegraph*. Accessed April 12, 2019. https://www.telegraph.co.uk/culture/tvandradio/10786379/Wanted-a-Family-of-My-Own-ITV-review-Empathetic-and-sensitive.html.

House, Laura. 2017. The Rarely Told Story of a Failed IVF Journey: Woman, 29, Shares Heartbreaking Picture of her Prepared Pregnancy Announcement After Trying for a Baby for Eight Years with No Luck. *Mail Online*. Accessed April 12, 2019. http://www.dailymail.co.uk/femail/article-4687506/The-rarely-told-story-failed-IVF-journey.html.

IAC. 2018. Have you Got What it Takes to Adopt a Child Transracially. *IAC: The Centre for Adoption*. Accessed April 12, 2019. http://www.icacentre.org.uk.

International Adoption Guide. 2018. Welcome to the International Adoption Guide. *International Adoption Guide*. Accessed April 12, 2019. http://www.internationaladoptionguide.co.uk.

Jensen, Robin. 2016. *Infertility: Tracing the History of a Transformative Term*. Pennsylvania: Pennsylvania State University Press.

Jones, Cambridge. 2007. Cambridge Jones: Making a Difference with Award Winning Photography—Heart Gallery Project Outline 2007. *Cambridge Jones*. Accessed April 12, 2019. http://www.cambridgejones.com/HeartGaleries.html.

———. 2018. Forthcoming Books and Exhibitions. *Cambridge Jones*. Accessed April 12, 2019. http://www.cambridgejones.com/books+exhibitionsmenu.html.

Kewcumber. 2016. Adopting Our 3rd Child. *Mumsnet*. Accessed April 12, 2019. https://www.mumsnet.com/Talk/adoptions/2616226-Adopting-our-3rd-child.

Kristof, Nicholas. 2013. When Children Are Traded. *The New York Times*. Accessed April 12, 2019. https://www.nytimes.com/2013/11/21/opinion/kristof-when-children-are-traded.html#story-continues-2.

Krlstina. 2016. Adopting Our 3rd child. *Mumsnet*. Accessed April 12, 2019. https://www.mumsnet.com/Talk/adoptions/2616226-Adopting-our-3rd-child.

ktbeau. 2010. Could I Hear Your Adoption Success Stories? *Mumsnet*. Accessed April 12, 2019. https://www.mumsnet.com/Talk/adoptions/821001-Could-I-hear-your-adoption-success-stories.

Letherby, Gayle. 1999. Other Than Mother and Mothers as Others: The Experience of Motherhood and Non-Motherhood in Relation to Infertility and

Involuntary Childlessness. *Women's Studies International Forum* 22 (3): 359–372.

———. 2003. Battle of the Gametes: Cultural Representations of 'Medically' Assisted Conception. In *Gender, Identity and Reproduction: Social Perspectives*, ed. Sarah Earle and Gayle Letherby, 50–65. London: Palgrave Macmillan.

longtermfamilyplanning. 2009. Could I Hear Your Adoption Success Stories? *Mumsnet*. Accessed April 12, 2019. https://www.mumsnet.com/Talk/adoptions/821001-Could-I-hear-your-adoption-success-stories.

looseleaf. 2009. Could I Hear Your Adoption Success Stories? *Mumsnet*. Accessed April 12, 2019. https://www.mumsnet.com/Talk/adoptions/821001-Could-I-hear-your-adoption-success-stories.

Lubbock Interagency Adoption Council. 2018. Children of the Heart Gallery. *Lubbock Interagency Adoption Council*. Accessed April 12, 2019. http://adoptinlubbock.org/heartgallery/.

Madsen, Charlotte. 2014. Infertility on Film and Television—Part 2: Rules, Housewives and Friends. The Road to Baby Madsen: Our IVF Journey. Accessed April 12, 2019. http://roadtobabymadsen.blogspot.com/2014/06/infertility-on-film-and-television-part.html.

Mapes, Diane. 2016. It Takes More Than Love: What Happens When Adoption Fails. *Today*. Accessed April 12, 2019. https://www.today.com/parents/it-takes-more-love-what-happens-when-adoption-fails-918076.

Marsh, Margaret, and Wanda Ronner. 1999. *The Empty Cradle: Infertility in America from Colonial Times to the Present*. London: Johns Hopkins University Press.

McDermott, Mark. 2018. Understanding Independent Adoption. Adoptive Families: The How-to-Adopt and Adoption Parenting Network. Accessed April 12, 2019. https://www.adoptivefamilies.com/how-to-adopt/understanding-independent-adoption/.

meandyouplustwo. 2016. Adopting Our 3rd Child. *Mumsnet*. Accessed April 12, 2019. https://www.mumsnet.com/Talk/adoptions/2616226-Adopting-our-3rd-child.

Mills, Brett. 2009. *The Sitcom*. Edinburgh: Edinburgh University Press.

Mohan, Isabel. 2016. *The Coopers vs The Rest* has Promise but Feels Like a Poor Imitation of *My Family*. Review. *The Telegraph*. Accessed April 12, 2019. https://www.telegraph.co.uk/tv/2016/08/29/the-coopers-vs-the-rest-has-promise-but-feels-like-a-poor-imitat/.

Myall, Steve, and Geraldine McKelvie. 2016. Will You Be My Forever Parents? Heartbreaking Story of Boy Who Wants to Be Adopted. *Mirror*. Accessed April 12, 2019. https://www.mirror.co.uk/news/uk-news/will-you-forever-parents-heartbreaking-905830.

Narey, Martin, and Mark Owers. 2018. Foster Care in England: A Review for the Department for Education. *Department for Education*. Accessed April 12,

2019. https://assets.publishing.service.gov.uk/government/uploads/system/uploads/attachment_data/file/679320/Foster_Care_in_England_Review.pdf.

National Adoption Center. 2018. There Are No Unwanted Children ... Just Unfound Families. *National Adoption Center*. Accessed April 12, 2019. http://www.adopt.org.

National Adoption Day. 2018. November Eighteenth. *National Adoption Day*. Accessed April 12, 2019. http://www.nationaladoptionday.org.

Neil, Elsbeth. 2007. Post Adoption Contact and Openness in Adoptive Parents' Minds: Consequences for Children's Development. *The British Journal of Social Work* 39 (1): 5–23.

———. 2009. The Corresponding Experiences of Adoptive Parents and Birth Relatives in Open Adoptions. In *International Advances in Adoption Research for Practice*, ed. Gretchen Wrobel and Elsbeth Neil, 269–294. Chichester: Wiley.

Neil, Elspeth, Mary Beek, and Emma Ward. 2013. Contact After Adoption: A Summary of Key Findings for Adoptive Parents. Centre for Research on Children and Families. Accessed April 12, 2019. https://www.uea.ac.uk/documents/8033393/8214983/CRCF+Adoptive+Parents+Final.pdf/6ddfcab8-5c64-4a41-831f-1fd87185f426.

———. 2015. *Contact After Adoption: A Longitudinal Study of Adopted Young People and Their Adoptive Parents and Birth Relatives. British Association for Adoption and Fostering*. London: BAAF. Accessed April 12, 2019. https://corambaaf.org.uk/books/contact-after-adoption-summary.

Nelson, Lloyd. 2017. US VS. UK: International Differences in Fostering and Adoption. *News From Our Heart. Foster Care Newsletter*. Accessed April 12, 2019. http://foster-care-newsletter.com/us-vs-uk-international-differences-in-fostering-and-adoption/#.Wug6Sy%2D%2DLVp.

neverjamtoday. 2009. Could I Hear Your Adoption Success Stories? *Mumsnet*. Accessed April 12, 2019. https://www.mumsnet.com/Talk/adoptions/821001-Could-I-hear-your-adoption-success-stories.

NHS. 2018a. Your Adopted Child's Health Needs. *NHS*. Accessed April 12, 2019. https://www.nhs.uk/Livewell/adoption-and-fostering/Pages/adopted-children-medical-and-health-needs.aspx.

———. 2018b. Adopting a Child: Your Health and Wellbeing. *NHS*. Accessed April 12, 2019. https://www.nhs.uk/Livewell/adoption-and-fostering/Pages/Adoption-your-health-and-wellbeing.aspx.

———. 2018c. We Adopted After IVF. *NHS*. Accessed April 12, 2019. https://www.nhs.uk/Livewell/adoption-and-fostering/Pages/andrew-mcdougall-we-adopted-after-IVF.aspx.

Nikol aka Not Just a Beauty Blogger. 2017. The Best Prescription Your Doctor Has Ever Written: Advice from Two Girls in the Know. *Not Just a Beauty*

Blogger. My Fashionable Journey Through IVF. Accessed April 12, 2019. http://www.notjustabeautyblogger.com/tag/unexplained-infertility/.

Oakley, Ann. 1979/81. *From Here to Maternity: Becoming a Mother*. Middlesex: Penguin.

OPA. 2018. Open Adoption: Could Open Adoption Be the Best Choice for You and Your Baby. *Office of Population Affairs*. Accessed April 12, 2019. https://www.childwelfare.gov/pubPDFs/openadoption.pdf.

Padi Productions. 2011. Catwalk Kids. *Padi Productions*. Accessed April 12, 2019. http://www.padiproductions.com/otro.php?func=1&id=11&ids=13&idioma=.

Parents.com. 2019. The Adoption Process: Agency vs. Independent Adoption. Accessed April 25, 2019. https://www.parents.com/parenting/adoption/facts/agency-vs-independent-adoption/.

Patterson, Claire. 2018. Disruption Support Group. Adoption Disruption UK: Parent Support & Care Orders. Accessed April 12, 2019. https://adoptiondisruptionuk.com.

Pemberton, Becky. 2018. Home is Where the Heart is: How Many Adoptions are there in the UK Each Year, How Do You Adopt a Child and How Long Does it Take. *The Sun*. Accessed April 12, 2019. https://www.thesun.co.uk/fabulous/5301173/adoptions-uk-each-year-adopt-child-long/.

Phillips, Natasha. 2016. Fashion Shows Where Kids in Care Are Paraded For Adoption? Welcome to Middle America. *Researching Reform*. Accessed April 12, 2019. https://researchingreform.net/2016/08/25/fashion-shows-where-kids-in-care-are-paraded-for-adoption-welcome-to-middle-america/.

Ratcliffe, Rebecca. 2017. Most Adopted Children Never Meet Their Birth Family. Is That All About to Change? *The Observer*. Accessed April 12, 2019. https://www.theguardian.com/society/2017/mar/26/adopted-children-meet-birth-families-face-to-face-contact.

Robinson, Sonya. 2017. Child Welfare Social Workers and Open Adoption Myths. *Adoption Quarterly* 20 (2): 167–180.

Sandelowski, Margarete. 1990. Failures of Volition: Female Agency and Infertility in Historical Perspective. *Signs* 15 (3): 475–499.

Sandelowski, Margarete, and Sheryn de Lacey. 2002. The Uses of a Disease: Infertility as Rhetorical Vehicle. In *Infertility Around the Globe: New Thinking on Childlessness, Gender, and Reproductive Technologies*, ed. Marcia Inhorn and Frank Van Balen, 33–51. Berkeley: University of California Press.

Scott, Ryan, Gardenia Harris, Donna Brown, Doris Houston, Susan Livingston Smith, and Jeanne Howard. 2011. Open Adoptions in Child Welfare: Social Worker and Foster/Adoptive Parent Attitudes. *Journal of Public Child Welfare* 5 (4): 445–466.

Selby, Julie. 2015. *Infertility Insanity: When Sheer Hope (and Google) are the Only Options Left*. Canada: Influence Publishing.

246   R. FEASEY

Selwyn, Julie; Dinithi Wijedasa, and Sarah Meakings. 2014. Beyond the Adoption Order: Challenges, Interventions and Adoption Disruption. *Department for Education*. Accessed April 12, 2019. https://assets.publishing.service.gov.uk/government/uploads/system/uploads/attachment_data/file/301889/Final_Report_-_3rd_April_2014v2.pdf.

Siegel, Deborah. 2008. Open Adoption and Adolescence. *Families in Society: The Journal of Contemporary Social Services* 89 (3): 366–374.

———. 2012. Growing Up in Open Adoption: Young Adults Perspectives. *Families in Society: The Journal of Contemporary Human Services* 93 (2): 133–140.

———. 2013. Open Adoptions: Adoptive Parents. Reactions Two Decades Later. *Social Work: A Journal of the National Association of Social Workers* 58 (1): 43–52.

Sloan, Jenna, Kate Jackson, and Katy Docherty. 2016. Could You Be a Forever Family For These Kids? Ten Years Supporting National Adoption Week. *The Sun*. Accessed April 12, 2019. https://www.thesun.co.uk/archives/news/1027817/could-you-be-a-forever-family-for-these-kids/.

Stanford, Peter. 2017. Are Adoption Parties the Best Way to Help Children Find Their Forever Family? *The Telegraph*. Accessed April 12, 2019. https://www.telegraph.co.uk/women/family/adoption-parties-best-way-help-children-find-forever-family/.

The Adoption Exchange. 2016. Tim Wieland Awarded with 2016 Adoption Excellence Award. *The Adoption Exchange*. Accessed April 12, 2019. https://adoptex.wordpress.com/2016/12/12/tim-wieland-awarded-with-2016-adoption-excellence-award/.

———. 2018. Partnerships: Wednesday's Child Partnerships. *The Adoption Exchange*. Accessed April 12, 2019. https://www.adoptex.org/get-involved/partnerships/.

The Washington Times. 2001. Fashion Show Lets Parents Shop for Children to Adopt. *The Washington Times*. Accessed April 12, 2019. https://www.washingtontimes.com/news/2001/may/3/20010503-022849-5099r/.

thomassmuggit. 2018. Adoption in Film and TV. *Mumsnet*. Accessed November 9, 2018. https://www.mumsnet.com/Talk/adoptions/3233363-Adoption-in-Film-and-TV.

Thornton, Lucy, and Joanna Lovell. 2017. These Adorable Siblings Have Made a Heartbreaking Plea to Find a New Family. *HullLive*. Accessed April 12, 2019. https://www.hulldailymail.co.uk/whats-on/family-kids/adorable-siblings-made-heartbreaking-plea-648257.

Wallace, Kelly. 2016. Infertility: When Adoption is Not an Option. *CNN*. Accessed April 12, 2019. https://edition.cnn.com/2016/10/10/health/feat-infertility-when-adoption-not-option/index.html.

Wallwork, Ellen. 2017. 15 Things You Should Know About Adopting A Child. *HuffPost*. Accessed April 12, 2019. https://www.huffingtonpost.co.uk/2015/03/17/15-things-you-should-know-about-adopting-a-child_n_7315868.html.

Wollaston, Sam. 2017. *Finding Me a Family* Review: Matchmaking Children and Parents. *The Guardian*. Accessed April 12, 2019. https://www.theguardian.com/tv-and-radio/2017/dec/06/finding-me-a-family-review-matchmaking-children-parents.

Young, J., and Elsbeth Neil. 2009. Contact After Adoption. In *The Child Placement Handbook: Research, Policy and Practice*, ed. Gillian Schofieldand John Simmonds, 241–259. London: BAAF.

Zill, Nicholas. 2011. Better Prospects, Lower Cost: The Case for Increasing Foster Care Adoption. *Adoption Advocate*. Accessed April 12, 2019. http://www.adoptioncouncil.org/images/stories/NCFA_ADOPTION_ADVOCATE_NO35.pdf.

CHAPTER 6

Conclusion: Future Research Directions

This volume introduces us to the 'exquisitely intricate orchestration of hormones and engineering' that are necessary to make a baby (Sterling 2013, p. 121), while reminding us that this orchestration is a hope-fuelled and frustrating fantasy for one in seven couples in the UK and one in eight couples in the US. Although fertility diagnoses, reproductive technologies and legal frameworks have changed over the past three decades, we continue to live in a pronatal environment in which treatments such as IVF fail more than they succeed. In the late 1980s, *Life* writers noted that '[o]nce upon a time, there was a man and a woman. They met, fell in love, and married. And very soon they decided to have a family. They made love, and within a year, their first child was born. That one was very soon followed by others. And they lived happily ever after' (Quindlen cited in Sterling 2013, p. 70). We are of course reminded that this traditional narrative 'is a fairytale … as patently fantastic as *Sleeping Beauty*' for those women and couples who have been affected by an infertility diagnosis or loss (Quindlen cited in Sterling 2013, p. 70). Moreover, *Sleeping Beauty* is a well-known fairy tale, passed down through generations, the popular narrative is told and retold through film, television, literature and wider re-imaginings in popular media culture, and yet, while the fantastical narrative of sleeping beauty is far-reaching, the reality of contemporary fertility and the commonality of infertility and pregnancy loss are rarely acknowledged or understood by those unaffected.

© The Author(s) 2019
R. Feasey, *Infertility and Non-Traditional Family Building*,
https://doi.org/10.1007/978-3-030-17787-4_6

249

We should be reminded that women seeking advice and support relating to an infertility diagnosis routinely turn to online platforms in general and the family building blogosphere in particular. The blogosphere encourages infertility camaraderie but leaves little space or support for those women who look to get off the assisted reproductive treadmill before finding their happy 'healthy newborn' ever after. Women who experience involuntary childlessness speak of stigma, shame and self-blame, which are compounded in these ostensibly safe online spaces. Although the topic of infertility is widely discussed and debated online, there appears to be a shared consensus amongst bloggers whereby infertility is inextricably linked to family building. In this way, there is no such thing as an infertility blog, the term is a misnomer, because what are presented to interested and invested readers is a set of family building narratives, with an infertility back story. Such blogs remind us that we are living in a pronatal period, where mature womanhood continues to be equated with motherhood. As such, it is disappointing to note that while the blogosphere focuses on family building narratives over and above a more difficult conversation about involuntary childlessness, factual programming weaves family building through its representations of infertility. In the same way that a cursory glance at the infertility blogosphere leaves readers optimistic about their chances of conception, so too these screen depictions leave women in the audience with a sense of hope that they too will get the chance to experience a healthy pregnancy outcome, irrespective of age or finances. Other voices are seldom heard or seen that counter this positive narrative, irrespective of the realistic chances of pregnancy success.

While the subject of loss is being addressed more candidly on social media, be it through blogs, vlogs, Facebook or Twitter, there is a current disconnect between the voices heard and the feelings of isolation and loneliness that are said to be felt by women who have experienced miscarriage, stillbirth, ectopic or molar pregnancy. While a myriad of online faces and voices urge women to share, support and reach out to one another, they acknowledge the shroud of secrecy and the shared silence that often accompanies loss. Indeed, there is a self-fulfilling circularity to those cases where women who speak of their loneliness themselves self-censor. From a diagnosis of infertility, through assisted reproductive treatments and narratives of loss, women are routinely informed not only of the importance of motherhood to womanhood, but also of the social hierarchy that exists in relation to family building. We are reminded that biological motherhood is the gold standard, be it natural, through reproductive assistance or gestational surrogacy, with egg donation and adoption being presented as preferential to childlessness, but not on a parenting par with their genetically related maternal counterparts.

We can find a wealth of information about infertility, assisted reproductive treatments, pregnancy loss and adoption through a myriad of personal narratives, public campaigns, charities and support groups, but the suggestion is that we are not looking until we need them. This means that the circle of support remains limited, restricted to those who have experienced infertility or loss. In this way, mainstream media has a crucially important role to play in helping to smash the silence, quash the secrecy and debunk societal taboos as they relate to reproductive disruption.

Infertility, loss and non-traditional family building are important areas of research within such diverse fields as anthropology, sociology, psychology and behavioural health science. After all, they have become a discursive site for the examination and critique of a wide variety of phenomena, including human agency and objectification; the culture of risk, the politics of gender, genealogical bewilderment, class, capitalism, and the commodification of human life; deviance and stigma, hegemony and concordance; and even discourse itself (Sandelowski and de Lacey 2002, p. 33). On the back of such research, an understanding of the ways in which infertility, loss and non-traditional family building are being represented in the contemporary media landscape is of crucial importance to those who have a diagnosis, those looking to offer support and those media researchers, creatives, practitioners and commissioners who are in a position to bring these topics to our collective attention.

A myriad of sites, resources and networks have been set up locally, nationally and internationally to support women affected by an infertility diagnosis. So many in fact that we are told that physicians see 'no reason for anyone to struggle with infertility anymore, especially alone' (Marsh and Ronner cited in Sterling 2013, p. 12). However, even a cursory glance at the blogosphere, vlogosphere, social media platforms, screen appearances and broader channels of discourse makes it clear that, irrespective of changes to available treatments and the emergence and growth of bespoke support groups, women affected by infertility continue to feel isolated and alienated from friends and family who have not themselves experienced involuntary childlessness. It is not enough for infertility, pregnancy loss or non-traditional families to appear fleetingly across mainstream popular media culture; rather, realistic depictions must be presented throughout the entertainment arena, be it factual or fictional, highbrow or lowbrow, commercial or public service, online or onscreen. Only when candid depictions of infertility, miscarriage, ectopic and molar pregnancy, stillbirth and non-traditional forms of family building become commonplace can we open up a meaningful dialogue, replacing current experiences of shame and silence with genuine understanding and realistic life options for women within and beyond a maternal role.

I have looked at a number of factual, first-person, reality and documentary texts that focus on infertility; what I have therefore overlooked is the ways in which the themes of infertility and non-traditional family building are currently being depicted in fictional entertainment, spanning mediums, formats and demographics. Erin Donnelly asks us 'why are women with fertility issues so often portrayed as evil' in mainstream fiction? By way of an example she announces that while 'blonde women were overwhelmingly rich, entitled, and cold' during Hitchcock's cinematic reign, their contemporary counterparts are 'rich, entitled, cold, *and* struggling with fertility' (Donnelly, E 2017, emphasis in original). Indeed, 'from *Mad Max: Fury Road* to ... *Juno*, women are often divided into "breeders" and "the barren," with the latter coming off as cool and distant at best, and malicious and desperate at worst' (Ibid.). Whether it be Black Widow/Scarlett Johansson in *Avengers: Age of Ultron* (2015), the wives of Gilead in *The Handmaids Tale* (2017–) or, at the time of writing, a potential narrative arc in *Suits* (2011–), an examination of such fictional representations are crucial, not because they are based in verisimilitude or an authentic infertility experience, but rather because they are not. In her work on cultural values, popular media and infertility, Brooke Edge proposes the idea that in 'departing from realism, such representations have the power to condition cultural understandings of minority populations, especially those that are stigmatized and not always spoken of openly' (Edge 2015, p. 7).

While further research is needed on the representations of infertility, loss and the non-traditional family in fictional entertainment, research is also needed on the portrayal of male-factor infertility, black minority ethnic family building via assisted reproduction and representations of global infertility. After all, the experience and depiction of infertility, miscarriage, stillbirth, IVF, surrogacy and adoption are not limited to the UK or the US. Indeed, global differences in terms of state support, religious teachings and educational programmes vary widely, as do the depictions in media texts as they span developed and developing countries (Van Balen and Inhorn 2002; Ginsberg and Rapp 1995).

Men are diagnosed with infertility and they too experience assisted reproductive treatments, miscarriage and stillbirth (Barnes 2014). Like many of their female counterparts men 'feel stigmatized in a childless situation since cultural ideals about manhood are often intertwined with cultural ideas about fertility and virility' (Sterling 2013, p. 15). Indeed, 'when a man cannot "get his wife pregnant," he may feel that others (including his own partner) view him as less of a man' (Ibid.). Hegemonic masculinity is rarely equated with sensitive or connected iterations of fatherhood (Connell 1995, 1998; Feasey 2008; Kaufman 2013), rather, the pinnacle of hegemonic manhood speaks of 'a man *in* power, a man *with* power, and a man *of* power' (Kimmel 2004, p. 184, emphasis in original), with fertility as a key demonstration of appropriate masculinity here. Esmée Hanna and Brendan Gough worked with Britain's national fertility charity, Fertility Network UK, in order to understand the ways in which men experience involuntary childlessness on the back of an infertility diagnosis, and their findings foreground feelings of shame and stigma because these men associate healthy masculinity with procreation (Hannah and Gough 2017).

It is rare for men affected by infertility to speak out about their diagnosis, much less so, openly. When a couple is diagnosed with infertility, men speak of trying to manage their own disappointment, isolation and fear with a desire to stay strong for their partners. This desire to stay strong is rooted in the hegemonic model of masculinity. However, this desire to maintain hegemonic credentials puts men under greater stress as they struggle, routinely in silence and isolation, with the lived reality of an infertility diagnosis (Clothier 2017). As I have argued elsewhere, there is the suggestion that the silence, stigma and shame that surround male-factor infertility might be changing; after all, bespoke online spaces and support services exist for those men who wish to share their experiences with other men who understand the social, sexual and relational problems that can stem from a diagnosis. However, the fact that these voices are routinely anonymised and removed from their friends, family and lived experiences means that this dialogue does little to negotiate the wider stigma, quell the silence or debunk the long-standing and ubiquitous link between masculinity and virility (Lundin 2002; Mason 2003; Wischmann and Thorn 2013; Feasey 2019).

Furthermore, it is important that this dialogue speaks not just to those white, heterosexual, middle-class, married couples looking to conceive, but to all those affected by infertility. In the first instance, further research needs to acknowledge the black minority ethnic experience as it relates to infertility (Chandra et al. 2013), IVF success rates (Maalouf et al. 2017), cross-racial gestational surrogacy arrangements (Harrison 2016) and prospective adopters (Farmer et al. 2010; Department for Education 2011). While a national health statistics report shows black women are one and a half times more likely to experience infertility than their white counterparts (Chandra et al. 2013), recent research from the *International Journal of Obstetrics and Gynaecology* has suggested that ethnicity is a significant independent factor in determining the chances of successful IVF or ICSI treatment (Maalouf et al. 2017). Recent findings make it clear that 'South Asian Indian, South Asian Bangladeshi, South Asian Pakistani, Black African, and Other Asian women ha[ve] significantly lower odds of a live birth than White British women' going through IVF or ICSI treatment (Ibid., p. 906). The creative media industries have an important role to play here in speaking to and about those black and ethnic minority women within and beyond the UK as they have been affected by an infertility diagnosis and assisted reproductive efforts.

In a recent short-form documentary on the topic of infertility, a group of 30-something women, when asked about infertility and assisted reproductive treatments and technologies, said that they had little to no idea about the success rates of assisted reproductive treatments or technologies (Levy and Farrar 2018). At the same time, Professor Robert Winston, fertility expert and Chairman of the Genesis Research Trust, could be seen telling daytime television audiences that private IVF treatments are 'peddling in failure' (Winston cited in Corner 2018). He goes as far as to suggest that he is 'haunted by the fact that only one in four cycles of IVF treatment actually result[s] in a live baby' (Ibid.). Winston makes the point that infertility clinics would rather treat people through seemingly ineffectual assisted reproductive technologies and expensive add-on treatments than help promote further research on infertility (Winston 2017). At the time of writing, the Royal College of Obstetricians Gynaecologists, the British Fertility Society and the HFEA are signing a 'consensus statement calling for private IVF clinics to stop charging patients costly optional add-on treatments that are not proven to work' (Patel 2018) in order to 'create a culture change among fertility professionals in the UK' (HFEA 2019).

With the themes of loneliness, isolation and miscommunication in mind, one might suggest that the ways in which the media frame medical

6 CONCLUSION: FUTURE RESEARCH DIRECTIONS   255

information and its accompanying emotional impacts are failing to 'advanc[e] public education on reproductive health issues' (Sangster and Lawson 2015, p. 1073). Further research, information, education and communication are key in conveying the reality of infertility, loss and non-traditional family building to a broad audience (British Fertility Society 2018a, b; Hepburn 2018; MFM 2018; Harper et al. 2019). From this estimation then, I hope that readers, researchers, educators, creatives and those who commission content will find this book a useful introduction to the representation of infertility, IVF, loss and adoption in first-person, confessional and factual media, and use it as a springboard for further dialogue, debate and meaningful representations.

REFERENCES

Barnes, Liberty. 2014. *Conceiving Masculinity: Male Infertility, Medicine, and Identity*. Philadelphia: Temple University Press.

British Fertility Society. 2018a. Modern Families Education Project. *British Fertility Society*. Accessed April 12, 2019. https://britishfertilitysociety.org.uk/fei/#link5.

———. 2018b. Fertility Fest—The Modern Families Project. *British Fertility Society*. Accessed April 12, 2019. https://www.fertilityfest.com/the-modern-families-project.

Chandra, Anjani, Casey Copen, and Elizabeth Stephen. 2013. Infertility and Impaired Fecundity in the United States, 1982–2010: Data From the National Survey of Family Growth. *National Center for Health Statistics* 67: 1–18.

Clothier, Richard. 2017. Male Infertility: I Felt So Guilty That I Couldn't Come up With the Goods. *The Telegraph*. Accessed April 26, 2019. https://www.telegraph.co.uk/men/fatherhood/male-infertility-felt-guilty-couldnt-come-goods/.

Connell, R.W. 1995. *Masculinities*. Berkeley: University of California Press.

———. 1998. Masculinities and Globalization. *Men and Masculinities* 1 (1): 3–23.

Corner, Natalie. 2018. Fertility Expert Professor Robert Winston Says Expensive Private IVF Clinics are "Peddling in Failure"—And He's "Haunted" by How Few Cycles of Treatment Actually Result in a Baby. *Mail Online*. Accessed April 12, 2019. http://www.dailymail.co.uk/femail/article-5942225/Infertility-expert-Professor-Robert-Winston-shares-downfalls-costly-private-IVF.html.

Department for Education. 2011. An Action Plan for Adoption: Tackling Delay. *Department for Education*. Accessed April 12, 2019. https://assets.publishing.service.gov.uk/government/uploads/system/uploads/attachment_data/file/180250/action_plan_for_adoption.pdf.

Donnelly, Erin. 2017. Why are Women with Fertility Issues so Often Portrayed as Evil? *Refinery29*. Accessed April 12, 2019. https://www.refinery29.com/en-gb/2017/01/162817/infertile-female-villains-in-movies-tv-characters.

Edge, Brooke. 2015. Barren or Bountiful? Analysis of Cultural Values in Popular Media Representations of Infertility. PhD diss., University of Colorado. Accessed April 12, 2019. https://scholar.colorado.edu/jour_gradetds/25/.

Farmer, Elaine, Cherilyn Dance, Jeni Beecham, Eva Bonin, and Danielle Ouwejan. 2010. An Investigation of Family Finding and Matching in Adoption. *Briefing Paper*. Accessed April 12, 2019. http://www.adoptionresearchinitiative.org.uk/briefs/DFE-RBX-10-05.pdf.

Feasey, Rebecca. 2008. *Masculinity and Popular Television*. Edinburgh: Edinburgh University Press.

———. 2019. Male Factor Infertility and the Media. *Viewfinder*. Accessed May 1, 2019. https://learningonscreen.ac.uk/viewfinder/articles/male-factor-infertility-and-the-media-masculinity-and-the-hegemonic-hierarchy/.

Ginsberg, Faye, and Rayna Rapp, eds. 1995. *Conceiving a New World Order: The Global Politics of Reproduction*. Berkeley: University of California Press.

Hannah, Esmée and Gough, Brendan. 2017. It Made Me Feel Less of a Man Knowing I May Never be a Dad: The Hidden Trauma of Male Infertility. *The Conversation*. Accessed April 26, 2019. https://theconversation.com/it-made-me-feel-less-of-a-man-knowing-i-may-never-be-a-dad-the-hidden-trauma-of-male-infertility-84414.

Harper, Joyce, Jessica Hepburn, Gabby Vautier, Emma Callander, Tian Glasgow, Adam Balen, and Jacky Boivin. 2019. Feasibility and Acceptability of Theatrical and Visual Art to Deliver Fertility Education to Young Adults. *Human Fertility* 1: 1–7.

Harrison, Laura. 2016. *Brown Bodies, White Babies: The Politics of Cross-Racial Surrogacy*. New York: New York University Press.

Hepburn, Jessica. 2018. Jessica Hepburn. *Jessica Hepburn*. Accessed April 12, 2019. https://www.jessicahepburn.com.

HFEA. 2019. Fertility Regulator Calls for Clinics to be More Open about Treatment Add-ons. *Human Fertilisation and Embryology Authority*. Accessed April 12, 2019. https://www.hfea.gov.uk/about-us/news-and-press-releases/2019-news-and-press-releases/fertility-regulator-calls-for-clinics-to-be-more-open-about-treatment-add-ons/.

Kaufman, Gayle. 2013. *Superdads: How Fathers Balance Work and Family in the 21st Century*. New York: New York University Press.

Kimmel, Michael. 2004. Masculinity as Homophobia: Fear, Shame, and Silence in the Construction of Gender Identity. In *Feminism and Masculinities*, ed. Peter Murphy, 182–199. Oxford: Oxford University Press.

Levy, Claire, and Ruth Farrar. 2018. *Infertility, The Media & Me*. Film.

Lundin, Susanne. 2002. The Threatened Sperm: Parenthood in the Age of Biomedicine. In *New Directions in Anthropological Kinship*, ed. Linda Stone, 139–155. Oxford: Rowman and Littlefield.

Maalouf, Wadih, Bruce Campbell, and Kannamannadiar Jayaprakasan. 2017. Effect of Ethnicity on Live Birth Rates After In Vitro Fertilisation/Intracytoplasmic Sperm Injection Treatment: Analysis of UK National Database. *BJOG, An International Journal of Obstetrics and Gynaecology* 124 (6): 904–910.

Mason, Mary-Claire. 2003. *Male Infertility—Men Talking.* London: Routledge.

MFM. 2018. Innovation in Sex Education. *My Fertility Matters Project.* Accessed April 12, 2019. http://www.mfmprojectuk.org.

Patel, Rikita. 2018. HFEA Calls for Culture Change on IVF Add-ons. *BioNews.* Accessed April 12, 2019. https://www.bionews.org.uk/page_139908.

Sandelowski, Margarete, and Sheryn de Lacey. 2002. The Uses of a Disease: Infertility as Rhetorical Vehicle. In *Infertility around the Globe: New Thinking on Childlessness, Gender, and Reproductive Technologies*, ed. Marcia Inhorn and Frank Van Balen, 33–51. Berkeley: University of California Press.

Sangster, Sarah, and Karen Lawson. 2015. Is Any Press Good Press? The Impact of Media Portrayals of Infertility on Young Adults' Perceptions of Infertility. *Journal of Obstetrics and Gynaecology, Canada* 37 (12): 1072–1078.

Sterling, Evelina. 2013. From No Hope to Fertile Dreams: Procreative Technologies, Popular Media, and the Culture of Infertility. PhD diss., Georgia State University. Accessed April 12, 2019. https://scholarworks.gsu.edu/cgi/viewcontent.cgi?article=1069&context=sociology_diss.

Van Balen, Frank and Marcia Inhorn. 2002. "Introduction: Interpreting Infertility: A View from the Social Sciences." In *Infertility Around the Globe: New Thinking on Childlessness, Gender and Reproductive Technologies*, edited by Marcia Inhorn and Frank Van Balen, 3-32. London: University of California Press.

Winston, Robert. 2017. Why I'm Ashamed of the Exploitation in the IVF Industry. *Mail Online.* Accessed April 12, 2019. http://www.dailymail.co.uk/debate/article-4471742/Why-m-ashamed-exploitation-IVF-industry.html.

Wischmann, Tewes and Thorn, Petra. 2013. (Male) Infertility: What Does it Mean to Men? New Evidence from Quantitative and Qualitative Studies' Reproductive. *BioMedicine Online* 27 (3): 236–243.

Useful Websites UK

Adoption Plus http://www.adoptionplus.co.uk

CoramBAAF: Adoption & Fostering Academy https://corambaaf.org.uk

Cruse Bereavement Care https://www.cruse.org.uk

Ectopic Pregnancy Foundation http://www.ectopicpregnancy.co.uk

Family Futures https://www.familyfutures.co.uk

Fertility Network UK http://fertilitynetworkuk.org

Kicks Count https://www.kickscount.org.uk/why-we-want-home-doppler-sales-to-be-regulated

Miscarriage Association https://www.miscarriageassociation.org.uk

Molar Pregnancy Support & Information http://www.molarpregnancy.co.uk

NHS Choices https://www.nhs.uk/pages/home.aspx

SANDS (Stillbirth and Neonatal Death Society) https://www.sands.org.uk

The Agency for Adoption & Permanency Support https://www.pac-uk.org

The Ectopic Pregnancy Trust https://www.ectopic.org.uk

© The Author(s) 2019

R. Feasey, *Infertility and Non-Traditional Family Building*,
https://doi.org/10.1007/978-3-030-17787-4

INDEX

A

Abbey, Antonia, 41
Abbott, Jodi, 156, 172, 173
Abetz, Jenna, 50
Abuse, 24, 191, 213, 214, 217, 229, 231, 234–236
Action for Children, 213, 218, 235
Activity days, 212, 213, 217–226, 228–231
ACW, 200
Adams, Stephen, 20, 43, 44, 120
Adamson, G.D., 10
Adoption
   adoption.com, 195
   The Adoption Exchange, 220, 223, 224, 228, 229
   The Adoption Party (2014), 212
   adoption plus, 259
   The Adoption Register, 192, 196
   Adoption UK, 191–193, 209, 234
   adoptive parents, 19, 190, 191, 194–196, 198, 202, 203, 206–209, 211, 212, 216, 217, 219, 222, 224, 229, 234–237
   AdoptUSKids, 196, 198, 224

   after infertility, 198–206
   The Agency for Adoption & Permanency Support, 259
   American Adoptions News, 195
   assessments, 192, 195
   breakdown, 232–237
   Britain's Adoption Scandal (2016), 212
   The Children and Adoption Act 2006, 193
   closed adoption, 208, 229
   displacement, 233
   disruption, 232, 235, 236
   dissolution, 233
   The Donaldson Adoption Institute, 197
   facilitator, 196
   matching stage, 192
   National Adoption Center, 190, 196
   National Adoption Day, 228
   National adoption information service, 194
   National Adoption Week, 225, 226, 228

© The Author(s) 2019
R. Feasey, *Infertility and Non-Traditional Family Building*,
https://doi.org/10.1007/978-3-030-17787-4

262 INDEX

Adoption (*cont.*)
National Center on Adoption and
Permanency, 190
network, 24, 189
Older Parent Adoption, 195
open adoption, 195, 206–209
placement issues, 213, 235
placement process, 196
post-adoption surprise pregnancies,
212
private agency adoption, 196, 197
private re-homing, 235
process, 70, 189, 190, 192–197,
200, 201, 205, 207, 212, 213,
219, 237
prospective adopters, 23, 189, 191,
192, 197, 212, 214, 215, 219,
220, 223, 224, 229–230, 254
public agency adoption, 196
restrictions, 193
semi-open adoptions, 208
Unlicensed agency adoption, 196
Adopt Me I'm a Teenager (2005), 210
Advertising, 220, 224
Age out, 190, 230, 235
Aggressive behaviours, 213, 235
Aggressive marketing, 213, 224, 228,
230, 231
Akass, Kim, 204
Alex Jones: Fertility & Me (2016), 87,
116, 126
A Little Pregnant, 41, 54, 55, 69
Alvarez, Frank, 232
Amateur Nester, 74
American Pregnancy Association, 147,
148
American Society for Reproductive
Medicine (ASRM), 43, 90, 92,
99
Anderson, Eric, 169
Andersson, Gunvor, 238

Andrews, Frank, 41
Ang, Lawrence, 60, 169
Anger/angry, 18, 38–44, 52, 57, 60,
61, 68, 72, 73, 144, 146, 154,
155, 201, 213, 235
Annie (2014), 210
Anonymity, 55, 56, 94
Anonymous, 19, 62, 77, 95, 115, 158,
206
Anonymous Father's Day (2011), 115
Arnold, Ben, 211
Artificial insemination, 10, 88
Arya, Jitendra, 6
Ashton, Dan, 18
Assisted reproduction, 3, 10–13, 78,
87–133, 170, 252
assisted reproductive technologies,
10, 12, 13, 18, 21, 28, 64, 87,
90, 92, 93, 112, 113, 115,
120, 129–132, 254
assisted reproductive treatments, 12,
13, 15, 19, 20, 22–24, 27, 28,
52, 56, 66, 78, 89, 95, 102,
103, 114, 116, 132, 143, 165,
194, 199–202, 216, 217, 236,
250, 251, 253, 254
intracytoplasmic sperm injection
(ICSI), 10, 13
intrauterine insemination (IUI), 10,
12, 100
in vitro fertilisation (IVF), 10, 12,
13, 23, 59, 66, 93, 105, 115,
132, 199, 201
Astbury, Jill, 90, 120
Attachment difficulties, 213, 235,
236
Attain Fertility, 13
Attorney adoption, 196
Aufderheide, Patricia, 114
Avengers: Age of Ultron (2015), 252
Awareness Days, 228

B

Babycenter community, 169
Baby Cotton, 107, 108
Babyloss Awareness Week, 155
Baby M, 109
The BabyMakers (2012), 44
Baby Makers: The Fertility Clinic (2013), 115
Baby Mama (2008), 44, 112
Baby Maybe, 52, 72
Back-Up Plan (2010), 112
BabyWanted: ApplyWithin, 55
Bad mother, 5
Banet-Weiser, Sarah, 64
Barnes, Liberty, 253
Barren, viii, 4, 252
Barren Mare, 55
BBC, 17, 107, 116, 133, 210
BBC News, 173
BBC2, 87, 117, 127, 211
Beattie, Keith, 114
Becker, Gay, 28
Beecham, Jeni, 254
Beek, Mary, 208
Belkin, Lisa, 199, 200
Bell, Sarah, 95, 96
Benward, Jean, 94, 95, 99
Bernardi, L.A., 145
Berridge, Susan, 1
Berryman, Rachel, 169
Betton, Victoria, 170
Bewley, Susan, 44
Big Love (2006–11), 113
Biological, 8, 9, 15, 66, 68, 70, 94, 100, 102, 104, 106, 107, 109, 111–113, 116, 123, 126, 197, 199, 200, 202–206, 208, 210, 212, 216, 237, 238, 250
Biological children, 15, 24, 26, 48, 66, 125, 131, 203, 204, 212–216
Birth announcement, 71, 74, 78

The Blind Side (2009), 210
Blogs
 bloggers, 28, 49–55, 57, 59–61, 68, 71, 72, 74–78, 100, 131, 157, 158, 171, 205, 250
 blogosphere, 21, 23, 26, 37, 49, 50, 55, 57, 60, 62, 65, 68, 71, 75–78, 158, 250, 251
Blyth, Eric, 94–96, 98, 99, 106–108
BOB, 219
Bodkin, Henry, 130
Boggs, Belle, 12
Boivin, Jacky, 5, 212
Bologna, Caroline, 175
Bonin, Eva, 254
Bray, Catherine, 115
Breeders: A Subclass of Women? (2014), 115
Brent, Tyler, 50
Brian, Kate, 6
British Fertility Society, vii, 20, 43, 44, 107, 254, 255
Bronstein, Jenny, 4, 26, 52, 67
Brooklyn Nine-Nine (2013–), 210
Brown, Donna, 208
Brown, Lesley, 11, 12
Brown, Louise, 11, 12, 87, 105, 107
Bubbles and Bumps, 18, 28, 37, 61, 65
Bui, 47
Bullock, Anne-Marie, 44
The Bump (magazine), 103
Burr, Vivien, 8
Busted Plumbing, 69
Butterflymum79, 203

C

Campbell, Angela, 110
Campbell, Bruce, 254
Campbell, Pam, 143

264 INDEX

Candace of Our Misconception, 69, 70
Carr, Elizabeth, 12
Carr, Judith, 12
Catwalk Kids (2011), 189, 212–214, 217, 224, 227, 228, 230, 231
Celeb News, 128
Center for Bioethics and Culture, 115, 116
Center for Human Reproduction, 94
Centers for Disease Control and Prevention (CDC), 7, 10, 24, 90, 101, 102, 143, 147
Cesare, Nina, 156, 175, 176
Challoner, Jack, 12
Chambers, Ruth, 143
Chandra, Anjani, 254
Chen, Laurie, 211
Chez Miscarriage, 55, 60
Childfree, 25, 70, 118
Childlessness, 5, 15, 25, 38, 39, 42, 43, 45, 49, 64, 66, 71, 75, 76, 96, 106, 174, 193–195, 200, 202–204, 250, 251, 253
Children of Men (2006), 17, 44
Children Who Wait, 192
Child Welfare Information Gateway, 196–198, 207
Christiansen, O.B., 145
Clarity (2015), 210
Clarke, V. E., 120
Clinical Commissioning Groups (CCG), 88, 89
Closure (2013), 210
Cockerell, Jennifer, 175
Codrea-Rado, Anna, 170
Cohn, Victor, 12
Collins, Catherine, 144
Commercial surrogacy, 107, 110
Commissioning parents, 108, 110
Communicable diseases, 12

Community, 4–6, 23, 46, 49–59, 61, 62, 64, 66, 68, 72–74, 76, 78, 95, 101, 105, 148, 155, 157, 169, 172, 175, 199, 226
Connell, Claudia, 94
Connell, R.W., 253
Contact After Adoption, 208
Control, 5, 42, 46, 52, 54–57, 126, 132, 146, 159, 177
Conway, Kerry, 175
The Coopers vs The Rest (2016), 210
Copen, Casey, 254
CoramBAAF: Adoption & Fostering Academy, 222
Corner, Natalie, 254
Coronation Street (1960–), 79, 113, 167
Costs, 66, 87, 89, 91, 94–96, 108, 114, 115, 121, 124, 197, 230, 232
Coulson, Neil, 40, 42, 46, 51, 56, 57, 61
Counselling/ counseling, 16, 46, 68, 77, 89, 154, 156
Couser, Thomas, 46, 49
Crary, David, 189
Creating a Family, 37, 38, 41, 68, 69, 71, 72, 74–76
Crowe, Christine, 11
Cruse Bereavement Care, 155
Cult of True Womanhood, 211
Cycle buddies, 56, 72

D

Dance, Cherilyn, 254
Danielsson, Krissi, 145, 150
The Dark Matter of Love (2012), 210
Davenport, Dawn, 100, 200, 201
Dave Thomas Foundation for Adoption, 229
Davies, Iwan, 107

INDEX 265

De Lacey, Sheryn, 8, 202, 251
De Mouzon, J., 10
De Neubourg, Diane, 10
Dean, Will, 212
Declercq, Eugene, 156, 172, 173
Demory, Pamela, 113
Department for Education, 189, 192, 193, 254
Department of Health and Social Care, 108
Depression, 14, 39, 52, 57, 154, 155
Desperate, 16, 27, 39, 40, 91, 202, 216, 219, 225, 252
Desperate Housewives (2004–12), 167
Despicable Me (2010), 210
Devroe, Sarah, 10
DiLapi, Elena, 2, 100
Dinwoodie, April, 195, 197
Disability, 98, 144, 191, 193, 213, 214, 235
Documentary, 19, 20, 23, 26, 79, 113–127, 132, 133, 175, 189, 190, 210, 212, 219, 221–224, 226, 230–232, 236, 237, 252, 254
Docherty, Katy, 225
Donato, Jill Di, 129
Donnelly, Erin, 252
Donnelly, Laura, 89
Donor insemination, 10, 13, 50, 94, 101, 102, 106
Donor Mum: The Children I've Never Met (2011), 115
Donors, 10, 88, 92–96, 106
Donor Sibling Registry, 95
Don't Count your Eggs, 74
Douglas, Susan, 1
Doward, Jamie, 110
Drinkwater, Jane, 234
Dual approval, 197
Due, Clemence, 144
Dugan, Emily, 111

Dugas, Timothy, 50
Duner, Alex, 145

E
Earle, Sarah, 27
Edelman, Joni, 26
Edge, Brooke, 3, 5, 18, 21, 27, 38, 39, 103, 113, 126, 129, 130, 210–212, 252
Education, vii, 3, 25, 38, 43, 44, 115, 117, 121, 148, 190, 219, 226, 236, 237, 255
Egg donor/ egg donation, 10, 13, 14, 16, 50, 64, 89, 93, 94, 96, 99, 100, 102, 104, 106, 115, 123, 124, 130, 131, 202, 251
Egg freezing, 100, 115
Eggs for Later (2010), 114
Eggsploitation (2010), 115
Elgot, Jessica, 95
Embrace Fertility, 39
Embryo transfer, 11, 14, 90, 113, 124
Ending treatment, 62–71
End-of-pregnancy management, 149, 150, 153, 154
Epstein, Yakov, 57
Evans, Oliver, 59
Exchange events, 219–226
Exposure: Don't Take my Child (2014), 212

F
Factual entertainment, 23
Fallopian tubes, 7, 11, 12, 39, 49, 150, 151, 153
Family Addition with Leigh Anne Tuohy (2013–), 212
Family building blogs, 22, 37, 49–53, 55, 58–62, 68, 69, 72, 74, 76, 78, 158, 163

266   INDEX

Family Futures, 259
Farmer, Elaine, 254
Farrar, Ruth, 20, 176, 254
Farquharson, R.G., 145
Fashion shows, 217, 220, 224,
   226–232
Fault, 4, 43, 145, 173
Feasey, Rebecca, vii, 1, 18, 21, 44, 72,
   98, 104, 127, 128, 131–133, 253
Fertility
   clinics, 58, 65, 87–133
   Fest, vii, 18
   Network UK, 253
   specialists, 11, 43, 102–105
   tourism, 89, 95
   treatment abroad, 89, 92
Fetal Medicine Unit, 91
15,000 Kids and Counting (2014),
   189, 199, 212–217, 219, 220,
   224, 225, 238
Finding Me a Family (2017), 189,
   212, 215–217, 220, 221, 223,
   225, 232
Finding Mum and Dad (2014), 189,
   212, 214, 215, 217, 218,
   220–223
First4Adoption, 191, 194–196, 199
Fit Pregnancy magazine, 103
Fixmer-Oraiz, Natalie, 98
Fixsen, Amanda, 190
Fogle, Asher, 167–169, 189, 190,
   198, 213
Forever Infertile, 40, 75
Foster
   care, 38, 189–191, 196–198, 213,
      224–229, 232, 235–237
   early permanence, 197
   foster-for-adoption, 195, 197, 198,
      207
   fostering, 9, 22, 198
   Fostering Change for Children, 197
Frank, Arthur, 49

Franklin, Sarah, 104, 107
Freddie Mac, 228, 229
Freedman, Mia, 131
Freeman, Michael, 109
Freer, Bridget, 233
Free Willy (2003), 210
Friedman, May, 54
Friends (1994–2004), 44
Froelker, Justine Brooks, 201
Funding, 89, 95
Future Baby (2016), 115, 116

G

Gallup, Caroline, 65, 67
Gamble, Natalie, 107, 108
Game of Thrones (2011–), 2
Gander, Kashmira, 108
García-Rapp, Florencia, 169
Garnefski, Nadia, 2
Gatrell, Caroline, 43, 130
Gender queer, 99
Genesis Research Trust, 254
Geriatric primigravida, 118
Gestational surrogacy, 106, 107, 111,
   251, 254
Ghevaert, Louisa, 111
Gibbings-Jones, Mark, 211
Gibbs, Samuel, 58
Gibson, Allison, 159, 160
Gibson, Margaret, 163, 169
Gilmore Girls: A Year in the Life
   (2016), 113
Ginsberg, Faye, 253
Girlfriends (2000–08), 167
The Girl on the Train (2016), 17, 167
Girls (2012–2017), 2
Giuliana & Bill (2009–), 44, 111, 167
Goddijn, M., 145
Goldberg, Haley, 167
Gonzalez, Lois, 132
Goodenoughmam, 206

INDEX 267

The Good Girl (2002), 44
Goossen, William, 169
Gordon, Baker H. W., 90, 120
Gorfinkel, Iris, 145, 146
Grace (2009), 44, 167
Grant, Amanda, 207
Grant, Theresa, 215, 218
Greil, Arthur, 28, 97
Grey's Anatomy (2005–), 167, 211
Grief/grieving, 38–44, 52, 56, 62, 63,
  155, 163, 165, 166, 171
Griessner, Lanay, 115
Griffiths, E., 5, 212
Guilt, 6, 38, 72, 154, 157, 160, 162,
  164, 176, 178

H
Haase, Jean, 107
Haberman, Clyde, 109
Hall, Stephen, 129
Hallett, Alicia, 103
Halman, Jill, 41
Hammarberg, Karin, 90, 120
The Handmaid's Tale (2017–), 17
Hanson, Clare, 104
The Hardest Quest, 69
Hard to place, 213, 218
Harris, Gardenia, 208
Harrison, Laura, 254
Harrison, Phil, 211
Harte, Alys, 234
Health, vii, viii, 2, 5, 8, 15, 18, 21,
  23–27, 43, 48, 50, 58, 59, 63, 68,
  77, 87, 91, 93, 96, 97, 99, 102,
  109, 116, 117, 120, 121, 126,
  144–149, 152–154, 156–158,
  161, 169, 170, 174, 175, 178,
  193–195, 198, 201, 213, 228,
  231, 234, 235, 251, 254, 255
Health information, 58, 77
Health issues, vii, 59, 255
Heart Gallery of America, 227

The Help (2011), 167
Hemenway, Nancy, 57
Henderson, Meg, 213, 217, 233
Hepburn, Jessica, vii, 25, 40, 255
Hepworth, Rosemary, 21, 51, 57, 65
Hill, M.A., 106
Hilpern, Kate, 234, 237
Hinton, Lisa, 38, 41, 51, 53, 57, 67
History of abuse, 24, 213, 234, 235
History of neglect, 24, 234
History of trauma, 24, 213, 235
Hobson, Katherine, 146, 159, 177
Hogan, Michael, 212
Holder, Angela, 109
Holman, Rebecca, 146, 161, 170,
  172, 174–176
Home study, 196
Hope, viii, 20, 25, 39, 41, 47, 48, 52,
  61–63, 65, 66, 68–71, 78, 87,
  102, 105, 109, 117, 118,
  124–127, 131, 132, 157, 158,
  172, 173, 176, 191, 219, 231,
  238, 249, 250, 255
Horsey, Kirsty, 111
Horton, Helena, 167
Hosey, Sara, 2
Host surrogacy, 13
Hotel for Dogs (2009), 210
House, Laura, 62, 63, 199
Houston, Doris, 208
Howard, Jeanne, 208
How I Met Your Mother (2005–14), 44
Howlett, Paul, 211
Huh, Jina, 170
Human Fertilisation and Embryology
  Act 1990, 88
Human Fertilisation and Embryology
  Act 2008, 108
Human Fertilisation and Embryology
  Authority (HFEA), 6, 7, 10, 77,
  88–90, 93–95, 99, 107, 254
Hurley, Richard, 105
Hyper-fertility, 98

268 INDEX

I

IAC: The Centre for Adoption, 193
Identifying information, 207, 208
Inconceivable (2005–), 44
InConceivable: Our Journey Through
  In vitro fertilisation, 46
Independent adoption, 191, 195, 196
Independent voluntary adoption
  agency, 196
Indichova, Julia, 46–49
Infertile Myrtle: Life as an Infertile
  Couple, 72, 73
Infertile Myrtle's Blog, 73, 74
Infertility
  age-related, 13, 23, 43, 45, 48, 87,
    101–103, 115–120, 123,
    127–133
  anticipated, 9, 100, 114–115
  blogs, 22, 37, 38, 52, 54–58, 75, 250
  celebrity, vii, 17, 21, 128, 129, 131,
    132
  diagnosis, 3, 9–16, 19, 20, 23–24,
    27, 28, 37, 41–43, 46, 48, 51,
    52, 57–59, 64, 66, 68, 69, 72,
    74, 76, 77, 87, 93, 95, 97,
    117, 122–123, 128, 190,
    198–200, 202, 204, 205, 210,
    236, 237, 249–251, 253, 254
  diaries, 75
  idiopathic, 8
  secondary, 7, 25, 48, 52
  social, 1, 9, 12, 39, 215
  stigma, 41
  support, 41
  unexplained, 6, 42, 206
The Infertility Journey, 47, 105
The Information Standard, 77
Inhorn, Marcia, 26, 27, 96, 97, 144,
  253
Inkpen, Kori, 170
Instagram, 175
Intended parents, 108, 110
Intensive mother, 5

Intercountry adoption, 192, 193
International Adoption Guide, 193
The International Council on
  Infertility Information
  Dissemination (INCIID), 48
Involuntarily childless, 20, 202, 217
Ishihara, O., 10
Isolation, vii, 19, 23, 39, 41, 51,
  57–58, 77, 145–147, 155–159,
  161, 163, 167, 172, 175, 176,
  236, 250, 253, 254
It81, 19
IVF One Day at a Time, 66
I Wasted all that Birth Control, 55

J

Jackson, Kate, 225
Jamie, 47
Jayaprakasan, Kannamannadiar, 254
Jay Z, 175
Jealous/ jealousy, 40, 61, 155
Jenkins, Julian, 143
Jensen, Robin, 4, 5, 212
Johnson, Robert, 9
Jones, Allie, 170
Jones, Cambridge, 227
Jones, Samantha, 167
Jones, Sarah, 111
Jordan, Lauren, 50, 60
Julianelle, Mike, 168
Juno (2007), 17, 252

K

Kahana, Jonathan, 114
Kahlor, LeeAnn, 51, 52, 58, 77
Katz Rothman, Barbara, 163
Kaufman, Gayle, 253
Kavka, Misha, 169
Keeping Up with the Kardashians
  (2007–), 44
Keough, Peter, 116

Kerrigan, Susan, 114
Kessler, David, 155
Kewcumber, 204, 211
Khamis, Susie, 60, 169
Khanapure, Amita, 44
Kicks Count, 259
Kimball, Alexandra, 175
Kimmel, Michael, 253
Kingdom (2014–), 167
Kitesurfercarly, 199
Kitten of Forever Infertile, 53, 75
Klein, Amy, 16
Knapton, Sarah, 154
Knocked Up (2007), 17
Knoll, Maria, 3, 26, 52, 67
Kohn, Ingrid, 17, 146
Kolte, A.M., 145
Korolczuk, Elzbieta, 62, 63, 78
Kouri, Prikko, 170
Kraaij, Vivian, 2
Kramer, Ryan, 95
Kramer, Wendy, 95
Kristof, Nicholas, 235, 236
Kritzer, Naomi, 57, 60, 75
Ktbeau, 206
Kübler-Ross, Elisabeth, 155
Kumar, Naina, 27
Kung Fu Panda 2 (2011), 210
Kurinczuk, Jennifer, 38, 41, 51, 53, 57, 67

L
Lacobucci, Gareth, 121
Lacour, Alyssa, 50
Lahl, Jennifer, 116
Lampi, Elina, 120
Landau, Ruth, 106, 107
Lankston, Charlie, 171
Lawson, Karen, 59, 255
Lea, Laura, 95
The Leery Polyp, 55
The Legend of Tarzan (2016), 210

Lemish, Dafna, 18, 75, 102
Lemon Stripes, 157, 158
Lemonwater, 78
Lesbian, 2, 9, 12, 23, 50, 99, 118, 132, 169, 214
Letherby, Gayle, 9, 15, 16, 25, 27, 99, 100, 106, 202, 203
Levy, Claire, 20, 176, 254
Lewin, Ellen, 2
LGBT+, 98, 190
Licensed private agency adoption, 196
Licensed2Love: Life of a wife, mom & nursing student, 71
Licensing, 87–93
The Life on an Infertile Myrtle, 73
Life Without Baby, 76
The Light Between Oceans (2016), 17, 167
Lion (2016), 210
Lisa of Amateur Nester, 74
Liu, Leslie, 170
Live birth rate, 90, 131
Living without children, 9, 25
Local authority, 191, 198, 220, 232, 233, 236
Lonely/loneliness, 40, 41, 145–147, 155–158, 163, 168, 172, 176, 250, 254
Longtermfamilyplanning, 205
Looseleaf, 206
Lopez, Lori Kidom, 51
Lovell, Joanna, 225
Lovelock, Michael, 169
Lubbock Interagency Adoption Council, 227

M
Maalouf, Wadih, 254
Macaluso, Maurizio, 9
Mackert, Michael, 51, 52, 58, 77
Mad Max: Fury Road (2015), 252
Madsen, Pamela, 120, 133

270 INDEX

Magee, Anna, 89, 90
Maher, Jennifer, 17, 112
Make Me a Baby (2007), 114
Male factor infertility, 10, 27, 39, 122, 252, 253
Malik, Sumaira, 40, 42, 46, 51, 56, 57, 61
Mamo, Laura, 39, 66, 93, 99
The Maniscalco Journey, 55, 70, 71, 73
Mansour, R., 10
Mapes, Diane, 234
Marketing, 28, 99, 101, 105, 169, 214, 219–232, 237
Marley and Me (2008), 167
Marsh, Margaret, 3, 21, 43, 212, 251
Martin, Lauren, 9, 12, 90, 92, 100
Maternity and Infant (magazine), 103
Matthews-King, Alex, 59
Mayo Clinic, 150, 154
Mazza, Danielle, 120, 133
McCarthy, Patrice, 41, 67
McDermott, Mark, 196
McIntyre, Phillip, 114
McKelvie, Geraldine, 226
McLaughlin, Hugh, 28
McQuillan, Julia, 97
Meakings, Sarah, 232, 234
Meandyouplustwo, 205
Meet the Robinsons (2007), 210
Memoirs, 9, 18, 20, 39, 45, 49, 57, 79, 164, 175, 192
MFM, *see* My Fertility Matters
Miah, Andy, 178
Michaels, Meredith, 1
Miller, Cheryl, 9, 39, 49, 50, 52, 54–57, 63, 64, 75
Miller, Kelsey, 171
Mills, Brett, 211
Mills, Emma, 171
The Mindy Project (2012–2017), 44
MineOpine, 199

Miscarriage
#ihadamiscarriage, 175
chemical pregnancy, 122
as a component of infertility, 165
delayed, 149, 150
due to an ectopic pregnancy, 144, 147, 150, 151, 153
due to a molar pregnancy, 20, 25, 26, 143, 144, 147, 150, 151, 153, 154, 177, 250, 252
ectopic pregnancy, 150, 151, 153, 154
Ectopic Pregnancy Foundation, 155
The Ectopic Pregnancy Trust, 154
Miscarriage Association, 143, 144, 148, 150–156, 175
Miscarriage Care campaign, 155, 156
missed/silent, 127, 143, 147, 150, 151, 153, 174, 177
molar pregnancy, 25, 26, 147, 150, 151, 153, 154, 177, 250, 252
Molar Pregnancy Support & Information, 259
pregnancy loss, 17, 25, 133, 144, 145, 147–158, 162, 164, 167, 169, 172, 173, 175, 176
recurrent, 147, 149, 152–154, 165, 173, 214
Mistresses (2013–2016), 113
Modern Family (2009), 210
Moffitt, Perry-Lynn, 17, 146
Mohan, Isabel, 211
Mom (2013–), 210
Moore, Julia, 50
Morgan, Polly, 12
Morris, Max, 169
Morton, Natalie, 95, 96
Moscrop, Andrew, 159
Mosquera, Susan, 175
Mother and Baby magazine, 103

Mother and Child (2009), 210
The Mothering magazine, 103
Mother/motherhood, vii, 1, 38, 87, 148, 193, 250
Mrs. Spit, 76
Mulkay, Michael, 65
Multiple births, 91
Multiple gestations, 91
Multiple pregnancies, 89–91, 152
Mumsnet, 155, 156, 203, 205, 206, 209–211
Mum & Tots magazine, 103
Murdoch, Cassie, 62, 161, 174, 176
Murphy, Judy, 169
Murphy, Patricia, 170
Mutcherson, Kimberley, 10
Myall, Steve, 226
My Fertility Matters (MFM), 25, 43

N
The Naked Ovary, 55
Narey, Martin, 232
National Gamete Donation Trust, 96
National Health Service (NHS), 7, 8, 13, 24, 88, 89, 91, 93, 95–97, 118, 119, 121–123, 143, 147–154, 156, 166, 191, 193–195, 199
National Institute for Health and Care Excellence (NICE), 6, 7, 10, 12, 13, 88, 89
National Sperm Bank, 94, 95
Natja, 47
Needleman, Sima, 7
Neil, Elspeth, 207–209
Nelson, Lloyd, 195, 197
Neogi, Tina, 170
Neporent, Liz, 130
Neverjamtoday, 206
Newborn, 17, 22, 74, 104, 153, 191, 197, 213, 217, 219

The New Normal (2012-13), 17, 99, 113
The Next 15000 Days, 76
19 Kids and Counting (2008-2015), 167
90210 (2008–2013), 167
Non-identifying information, 206–207
Non-traditional mothering, vii, 1, 2, 17, 22
Norcross, Sarah, 111
Not Just a Beauty Blogger, 37
Novels, 20, 61, 99, 175
Nsoesie, Elaine, 156, 175, 176
Nygren, K., 10

O
Oakley, Ann, 216
Obama, Michelle, 129, 173
The Odd Life of Timothy Green (2012), 17, 44
Offending behaviours, 213, 235
Office for National Statistics (ONS), 7, 131, 152
Office of Population Affairs (OPA), 207, 208
Ollove, Michael, 92
The Omen (1972/2006), 210
Oncofertility, 93
One Day at a Time, 66
On Flunking Applied Biology 101, 55
O'Reilly, Andrea, 2
Orphan (2009), 210
Osborne-Thompson, Heather, 21, 64
Our Misconception: Chasing Dreams, Babies, and a Mini-human, 69, 70
Ouwejan, Danielle, 254
Owers, Mark, 232

272 INDEX

P

Padi Productions, 224, 230
Panorama: Inside Britain's Fertility Business (2016), 115
Paper Dream (2012), 210
Parental Order, 108, 111
Parenthood For Me, 69
Parenting Advice for Foster Carers and Adopters, 223, 232
Parenting magazine, 65, 75, 103, 130, 163
Parents-in waiting, 39, 66, 93
Parfitt, Rebecca, 158, 160
Park, Hyeoun-Ae, 170
Parnell, Jade, 170
Patel, Rikita, 254
Pathographies, 46, 49, 57, 78
Pathology, 6, 8, 39, 98
Patterson, Claire, 236, 237
Pedersen, Sarah, 60
Pemberton, Becky, 190
Peoplebabies, 103
Permanence, 17, 19, 23, 197, 213, 217, 219, 230
Petrucelli, Elizabeth, 145, 173
Phillips, Natasha, 228, 231, 232
Phoenix, Ann, 3
Photographic exhibitions, 17, 224, 228
Plum magazine, 103
Poetry, 157, 163, 175
Portwood-Stacer, Laura, 1, 64
Postmenopausal, 23, 93, 98, 99, 132
Pratt, Wanda, 170
Preece, Jennifer, 169
Pregnancy After Loss (PALS), 155
Pregnancy announcement, 23, 160, 167–171, 173, 174
Pregnancy Life & Style magazine, 103
Pregnancy & Newborn magazine, 103
Pregnancy rate, 89, 90
Preimplantation genetic diagnosis (PGD), 10, 12

Press Association, 12
Prima Baby & Infant magazine, 103
Primary infertility, 7
Pritchard, Louisa, 156, 172, 173
Pritchard, Sarah, 91
Private clinic, 89, 121
Private Practice (2007–2013), 44
Private treatment, 87, 89, 122
Promotion, 162, 169, 224, 226
Pronatal, viii, 2, 20, 26, 38, 63, 64, 66, 71, 76, 78, 79, 126, 132, 162, 203, 237, 249, 250
Psychogenic infertility, 5, 43, 212
Publicity, 131, 171, 177, 224
Public service, 22, 25, 116, 189, 211, 222, 226, 236, 252
Pullen, Christopher, 113
Pulver, Amy, 9
Purdie, Jennifer, 159, 168, 177
Pvedadmin, 131

Q

Quenby, S., 145
Question, 4, 14, 18, 19, 21, 24, 26, 28, 37, 38, 47, 48, 58–61, 63, 69, 71, 72, 77, 78, 90, 92, 94, 96, 97, 103, 108, 109, 112, 114–117, 120–124, 148, 153, 157, 159, 160, 167, 169, 170, 173, 174, 177, 198, 203, 206–208, 213, 215, 216, 221, 222, 224, 228

R

Rahman, Grace, 211
Rainbow baby, 158
Rapp, Rayna, 253
Rare, 19, 76, 165, 166, 253
Ratcliffe, Rebecca, 207–209
Ratliff, Clancy, 55, 59, 61

Rauch, Melissa, 145
Regan, Maureen, 47
Regulation, 87–94
Reimer, Vanessa, 38
Reproductive disruption, 18, 25,
    144–145, 251
Reproductive stratification, 97
Repro-lit, 9, 38–49, 57, 68, 158, 159,
    163, 173
Resolve; The National Infertility
    Association, 7, 37, 41
Rich, Emma, 178
Richards, Mandi, 175
Riggan, Kirsten, 90
Riggs, Damien, 144
Riley-Smith, Ben, 129
The Ring (2002), 210
Risk taking behaviours, 213, 235
Rissanen, Marja-Liisa, 170
The Road to Baby Madsen
    Our IVF Journey, 113, 210
Robinson, Sonya, 208, 209
Rogers, Angelica, 145
Rojek, Chris, 60
Role models, 41, 42, 58, 66, 71, 72,
    128
Romero, Natalie, 146, 175
Ronner, Wanda, 3, 21, 43, 212, 251
Rosenberg, Helane, 57
Ross, Ryan, 59
Ross, Sherry, 93
Roston, Michael, 145
Rotman, Dana, 169
Rotten Eggs, 55
Roy, Deanna, 175
Ryan, Maura, 2

S
Sable, David, 41
Saccone, Anna, 175
Sahagian, Sarah, 38

Same-sex couples, 88, 93–95, 99
Samglo, 199
Sanchez, Kiele, 144, 158, 159, 165
Sandelowski, Margarete, 5, 6, 8, 202,
    212, 251
Sanghani, Radhika, 173
Sangster, Sarah, 59, 255
Sarah, 200
Satterwhite, Catherine, 9
School issues, 213, 235
Schroevers, Maya, 2
Scott, Lee, 112
Scott, Megan, 166
Scott, Ryan, 208
Scully, Anne-Marie, 7, 13, 15, 18, 26,
    39–42, 49, 56, 57, 64, 164
Secrecy, 19, 25, 146, 156, 163, 173,
    176, 250, 251
Secrets and Lies (1996), 44
Selby, Julie, 42, 48, 54, 98, 192
Self-help, 20, 45, 46, 48, 49, 57, 64,
    78, 163
Self-regulation, 92
Selwyn, Julie, 198, 232–234, 236,
    237
Sex and the City (1998–2004), 44,
    211
Sexualised behaviour, 213, 235
Shalev, Shirley, 18, 75, 102
Shame, 3, 19, 20, 40, 63, 72,
    143–178, 250, 252, 253
Shapiro, Connie, 20, 120, 133
The She Is Project, 9
Siegel, Deborah, 207, 208
Sifferlin, Alexandra, 145
Silence, 17, 18, 23, 25, 42, 143–178,
    250–253
Silent Sorority, 56
Simonds, Wendy, 163
Singh, Amit, 27
Single Mothers by Choice (SMC), 50,
    101

274 INDEX

Single women, 9, 88, 99, 101, 102, 214, 237
Six Feet Under (2001–2005), 167
Sloan, Jenna, 225
Smith, David, 129
Smith, Natalie, 111
Smith, Susan Livingston, 208
Social media, 19, 20, 22, 23, 116, 143, 147, 155, 156, 167–170, 172–177, 205, 209, 226, 250, 251
Social parents, 106, 108, 203
Social workers, 192, 208, 212–215, 218–223, 229, 232, 236
Society for Assisted Reproductive Technology (SART), 90
Soelmark, Nathalie, 170
Sohr-Preston, Sarah, 49–52, 54, 58, 59, 74, 156
Sperm, 7, 8, 10, 11, 13, 14, 16, 43, 64, 88, 92, 94–96, 105, 106, 118, 122, 123, 151
Sperm donor/donation, 10, 16, 23, 93–95, 100, 115, 132
Sperm Palace Jesters, 55
Spontaneous abortion, 144–145
Stanford, Peter, 222
Stealing Baby Kisses, 69
Stephen, Elizabeth, 254
Stephenson, M.D., 145
Sterile, 4, 5
Sterling, Evelina, 7–9, 18, 27, 28, 38–40, 42, 43, 47, 55, 59, 61, 65, 92, 93, 97–104, 106, 111, 129, 130, 132, 165, 249, 251, 253
Stern, Carly, 171
Stigma, 3, 41, 54, 63, 132, 173, 175, 236, 250, 251, 253
Stillbirth, 7, 20, 23, 25, 26, 44, 58, 116, 143, 147–156, 158, 160, 164–167, 177, 214, 250, 252, 253

Stillbirth and Neonatal Death Society (SANDS), 155
Stirrup Queens, 55, 69
Stopping treatment, 202
Straight surrogacy, 106
Striff, Erin, 2, 41, 51, 55, 57, 60, 100, 129
Stubbs, David, 211
Stuck (2013), 210
Stylist, 156, 157, 159, 160, 162, 163
Sub-fertility, vii, 7, 132
Suffering, 4, 8, 14, 25–27, 57, 65
Suits (2011–), 252
Suleman, Nadya, 98
Sulleyman, Aatif, 155
Sullivan, E., 10
Sunny Day Today Mama, 69
Superman (1978), 210
Surrogacy, 13, 14, 16, 18, 21–23, 28, 50, 58, 61, 63, 64, 70, 75, 78, 104, 106–112, 116, 132, 251, 252, 254
The Surrogacy Arrangements Act 1985, 110
Surrogacy view, 110
Surrogate, 26, 70, 92, 106–113, 115, 122, 202, 214, 215
Surrogate Parenting Services, 106
Surugue, Lea, 98
Swift, Rebecca, 169
The Switch (2010), 112

T

Taylor, Verta, 163
Third party assisted conception, 44, 106, 107, 111
30 Rock (2006–2013), 210
This is Us (2016–), 167
Thomassmuggit, 210
Thorn, Petra, 253

Thornton, Lucy, 225
Throsby, Karen, 7, 9, 11, 12, 14, 15, 27, 28, 38, 40, 64–66, 68, 76, 93, 97–100, 104, 105
Tia & Tamera (2011–2013), 44
The Time Traveller's Wife (2009), 167
Today's Parent magazine, 103
Tomlins, Jacqueline, 8, 10, 11, 14, 101, 106, 144, 148, 149, 159, 163–165
Tomlinson, Victoria, 170
Tommy's, 143, 150, 152, 154, 155
Too Old to Be a Mum? (2010), 115
Traditional surrogacy, 109
Trauma, 24, 26, 191, 198, 213, 235
Treatment cycle, 90, 93
Tri Health, 12
True Detective (2015), 2
Tuft, Ben, 95
Tuhus-Dubrow, Rebecca, 45
TV Tropes, 167
Twinsters 2015, 210
The 2 Week Wait, 69

U

Uncommon, 166, 232
United Nations, Department of Economic and Social Affairs, 37
UP (2009), 19

V

Van Balen, Frank, 4, 6, 26, 27, 96, 97, 144, 253
Van de Wiel, Lucy, 115
Vanderpoel, S., 10
Vargo, Julie, 47
Vegas Baby (2016), 116
Venetis, C., 5, 212

Very common, 17, 23, 26, 143, 158, 166, 170, 177
Victorian Assisted Reproductive Treatment Authority (VARTA), 10
Video diaries, 175
Vloggers, 60, 170, 171, 176, 205
Vlogosphere, 26, 251
Vlogs, 19, 20, 143, 170, 177, 250

W

Wakley, Gill, 143
Wallace, Kelly, 201
Wallwork, Ellen, 209
Wanted: A Family of My Own (2014), 189
Ward, Emma, 208
Warnock Report, 87, 88
The Washington Times, 231
Weber, Patrick, 169, 170
Wednesday's Child, 228, 229
Welcome to the Desert, 55
Welling, Raymond, 60, 169
Wells, Chandra, 50, 55, 59–61
Wertman, Tonya, 129
What the Blog?, 69
What to Expect When You're Expecting (2012), 17, 113, 167, 210
Whiteford, Linda, 132
Who Shot My Stork, 55
Wijedasa, Dinithi, 232, 234
Wild, Leah, 104
Win a Baby (2012), 115
Winderman, Emily, 167
Winston, Robert, 15, 38, 64, 71, 76, 124, 254
Wischmann, Tewes, 253
Withnall, Adam, 154
Wohlmann, Anita, 6, 28, 45–47, 49, 52

276 INDEX

Wollaston, Sam, 221, 232
Woman's problem, 27
Wondercat, 19
Woods, Heather, 167
Woollett, Anne, 3, 65
World Health Organisation (WHO), 6, 37
The World's Oldest Mums (2009), 114
Wright-Schnapp, Tracie, 9
A Wrinkle in Time (2018), 210

Y
Yip, 200
Young, J., 207
Your Pregnancy, 103

Z
Zegers-Hochschild, F., 10
Ziebland, Sue, 38, 41, 51, 53, 57, 67
Zill, Nicholas, 232
Zuckerberg, Mark, 155, 172–174, 177

9783030177898

9781138870642